Theory and Practice of Ethnography

Theory and Practice of Ethnography

Readings from the Periphery

Editors

ESWARAPPA KASI

RAMESH C. MALIK

Indira Gandhi Rashtriya Manav Sangrahalaya, Bhopal

(National Museum of Mankind)

RAWAT PUBLICATIONS

Jaipur • New Delhi • Bangalore • Mumbai • Hyderabad • Guwahati

ISBN 81-316-0306-7

Published by

Indira Gandhi Rashtriya Manav Sangrahalaya
Shamla Hills, Bhopal 462 013
email: directorigrms@gmail.com

and

Prem Rawat for **Rawat Publications**
Satyam Apts., Sector 3, Jawahar Nagar, Jaipur 302 004 (India)
Phone: 0141 265 1748/7006 Fax: 0141 265 1748
E-mail: info@rawatbooks.com
Website: www.rawatbooks.com

New Delhi Office
4858/24, Ansari Road, Daryaganj, New Delhi 110 002
Phone: 011 2326 3290

Also at Bangalore, Mumbai, Hyderabad and Guwahati

Typeset by Rawat Computers, Jaipur
Printed at Chaman Enterprises, New Delhi

Contents

Preface ix

Introduction: Theory and Practice of Ethnography 1
Ramesh C. Malik and Eswarappa Kasi

I
Practice of Ethnography

1 Ideology and Practice in Ethnographic Research 13
Kamal K. Misra

2 Interpreting Women's Protest: Ethnographic Research with Women Survivors of the Bhopal Gas Disaster 22
Brian J. Mooney

3 Empowerment and Social Change in Tripura Tribal Community of Bangladesh 43
Khurshed Alam

4 'Salwa Judum' and Loss of Cultural Practices among Tribes of Bastar: An Anthropological Concern 61
Devesh K. Sahu and Ankita Arya

5 Scientific and Cultural Gap in Explaining Health: An Ethnographic Analysis of Reproductive Morbidity among Tribal Women in Kerala 67
O.G. Sajitha

6 The Ethnographic Imagination 76
Mohan Ramanan

7 Ethnography Training for Translators 79
Ramesh C. Malik

II
Language, Literature and Culture: An Enthnographic Appraisal

8 How did the Oriya Language Catch 'Fire'? 93
Panchanan Mohanty

9 Question-Words and its Morpho-Syntactic Study of Rongmei Language 100
Haireisim Newme

10 *Trajectory of Extinction:* Forgotten Spirit of Arabic-Malayalam 108
Yasser Arafath P.K.

11 Narrating the Voice of the Voiceless: A Critical Interrogation of Marginality in Modern Indian Fiction 121
K. Venugopal Reddy

12 The 'Other' Amidst 'Us': The Narrative of the Domestic Worker 142
Tutun Mukherjee

13 Depiction of Women in Ao-Naga Folk Tales 153
Resenmenla Longchar and J. Limainla Ao

III
Rethinking History and Deconstruction of Ethnographic Realism

14 Under Surveying Eyes: Ethnographical Profiling and the Construction of 'Identities' in the Colonial Writings in the Garo Hills 165
Babitha Justin

15 Creating Identities: British Rule and the Hos of Singhbhum, 1820–1932 174
Sanjukta Dasgupta

16 Challenging the Sanskritic Order: Emergence of the Sudra to Subaltern Consciousness in Pre-Colonial Orissa 191
Basanta Kumar Mallik

17 The 'Savage Other' in Naga Historiography: Condition and Paradigm 200
Temjenwabang

18 Rethinking the Concept of Tribe Construction and Re-construction of *Adivasi* Identity 220
Netrapal Singh

IV
Social Development and Ethnographic Discourses

19 The Rational and the Relative: History and Tradition in the Construction of Social Knowledge 253
Upendra

20 Political Economy of Drought and Sustainability: A Village Study in Chittoor District of Andhra Pradesh 264
P. Raghupathi, K. Gangaratnam and V. Subramanyam

21 Land and Dalits: A Village Study 287
E. Krishna Rao

22 Improved Biophysical Management and Livelihood Security: Said and Done through Community Watersheds? 308
R.P. Mula, N.V. Thang, T. Wangkahart, S.P. Wani and Y. Supama

23 Perspectives on Higher Education: Affirmative Action for the Marginalized 326
Md. Irfan Basha

24 Poverty and Vulnerability among Tribal People: A Case of Sugalis 337
Eswarappa Kasi

Contributors 355

Preface

The volume comprises a selection of papers presented at the *Ethnographic Discourse of the Other* an International Conference, organized by School of Humanities and School of Social Science, University of Hyderabad, July 3–5, 2007. It presents papers which conglomerate four special themes highlighted and briefly discussed at the conference, namely, the theory and practice of ethnography, language, literature and culture, rethinking history and social development.

This is our privilege to express our deep gratitude to the anonymous referees for insightful suggestions integrated in the present volume. We would like to remember here all the institutions and individuals who have provided sponsorship, encouragements and various kinds of helps without which this volume would never have seen the light of academic genre. First of all, we would like to thank the following institutions for sponsoring financial help: Indira Gandhi Rashtriya Manav Sangrahalaya, Bhopal; Centre for World Solidarity, Secunderabad; Dean, School of Humanities, School of Social Sciences and Dean, Students Welfare, University of Hyderabad, Hyderabad.

We are highly grateful to all those participants and our teachers, Profs. Panchanan Mohanty, Mohan Ramanan, Kamal K. Misra, E. Haribabu, Siva Prasad and M.N. Rajesh who helped to lay the foundation of our ethnographic understandings in interdisciplinary way. We must indebted to our friends, at University of Hyderabad for helping us blending these suggestions with their own wise advice. A special thanks goes to Prof Kishor K. Basa, the Director of IGRMS and Surya K. Pandey and Suchir Shrivastava, for their continuous encouragement and every support for materializing this event. We are also thankful to Rawat Publications for bringing out the volume beautifully and in right time.

Ramesh C. Malik and Eswarappa Kasi

Introduction

Theory and Practice of Ethnography

RAMESH C. MALIK AND ESWARAPPA KASI

The concept of ethnography is evolved from the tradition of cultural anthropology, which manifests the scientific study of human beings and its surrounding culture. In a broad sense ethnography is an interdisciplinary in nature and it deals with the disciplines those are studying on human culture, cognition, language, and society. Though, it is a structural branch of anthropology some times it is included also in the discipline of humanities (folklore, linguistic, literature), history, and sociology. So, you can say it is not only the branch of social science but also an allied branch of humanities. Before discussing the theme and perspectives of ethnography, a few remarks need to remembered, i.e., meanings of ethnography, nature of ethnography, and tasks for ethnographer. Because, it may useful to understand the ethnographic description as well helps to evaluate an ethnographic texts. Literarily, ethnography means writing about people, or writing an account of the ways of life of a particular people (Hammersley, 2007: 1479). On the other hand, ethnography is the study of people's behaviour in naturally occurring ongoing setting, with a focus on the cultural interpretation of behaviour (see also Firth, 1961; Hymes, 1982). It shows that ethnography is a source of cultural communication or transformation from one form to another form. In one way, ethnography is a process and other way it is a product. In the theme of process the ethnography gives ideas about data collection, participant observation, interviews, and recoding of human actions in natural settings and secondly it also gives the road map of describing cultural practices of the people and their society. In other way, ethnography as a product, which means a documentation of the entire cultural behaviour of people or group of people including their livelihood, social institution, rituals, beliefs, culture poverty, economy, cultural dynamics, indigenous knowledge, knowledge shifting, language, literature, history, and all related biological and ecological informations. So, the term has a double meaning, referring to a form of research and to product of that research: ethnography as a practice produces ethnographies (Hammersley, 2007: 1479). To read, write and understand ethnography and its interdisciplinary functions we should have satisfactory definitional knowledge about ethnography, which will help to get a clear structural and functional properties of ethnography.

Working Definitions of Ethnography

1. Ethnography is the art and science of describing a group or culture (Fetterman, 1998: 1).
2. In its most characteristic form it involves the ethnographer practising, overtly or covertly, in people's daily lives for an extended period of time, watching what happens, listening to what is said, asking questions—in fact, collecting whatever data are available to throw light on the issues that are the focus of the research (Hammersley and Atkinson, 1995: 1).
3. Ethnography is a research process in which the anthropologist closely observes, records, and engages in the daily life of another culture—an experience labelled as the fieldwork method—and then writes accounts of the culture, emphasizing descriptive details. These accounts are the primary form I which the fieldwork procedures, the other culture, and the ethnographer's personal and theoretical reflections are accessible to professionals and other readerships (Marcus and Fischer, 1986: 18).
4. Ethnography is the study of people in naturally occurring settings or 'fields' by means of methods which capture their social meaning and ordinarily activates, involving the researcher participating directly in the setting; if not also the activities, in order to collect data in a systematic manner without meaning being imposed on them externally (Brewer, 2000: 10).

Above definitions of ethnography claim at least two dimensional meaning, on the one hand, it refers to data collection procedure and other hand, it refers to that product of entire exercise that is a monographic description of research work where researcher engaged.

The Nature of Ethnography

The first takes the task of ethnography to be documenting stable cultures, patterns of social interaction, institutions, and so on, as they exist in the world independently of the researcher. By contrast, constructionism is concerned with the interactional or discursive processes whereby cultures, institutions, etc., are continuously and contingently produced and sustained. In line with this, constructionist do not use informants' accounts as a source of information about the world, or even about informants' own experience, but rather study them as exemplifying discursive practices, narrative strategies, or distinctive voices. Moreover, in its more radical forms constructionism treats the social phenomena studied by ethnographers as effectively constituted in and through the research process itself, and especially through the process of writing (Clifford and Marcus, 1986). Indeed, de Certeau argues that the writer of ethnography first appears in the guise of the woman because ethnography is initially in competition with an 'older' form of writing, that is, the contemplation of and transcription of biblical revelation (cf from Clough, 1992: 16–17). Ethnography instead proposes a writing that seemingly owes nothing to the contemplation of historical tradition and everything to the observational methodology of empirical scientific research. Ethnography, therefore, founds itself on "a form (a network of formal relations)" that "consists more in what scientific research gives itself as work rules than in what it receives a law of history" (Clough, 1992: 16–17). As a set of methods, ethnography is not far removed from the means that we all use in everyday life to make sense of our surroundings. However, it involves a more deliberate and systematic approach and, also, distinctive mentality. This can perhaps best be summarized as seeking to make the strange familiar, in the sense of finding intelligibility: and rationality within it, and making the familiar strange, by suspending those background assumptions that immediately give apparent sense to what we experience (Hammersley and Atkinson, 1995). The ethnography can be written in many styles and in many formats. A typical ethnography describes the history of the group, the geography of the location, kinship patterns, symbols, politics, economic systems, educational or socialization systems, and the degree of contact between the target culture and mainstream culture. Specialized ethnographies may focus on specific elements of socialization of the young or the role of a significant person such as the principal (Fetterman, 1998: 12, cf. Wolcott, 1973). In his recent paper "ethnography" Martyn Hammersley laid down significant nature of the ethnography and he states in practical terms, as a method, ethnography usually involves most of the following features:

1. People's actions and accounts are studied primarily in everyday contexts rather than under conditions created by the researcher, such as in experiments or highly structured interview situations. In other words, research takes place 'in the field'.
2. Data are gathered from a range of sources, including documentary evidence, but participant observation and/or relatively informal conversations are usually the main ones.
3. Data collection is 'unstructured' in the sense that it does not involve following through a fixed and detailed research design set up at the beginning. Nor are the categories that will be used for interpreting what people say or do built into the data collection process itself via prestructuring of observation, interviews, or documentary analysis.
4. The focus is usually on a small number of cases, perhaps a single setting or group of people, typically small scale, with these being studied in depth.
5. The analysis of the data involves interpretation of the meanings and functions of human actions and how these are implicated in local and wider contexts. What are produced, for the most part, are verbal descriptions, explanations, and theories; quantification and statistical analysis play a subordinate role at most.

The Task of Ethnographer

Primary goal of ethnographer is to provide a description of cultural forms. In this context, Malinowski's frontispiece suggests what events that narrative would typically dramatize in the name of empiricism: the trials of the researcher in the field. In entering the field, the discipline and dispassion of the ethnographer's empirical methodology are put on trial; they are shown to be triumphant only when, having suffered the experience of fieldwork, the researcher is able to leave the field and return home to write (Clough, 1992: 17).

The ethnographer's task is not only to collect information from the emic or insider's perspective but also to make sense of all the data from an etic or external social scientific perspective. John D.Brewer suggests that in doing and writing up ethnographic research, ethnographers should:

1. Establish the wider relevance of the setting and the topic, and clearly identify the grounds on which empirical generalizations are made, such as by establishing the representativeness of the setting, its general features, or its function as a special case study with a broader bearing.
2. Identify the features of the topic that they are addressing in the study and those left unresearched, and discuss why these choices have been made and what implications follow from these decisions for the research findings.
3. Identify the theoretical framework they are operating within and the broader values and commitments (political, religious, theoretical and so on) they bring to their work.
4. Establish their integrity as researcher and author, by outlining:
   (i) the grounds on which knowledge claims are being justified (length of fieldwork, the special access negotiated, discussing the extent of the trust and rapport developed with respondents, and so on);
   (ii) their background and experience in the setting and topic;
   (iii) their experiences during all stages of the research, especially mentioning the constraints imposed therein;
   (iv) the strengths and weaknesses of their research design and strategy.
5. Establish the authority of the data, by:
   (i) discussing the problems that arose during all stages of the research;
   (ii) outlining the grounds on which they developed the categorization system used to interpret the data, identifying clearly whether this is an indigenous one, used by respondents themselves, or an analyst-constructed one; and if the latter, the grounds which support this;
   (iii) discussing rival explanations and alternative ways of organizing the data;
   (iv) providing sufficient data extracts in the text to allow readers to evaluate the inferences drawn from them and the interpretations made of them;
   (v) discussing power relations within the research, between researcher(s) and subjects and within the research team, in order to establish the effects of class, gender, race and religion on the practice and writing up of the research.
6. Show the complexity of the data, avoiding the suggestion there is a simple fit between the social world under scrutiny and the ethnographic representation of it, by:
   (i) discussing negative cases which fall outside the general patterns and categories employed to structure the ethnographic description, which often serve to exemplify and support positive cases;
   (ii) showing the multiple and often contradictory descriptions proffered by respondents themselves;

(iii) stressing the contextual nature of respondents' accounts and descriptions, and identifying the features which helps to structure them (2001: 104–105).

It means ethnographer is a good surgeon who used to do culture operations. Theses are the preliminary intuition to entering the culture operation, the ethnographer or surgeon should more optical about above-mentioned procedures of doing and writing ethnographic research.

Ethnographic Discourse of the Others

The "Ethnographic Discourse of the Others", broad theme interestingly elaborates the theoretical and empirical layout of the research process and product from the genre of allied disciplines such as anthropology, linguistic, literature, history, and sociology. In our context, we have considered the esthetic of the 'Other' is confined on the subhuman society mainly, woman, tribal, downtrodden, savage and marginalized people across the world, who are living under the deprivations, economically, socially, culturally, and linguistically. Applying the methodological tools of ethnography how the ethnographer or researcher can experiment the social realities from the different time and space consciously is the focal task of the exercise. For us ethnography is a process, also a product. Let us see how the theoretical processes and empirical products are offering beautiful flavours from different blossoms.

Practices of Ethnography

Ethnography is both method and methodology. Method refers the data collection techniques and methodology implies the theoretical and philosophical framework. First paper of the book is introducing the syntax of ethnography and its relevance to preparing ethnographic discourse in the discipline of social sciences by *Kamal K. Misra*. He vividly discussed on the nature and role of ethnography and its theoretical juncture from the different point of views. In social construction, the role of women and their resistance against dominance is very vibrant to recall their social justice and gender identity. *Brian Mooney's* paper analyses the women's speeches to understand how the women represent themselves as women within the context of a dominant discourse of women's subjectivity in contemporary Indian society that equates 'woman' with 'wife' and 'mother', and it engages with contemporary Indian scholarship on those issues of women's subjectivity and discourses of gender. The study of *Khurshed Alam* concentrates on the theme of empowerment and social changes in Tripura tribal community of Bangladesh. He discusses on the scope of improvement of their situation prevailing and in which they have to be figured out and plan has to be made to improve their situation further keeping conformity with their culture, ecological setting, access to local resources availability. *Devesh K. Sahu* and *Ankita Arya* have focused on the issues of human rights and destroying the traditional lives of indigenous peoples in entire Bastar division of Chhattisgarh, commonly called as 'Naxalite affected area of the state'. *O.G. Sajitha's* paper aimed to analyse and compare the explanatory models suggested as the cause of abortion, gynecological morbidity and antenatal, natal and post-natal morbidity by three different tribal groups in

Kerala. The ideology of ethnographic can bridge the gap between humanities and social sciences. *Mohan Ramanan* suggests that anthropology and the ethnological dimensions of the subject are of great importance in our present times. This is because we do not live in a world of easily held beliefs and certainly any essential formulations like Man, Justice or Love are looked upon with a degree of scepticism. And the paper of *Ramesh C. Malik*'s claims that ethnography training is important for translators to prepare faithful translation and ethnography training can reject the cultural divination of translation.

Language, Literature and Culture: An Ethnographic Appraisal

Language, literature and culture are integral part of the culture and society. By the mid-twentieth century, anthropological approaches had influences common beliefs about culture, especially: (1) that human societies cannot be explained simply by natural environment or human biology; (2) that cultural possibilities are innumerable; (3) that cultures are diverse; (4) that different elements within a culture are patterned and interconnected; (5) that elements of culture must be understood by pacing them in their context, rather than by treating them in isolation (Spillman, 2007: 922). "Language constitutes the most distinctive feature of a culture, which maybe described in a simplistic manner as the totality of the beliefs and practices of a society. And although a language may be regarded as a relatively small part of a culture, it is indispensable for both the functioning and the perpetuation of the culture" (Nida, 2002: 13). Because language is a part of culture, and linguistics from the point of view, may be consider a branch of cultural anthropology, the relationship between language and other aspects of culture has naturally become a concern of anthropological linguistics. This rather vague area of knowledge is often called ethno-linguistic (Greenberg, 1971: 293). In this genre, *Panchanan Mohanty* discovered a road map between two language family, Dravidian and Indo-Aryan. By following ethno-methodology, first, he possesses a sound knowledge of phonology and morphology in order to decipher the etymological history of a word. Second, the Oriya word for fire,/niā:/has a Dravidian source and it is indicative of the importance of Dravidian substratum in the Oriya language and culture. *Haireisim Newme* discussed on "Question-Words and its Morpho-Syntactic Study of Rongmei Language". Mainly his interest goes to linguistic analysis of simple and complex sentences and assertive and questions sentences. He found that morphemes, with clear-cut boundary between them, carrying grammatical functions such as tense, number, person, gender, and genitive, etc.

Language as an identity is raised by *Yasser Arafath. P.K.* His intuition devoted on forgotten spirit of Arabic-Malayalam and the historical evident shows how a linguistic community is journeying through the language endangerment. Literature is probably most useful, however, as a tool to help ethnographers to communicate their insights (1998: 126). So, *K. Venugopal Reddy* discussed on Indian English fictions by Mulk Raj Anand's *Untouchable* (1935), and Kamala Markandaya's *The Nectar in a Sieve* (1954). He demonstrates the narrative reality through their admirable portrayal the social and economic forms of marginalization in India. Literary texts can claim to be sources of ethnography. In her paper, "The 'Other' amidst 'Us': The Narrative of the Domestic Worker" *Tutun Mukherjee* explores ethnographic motivations in literary texts. Her study focuses on two literary texts: *The Diary of a Maidservant*, a translation of Krishna Baldev Vaid's Hindi novel *Ek Naukrani ki Diary* and *A Life Less Ordinary* by Baby Haldar translated into English from Bengali original *Alo Andhari*. Folktales are important to both literate and non-literate societies. They crystallize an ethos or a way of being. Cultures often use folktales to transmit critical cultural values and lessons from one generation to the next. Folktales usually draw on familiar surroundings and on figures relevant to the local setting, but the stories themselves facades (Fetterman, 1998: 60). A co-authored paper by *Resenmenla Longchar* and *J. Limainla Ao* propose the process of recovering history from the folklore is complex but not impossible task and here a rich diversity of sources with their multiple representations can be highlighted. In the Ao-Naga women's context, the different strategy can reveal a set of ideas, desires, imagination in which some facet of society are given in different treatment which is not consonant with regular narratives. It is this aspect, which reveal the process of 'Othering' within the Ao-Naga society which helps to understand the past in a more wholesome and objective manner.

Rethinking History and Deconstruction of Ethnographic Realism

Ethnography presents as factual representations of cultural perspectives, historical events, and social situations (Clough, 1992: 17).Therefore, the descriptions of cultural, social and historical situations that the ethnography puts forth in the relative terms of empirical correspondences depend for their authority on the narrative construction of the subject (Clough, 1992:18). In literate societies, written documents are one of the most valuable and timesaving forms of data collections (Fetterman, 1998: 58). *Babitha Justin* presents an ethnographical profiling and the construction of 'Identities' in the Colonial writings in the Garo Hills. She argues that the early attempts at ethnography have a long-lasting effect in the sense that these books are used as source texts for information on the Garo culture before written Garo was introduced. These books also contain definitions helped create a different 'identity', completely antithetical to the localized and parochial identity, which was gradually forged into the larger concept of 'nationhood'. In the same direction, *Sanjukta Dasgupta*'s essay demonstrates the historical perspective on Ho tribe of Singhbhum, particularly in colonial period from (1820–1932). Her argument is British rule undoubtedly created categories and policies that impacted in a major way on indigenous identities, we should remember that tribal people were not simply passive participants in the making of their destinies but they too sought to actively recreate their self-identity in keeping with the socio-economic and political culture of the time. *Basanta Kumar Mallik* challenges in historical religious movement in medieval Orissa, particularly the subaltern writers are confronted to reject the goggle-de-gook of Sanskrit literary discourses. Further, he argues the subaltern writers discontent against the contemporary society, priests, ruling class and their sincere efforts for scholarly enquiry are clearly discernible in their writings. *Temjenwabang* concentrated on "the 'Savage Other' in Naga Historiography: Condition and Paradigm" and he persistent discourse of the early Nagas as the savages other in the colonial sources 'conditioned' most of the post-colonial writers. For, a sensible consideration arguably indicates that the colonial construct of other inferior societies was also justifiable, though the metaphors and allusions to portray these societies were often derogatory at the same time. *Netrapal Singh* gives the historical development of tribe or tribal concepts by native and non-native social scientists. He briefly demonstrates the theory of tribe and its horizontal application in different context.

Social Development and Ethnographic Discourse

Social development consists of two interrelated aspects, one ethnographic learning and policy making which can help to discovers better ways to fulfil social aspirations and it develops organizational mechanisms to express that ethnographic knowledge to achieve its social and economic goals. The process of ethnographic discourse manifesto the human consciousness to mobilize the social developmental knowledge from one to another. In this aspect, *Upendra* imagination theorizes the Rational and the Relative: History and Tradition in the Construction of Social Knowledge which answers the questions rose above with respect to different knowledge systems like social knowledge and moral knowledge. The central purpose of the paper is to describe the friendly connection between generic knowledge that has autonomous value, and other forms of knowledge that are grounded in cultures, histories, traditions and other contingent factors. *P. Raghupathi* and his co-authors are tried to analyses the crop diversification that led to sustainability of rural mass in various ways. And how it paves the way for livestock development, which in its turn leads to further development of dairy industry. Moreover, how the dairy industry become as a significant and subsistence occupation to the all sections of population at a drought-prone village level as a whole. *E.Krishna Rao*'s paper on land and Dalits in Andhra Pradesh where found land creates social deprivation. So his paper tried to give some input to revive the policy on land renovation. Further, he suggests government should provide alternative employment through the self-employment programmes to these landless SCs. *R.P. Mula* and others presents on the natural resource management while simultaneously securing livelihoods of farm households. Based on a study conducted in four watersheds in Thailand and Vietnam, interventions implemented to improve the biophysical resources correspondingly improved livelihoods of resource-poor farm households under conditions of strong capacity building and user sensitivity. *Md. Irfan Basha's* ethnographic "Perspective of Higher Education and its Affirmative action for the Marginalized" gives wide perspective on issues relating to the education of Muslims in India and particularly in Andhra Pradesh. He states the Muslims are at a double disadvantage with low levels of education combined with low quality education; their deprivation increases manifold as the level of education rises. In some instances the relative share for Muslims is lower even than the SCs who are victims of a long-standing caste system. Eventually, *Eswarappa Kasi* speaks on culture of "Poverty and Vulnerability among Tribal People: A Case of Sugalis of Ananthapur". His empirical notions are dealing with the subjectivity of vulnerability which can be understood by analyzing the real life situations and strategies adopted by the people to manage their livelihoods.

Conclusion

The cognitive process of human, as a result, creates some sorts of textual vignette in his/her thoughts. Ethnographic is a set of cognitive processes which claims a structural and functional product of the human race, caste, religion, language, culture, belief, social structure, historiography, and other internal and external constituent elements of the human society. To construct an ethnographic text, the process itself covers the methodological practices of the authority concerned, which may be an anthropologist, sociologist, linguist, writer, historian, and scholar of the interdisciplinary studies. The final product takes a filtering composition from the base of the methodological wombs that, alternatively, demands an ethnography form of that whole cluster. It conveys that the process of social practices as well as products is reciprocal in some points though they are not synonymous, but the pragmatic nuances of the textual abilities formulate a synonymous situation. So, it contains a broad generic experimentation and explanation of particular modes and objectives can ideally make the different flavour from different angle which are implanted in this volume.

References

Brewer, J.D., (2000), *Ethnography*, Buckingham: Open University Press.

———, (2001), "The Ethnographic Critique of Ethnography: Sectarianism in the RUC", Alan Bryman (ed.), *Ethnography*, Vol. IV, London: Sage Publications.

Bromley, YU. V., (1984), *Theoretical Ethnography*, Moscow: Nauka Publishers.

Clifford and Marcus, (1986), *Writing Culture: The Poetics and Politics of Ethnography*, Berkeley: University of California Press.

Clough, Patricia Ticineto, (1992), *The End(s) of Ethnography from Realism to Social Criticism*, New York: Sage Publications.

Fetterman, D.M., (1998), *Ethnography Step by Step*, (2nd edition), Thousand Oaks: CA, Sage Publications.

Firth, R., (1961), *Elements of Social Organization*, Boston: Beacon.

Greenberg, Joseph H., (1971), "The Science of Linguistics", Anwar S. Dil (ed.), *Language, Culture and Communication*, California: Stanford University Press.

Hammersley, M. and Atkinson, P., (1995), *Ethnography*, (2nd edition), London: Routledge.

Hammersley, M., (2007), *Ethnography*, George Ritzer (ed.), *The Blackwell Encyclopedia of Sociology*, Vol. II, Oxford: Blackwell Publishing Ltd.

Hymes, D., (1982), *What is Ethnography?* in P. Gilmore and A.A. Glatthorn (21–32). Washington, DC: Centre for Applied Linguistics.

Marcus, G.E. and Fischer, M.M.J., (1986), *Anthropology and Cultural Critique: An Experimental Moment in the Human Science*, Chicago: University of Chicago Press.

Nida, Evgene A., (2002), *Contexts in Translating*, Amsterdam: John Benjamins Publishing Company.

Spillman, Lyn, (2007), *Culture*, George Ritzer (ed.), *The Blackwell Encyclopedia of Sociology*, Vol. II, Oxford: Blackwell Publishing Ltd.

Wolcott, H.F., (1973), *The Man in the Principals Office: An Ethnography*, New York: Holt, Rinehart and Winston, (Reissued by Waveland Press).

I
Practice of Ethnography

1 Ideology and Practice in Ethnographic Research

KAMAL K. MISRA

The trajectory of discourses on the nature and role of ethnography in social science research has drawn the attention of many anthropologists and students of cultural studies since it was recognized as an inevitable instrument in collecting reliable and scientific empirical data for further analysis and preparation of research reports. Many anthropologists divide ethnographic practices into two kinds: 'traditional ethnography' and 'alternative writings'. Traditional ethnography applies to "... certain writing conventions aimed to fulfill the scientific paradigm—particular narrative structure that claims to represent totality of social or cultural life, scientific observer image, 'people' image, native point of view, rapport, and objective and generalizable style" (Klumbyte, 2001). This practice is dated prior to 1960 and critiqued as being subjective, contextual and ideological, failing to deal with history, change, political economy, and situational issues. Consequently, alternative writing emerged in the post-1960 period to address the aforementioned shortcomings of the traditional ethnography and primarily advocated new writing strategies that are sensitive to anthropologist, viz. informant relations, social and contextual situatedness of the researcher, relevance of political economy and history, as well as ethical and political circumstances. As a result, this new style included subjectivity, reflexivity, dialogue, different perspectives, openness, and conflict situations as a part of ethnographic writing (ibid.). In this paper, while I am inclined to give full credit to the critiques of the traditional ethnography for many of its failures, I argue that alternative writings do not at once transcend all the problems of traditional ethnography and are far from problematic themselves. The problems of subjectivity/objectivity issues, author-centred texts, prevalence of anthropologist's authority over final analysis, ethical and political sensitivities, the limits of new theoretical paradigms (social history, political economy), native anthropology, etc., continue to engage anthropologists in critical discussions even now. I contend that ethnographies are largely textual constructions, they are shaped by political and historical contexts, moral and ideological imperatives, bound to disciplinary constraints, and limited to the theoretical models they apply. There are also certain inherent problems in our tradition of fieldwork that regulate the nature and texture of these textual constructions that are bound to reflect on the reliability, validity and authenticity of ethnographic writing that every ethnographer has to bear in mind. What are the options then before us as ethnographers? Should we abandon ethnographic practice and writing altogether? If not, instead of mere critiquing the ethnographic practice and writing, I would appeal for a more conscientious and reflexive ethnography. I resolutely believe that in ethnographic practice and writing although perfect objectivity may not be attainable, it can be approximated. I also contend that scientific standards and procedures available in social sciences should be meticulously maintained in order to achieve an impartial perspective on cultural data to raise their level of validity and reliability. Since absolute value neutrality is near impossible in ethnographic research and writing, starting with the personal prejudices of the ethnographer to the very nature of fieldwork, the ethnographer should cultivate the habit of honestly declaring the possible sources of prejudices that might inflict the ethnography. I hope this will neutralize the contentious issues of authenticity and authority in ethnographic practices.

Ethnography in Perspective

Before I proceed further, it is imperative to understand what the word 'ethnography' means. Ellen (1984), for example, alludes to at least five different meanings of ethnography, although their differences are subtle in nature. In common parlance it is used to refer to empirical accounts of the culture and social organization of particular human populations. This implies that ethnography is a product of intensive data collection and their meticulous analysis. This meaning of ethnography immediately changes when it is opposed to 'theory'. While theory is generally concerned with an organized way of thinking about a given subject, ethnography is a tool that helps in this process of organization of thought. Further, 'an ethnographic account' (of a living people) is characteristically different from the historical or archeological account, as the latter requires altogether different tools to arrive at any conclusion. Apart from these distinctions, when the term is used to indicate a set of research procedures, it accounts for an intensive qualitative study of small human groups through 'participant observation'. And finally, 'ethnography' may refer to an academic subject that revolves round the comparative study of ethnic groups or races of men. Therefore, Ellen suggests, "... ethnography is something you may do, study, use, read or write. The various usages reflect ways in which different scholars have appropriated the term, often for perfectly sound conceptual reasons" (1984: 8).

Despite its many definitions and varied ways in which it is described, for the purpose of this paper, I understand ethnographic research as a broad rubric for investigations described variously as qualitative research, case study research, field research, anthropological research, or ethnography (Smith, 1974, 1979). Characteristics of ethnographic research include "... participant and non-participant observation, focus on natural settings, use of participant constructs to structure the research, and investigator avoidance of purposive manipulation of study variables. Although these approaches are most common in sociology and anthropology, they are used to some extent by all social science disciplines" (LeCompte and Goetz, 1982).

The end-product of an ethnographic exercise is the text, which purports to deal with 'objective' facts. In other words, text is the result of a serious process of objectivization and an ultimate product of a complex interaction between 'self, and the 'other'. This supposedly objectivization of complex interaction between the ethnographer and the informants and its presentation in written texts has created an epistemological crisis in social sciences. It has raised many pertinent questions since the publication of *Writing Culture: The Poetics and Politics of Ethnography* edited by Clifford and Marcus (1986), and Marcus and Fischer edited *Anthropology as a Cultural Critique: An Experimental Moment in Human Sciences* (1986). Of course, prior to these outstanding publications, Edward Said's *Orientalism* (1979) had already stiffed the conscience of the ethnographers, when he examined the rhetoric of Western scholarship in colonial and neo-colonial settings and questioned its authority over the 'objective' portrayal of non-Western societies and cultures. This was the time when within the discipline of anthropology, Mead-Freeman, Redfield-Lewis controversies and the bitterness over the publication of Malinowski's field diary, etc., had already put the conventional ethnographic writing into utter disrepute. Since social science literature is replete with a plethora of references on this subject, it is not my intention to rehearse or refine the issues commonly engendered in the labels of 'post-modern' or 'reflexive' or 'auto-critical' writings again in this paper. However, suffice it to say that these critiques "... swept away many of the assumptions about the objects of ethnography: primitiveness, isolation, ahistoricity, statism, resistance to modernity. Acknowledgment of change, temporality, movement, wide-ranging circulations, and transnationalism led to questioning the relevance of all interpretations and explanatory theories based solely on cultural frames and on information gathered through fieldwork experience alone" (Borneman and Hammoudi, 2007).

Ethnographic Fieldwork and the Problem of Subjectivity

As a branch of social sciences in general, and social and cultural anthropology in particular, ethnography is an outcome of usually prolonged fieldwork in a community. Going by the definition of Hammersley and Atkinson (1995), the term ethnography refers "... primarily to a particular method or sets of methods. In its most characteristic form it involves the ethnographer participating, overtly or covertly, in people's lives for an extended period of time, watching what happens, listening to what is said, asking questions—in fact, collecting whatever data are available to throw light on the issues that are the focus of the research." Similarly, Johnson (2000) defines ethnography as "... a descriptive account of social life and culture in a particular social system based on detailed observations of what people actually do." These and other definitions of ethnography are emphatically rooted in the convention of fieldwork, which has some inherent problems that eventually lead to the problem of subjectivity. However careful the ethnographer might be and whatever precautions s/he might take to be objective and free from all prejudices, there is a possibility of subjectivity unconsciously creeping into ethnography. I shall enlist below some of these possibilities.

It should be realized that the fulcrum of fieldwork is essentially a human equation—an equation between the researcher and the informants. In other words, fieldwork is impossible without human company. Hence, it has to be collaborative in its essence and spirit. In this collaborative exercise, the researcher and its promise to be objective constitute only one half of the possibility of ethnography being free from subjective considerations, as the other half depends entirely on the informants and their resolute commitment to share only objective realities with the researcher. Therefore, it is evident that the outcome of fieldwork depends not only on the skills and motivations of the researcher, but also on the behaviour of the informants. Since exaggeration of selected events, suppression of significant facts, projection of self and the deeds of a particular actor beyond a required threshold, deliberate distortion of facts by the informants, etc., are common experiences encountered by the researcher, these make the resultant ethnography subjective on which s/he has very little control.

As suggested earlier, a typical ethnographic fieldwork is for a prolonged period in a community, usually lasting for at least one calendar year or more. The idea is that prolonged stay of the researcher in the midst of the community helps in frequent participant observation of many crucial social and cultural events that could not be otherwise experienced by the researcher. In fact, participant observation is the most powerful tool of a researcher, particularly if the community studied is largely a homogeneous one. But the problem arises with regard to the acceptability of the researcher by the host community, although the former is all prepared for a longer stay. The prime requirement for a longer and better fieldwork is the unpretentious acceptability of the researcher by the host community, which is difficult to come by. Whatever tall claims the researcher might make regarding his/her total acceptance by the hosts, it is a proven fact that for all practical purposes, the researcher belongs to the category of 'others' for the hosts. Therefore, Freilich (1970) is right when he remarks that the researcher can at best assume the role of a 'marginal native'. Under these circumstances, when the presence of the researcher in the community is looked with suspicion, the quality of data, on which the ethnography is based, is under severe threat.

Subjectivity during fieldwork and empirical data collection also creeps in, if the researcher and the informants are at different levels of intellectual orientation. It is more so, if the researched community is pre-literate. When the researcher places before the informants a question or a volley of questions, it is expected that the informants have understood the questions(s) and answer accordingly. But, in fact, most often than not, the questions are either not properly understood or misunderstood, and therefore, the answers that constitute the background of the data are either partial truths or non-truths. The researcher has in this case no control over the informants and considers the answers as the final truths that lead to subjectivity in ethnographic analysis and writing. In conventional ethnographic research since ethnography is about 'other' cultures and communities, lack of language competence of the study culture or community on the part of the researcher ends up with the data, which are, what Geertz (1973) calls, the interpretations of interpretations of interpretations. Sometimes, the interpreters engaged by the researcher due to his/her lack of knowledge of the local language/dialect manoeuver the data intentionally or unintentionally, thus bringing in subjectivity to ethnographic research and writing. Further, there are certain elements in a culture, which we may term as 'sensitive' or 'private', to which the researcher does not have an easy access even after a prolonged tenure of fieldwork. As a result, the ethnography turns out to be incomplete or partial, and the researcher has to satisfy himself/herself with whatever data available for writing ethnography.

Perhaps the most important source of subjectivity in ethnography is due to the fact that the researcher has to get entangled with at least three distinct cultures and has to get him/her properly acquainted with all three of them, which is a Herculean task. One of them is the 'culture of orientation', the second, 'the native culture', and the third, 'the fieldwork culture'. Most often, these three cultures are at crossroads, and in some extreme cases, are mutually contradictory. The researcher has to strike a precarious balance in this situation to free him/her from the prejudices, and if not balanced, subjectivity is bound to get into the researcher's perception of the community and its culture.

It is not only the researcher, but also the conditions and techniques of ethnographic fieldwork that impose many challenges to the ethnographer to present an objective picture of the cultural reality. If the right kinds of informants are not selected, if the micro-cosmic location of fieldwork is not representative of the macro-cosmic universe of the study that spreads over a region, and if the time frame of fieldwork falls short of some cultural practices that extend well beyond the period of fieldwork, portrayal of cultural reality through ethnography is at serious stake. The other problem emanates from the theoretical position and concomitant hypotheses formulated by the researcher that orients his/her fieldwork. Since the researcher usually collects information consistent with his/her theoretical orientation and hypotheses, in all probability many counterevidences are deliberately ignored and underestimated, undermining the objectivity of ethnography. There are also personal and ethical considerations that limit the information sharing process. The social status and life experience of the researcher invariably colour the interpretation of the cultural data, bringing in subjectivity to ethnography. Further, if the ethnographer realizes that disclosing of some data and their sources might adversely impact communal harmony or otherwise prove harmful for the study community, such data are consciously suppressed and not reflected in the ethnography. This certainly undermines objectivity of the ethnography in question.

Besides these sources of subjectivity in ethnographic fieldwork, another important source is the nature of research itself. In social sciences, largely the problem of study is a matter of choice for the researcher. And this choice is usually governed by major ideological tendencies and political priorities of a given historical period. Within the domain of anthropology, we know that until recently ethnography meant the study of the 'other' non-White cultures in the colonies of the East by the Western scholars who were Whites. When the Western scholars were explaining social processes of the 'natives', they were necessarily evaluating these processes, and evaluation always presupposed a framework of values. Since values, and judgements based on these values, differ remarkably from one researcher to another, reliability or repetitiveness of ethnographic data was always a problem for the ethnographers. Therefore, it is possible that two different researchers may produce contradictory accounts of the same culture.

This situation has occurred several times and I have in mind the ugliest ever controversy on the analysis of child-rearing practices and adolescent behaviour among the Samoans of Polynesia. Margaret Mead's (1928–2001), culturological approach, for example, was based on a hypothesis that adolescent behaviour, and, in particular, adolescent crises typical in American family life, was culturally determined and not influenced by biological indicators, such as hormonal changes during maturation. Accordingly, she concluded that the Samoan parents raised their children in a permissive manner which brought them to a healthy adulthood in contrast to the anxieties and frustrations of American teenagers. Contrarily, another fellow anthropologist, Derek Freeman (1983), who carried out a study of the same culture suggested that Samoan adolescence was just as restrictive and turbulent as the American experience and that both reflected universal biological tendencies. This shows how ethnography largely depends on individual researcher and his/her perception of the study culture and community. John Beattie (1966) has stressed on the point as to how radical opposition has assumed prominence in ethnographic writings, as different researchers have conceived their universe of study differently. In addition to these problems, McGrath has drawn our attention to the fact that how difference in methodology makes a difference in the quality of data that have a bearing on the ethnographic research and writing.

Participant observation was conceived and popularized by Malinowski as an essential tool in ethnographic fieldwork. But it needs to be appreciated that total participation is neither necessary nor possible. Being a 'marginal native', the ethnographer has limited and conditional access to certain actions and performances in the field. Even if the ethnographer claims to be a participant observer of actions and events, more often than not he/she interprets these actions and events from the perspective of his/her culture of orientation. A great scholar like Verrier Elwin (1964) even after spending nearly his whole life in India and marrying two tribal women of Indian origin conceded that he never ceased to be an Englishman he was.

From Fieldwork to Ethnographic Writing

Closely associated with the problem of subjectivity in fieldwork, or what I would call 'ethnographic practice', outlined in the preceding section, ethnography as a product suffers serious setbacks as well. It is imperative to clarify that ethnography as a product is the 'text' based on empirical data collected by the ethnographer during his/her prolonged stay in the midst of the study community. Clifford and Marcus (1986) argue that ethnography begins "not with participant observation or with cultural texts (suitable for interpretation), but with writing, the making of texts". Writing texts on the basis of empirical data in itself is a complex process. Geertz (1973) for example, says, "the ethnographer 'inscribes' social discourse. *He writes it down.* In so doing he turns it from a passing event, which exists only in its own moment of occurrence, into an account, which exists in its inscription and can be reconsulted". Writing text, therefore, is a rhetorical activity, and Geertz argues, "We measure the cogency of our explications not against a body of uninterpreted data ... but against the power of the scientific imagination to bring us into touch with the lives of strangers" (ibid.). The ethnographer's use of rhetoric is, therefore, the process of transforming data into texts. As regards cultural representation of these texts, it is said, "The imaginative power which wins readers' assent is a matter not simply of knowledge but also of rhetorical skill. Ethnographies persuade readers not by the power of factual description but by employing the narrative structures, textual tropes, and argumentative topoi developed by the ethnographic genre. Geertz's own notion of 'thick description' is a case in point. It is a highly stylized form of verisimilitude that has become a standard in discussions of ethnographic method and functions as a textual strategy authorizing attempts at ethnographic realism" (Herndl, 1991). Therefore, writing ethnography is thoroughly a textual practice, and it is construed as a product of research rather than as a research method.

The textual practice of writing ethnography and the use of rhetoric in it has raised many questions. The central question to this practice is ethnographic authority, which James Clifford (1983) has articulated as: "How is unruly experience transformed into an authoritative written account? How, precisely, is a garrulous overdetermined, cross cultural encounter shot through with power relations and personal cross purposes circumscribed as an adequate version of a more-or-less discrete 'other world' composed by an individual author?" More often than not 'scientific' ethnographic research is transformed into another literary genre, that is the text, where "Literary processes metaphor, figuration, narrative—affect the ways cultural phenomena are registered, from the first jotted 'observations' to the completed book, to the ways these configurations 'make sense' in determined acts of reading" (Clifford and Marcus, 1986). Clifford and Marcus, therefore, assert that ethnographic truths are inherently partial—committed and incomplete.

Epilogue

There is no denying to the fact that in recent years the ideology and practices of traditional ethnography are increasingly under severe criticism. Doubts have been aptly expressed regarding the adequacy of traditional ethnographic methods and concepts to the intellectual and political challenges of the contemporary post-colonial world. Criticisms are abound against the construction of ethnographic texts, against the structure and practices through which the ethnographer establishes relationship with the informant in the field, against the efficacy of traditional ethnographic practices in a seemingly globalized and deterritorialized world, etc. (Gupta and Ferguson, 1997). But should we abandon the ideology and practice of ethnography, which has been a hallmark of social sciences in general, and anthropology in particular, for more than a century? What should be the way out? How ethnographic practice and writing can gear itself to the demands of the contemporary world? To me, it seems, although perfect objectivity in ethnographic data may not be attainable, it can nevertheless be approximated. And this is possible, if the ethnographer meticulously maintains the scientific standards and procedures available in social sciences to raise the levels of validity and reliability of ethnographic data. Further, since absolute value neutrality is nearly impossible in ethnographic research and writing, as subjectivity creeps in starting from the personal prejudices of the ethnographer to the very nature of fieldwork, the ethnographer should cultivate the habit of honestly declaring the possible sources of prejudices that might inflict the ethnography. I hope this will neutralize the contentious issues of authenticity and authority in ethnographic practices and writing. Reflecting on ethnographic practices in Anthropology, Gopala Sarana (1973) aptly maintains, "Anthropology has a humanistic element in its approach but it is not one of humanities. Its overall orientation is scientific rather than humanistic. But it is a science with a difference and sports a very high degree of procedural autonomy".

References

Beattie, John, (1966), *Other Cultures: Aims, Methods and Achievements in Social Anthropology*, New York: Free Press.

Borneman, John and Abdellah, Hammoudi (eds.), (2007), *The Future of Ethnographic Practices*, Chapter 1, Taipei: Academia Sinica and Department of Anthropology, National Chi Nan University http://www.ioe.sinica.edu.tw/chinese/seminar/07060203/qBornemqn.2dt.

Clifford, James, (1983), *On Ethnographic Authority*, Representations, 1 (2), 118–146.

Clifford, James and Marcus, G.E. (eds.), (1986), *Writing Culture: The Poetics and Politics of Ethnography*, Berkeley: University of California Press.

Ellen, R.F. (ed.), (1984), *Ethnographic Research: A Guide to General Conduct*, London: Academic Press.

Elwin, Verrier, (1964), *The Tribal World of Verrier Elwin: An Autobiography*, Oxford: Oxford University Press.

Freeman, Derek, (1983), *Margaret Mead and Samoa: The Making and Unmaking of an Anthropological Myth*, Cambridge: MA, Harvard University Press.

Freilich, Morris (ed.), (1970), *Marginal Natives: Anthropologists at Work*, New York: Harper and Row.

Geertz, Clifford, (1973), *Interpretations of Culture: Selected Essays*, New York: Basic Books.

Gupta, Akhil and James, Ferguson (eds.), (1997), *Anthropological Locations: Boundaries and Grounds of a Field Science*, Berkeley: University of California Press.

Hammersley, Martyn and Atkinson, Paul, (1995), *Ethnography: Principles in Practice*, (2nd edition), London: Routledge.

Herndl, Carl G., (1991), Writing Ethnography: Representation, Rhetoric and Institutional Practices, *College English*, 53 (3), 320–332.

Johnson, Allan G., (2000), *The Blackwell Dictionary of Sociology*, (2nd edition), Oxford: Blackwell Publishing.

Klumbyte, Neringa, (2001), "Problems of Ethnography Writing: Critics of the Traditional and Alternative Conventions", *Lietuvos Etnologija*, I (10).

Kulick, Don and Willson, Margaret (eds.), (1995), *Taboo: Sex, Identity and Erotic Subjectivity in Anthropological Fieldwork*, New York: Routledge.

LeCompte, Margaret D. and Judith, Preissle Goetz, (1982), "Problems of Reliability and Validity in Ethnographic Research", *Review of Educational Research*, 52(1), 31–60.

Marcus, George E. and Michael, M. Fischer, (1986), *Anthropology as a Cultural Critique: An Experimental Moment in the Human Sciences*, Chicago: University of Chicago Press.

Mead, Margaret, (1928/2001), *Coming of Age in Samoa: A Psychological Study of Primitive Youth for Western Civilization*, New York: Harper Collins Publishers.

Sarana, Gopal, (1973), "Anthropological Method and Indian Anthropology, (The L.K. Anantha Krishna Aiyar Birth Centenary Lectures, 1972–73)", Madras: University of Madras Press.

Smith, L.M., (1974), "Reflections on Trying to Theorize from Ethnographic Data", *Anthropology and Education Quarterly*, 5 (l), 18–24.

———, (1979), "An Evolving Logic of Participant Observation, Educational Ethnography and Other Case Studies", *Review of Research in Education*, 6, 316–377.

2 Interpreting Women's Protest

Ethnographic Research with Women Survivors of the Bhopal Gas Disaster

BRIAN J. MOONEY

> You are human, I too am human ... Gandhiji didn't divide anyone up, not Hindus and not Muslims. Our offspring should not be made Hindu or Muslim. People here have been divided up and have been made Hindus and Muslims. People are divided into their castes and are divided up into their parties.
>
> To make differences between people, four days ago in Rajasthan riots were incited. There was a curfew. I don't accept any of this. In Ajmer Sharif (a Muslim pilgrimage centre) millions of people were joined together in faith and belief. A Hindu-Muslim riot was incited in the name of the shrine in that city. What a big shame. It's a shame for the whole country. I saw a Bhojpuri boy making an offering at the door to the shrine. What faith, what belief! Today, what happened in Ajmer Sharif is such a shameful thing and no politician could do anything to stop it. Only society, only people can stop this.
>
> A member of Bhopal Gas-Affected Women Workers' Organization[1]

Since the days in the immediate aftermath of the 1984 Union Carbide gas disaster in Bhopal, activist organizations of survivors of the disaster have been struggling against Union Carbide Corporation and the Government of India for medical treatment, compensation, and occupational rehabilitation. For example, at the weekly Saturday rallies of the *Bhopal Gas Peerit Mahila Udyog Sangathan* (Bhopal Gas-Affected Women Workers Organization),[2] that continue even today, gas-affected women stand up in Bhopal's Shahjehani Park before an audience of 100–200 other women, and some men too, and deliver impassioned speeches to encourage their sisters and friends to continue their now 22 year-long struggle. The women in the Sangathan, whose behaviour and appearance is otherwise appropriately modest according to the conservative standards of Bhopal, also plan and execute frequent public protests and civil disobedience to secure their claims as survivors, including climbing over police barricades or marching themselves directly into a jailhouse to provoke arrest, just to mention two examples.

In their speeches, the women address their immediate concerns as Bhopal survivors demanding medical treatment, occupational rehabilitation, and compensation. Quoted above, however, is a sample of speech that appears to bear no direct relationship to the demands of the survivors of the Bhopal disaster for compensation and treatment. The women speak passionately about other compelling political, social and economic issues in contemporary India, such as communal violence and religious politics, corruption, the impact of foreign-branded products on their households, economic globalization and economic liberalization, elections, and even the significance and value of India's independence in 1947. While the primary purpose of the Sangathan is to agitate against Union Carbide and the Government of India to fulfil those demands for treatment, rehabilitation and compensation, the women of the Sangathan frequently address themselves to these other compelling and divisive contemporary issues of concern to poor people throughout India.

This paper concerns how and why such a marginalized group—poor women survivors of the Bhopal gas disaster—have come to embrace such a broad critique of contemporary India into their otherwise narrowly defined set of concerns. The paper analyses the women's speeches to understand how the women represent themselves as *women* within the context of a dominant discourse of gender in contemporary Indian society that reduces 'woman' to 'wife' and 'mother' in the subjectivity ascribed to women. By confining the form of their speeches to this protected domain of stereotyped expectations of women, the women of the Sangathan are able to radicalize the content of their speech and to extend their concerns beyond the particular concerns of Bhopal survivors.[3] In their speeches, the women ostensibly embrace that subjectivity in their public concerns as wives and mothers who have survived the Union Carbide gas disaster. But they also use that embrace of the dominant discourse about women to subversive effect as they find their agency and political voices in articulating their positions on those other compelling and controversial political topics. Ultimately, by embracing the very subjectivity that would marginalize women in political discourse, the women of the Sangathan find space for expression of their political agency.

The Disaster: An Overview

In December 1984, Union Carbide was operating a pesticide factory on the outskirts of the city of Bhopal. On the night of December 2–3, a tank containing highly toxic methylisocyanate gas exploded and the gas escaped. The gas was heavier than air so it settled to the ground where it was carried by the wind through the most heavily populated and poorest sections of the old city of Bhopal. With no emergency evacuation plans in place and no understanding of what was happening to them, about 5,00,000 people fled for their lives in the middle of the night in a mass exodus, but hundreds of thousands were injured when they inhaled the gas or when it came in contact with their eyes. The fatality estimates vary from the official government number of about 2,500 dead, to the numbers quoted by people on the street in Bhopal of 50,000 dead, and to a middle estimate by survivor organizations of about 15–20,000 dead. At first, the local medical authorities were not even sure what the chemical composition of the gas had been. Even after it was disclosed by Union Carbide to have been methylisocyanate, there were no protocols for treating the many thousands of people exposed to it. The city and the survivors struggled to cope not only with the massive scale of injuries, but also with thousands of cremations and burials. Lung and eye damage caused by exposure to the gas left many survivors unable to return to work since most were employed in some form of physical labour.

In 1987, after three years of legal manoeuvring in lawsuits commenced by the Indian survivors in American courts, the United States District Court in New York decided that India was the more appropriate forum for hearing the cases and dismissed them on the condition that Union Carbide submit to the jurisdiction of the Indian courts. The case against Union Carbide began all over again in the District Court in Bhopal where the local judge ordered Union Carbide to pay interim relief to the survivors. During an appeal of that order in 1989 to the Supreme Court of India, the Supreme Court ordered a settlement between Union Carbide and the Government of India (which had been authorized in 1985 by legislation of the Indian Parliament to represent the individual survivors) in order to accelerate relief to the survivors and to avoid an unprecedented litigation that seemed to be beyond the resources of the Indian judicial system. The survivors themselves were not notified in advance of the settlement and were not parties to the negotiations that seemed to take place in collusive secrecy between the Supreme Court, the Government of India, and Union Carbide. After appeal proceedings affirmed the settlement in 1991, Union Carbide paid $ 470 million to the Government of India. The government then took over the administration of all compensation and relief efforts. Having paid its settlement, Union Carbide ceased operations in India altogether and has disclaimed all further liability.[4]

During the many years of litigation, the Government of India and the local government in Bhopal undertook medical and rehabilitation relief efforts there. In the meantime, survivors in Bhopal began protesting against Union Carbide's lack of response to the disaster while the litigation was pending and also against the inadequacy of the government's own relief efforts. Survivor organizations formed and stepped up their agitations for relief. When the Supreme Court of India ordered the settlement in 1989, huge protests broke out in Bhopal and New Delhi as the survivors were enraged both at their exclusion from the settlement negotiations and at what seemed to be collusion between the Supreme Court, the Government of India, and Union Carbide. Those organizations, including the Sangathan, continue to agitate for better medical treatment for the survivors from a government medical bureaucracy established specifically for that purpose pursuant to the settlement agreement.[5]

Gendered Protest

> Gas-affected friends, it is important to me to work energetically to advance our organization. We must not sit by and rest on our laurels. Now it is May-June weather will arrive. Schools and colleges will close. Our children are sitting at home, our children who wanted jobs at Indira Gandhi Hospital. They should come every Saturday here to Shahjehani Park ... .
>
> In our hands, in our bodies there is complete strength. We will cause blood and sweat to flow continuously. We will perform non-violent resistance just like Gandhiji and we will chase off the plunderers who have come from afar.

> We say with a vow that we will forcefully advance our struggle and we will not withdraw. And as many desires as you have, you should always remember them. I want to say just this much and I'll stop my speech.
>
> Kamla Sharma[6]
> Member of Bhopal Gas-Affected
> Women Workers' Organization

The female-gendered subjectivity 'woman' foregrounded in both the Sangathan's name and in its protest practices emerges from the construction of that subjectivity in colonial India and from its elaboration in nationalist and post-colonial discourses (Chatterjee, 1993; Mani, 1989). By 'subjectivity', following Foucault, I refer to the shaping of women's social roles, social positions, and norms of behaviour that take place within relations of power; the dominant subject position for women has been the roles of wives and mothers subordinated to male authority. Subjectivity is uncovered through the analysis of the construction of subject positions in hegemonic discourses but also through the analysis of the agency of the subaltern made manifest in their "ability to engage with, appropriate, challenge, or subvert hegemonic discourses" (Mankekar, 1999: 28). Here, I examine the colonial and post-colonial representations of the category 'woman' as well as the ways in which women's agency in India has been visible and invisible in public activism.

I will consider the potential for women's activism to transcend the limitations of the dominant constructions of their subjectivity as wives and mothers and how this subject position contains the potential for agency in women's activism. The Sangathan is typical of women's activism and protest in India in ways that reproduce the hegemonic construct of the subject position 'woman'. But, as I will argue later, the deployment of 'women' in the Sangathan has had counter-hegemonic effects as Bhopal's women survivors find space in their public protests for the exercise of agency even while they ostensibly embrace the dominant construction of their subjectivity as women, as wives and mothers.

Female-gendered subjectivity in contemporary India emerges out of the deployment of the category of 'women' by 19th century Indian nationalists who were engaged with the discourse of British colonial rule. Lata Mani has argued, for example, that the discourse of colonial rule simultaneously produced the categories of 'tradition' and 'modernity' and in this discursive field, Indian nationalist reformers located 'women' within the realm of tradition, thereby claiming for Indian nationalists the prerogative to debate the rights and status of women in society (Mani, 1989: 90). Similarly, Partha Chatterjee has argued that in the early history of nationalism, the 'women's question', that is, questions of social reform relating to women such as *sati* and widow remarriage, became confined to the private, domestic sphere. By locating women and these questions within the domestic sphere, nationalists succeeded in locating them "in an inner domain of sovereignty, far removed from the arena of political contest with the colonial state" (Chatterjee, 1993: 117).

The association of 'woman' with 'tradition' and the 'domestic' in nationalist discourse constructed a subject position for women bearing particular moral and personal qualities, either thought to be inherent in femininity itself or to be cultivated through education of women (Chatterjee, 1993: 129–31). These qualities of modesty, purity, spirituality, and filial devotion came to mark women as distinct from the modern world external to the home (Chatterjee, 1993: 130–31; Sunder Rajan, 1993: 109). In this image women stand as signs for the 'nation' through their "spiritual qualities of self-sacrifice, benevolence, devotion, religiosity, and so on ... making it possible for her to go into the world under conditions that would not threaten her femininity" (Chatterjee, 1993: 131). The association of these signs of tradition with women meant that women could be effectively deployed in the nationalist struggle. But it was a subject position that sought to contain women's agency and that refused to acknowledge women as political actors, choosing instead to impute their overt political actions to the domestic influences of men (Visweswaran, 1996: 89).

Thus, women emerge in to the field of the modern and the political as the bearers of tradition in the form of moral and spiritual purity. Given these roles, women participated prominently in the nationalist and independence movements (see Kumar, 1993). Gandhi had faith in the central role of women in non-violent resistance due to their capacity for 'heroic non-violence' that he characterized as an "ancestral treasure lying buried in a corner of the house unknown to the members of the family" (Iyer, 1991: 387). He even argued that given this spiritual purity, it was women's *dharma* to dedicate themselves to the nation, whether it be within the home using a spinning wheel to produce their own cloth, or outside the home engaging in political protest and *satyagraha* (Mankekar, 1999: 109).

This figure of the properly feminine woman as domesticated bearer of tradition nevertheless bearing the public duty of salvation of the nation persists in popular representations of women in post-colonial India. Rajeswari Sunder Rajan (1993) argues that the pervasive image of the woman as self-sacrificing for family and nation, typified in the film *Mother India* (1957),[7] provides an almost mythic appeal for the public service of women, including, most notably, Indira Gandhi (Sunder Rajan, 1993: 109).

Other similar contemporary representations come from India's national television station, Doordarshan. Purnima Mankekar (1999) traces the history of Doordarshan's programming into the 1990's when broadcasting exploded through the construction of extensive transmission networks for television and through the simultaneous availability of televisions not only in middle class homes but in less wealthy homes as well (Mankekar, 1999: 5–6). Mankekar finds that Doordarshan's melodramatic serials routinely represent women as conforming to the ideal for the 'Indian woman' through such visible conventions of modesty as having her hair pulled back, through attention to tradition by wearing the *mangalsutra*, and through mindfulness of domestic feminine duties by showing devotion to her husband (Mankekar, 1999: 89). While generally confined to the home in these narratives, occasionally there are women characters who do venture forth from the home, but these characters hew to yet another ideal for Indian women: the woman devoted to the purity of her nation and to such other modern causes as 'national integration' and anti-communalism. For example, the title character of one serial, Kalyani, becomes a police officer who is dedicated by day to rooting out crime and corruption and by night to her duties as wife, mother and daughter (Mankekar, 1999: 119–21). She harnesses her 'traditional' domestic purity to the cause of national salvation and her 'modernity' is continuous with traditional domestic role rather than emerging from any independent source of female subjectivity (Sunder Rajan, 1993: 135). Her public life is never concerned with feminism or more loosely with 'women's issues' except insofar as those issues relate to women's 'traditional roles' (for example, women's activism against 'eve-teasing', a euphemism for sexual harassment). Rather, images of the 'new Indian woman' continue to represent women as bearers of tradition in their concerns for family, modesty and domesticity in a balance between "(deep) tradition and (surface) modernity" (Sunder Rajan, 1993: 133).

This representation of women extends to the ways in which women's activism and, indeed, militancy is represented in the context of contemporary social and political movements in India.[8] Tharu and Niranjana (1996) describe the ways in which women's activism in India has become both common and highly visible, but also the ways in which that activism (and representations of it) reproduces women's traditional roles, finding a "familial impulse behind women's militancy" and a responsibility for "rescuing not only their families but also 'saving the nation'" (Tharu and Niranjana, 1996: 256). Tharu and Niranjana warn against the 'undertow' of dominant discourses of the modern state on the feminist potential of women's movements (Tharu and Niranjana, 1996: 260). Kannabiran and Lalitha find that in the contemporary mobilization of women for political action, women's subjectivity as wives and mothers is strategically deployed even while women's agency as women is otherwise contained. Women are expected to participate politically within the gendered boundaries that highlight their purity, honesty and concern for the greater good of the nation while never challenging their subordinate status (Kannabiran and Lalitha, 1989: 183–87, 198).

In Bhopal, similarly, participation in the Sangathan has enabled women survivors of the Bhopal disaster to escape their marginalization as women, but in complicated ways. Not only did Union Carbide's gas literally drive women from their homes, it produced a social dysfunction so severe and widespread that women were mobilized in large number to engage in protest. In the following section, I will examine in detail the ways in which the subjectivity of women as wives and mothers is effectively mobilized in the Sangathan through its gendered practices of protest, specifically, through the form of the women's speeches and in their identification with domestic concerns. Bhopal women's mobilization is consistent with other cases of women's political activism in India insofar as it takes advantage of the location of women's subjectivity in the realm of 'tradition' and the domestic. It is also a mobilization, however, in which women's agency escapes, if temporarily, its domestic confinement as a result of the ways in which the Bhopal disaster has affected women in their lives in the home. As I will discuss below, in their participation in the Sangathan's protests, the Bhopal women survivors articulate their domestic experience of the Union Carbide gas disaster in ways that create meaningful links between the events of the night of the disaster and broader critiques of the social, political and economic circumstances of contemporary life in Bhopal.

The Sangathan and Women's Protest

The Bhopal Gas Peerit Mahila Udyog Sangathan was founded in December, 1987, by women survivors of the disaster who were protesting against the closure of an occupational rehabilitation programme being offered by the Government of Madhya Pradesh on behalf of the survivors of the Bhopal disaster. Soon after its formation, the Sangathan selected a prominent male Bhopal activist, Abdul Jabbar Khan, to lead the organization.[9] The occupational rehabilitation programme was to train women in sewing, a form of occupational rehabilitation that was considered appropriate for the women survivors given the physical limitations caused by exposure to the gas. The state government considered the sewing centres to be temporary training centres and not sources of permanent employment for the women, so it closed the training centres. In the meantime, the state continued to provide food commodities free of charge to the survivors. Jabbar and the Sangathan argued, however, that economic rehabilitation and employment were what the survivors needed over the long-term, not temporary handouts. Although the Sangathan succeeded in having the sewing centres reopened for a brief period, in the process the Sangathan had become actively engaged along with other survivor and activist organizations in the legal challenge against the Union Carbide settlement. No longer focused only on occupational rehabilitation, the Sangathan began agitating more broadly on behalf of the survivors also for medical research and treatment and for compensation.

The Sangathan is best known in Bhopal for its weekly protest rallies in Shahjehani Park, a public park on the edge of Bhopal's old city. On Saturdays at around 12:30 pm, the Sangathan's women members, some with children in tow, begin to gather and sit under the shade of the small trees behind the park's community house and under its verandah. Some women prepare their own *paan* out of little metal boxes or canisters they carry for this purpose. Others sit cutting up areca nuts with special nut cutters, then chew on the astringent cuttings. They chat quietly while the several men who work for the Sangathan hook up the loudspeakers and test them, repeatedly: "Hello, hello, hello ... ." They squat on the dusty ground and talk, the Muslim women lifting their black veils, although few bother to cover their faces anyway. Muslim and Hindu women sit together. They all have adopted a Muslim male custom: they gently shake each others' hands as a greeting, often using both hands. The women in the Sangathan are accustomed to foreigners and to Indians from Delhi or Bombay, journalists mostly, visiting the park on Saturdays. My first attendance drew little attention, but as I continued to come week after week over the course of three years, the women realized that I was not one of those foreign journalists who come and go quickly, especially because I was able to speak to them directly in Hindi. In the park, the women all greet each other by shaking hands, and some of the bolder women greet the men this way too. After I had become more of a permanent fixture at the meetings, some of the women even began to greet me this way, chose to sit near me, to invite me to a local tea stall, or to invite me to their homes.

I had assumed that during my stay in India—especially in as conservative a place as Bhopal—that I would have few occasions for direct interaction with women (particularly with women who were not of the English-speaking, educated classes). Except for my interactions with the women who worked in Sambhavna Clinic (another organization dedicated to assisting Bhopal survivors) and with the women who participated in the Sangathan, that was the case. I had read press reports about the Sangathan and about how the Muslim women in it had liberated themselves through the process of protesting the gas disaster. These reports had used the common trope of 'lifting the veils', which is to say, that the Muslim women, at least, had claimed their freedom and cast off their *burqas* and veils. The veil on the burqa for the Sangathan women is largely unused now and they arrive simply wearing the headcovering with the veil thrown back. Indeed, some of the women who had worn the burqa before the gas disaster no longer conceal themselves with the burqa at all. During an overnight train ride to Delhi to protest at the Parliament building on 15 August 1997, many of the women departed from Bhopal in the evening in a burqa and emerged in the morning from the train without them, instead wearing colourful salwar kamiz for their big trip to the capital. For Hindu women, visible signs of 'freedom' are more difficult to detect; the change would be whether the woman covers her hair with her dupatta or with the end of her sari.

The 'lifting of the veils' is a sign for a wider transformation in the women's behaviour as seen in their activism. During one of my early visits to the park on a weekday after the women were getting to know me as a more long-term presence, I was chatting with several of them and taking a few photographs before returning home to the United States for a few months. It happened that they were planning some civil disobedience for the following week: they were to march to the city jail, barge inside and get themselves arrested. I was surprised by this, but even more surprised that the person most enthusiastic about this Gandhi-inspired *satyagraha* was an elderly woman in a burqa, Shahida Bai. I asked incredulously, "You are going to march right into the jail and get arrested?" Shahida smiled proudly and wobbled her head to gesture her agreement. On another occasion, Shahida invited me to her house in the Old City. I was a bit nervous when I went, thinking that her male relatives would be angry or at least uncomfortable about a foreign man coming alone to call on one of the women of the household and the discredit that would bring upon the house. Instead, no one minded and I was given the usual Bhopali over-attentive hospitality.

The women's speeches in the Sangathan rallies pose complicated problems of context and interpretation. Sunder Rajan raises the problem of interpretation since subaltern groups and subaltern women "are users of language who are both excluded from and trapped within a sign-system that is not of their making" (Sunder Rajan, 1993: 89). Because subaltern women's speech is generally confined to the home, public speech is often marked by various forms of 'linguistic excess' (such as confession, polemic, diatribe, or profession of faith) that 'signify truth' by means other than reference to facts (Sunder Rajan, 1993: 88). "Women's memoirs in colonial Bengal were marked by a 'directness' and even an 'artlessness' that were 'appropriate for an authentic 'feminine' literary voice" (Chatterjee, 1993: 139). The Sangathan women's speeches, likewise, manifest such signs of excess, directness and artlessness: signs of inexperience in public speaking, speculation about facts, and also even diatribe and emotion. Nevertheless, and without romanticizing their subaltern speech as 'truth', I will credit it with a certain discursive power, even agency, of its own.

I respond to this problem of interpretation with a pair of related questions in mind. On the one hand, how do the speeches correspond in form and content to the hegemonic construct of women's subjectivity as being contained within the 'traditional' and the 'domestic' and within their social roles as wives and mothers? On the other hand, how do the women's speeches challenge those limitations placed upon them such that the speeches transcend those limitations and open up space for the exercise of women's agency as women, not only as wives and mothers? The response to the first question asks us to examine the form of the women's speeches as well as their content for signs of humility, domesticity and boldness. The response to the second question will highlight the ways in which the women of the Sangathan effectively transcend their marginalization as women and as Bhopal survivors. The women freely address a myriad of other controversial contemporary issues, such as communalism or globalization, of concern not only locally in Bhopal, but nationally as well.

Protesting within the Boundaries of Women's Subjectivity

Humility: Consistent with the hegemonic construct of women's subjectivity, images of which, according to Purnima Mankekar, are as close as the nearest television broadcast of the 'National Programme' (Mankekar, 1999), the Sangathan women present themselves, in the speeches they give at the public rallies, as humble yet bold protectors of the nation's purity nevertheless mindful of their domestic responsibilities. The speakers are self-consciously unrehearsed.[10] Although the women may have thought about what they wanted to say in general before deciding to get up and speak, the speeches have the grammatical inconsistencies, hesitant qualities and changes of subject of impromptu speech. In any case, none of the women speaks from prepared notes. Some of the women stumble over what they want to say, while the women who speak frequently are emotional and even compelling and articulate speakers. The women who hesitate and stumble signal to the audience not only the novelty of public speaking, but also the duty to speak—a duty that transcends the survivors' otherwise humble social status and lack of familiarity with public speaking.

The women's speeches are framed by utterances that mark the women as modest and unpractised, even though what they have to say is often bold. In this way, the stage becomes open for anyone who wants to speak and inexperience comes to be valued as an asset to the Sangathan. Participation is non-elitist and thereby maximizes the potential for women's involvement. For example, the women begin their speeches hesitantly or with self-conscious acknowledgment that they are not prepared to speak.

I do not know what I want to say ...

> It's true that sometimes nothing special to say comes to us. Even so, when someone speaks, then I also must speak up. Since we are all participating in the organization then why should there be any embarrassment in speaking? If we are coming to the meetings, then it everybody's own work.

> Brothers and Sisters. Greetings. I have no idea why I'm so happy today.

These hesitant beginnings probably signal the sincere feelings of stage fright and uncertainty that many of the women have when they step up to the speaker's platform. The pragmatic effect is to cause other potential speakers to identify with them and to encourage them to speak up. The speeches end just as abruptly with simple statements that end the speeches without any dramatic conclusion:

> I want to say just this much and I'll stop my speech.
>
> I'll say just this much and I'll stop now.
>
> On this, I'll stop what I have to say. Shukriya.
>
> Now I'll stop what I have to say.

The women signal their inexperience in public speaking and thereby identify themselves indirectly with their domestic lives. Although the apparent effect of such statements in speech might be to undermine the speaker's credibility, in this context, these framing comments serve instead to buttress the women's persuasiveness by associating them with purity of purpose located in women's subjectivity.

Domesticity: Through these speech acts, the women construct themselves as ordinary, humble and modest not only through the form of their speech. They also tell stories that reference their domestic duties and practical knowledge to make their points:

> I've just gone to buy some goats. The women there were wearing burqas and selling goats. The women might be helpless, but if they raise one kid goat then they think, "When he gets big then he will bring in money". And when there is a need for money, ... we take what we have raised, what we have brought up, and sell it so that we will get its fruit. This is the way of the gas victims too. If people will keep on fighting then we will find success.

This is an excerpt typical in its reference to trips to the bazaar, the price of household commodities and foods, and to other domestic activities. The women talk about their domestic lives in ways that indicate that domestic concerns, rather than militancy or critiques of modernity, are what they bring to the Sangathan as women. Their speeches presuppose connections between the disaster and other areas of their lives that are self-evident to the women. Because as women they are responsible for domestic life of their households, the Sangathan's women have identified the impact of the gas disaster on other aspects of their domestic lives, enabling them to extend the focus of their protests beyond the more narrow demands for medical treatment, compensation, and occupational rehabilitation. The Bhopal disaster becomes a sign of the social disaster that the women confronted before the gas disaster and continue to confront in ways that are now made sense of by reference to the event of the gas disaster. Women as interpreters of the disaster produce an awareness of its expansive social impact.

In this sense, again, the practices of the Sangathan and the women's articulations of their roles are continuous with the dominant images of women's activism in India. Not surprisingly, the Sangathan's speakers are explicit about the women's roles as pure, brave saviors. They even explicitly reference their roles as saviors of society in ways that resoundingly echo Gandhi's own imagining of the need for women's participation in political activism, as in an excerpt recited above. It also echoes dominant representations of women's activism in which women, as the 'pure' saviors of national honour, are called upon to embrace public roles in particular political contests, but roles that are circumscribed in particular ways.

For example, the women assume it is their duty to participate in the Sangathan because of its social usefulness. The idiom for expressing this duty is the idea of women's responsibility, *zimedari*, for the household which extends by analogy to the Sangathan's responsibility for the well-being of society as a whole:

> The responsibility for every household is ... especially the woman's. If this were seen then she would be the Home Minister of her house. She's the home minister and all of the systems in the house are in her hands. Men come and abuse their wives and behave arrogantly. This is what's going on. But now women must drive the households. The home ministers must drive the households. They have seen that if a small family is organized then running it is her responsibility. How can we run society? ... . Just as it is our responsibility to run the household, so too is it our responsibility to run the Sangathan because we must look after society. It's not only for our households. Society is our responsibility too. And responsibility for the country is upon us too ... . Our responsibility is very great.

One of the many interesting things to say about this excerpt is the speaker uses the idiom of politics to describe the responsibility of women for society.[11] She uses the metaphor of 'Home Minister' to describe women's domestic and social responsibility and in so doing, she claims for women the responsibility not only for voicing the Sangathan's demands but also for undertaking responsibility for society as a whole. By assuming this responsibility, she suggests that the care of society is a responsibility that the state itself fails to meet and that therefore can only be entrusted to women.

Boldness: At the same time that the women are enacting a feminine-gendered subjectivity as women unaccustomed to the public stage, they also perform as bold activists. They do this through provocative acts, such as marching into the city jail to get arrested, and also through their speech. Ostensibly the women meet in the park to plan their next civil disobedience or protest march, (although many also acknowledge that they like to come and see their friends and escape the turmoil of their households). They also come, though, to hear the speakers who in turn urge the women to come to the park, to speak and to bravely continue their struggle. Whatever their practical value, the meetings are sites in which the women as speakers and as audience represent their subjectivity as bold and fearless fighters, even if they are only sitting in a park most of the time. Often there were guest speakers from political parties and from other people's organizations urging solidarity in all kinds of peoples' struggles: those of indigenous people, of farmers and the poor, against police brutality. More recently, in August 2006, in response to news of the Israeli bombings in Beirut, Lebanon, the women undertook to protest that military action and all other forms of what they termed 'terrorism'. Hearing these invocations of peoples' solidarity in various struggles presents the opportunity for the women to articulate a wider meaning in their struggle.

I cited above Kamla Sharma's invocation of the women's boldness:

> In our hands, in our bodies there is complete strength. We will cause blood and sweat to flow continuously. We will perform non-violent resistance just like Gandhiji and we will chase off the plunderers who have come from afar.

The speeches are repetitive in their use of 'protest language' to talk about themselves:

> [W]e say with a vow that we will forcefully advance our struggle and we will not withdraw.
>
> We people are one and we will remain one up until death and we'll keep fighting.
>
> This Sangathan has been fighting continuously for thirteen years and is fighting even today and we'll keep fighting until death.
>
> Friends, we've been fighting for thirteen years now. And we'll keep fighting, for justice we'll keep fighting.
>
> I want to say that there is a story behind every human life and that in every human life there is a hero or a heroine.
>
> We've taken an oath that until we win we will keep fighting against the government.
>
> Day and night the Mahila Udyog Sangathan is shouting but the government here is not listening. It's committing treachery. As long as each child gets not a penny in judgment, then Gas Peerit Mahila Udyog Sangathan will not sit silently. In every alley, on every streetcorner, on every streetcorner we'll make our objections. Our Sangathan does not sit by silently.

The women speak openly about their fantasized, or possibly even sincere, desire to hang Warren Anderson (the Union Carbide chairman at the time of the disaster in 1984) using a tone that borders on murderous rage:

> That murderer Warren Anderson will surely be hanged. Long live the unity of the gas-affected ... . We'll keep fighting. We'll win!
>
> Warren Anderson should be brought to India and if the government is restrained or embarrassed to punish him, then he should be brought and left before the Sangathan.

Appropriately, the walls of the buildings nearby in the park where the women meet are covered with graffiti calling for Warren Anderson's hanging and drawings of his effigy hanging by a noose.

Salima Bee, quoted above, is a member of the Sangathan speaks nearly every week. She describes having lived quietly as a housewife in a burqa before the gas disaster. Now she still wears the black cape but never covers her face. Her speeches are a weekly fixture and are dramatic and emotional. Apart from the substance of what she has to say, she speaks with enormous force and emotion that begins to build with her first words. She can speak for fifteen, twenty, or even thirty minutes and in her waning moments her voice quakes with anger as she raises her fist in the air. She punctuates her angry tirades with a periodic return to calm when she addresses the crowd directly again: *Saathiyon!*

Salima's presence is not only marked by her emotionality. Her words themselves are dramatic and histrionic:

> We're not afraid of anyone at all, not anyone at all. We fear God above, we fear our husbands, and no one else strikes fear in us. We give respect to great and small. This is what our elders have taught us.

Although respectful of the male hierarchy that exists in domestic life, she uses both her performance and her words to manifest her lack of fear for anyone else, including the Sangathan men lurking at the microphone switch, anxious to bring her lengthy speeches to a hasty end. On that same day, Salima was not so polite to an imaginary politician whom she addressed hypothetically in her speech:

> Today we have brought about (your) election victory and we have seated you and you have turned your attention from us. We too are ordinary people, ordinary people. The people's wishes are with you, the well-wishes of the poor are on you ... but these poor people, each one can be struck down, but they will not bow their heads .... We're stubborn people, we cannot bow to you and if we come up against you, we'll upend you and throw you out of your bungalow and beat you with shoes .... We'll shout slogans for your death. We remember.

Salima uses a powerful trope of degradation and humiliation: the beating with shoes. Although Salima's threat to the imaginary politician was a hypothetical one, in other speeches the women refer to acts of civil disobedience that are closer to reality.

The women specifically invoke these acts of civil disobedience, or *satyagraha*, and thereby locate themselves within the Gandhian politics of Indian independence. In these references, the women are invoking the history of women's activism in the Independence movement, a history that calls upon their roles as 'saviors of the nation'. So while these excerpts appear to be bold, even brazen, they are nevertheless consistent with the hegemonic construct for women's subjectivity.

> [W]e are prepared to get locked up. There is spirit in you. Go and keep it in jail! Arrest us! To those people who are struck with fear that the police will come, "what will be will be". If there is a crime then be scared. What crime have the gas-affected committed? They are not afraid of police stations or courts. The people who understand keep on coming every Saturday (to the Park).

Part of the 'women's work' of the Sangathan is to get arrested. I already mentioned the day when the women were planning to march into the city jail to get arrested. On that day, I had arrived in the Park on a weekday as the women were calmly planning an act of civil disobedience in which they would omit the disobedience altogether and proceed directly to jail. That is, the disobedience would be to enter the jail illegally whereupon they would be arrested and jailed. A few weeks later, they did just that. The offenders included Shahida Bai, an elderly Muslim woman in burqa.

Some of the boldness carries over into the women's behaviour off the stage too. Kamla Sharma was insistent about taking me for tea and samosas at a local tea stall after meetings and for paying for me as well. Shahida Bai wanted my attention one day, so she whistled at me from inside her burqa. She then quickly escorted me to a relative's house nearby Bhopal's Lower Lake where I met her daughter-in-law and teenage granddaughter. She invited me to the roof of the house to enjoy the view of Bhopal's Lower Lake where she recited this rhyme:

Digvijay Singh sharm karo	Digvijay Singh, be ashamed
Hamaarii mangii puuraa karo	Fulfil our demands
Chhote talaab men duub maro	Go drown in the Lower Lake!

Reciting this, her face beamed with delight.

Using Women's Subjectivity to Expand the Boundaries of Protest

While the Sangathan women address in their speeches their domestic concerns as wives and mothers in the aftermath of the gas disaster, they nevertheless expand the scope of their commentaries beyond their immediate concerns as survivors to address other compelling contemporary issues. It is in these excerpts of the women's speeches given below that we see the women transcend the more limited scope of their gendered subjectivity to express their agency as women with arguments that are deeply political and public, not only domestic.

Elections: During my research in 1998, there were two parliamentary elections called as governing coalitions crumbled and new Prime Ministers had to be elected. To prevent multiple voting, after casting his or her vote, a voter's middle fingernail would be marked with an indelible stain at the bottom of the nail. Those fingernails had just barely grown out by the time the second set of elections were called—reminders to all of the potential for electoral futility.

The elections were a source of frustration for the Bhopal women in particular. Since 1984, government control had shifted between competing political parties (in particular, between Congress and BJP governments), both locally and nationally, several times. In their eyes, no government had fulfilled its promises or its legal obligations to the Bhopal survivors, leaving them with bitter feelings about politicians and the political process:

> Day and night the Women Workers' Organization is shouting but the government here is not listening. It's committing treachery. As long as each child gets not a penny in judgment, then Gas-Affected Women Workers' Organization will not sit silently. In every alley, on every streetcorner, on every streetcorner we'll make our objections. Our Organization does not sit by silently. This government wants us to take our judgment today and tomorrow will take out votes. But instead we'll give them our sandals. We won't give them our votes. We'll give them what our hearts want. They'll tell us "Give your votes to the "palms" (Congress Party)" but we won't give it to them. We want to throw our votes in the gutter.

> Whoever wins, whoever loses, on the matter of the rights of the gas-affected everyone remains silent. The politicians fill their stomachs, their families' stomachs. They tell all lies. No Congress Party has ever done anything, no Janta Party either. For ourselves, we have taken things ourselves. After this election we must perform non-violent resistance. We must strike and we will strike. We must never stop our work. We will continue to take our rights no matter who the government is and at risk of death we'll keep on fighting.

Corruption: People throughout Bhopal tell stories about their daily encounters with official corruption as they seek their legal entitlements to compensation and treatment following the gas disaster. They cite the bribes paid to court clerks to get their claims decided, to bank officers to get compensation funds released, or to hospital pharmacists to get otherwise unavailable medicines. The opportunities for bribery abounded in the compensation claims process and medical treatment bureaucracy established ostensibly for the benefit of the survivors. Accordingly, the women frequently raised their voices over official corruption in their speeches:

> In front of Kamla Park there is a road and it's a very good one. Even so, there's a machine there spreading tar. The machine is spreading tar and the meaning is this, a bill of 2,00,000 rupees. Don't they understand that there's no need for this resurfacing? There are many streets that are in quite bad condition. But the repairs won't be made there. Indeed, this is a matter of corruption not limited to the politicians. It's a cancer spreading through society. Corruption is flowing through the blood of society.

> Why does this government want to turn its face from its own responsibility? "We (politicians) want to keep sitting in our seats and put tens of millions of rupees in our pockets. In the bank and in our pockets and we haven't any responsibilities". (quoting an imaginary politician)

While the women experienced profoundly the physical pain of exposure to the gas in the Union Carbide disaster, they also experienced the sting of official corruption directly as their occupational rehabilitation centre was closed. They came to experience the disaster not only as an industrial one, but also as a failure of the state itself as they saw corruption eat away at their legal rights and entitlements and demean the very notion of justice.

Globalization: The strands of critique in these speeches against politics and corruption are woven together in the women's concerns about globalization and foreign investment in the Indian economy. They experience those economic changes through television advertising, through the marketing of branded products in their local shops, and through news about controversial foreign investments. The government's economic liberalization commencing in the early 1990's had enabled vast foreign investment and also the importation of foreign products. Formerly unbranded commodities are now overshadowed in competition with branded products bearing both foreign and domestic brand names. The Sangathan women imagine a nexus between corruption on the local and national levels and the wealth to be tapped from multinational corporations. The speeches venture beyond theories about the Bhopal disaster to condemn economic liberalization and corruption together. They use anecdotes that would be familiar to any woman listening in the audience and that concern the everyday stresses of meeting the material needs of family life in the context of an increasingly media—and advertising-saturated environment and a market increasingly dominated by foreign-branded products:

> When we get up in the morning, we are caught in the clutches of foreign companies. Why does our son say that he will brush his teeth with Close-Up? Why, we have brushed out teeth with the ashes of the gas disaster. We brush our teeth with neem twigs and you need Close-Up because the TV says so. This is the condition in our country that, "Son, it might well be that you don't even get roti. You go watch TV, and sit, watch the advertisements for bath soap, wash yourself and keep on watching TV".

> We people have fallen into the clutches of foreign companies. Since our independence, (politicians) have been seated in the name of the freedom fighters … . Why does this government want to turn its face from its own responsibility and give it all to foreign companies? We (politicians) want to keep sitting in our seats and put crores of rupees in our pockets.

> [T]hree years ago you did not find bottled water in the railway station. You journeyed and took a supply of water from the tap. Just as there used to be facilities now what is there? When you have ten rupees in your pocket then you won't drink water. Why won't you drink? Because now there is in the name of Ganga Jal, Yamuna Jal, Godvari Jal for sale in place of drinking water.

One adverse consequence of liberalization and other economic changes is that branded products increasingly compete with public conveniences like drinking water, with unbranded commodities and with folk remedies. Foreign-branded products must be particularly bitter signs in Bhopal since it was a multinational corporation that brought the gas disaster. On walls near the former Union Carbide plant, for example, Pepsi signs are often defaced with black paint. Television advertising and marketing have exploded with the expansion of broadcast media, inserting themselves into domestic life in order to manufacture desires for products that people have heretofore been able to survive without (Rajagopal, 2001). These are products that the Sangathan women believe are unnecessary substitutes for existing commodities—substitutes that the family could scarcely afford. In one women's comment, "we have brushed our teeth with the ashes of the gas disaster", the speaker figuratively connects the Union Carbide gas disaster to the desire for foreign-branded products. In this way, the Bhopal disaster becomes something more than an event that occurred during one night in 1984. Rather, the disaster becomes a symbol of foreign economic exploitation that this speaker saw continuing in the intimacy of her television-influenced home life and in her relationship with her son.

Religious Violence: Talk of the 1998 elections provoked talk of communalism as well, especially since the events in Ayodhya in 1992. The motives and involvement of the major national political parties were deeply suspect. The relationship between politics and communalism is not lost on the women of the Organization who survived the deadly 1992 riots and the eleven-day curfew that followed in Bhopal:

> You are human, I too am human. Allah is great, Bhagwan is the creator of all. Gandhiji didn't divide anyone up, not Hindus and not Muslims. Our offspring and your offspring should not be made Hindu or Muslim. People here have been divided up and have been made Hindus and Muslims. People are divided into their castes and are divided up into their parties. At one time Mahatma Gandhi was president. In his time, what kind of Hindu and Muslim things there were. His death too brought on the Hindu-Muslim thing. … But there's no need to be afraid. We people are one and will remain one until death. And we'll keep fighting no matter whether it's the BJP or the Congress.

> To make differences between people, four days ago in Rajasthan riots were incited. There was a curfew. I don't accept any of this. In Ajmer Sharif millions of people were joined together in faith and belief. In the name of that shrine in that city a Hindu-Muslim riot was made. What a big shame. It's a shame for the whole

> country. I saw a Bhojpuri boy making an offering at the door to the shrine. What faith, what belief! Today, what happened in Ajmer Sharif is such a shameful thing and no politician could do anything to stop it. Only society, only people can stop this.

The women's speeches also resound with declarations of the communal harmony among the members of the Sangathan in comparison to the exploitative uses of religion by politicians. Here, the women present themselves as virtuous preservers of that harmony and of those religious values.

Conclusion

While engaging with the dominant representation of women's subjectivity as wives and mothers in their participation in the Sangathan, the Sangathan women further a number of explicit and practical demands as survivors. The Sangathan has been directly responsible for forcing the Government of India to take notice of the demands of the survivors.[12] That is, although their participation in the Sangathan consists mostly of speech performances in Shahjehani Park, it is performance with practical effects that address their consistent and forceful demands as survivors for rehabilitation, treatment and compensation from Union Carbide and the Government of India. The women emphasize this practical success in obtaining these benefits and their successes in staging protests:

> We know this much that we must fight and fighting we must obtain our rights. For thirteen years we've had big, big protests and through them we're getting compensation, treatment and employment. Fighting for thirteen years the Sangathan's voice is reaching very, very far.

> Friends, you can indeed see the results. If you were not organized, then the employment you have gotten, you would not have gotten. And you would not have gotten the compensation either. You would not have gotten the treatment either.

> Whenever Bhagwan (God) gives us something we forget it. If we remember Bhagwan just like this, then we'll remember the Sangathan just like this. We are raising demands for treatment, we are raising demands for employment, so Inshallah we will obtain everything.

The members of the Sangathan have come a long way since the late 1980's when they were demanding simply to keep their positions in the sewing centres, a modest effort on their own parts, as individuals, to improve their household incomes. Now, their speeches embrace the most salient social and political issues in contemporary India, specifically, elections and politics, corruption, religion and communalism, and economic liberalization. In these ways, the Sangathan women stake out strong political positions and come to challenge the very assumptions of the modern state. Women in Bhopal are the links that connect the events that occurred one night in Bhopal in 1984 to the broader political, economic, and social issues that frame contemporary India. Almost subversively, the women take on these potent issues while seemingly standing before each other in the public park in Bhopal as humble wives and mothers—the dominant subjectivity that would otherwise confine them. In these subtle acts of nonconformity, the women exercise their agency as women and perhaps even marginally transform that dominant subjectivity in the process (Raheja and Gold, 1994).

The Sangathan is today an active organization, still meeting every Saturday for rallies. The women continue their protests even as time passes and others in middle-class areas of Bhopal that were unaffected in 1984 ask why the Sangathan women are still protesting, or in their minds, complaining since the government has paid them their compensation. The power of the state to marginally satisfy subjects with individual compensation and to thereby quiet any radical critique they may be articulating seems to be at work in Bhopal since participation in the Sangathan has certainly diminished over the years.[13] Each Saturday meeting ends with a slogan that the members shout while raising their fists in the air. It remains an open question whether the slogan indeed portends any lasting change in Bhopal:

Long live the country's people Long life!	Desh kii jantaa Zindaabaad Zindaabaad!
Long live the country's people Long life!	Desh kii jantaa Zindaabaad Zindaabaad!
We will fight/We will win!	Larenge Jiitenge!
The wage earner/He will eat!	Kamaane vaalaa Khaaegaa!
The one who loots/He will go !	Lootne vaalaa Jaayegaa!
A new age It will come!	Nayaa zamaanaa Aayegaa!
Raise your voice/We are one!	Aawaaz do Ham ek hain!

Acknowledgements

The field research for this paper, conducted during 1996–1998 and 2006, was supported by a Fulbright Fellowship, an American Institute of Indian Studies Junior Research Fellowship, a Social Science Research Council Predissertation Fellowship for Area Research, a National Science Foundation Ethnographic Training Award, and the University of Michigan. I would like to thank Ann Stoler, Brinkley Messick and Val Daniel for their suggestions on theoretical approaches to this material. I would like to thank Peter Hook for his advice on translations and transcriptions. Finally, Ilana Feldman, Rachel Heiman, Karen Strassler, Mani Limbert, and Laura Kunreuther provided invaluable assistance with detailed readings of the manuscript.

Notes

1. These speech excerpts are my translations of Hindi transcripts of recordings of speeches that I made during field research in Bhopal in 1997–98.
2. In Hindi, the *Bhopal Gas Peerit Mahila Udyog Sangathan,* I will use the Hindi *Sangathan* to refer to the Organization.
3. In other research, I examine how these broader concerns of Bhopal survivors have been excluded from the official legal, medical and bureaucratic discourses through which the aftermath of the Bhopal disaster has been officially articulated and narrated (see Mooney, 2002).
4. In 2001, Dow Chemical Corporation acquired Union Carbide Corporation. Union Carbide therefore no longer exists as a legal entity.
5. The Sangathan was joined by other survivor organizations in legal actions and protests, against the settlement. These include the Bhopal Group for Information

and Action, the *Bhopal Gas Peerit Stationery Karmchari Sangh* (Bhopal Gas-Affected Womens' Stationery Workers' Union), the *Bhopal Gas Peerit Nirashrit Pension Bhogi Morcha* (the Bhopal Gas-Affected Poor-persons' Pension Front) and others. Besides their generalized agitations against government mismanagement and inaction on disaster-related relief, each of these organizations like the Sangathan, was formed for voicing specific demands. The Stationery Sangh was specifically concerned with having its members regularized as state employees in their factory that produced government forms and government ledger books. The Pension Bhogi Morcha demanded that government pensions be paid to survivors of the gas disaster.

6. Although the womens' speeches are public and their names frequently appear in press reports of Sangathan activities, I am using aliases in this paper to protect their identities.
7. *Mother India*, for those not familiar with this cinematic epic, depicts the heroic struggle of a widowed village woman in Nehruvian post-independence India. She melodramatically overcomes all sorts of agrarian tragedies. The narrative culminates in her decision to place public duty over filial devotion and kill her own son, a young man who had fallen into a disrepute that threatened the reputation of the village.
8. Womens' protests in many places, not just in India, are grounded in womens' roles as wives and mothers. Temma Kaplans' work on political movements in early 20th century Barcelona resonates with womens' activism in India (Kaplan, 1992). Like the women in Bhopal, Kaplan found that the working women of Barcelona articulated their domestic demands for public hygiene and affordable prices within a discourse of womens' self-appointed right to defend humanity and human decency (Kaplan, 1992: 106). Intending at first to secure the material needs of their families in times of social crisis, women often find themselves ultimately challenging the "legitimacy of the government itself", but find themselves protected in their protests by their feminine roles (Kaplan, 1997: 185). Although Kaplan finds that womens' movements sometimes lack concrete proposals to replace the governments they come to find illegitimate, their challenges are powerful because they are addressed to "fundamental moral precepts" (Kaplan, 1997: 188). These parallels in the conduct of womens' protest pose interesting questions for cross-cultural research in feminist anthropology.
9. "Jabbar Khan Moulded Gas-Hit Women into Fighting Force", by Nasir Kamaal, The Free Press, Indore, 1994.
10. The speeches are spontaneous and unrehearsed, and I have tried to capture this improvisational quality in the translation from Hindi which intentionally produces sometimes awkward English.
11. The representation of women as 'household politicians' is a trope used in advertising to appeal to middle class women. For example, a newspaper advertisement in the *Times of India* for Tata Tea features the smiling face of a Hindu housewife with a 'bubble' over her head quoting her appreciation for the product. In the amalgam of Hindi and English that marks middle class speech especially, she asks "Daam na bare ... Ghar kaa budget thiik rahe. Ghar ke Finance Minister ko aur kyaa chahiye?" (The price won't increase ... the household budget will be OK. What more does the household Finance Minister need?). The advertisement continues in English that "the budget comes with its ups and downs, highs and

lows. But whatever the budget, Tata Teas' Asli Taazgii (pure freshness/refreshment) will not change". Again, Sangathan womens' representations of themselves articulate with other dominant representations of women, especially middle class media representations (Mankekar, 1999).

12. An example of one such success is the Supreme Court of Indias' retention of continuing and original jurisdiction over the Bhopal litigation (see Mooney, 2002). As a consequence, the survivor organizations frequently filed petitions to the Court demanding that the Court direct the Government to fulfil its obligations for treatment by making medicines and medical treatment for survivors freely available in Bhopal. In effect, this was to ask the Supreme Court to take action to undo the practices of corruption extending from the government ministries in Delhi to the hospital orderlies in Bhopal, quite possibly an impossible task even for a Supreme Court. The Supreme Court maintains that jurisdiction even now and it has also resulted in a 2004 order that the Government of India disperse to the survivors all remaining funds paid by Union Carbide in settlement of the survivors' claims in 1991.
13. The individuating effects of the dominant discourses of the state (Foucault, 1983; Caplan and Torpey, 2001; Scott, 1998), that is, the methods through which the government has provided compensation and rehabilitation to individual survivors, thereby seemingly satisfying their demands, has contributed to a reduced participation in the Sangathan. While the women expand the significance of Bhopal through their activism as women, the discourses of the state ensure that the women, satisfied as individuals, begin to lose focus on their common interests as survivors (see Mooney, 2002).

References

Caplan, Jane and Torpey, John, (2001), "Introduction", in *Documenting Individual Identification: The Development of State Practices in the Modern World*, J. Caplan and J. Torpey (eds.), Princeton: Princeton University Press.

Chatterjee, Partha, (1993), *The Nation and its Fragments: Colonial and Post-colonial Histories*, Princeton: Princeton University Press.

Foucault, Michel, (1983), "Afterword: The Subject and Power", in *Michel Foucault: Beyond Structuralism and Hermeneutics*, (2nd edition), H. Dreyfus and P. Rabinow (eds.), Chicago: University of Chicago Press.

Iyer, Raghavan (ed.), (1991), *The Essential Writings of Mahatma Gandhi*, Delhi: Oxford University Press.

Kannabiran, Vasantha and Lalitha, K., (1989), "That Magic Time: Women in the Telengana Peoples' Struggle", in *Recasting Women: Essays in Colonial History*, Sangari, K. and Vaid, S. (eds.), New Delhi: Kali for Women.

Kumar, Radha, (1993), *The History of Doing: An Illustrated Account of Movements for Womens' Rights and Feminism in India*, 1800–1990, New York: Verso.

Mani, Lata, (1989), "Contentious Traditions: The Debate on *Sati* in Colonial India", in *Recasting Women: Essays in Colonial History*, Sangari, K. and Vaid, S. (eds.), New Delhi: Kali for Women.

Mankekar, Purnima, (1999), *Screening Culture, Viewing Politics: An Ethnography of Television, Womanhood and Nation in Post-colonial India*, Durham: Duke University Press.

Mooney, Brian, (2002), The Bhopal Disaster: Discourse and Narrative in the Ethnography of an Event, Ph.D. Dissertation, submitted, Department of Anthropology, University of Michigan.

Raheja, Gloria Goodwin, and Gold, Ann Grodzins, (1994), *Listen to the Herons' Words: Re-imagining Gender and Kinship in North India*, Berkeley: University of California Press.

Rajagopal, Arvind, (2001), "Thinking About the New Indian Middle Class: Gender, Advertising and Politics in an Age of Globalisation", in *Signposts: Gender Issues in Post-Independence India*, Sunder Rajan, R. (ed.), New Brunswick: NJ, Rutgers University Press.

Sangari, Kumkum and Vaid, Sudesh, (1989), *Recasting Women: Essays in Colonial History*, New Delhi: Kali for Women.

Scott, James, (1998), *Seeing Like a State: How Certain Schemes to Improve the Human Condition Have Failed*, New Haven: Yale University Press.

Sundar Rajan, Rajeswari, (1993), *Real and Imagined Women: Gender, Culture and Post-colonialism*, New York: Routledge.

Tharu, Susie and Niranjana, Tejaswini, (1996), "Problems for a Contemporary Theory of Gender", in *Subaltern Studies IX: Writings on South Asian History and Society*, Amin, S. and Chakrabarty, D. (eds.), Delhi: Oxford University Press.

Visweswaran, Kamala, (1996), "Small Speeches, Subaltern Gender: Nationalist Ideology and its Historiography", in *Subaltern Studies IX: Writings on South Asian History and Society*, Amin, S. and Chakrabarty, D. (eds.), Delhi: Oxford University Press.

3 Empowerment and Social Change in Tripura Tribal Community of Bangladesh

KHURSHED ALAM

Tripuras are the third largest tribal group of population in the Chittagong Hill Tracts (CHT) region after Chakmas and Marmas. Tripuras call themselves Tipara or Tipra. Nearly 80 per cent of all Tripuras are now living in the CHT area. Their original residence was in the Indian state of Tripura, although some believe that they were in fact descendants of the Bodo group of people, considered as the forefathers of the peoples of Assam, Burma and Thailand.[1] Tripuras initially migrated to Comilla, Sylhet and Chittagong areas as well as to some other parts of the country like Noakhali, Dhaka, Faridpur and Barisal. In course of time, they have concentrated largely in the CHT area, especially in and around Ramgarh and Khagrachari. The 1881 census recorded the distribution of Tripura people as: CHT 15,054, Comilla 4, and Sylhet 101, Barisal 45, Noakhali 16, Dhaka 4, and Sylhet and other areas 268. The number of Tripuras in the CHT area was 79, 772 in 1991. This figure accounts for 6.6 per cent of the total tribal population in the CHT.[2] Available information shows that Tripuras are divided into at least 36 groups (dafas) of which 16 are living in Bangladesh. Some of those groups are divided into a number of subgroups where remarkably all groups and subgroups have their own dialects, dresses and ornaments.

The language of Tripuras (Kokborok) belongs to the Bodo group, which has its origin in the Assam branch of the Tibeto-Burma language. Kokborok was widely used in writing letters, demonstrating magic, and preparing lists of indigenous medicines. But the script is on the verge of extinction due to limited or no use.

Male and female of Tripura community wear different kinds of dresses. The traditional dress of a Tripura man include dhuti (a narrow piece of cloth clad round the waist and between the legs with a fringed end hanging down from the rear) and a khaban (turban). Tripuras wear a ruggedly sewn jacket in winter days. The dress of a Tripura woman is similar to that of a Chakma woman and in most cases it is petticoat with a blouse on the upper part of the body. In the past, married Tripura women usually did not wear anything to cover the breasts where unmarried girls distinguished themselves by wearing colourful clothes. Both men and women wear crescent shaped silver earring. The women wear necklace made of beads and shells, nose skewers and ornaments on the hair, neck, wrist and ankle.[3]

Tripuras have dual types of inheritance. Eldest son of a family can inherit father's property entirely but the right of the eldest son to inherit may be forfeited if he separates himself from the parents' family when father is still alive.

Tripuras are mainly Hindus by religion but their beliefs and religious practices are different from the Hindu caste system in many ways. They worship the God Shiva and the Goddess Kali along with other 14 gods and goddesses like many other Hindu communities. In addition to that they also believe in a number of evil spirits, incorporeal beings and demons, who have their habitat in jungles and who do harm to people by inflicting diseases. In order to prevent that Tripuras do sacrifice animals and birds in the name of their gods and goddesses. Like Hindus, Tripuras believe in life after death and believe that those who have done good work will live in ease and comfort in the next life but the wrong doers will face ceaseless toil and constant harassment.[4]

Tripuras have their own way of settlement. In one hill normally one household lives, and thus they need many hills to accommodate a few households in a nearest place. Usually they construct bamboo-wooden thatched house using local materials and own labour. They also live relatively in inaccessible areas and have traditional rights in land. Tripuras' main means of livelihood is collecting wood and other fruits from hill, growing some agricultural products like vegetables, pineapple, guava, cow and goat rearing, weaving, wine preparing or working as day labourer for forest department, etc. From all these they earn very little money by which they try to survive.

The present study has been carried out to know the process of empowerment and social change in the lives of the Tripura community in Mirsharai and Fatikchhari Upazillas (sub-districts) under Chittagong district by restoring their cultural heritage. The study areas are the Korerhat Union of Mirsharai and Dantmara and Bagan Bazar Union of Fatikchari Upazilla under Chittagong district.

The studied people are the target populations of an NGO project who are socially disadvantaged, vulnerable, poor and hardcore poor from the Tripura ethnic minority group. There are 652 Tripura families living in the study areas, and it is expected that total of 462 families will be associated with the project directly. The project started in January, 2003, which will end up in December, 2007.

The prime focus is the entire minority group, but the main focus is on women and children who have less access to other sources of income, especially widows, divorcees, and abused women. Although these vulnerable minority people are the direct beneficiaries of the project, the Bengali community living in the area is the indirect beneficiary from the project's proposed advocacy work, education programmes for children and mass awareness programmes.

Under the project 507 beneficiaries have been brought under a total of 51 groups up to June 2005. Of which, there were 19 (37%) male groups, 23 (45%) female groups and 9 (18%) mixed groups respectively. Among them, there were a total of 16 (31%) groups having 156 (31%) members in Fatikchhari Upazila and 35 (69%) groups having 351 (69%) members in Mirsharai Upazila respectively. The primary target people are 511 directly and 2,555 families indirectly from tribal community.

Objectives of the Study

The specific objectives are:

1. to assess the positive and negative social changes that have taken place among the Tripura community
2. to assess the security of their livelihood
3. to assess the level of empowerment that they have over the years; and
4. to make some recommendations to overcome those difficulties that they have.

Approach and Methodology

The study was carried out following both quantitative and qualitative analyses. The approach was participatory and obtained maximum information from all types of stakeholders including involved NGO staff. Both quantitative and qualitative field data were collected and analyzed using appropriate methods and techniques such as questionnaire survey, focus group discussion (FGD), key informants interview (KII), case studies, and Non-participatory Observation. Prior to conducting the study, local communities were made aware of the objectives and purposes of the study in order to get their maximum support for the investigation.

The researcher used multi-stage random sampling method. At the first stage, using a random sampling method, 17 groups were selected out of total 51 groups formed by a local NGO, proportionately from Mirsharai and Fatikchhari Upazilas. In the second stage, similarly using a random sampling method, 7 members from each of the sampled group were selected as respondents for the questionnaire survey. Thus, a total of 119 (17 × 7 = 119) group members were included under questionnaire survey. To reach the expected sample size e.g., 120 nos. an additional respondent from a random group was included in the study. Using an interview schedule, the research team conducted the quantitative survey on 120 numbers of households.

The researcher pursued some FGDs with the group members, local influential persons, UP chairmen/members, CBO leaders, Local NGO staff, school teachers, school managing committees, and guardians. Thus FGD representatives were selected purposively to cover all types of target members from different social groups. Likewise, the individual group members were selected for case studies on random basis. The researcher selected the cases from the different background of the respondents (such as, physical abuse, rape case, early marriage etc.) including some positive stories. Findings from case studies have also been considered here. All those findings might give a clear idea about the empowerment and social changes that have taken place among the Tripura community.

Major Findings

Under the study many basic points about the life of the Tripura community have been investigated. Detail findings on those issues have been noted below:

Formation of Groups

For the development of the community local NGO made an attempt to form their groups to organize them to give a structured and organized effort. The

Table 1 *Number of Group by CBOs*

Upazila	*CBO*	*Total groups*	*Total group members*
Fatikchhari	Shanirvor	6	67
	Bijoy	10	89
Mirsharai	Provati	21	213
	Prodip	14	138

researcher also made an attempt to assess the group formation status and their participation in the group activities. Among them, there are 19 (37%) male groups, 23 (45%) female groups and 9 (18%) mixed groups. It means number of female groups is higher than the male, which is a kind of positive discrimination deliberately made by the respective NGO there (OPCA, 2005). Data provided in Table 1 show that there are 16 groups having 156 members in Fatikchhari Upazila and 35 groups having 351 members in Mirsharai Upazila. Thus the NGO followed policy of formation of three types of groups to see the effectiveness of different types. That has been done considering the advantage of the formation of groups rather than having any other specific point in mind. For example, in case of market area they have formed male group only.

Training Received

Soon after the formation of a group, the next task was to impart training to them. The local NGO also imparted training to the group members to increase their ability to make best use of credit and other resources that they do have. During study attempt was also made to know about the types of training they have received. Data show that a total of 64 (53%) respondents received different types of training imparted by the local NGO as of June 2005. Imparted trainings were on vegetable cultivation (37.50%), cattle rearing (29.69%), goat and poultry rearing (23.44%), group formation (20.31%), education/leadership (14.06%), health and sanitation and HIV/AIDS prevention (10.94%), savings and credit management (6.25%), pig rearing and agricultural production (7.81%), maternity, CBO, NGO's activities, and health issues (3.13%) and gender issues (4.69%). Slowly, the organization will cover all the group members under their training programme. Collected FGD data show that whoever got credit with training, could utilize their acquired skill in a better way.

However, the opportunity cost of training for the group members is also very high. For example, for receiving training they have to forgo their daily income whatever meagre amount they could earn. So, training without training allowance is not a workable phenomenon for them.

Loan Disbursement Among the Respondents

As per field investigation (Table 2) 59 per cent received loan support from the local NGO as of June 2005. Collected data also reveal that among loan recipients about 68 per cent are from Mirsharai Upazila, which is relatively forward while 50 per cent from Fatikchhari Upazila which is relatively backward Upazila. Presented data also disclose that cent per cent recipient of the credit, indeed, received the first time loan while 44 per cent and only one per cent respondents received second and third times loan respectively. It means the dynamics is

Table 2 *Loan Received by the Respondent by Upazila*

Category of loan	*Mirsharai (%)*	*Fatikchhari (%)*	*All (%)*
1st Loan	100	100	100
2nd Loan	73.17	3.33	44
3rd loan	2.44	0	1
Total	100	100	100

there in case of loan receipt and a section of people has earned capacity to avail and utilize loan more than one time. In the middle of the project they could cover 59 per cent of the total group members, which means they would be able to cover the rest 41 per cent. It would be pertinent to note here that the Tripura community mentioned that this is the first time that they have received some kind of support from any agency for their development. So, the community was totally without support for last three decades of independence. Thus, they were not only socially and politically excluded but also developmentally excluded or bypassed.

Status of Loan Disbursement by Number of Loan Recipients

Collected data show that among the loan recipients 10 per cent received loan amounting to BDT 1,600–2,000 (US $ 1 = BDT 68), 89 per cent received loan amounting to BDT 2600–3000, 1 per cent received loan amounting to BDT 3,600–4,000, 41 per cent received loan amounting BDT 4,600–5,000 and 4 per cent received loan above BDT 5,000 respectively.

However, the interest rate is around 22 per cent although the NGO does call it as service charges rather than calling it interest. The donor agency also lends that money on interest to them at around 8 per cent interest rate. But to the borrowers the acceptable interest rate is 10–12 per cent. The targeting of the poor matches with the needs and objectives of the project about which there is hardly any disagreement. And they have their savings, which was not there earlier. It is further going to build up their economic strength. The process would mainly help them to remove their economic poverty although the project has targeted to remove other poverties as well. A big barrier is that the group cannot be given any greater amount of money as loan as they have income poverty. So, their repayment capacity is also very poor. As a result, if there is a will, still there is critical way. Their income largely depends on the economic growth of that area which is primarily beyond their control.

The micro-credit provided to them also had some impacts on their employment. Women have benefited more than men from the micro-credit. To a great extent poverty reduction is possible with micro-credit at the borrower level. It also helps to reduce household borrowing from informal lenders.

Credit and IGA Related Training

Data show that a total of 20 participants (38.46%), out of 52 received training on goat and pig rearing. Likewise, 1 person (1.92%) received training on IGA activities, 2 persons (3.85%) on agriculture, 18 persons (34.62%) on vegetable gardening, 1 person (1.92%) on livestock and poultry rearing, and 9 persons (17.31%) on savings and credit management from the local NGO since inception of the development project.

Above data also reveal that the highest number (38.46%) of participants is concentrated in goat and pig rearing training followed by vegetable cultivation (34.62%) and savings and credit management (17.31%) training respectively. It further reveals that the training courses preferred by the recipients is logical, as goat and pig rearing, vegetables cultivation and savings and credit management activities are feasible and suitable for them considering the geographical location and the needs of the participants.

Effects of Training

Training imparted to the group members has yielded benefit in many forms as they have undertaken different IGAs. Data presented in Table 3 reveal that almost 75 per cent of training recipients expressed that they have been benefited. Particularly about 3 per cent respondents mentioned that due to increased income they are in a position to spend some money on the occasion of their daughter's marriage, which was almost impossible for them earlier. Likewise about 26 per cent respondents opined that their household income has been increasing due to goat rearing, 5 per cent respondents mentioned that they are getting support during the crisis and 31 per cent respondents agreed that they have gained financially.

Likewise, about 18 per cent respondents feel that their interest for savings increased, 10 per cent respondents told that their awareness on savings, poultry and vegetables cultivation increased and 31 per cent agreed that their skill on pig rearing has also increased. All that show that many positive changes have been taking place in their life due to support from the local NGO.

Table 3 *Benefits Obtained from Getting IGA Training*

Training	*Mirsharai*	*Fatikchhari*	*All*
Spent money for daughter's marriage	4	0	3
Increase income due to goat rearing	28	21	26
Support during crisis period	4	7	5
Increase interest for savings	16	21	18
Awareness on savings, poultry and vegetables cultivation	8	14	10
Skill on pig rearing	12	0	8
Gained financially	28	36	31
Total	100	100	100

Effects of the Training

The study findings reveal that some significant changes on social issues and behavioural pattern of the respondent's households have taken place due to participation in the social awareness programme imparted by the local NGO. Data presented in Table 4 show that 88.46 per cent respondents in Mirsharai and 100 per cent participants in Fatikchhari reported that early marriage has been decreasing after receiving training. Similarly, 48.08 per cent respondents in Mirsharai and 61.54 per cent participants in Fatikchhari told that dowry has

Table 4 *Changes Occurred due to Participation in the Training Course*

Issues	*Mirsharai Status of Situation*						*Fatikchhari Status of Situation*					
	Decreased		*Increased*		*No Change*		*Decreased*		*Increased*		*No Change*	
	No.	*%*	*No.*	*%*	*No.*	*%*	*No.*	*%*	*No.*	*%*	*No.*	*%*
Early Marriage	46	88.46	1	1.92	13	25	52	100	0	0	7	13.46
Dowry	25	48.08	1	1.92	3	5.77	32	61.54	6	11.54	3	5.77
Divorce	42	80.77	0	0	1	1.92	50	96.15	1	1.92	3	5.77
Polygamy	41	78.85	1	1.92	2	3.85	51	96.15	0	0	4	7.69
Female education	0	0	52	100	0	0	0	0	52	100	0	0
Violence against women	52	100	5	9.62	1	1.92	52	100	4	7.69	0	0
Positive behaviour of religious leader and social leader	2	3.85	49	94.29	4	7.69	0	0	52	100	1	1.92
Cultural activities	0	0	52	100	0	0	0	0	52	100	1	1.92

Table 5 *Sources of Income and Average Annual Income of the Respondents by Family Members*

Male family members				*Female family members*			
Source of income	*No. of family members*	*%*	*Average annual income (Tk)*	*Source of income*	*No. of family members*	*%*	*Average annual income (Tk)*
Agricultural activities (paddy, bamboo and vegetables)	60	50	13,713	Agricultural activities (paddy, bamboo and vegetables)	14	14.43	7,321
Agricultural/Forest day labour	92	77	20,948	Agricultural/Forest day labour	62	51.67	11,805
Non-agril. labour	18	15	16,622	Non-agril. labour	13	10.83	9,925
Small trading (Retailer)	6	5	16,900	Small trading (Retailer)	1	0.10	7,200
Service	12	10	27,938	Service	5	5.15	18,092
Wine making	24	20	10,414	Beer producing	25	20.62	5,613
Mason	1	0.83	24,000	Mason	0	0	
Carpenter	1	0.83	72,000	Carpenter	0	0	
Motor driving	2	1.67	36,000	Motor driving	0	0	
Cloth making	2	1.67	3,250	Cloth making	2	2.06	3,250
Others	10	8.33	8,330	Others	2	2.06	750
	120	—	—	—	97	—	—

been decreasing after receiving training. Likewise, a significant per cent of respondents opined that divorce, polygamy and violence against women have decreased in both Mirsharai and Fatikchhari area.

On the other hand, it has been found that female education, practice of religious activities and positive behaviour of religious and social leaders have increased significantly in both Mirsharai and Fatikchhari areas. The given information indicates that trainings are making positive effects on the lives of the Tripura tribal community.

Income Source and Annual Income of Household Members

Data presented in Table 5, show that about 50 per cent of male and 14.43 per cent female family member are involved in agricultural activities (paddy, bamboo and vegetables) as means of their livelihood while the annual income of male and female family members are Tk 13,713 and Tk 7,321 respectively. About 77 per cent of male and 51.67 per cent of female family members are involved in agricultural/forest day labour activities, while the annual income of male and female family members are Tk 20,948 and Tk 11,805 respectively.

Similarly, about 15 per cent of male and 13 per cent female family member are involved in non-agri-activities while the annual income of male and female family members are Tk 16,622 and Tk 9,925 respectively. Likewise, about 20 per cent of male and 20.62 per cent female family member are involved in wine making process while the annual income of male and female family members are Tk 10,414 and Tk 5,613 respectively. Analysis of that data shows that the highest number of people are involved in agriculture/forest labour activities. The study findings reveal that the annual income of male family members is much more higher than that of female members in the households.

The quantitative survey findings (Table 6) reveal that 4 per cent of members' monthly income usually falls around Tk 1,700. Likewise, 19 per cent respondents' monthly income falls under Tk 1,667–2,500, 21 per cent respondents' monthly income falls under Tk 2,500–3,333, 29 per cent respondents' monthly income falls under Tk 3,334–4,166, 17 per cent respondents' monthly income falls under Tk 4,167–5,000 and 11 per cent respondents' monthly income falls under above Tk 5,000. It has also been revealed that the maximum number of respondents' monthly income group falls within Tk 2,083–4,583 which reflects a good income level for such vulnerable tribal community.

As per present survey the monthly average income is Tk 2,815. On the other hand average family size is 5.18 which means for each household at least for rice alone as per the present market rate requires Tk 40–45 per day and for rest items including medicine one household needs almost double of that for bare

Table 6 *Annual Income Group of the Respondents*

Income Group (Tk)	*Mirsharai (%)*	*Fatikchhari (%)*	*Total*
Upto 20,000	7	2	4
20,001–25,000	3	8	6
25,001–30,000	10	15	13
30,001–35,000	8	12	10
35,001–40,000	13	8	11
40,001–45,000	5	23	14
45,001–50,000	20	10	15
50,001–55,000	7	13	10
55,001–60,000	12	2	7
Above 60,000	15	7	11

subsistence. Each household therefore requires Tk 2,700–2,800 for bare subsistence. Even 23 per cent of the respondents do not earn enough for bare subsistence. However, it should be mentioned here that a poor household does not have guaranteed income round the year rather enough and inadequate food cycle is common in their life.

Condition of Food Security of the Respondents

Food security is a major element among all other issues of the livelihood condition of an individual. In regard to the food security round the year, the quantitative survey findings (Table 7) show that about 30 per cent households have no shortage of food round the year. It has also been revealed that there are about 12 per cent households who usually experienced food shortage for 1 month, 40 per cent households who usually experienced food shortage for 2 months and 12 per cent sample households who usually experienced food shortage for 3 months.

Table 7 *Status of Food Security of the Respondents*

Month	*Mirsharai (%)*	*Fatkchhari (%)*	*All (%)*
1 Month	13	10	12
2 Months	33	47	40
3 Months	15	8	12
5 Months	2	2	2
6 Months	2	2	2

Despite their poverty one important point that has been mentioned by the target beneficiaries is that at this stage nobody has to live without food, rather still there are some households who used to face difficulties to manage food for three times a day. Before launching the project activities, a significant per cent of target beneficiaries used to fulfil their food requirement by eating only boiled vegetables during the crisis period, but now, it is not required for any of them. It indicates that their level of food security situation has improved with the implementation of the project what is not only desirable but also possible. It was reported that earlier a significant per cent of target beneficiaries used to fulfil their food requirement by eating only boiled vegetables and bamboo roots during the crisis period, but now, it is not required for any of them. Moreover, whenever they have good income on any day they go for wine, meat, cigar etc., without thinking about a rainy day.

Food Intake of Households

In general, the poor people in the rural area cannot afford to have food like meat, milk, egg, fish due to high price. They usually think that those foods are for the rich people. In poor families people consume these types of foods occasionally, in time of any religious and social festivals. Consumption of costly food and frequency of taking these items depends on economic solvency of the household. An attempt has been made to know about that during the survey.

It has been found from the field survey that 2 per cent households are unable to take meat, 3 per cent households are unable to take fish, 15 per cent households are unable to take eggs and 48 per cent households are unable to take milk within a month (Table 8). Data presented in the same table also reveal that some 21 per cent households are taking meat once in a month, 28 per cent are taking twice in a month, 16 per cent are taking thrice in a month and 25 per cent are household taking meat four days in a month and so on.

Table 8 *Food Intake (comparatively costly food) taken by the Respondents*

Type of Food	Status of respondent households (Per month)																	
	None		Once a month		Twice		Thrice		Four days		Five days		Six days		Seven days		More than 7 days	
	Nos of resp.	%	Nos of resp.	%	Nos of resp.	%	Nos of resp.	%	Nos of resp.	%	Nos of resp.	%	Nos of resp.	%	Nos of resp.	%	Nos of resp.	%
Meat	2	2	25	21	33	28	19	16	30	25	2	2	3	3	3	3	3	3
Fish	3	3	6	5	17	14	18	15	46	38	8	7	6	5	2	2	14	12
Egg	18	15	12	10	30	25	9	8	21	18	7	6	5	4	3	3	15	13
Milk	57	48	12	10	22	18	5	4	4	3	5	4	0	0	0	0	15	13

All these information indicate that the overall economic situation of households has improved better over the years as per their report. In future, gradual increase of number of households in this category would indicate to the positive changes.

Usages of Safe Water and Sanitary Latrine

It has been observed that household members are aware about the importance of safe water and sanitary latrine. The field data show that (Table 9) only 11 per cent households are using tube well water of their own and 10 per cent households are using their own ring slab latrine.

All these information regarding safe drinking water and sanitary latrines, indicate an alarming and vulnerable situation of the target people, which requires support to avoid that grave situation. While conducting survey, people emphasized on that and set forth recommendations to the local NGO to think over the issue.

Table 9 *Usage of Safe Water and Sanitary Latrine by the Respondents*

Name of Facilities	*Mirsharai (%)*		*Fatikchhari (%)*		*Overall Status (%)*	
	Yes	*No*	*Yes*	*No*	*Yes*	*No*
Tube well	12	88	10	90	11	89
Own ring slab	20	80	0	100	10	90
Own pucca latrine	7	93	13	87	10	90

Source of Safe Water

Data presented in Table 10 has revealed that about 78 per cent respondents are using tube well water for drinking purpose, 39 per cent respondents are using for washing utensils and 32 per cent respondents are using for washing cloths. Field data indicate that a significant per cent of respondents have been using pond/ditch water, spring water and other sources of water for drinking, washing utensils and cloths etc., due to lack of opportunity for adequate number of tube wells in the Tripura community areas.

Gender Issue

The study findings reveal that the 'poor and hardcore poor people' of the Tripura tribal communities, both male and female were targeted as beneficiaries of NGO with a view to initiate a process of empowerment and social change. It was also found that the project addressed a total of 507 group members. Among them, there are 19 (37%) male groups, 23 (45%) female groups and 9 (18%) mixed groups respectively. Analysis of the above-mentioned information show that the NGO project addressed about 60 per cent female beneficiaries and 40 per cent male beneficiaries respectively, which show a genuine emphasis on the gender issues under that project.

Education

Group members reported that through participating in the Group Development Education (GDE) programme they have been benefited in different ways in their

Table 10 *Usage of Safe Water by the Respondents*

Source of water	Status of safe water used by the respondent households																	
	Mirsharai						Fatikchhari						Overall status					
	Drinking		Washing utensils		Washing cloths		Drinking		Washing utensils		Washing cloths		Drinking		Washing utensils		Washing cloths	
	Nos of resp.	%	No. of resp.	%	No. of resp.	%	No. of resp.	%	No. of resp.	%	No. of resp.	%	No. of resp.	%	No. of resp.	%	No. of resp.	%
Tube well	46	77	27	45	24	40	47	78	20	33	14	23	93	78	47	39	38	32
Pond/ditch	2	3	20	33	23	38	2	3	23	38	26	43	4	3	43	36	49	41
Spring	4	7	7	12	7	12	4	7	5	8	4	7	8	7	12	10	11	9
Other	8	13	4	7	5	8	6	10	14	23	15	25	14	12	18	15	20	17

daily lives. They informed that the following changes have been brought about by the intervention of the project:

- Due to inclusion of the members of group in the adult education programme, some of them are able to sign and earned numeracy.
- Increased interest for education among the group members has been claimed
- Raised voice among the group members to protest against Gender Based Violence (GBV), torture and harassment
- Increased awareness on education, environment, rights, health, personal hygiene practice, safe drinking water, immunization, birth control, safe motherhood etc.
- Increased literacy rate in the Tripura tribal community people.
- Improved dressing pattern, such as, now they are using lungi instead of lengti.

The overall performance of non-formal education for children programme was found satisfactory while the non-formal education component achieved tremendously. It has been reported that the activities of school programme, the average attendance of students, materials used for teaching and relevant documents was found organized, updated and well maintained.

It has also been reported that NGO schools have been practising the curriculum which include: health education, cultural activities (songs and dance), fine arts, story telling, reciting of rhyme and poem, religious education, conversation, sports and physical exercise and drama (short drama) etc., which is contributing to increase extra-curricula skills of the school students and making the learning more attractive. There are instances where even some Bengali guardians are also showing interest to send their children to NGO school leaving the government school.

Almost all the students expressed their view that since education is the most important element for the well-being of life, they will try their level best for obtaining higher education for their children as per their ability which is an important change in their aspiration due to intervention of the project.

As per discussion and opinion from different group of stakeholders, it has come out that education programme of the local NGO has many positive effects on the Tripura tribal communities. These include: increased awareness and interest of the ultra poor, created favourable atmosphere for education where a significant number of Tripura children are being self-motivation, almost all students got interest to get admission in the secondary level school after completion of primary education and finally created opportunity of education for the children living in remote areas who usually identified as the outreach group.

Institution Building

Meanwhile the project has formed 4 CBOs within one year and necessary office, constitution, management committees, and work plan are in place to perform/practice their assigned responsibilities. It is to enhance the capacity of CBOs leaded by the Tripura community people within very short period of time, as their academic level is often poor.

Field findings also reveal that 3 CBOs except one have been able to organize about 60 per cent meeting with the help of NGO staff as per rules and regulations. It was reported that one CBO could not perform their responsibilities as expected due to less attendance, less seriousness to adhere to time etc.

Positive and Negative Changes

Over the years some positive changes have taken place, which include:

- Increased interaction with other communities
- Change in lifestyle including clothing[5] and living which are more modern
- Have access to law enforcement agencies
- Can protest violation of human rights
- Are becoming literate and looking for non-traditional occupations
- Reducing food insecurity
- Having savings and access to credit
- Developing some kind of democratic leadership.

On the other hand some negative changes have also taken place, which include:

- Increasing vulnerability of women folk
- Insecurity as a community is also increasing
- Social solidarity with the dominant community (Bengali) has been reduced.
- Control over natural resources has been lost
- With the population growth means of livelihood has been reduced.

Challenges and Opportunities

There are some challenges and opportunities, which have been noted below:

1. Implementation of transformational development programme by local NGO within the present context of culture, belief, values, social structure of the project area is undoubtedly a challenging work.
2. Tribal community eviction by the forest department due to settlement in the forest department's land is another big challenge
3. Due to lack of alternative options for earning, some group members are involved in making wine (locally produced by rice) as income generating activities. Usually they sell it in the market of the Bengali communities while sometimes the Bengali people used to come to the Tripura communities for drink and often create some other social problems.
4. NGO staff faced some critical problems while doing rapport building work and implementation of the project activities, which includes language problem, and cultural practices, ill behaviour of Bengali community with Tripura community, illiteracy of the target group and remoteness of the working area.

Conclusions

Many positive and negative changes have taken place in Tripura community's life over the years. Their livelihood security has also increased with the external intervention. Tripuras are also empowered as now they can protest against the misuse of power by the forest departmental officials or other government agencies including law-enforcing agencies. A new economic discipline has been in place, which is going to replace their traditional dependent economic system.

Recommendations

1. Since a part of the project area is very far with no transportation system, instalment collection can be done on weekly basis or the group leader can cover a part of the way everyday and a part by the NGO worker like relay race. But to disseminate the social development information there should have weekly meeting with the group members.
2. Goat distribution and rearing process is an innovative idea,[6] which should continue further as the process was liked and used by the Tripura community people.
3. Although the sanitation training is given to all the group members and are found aware of it including the school children, a mechanism should be worked out to avail the sanitary latrine. Present difficultly is to carry the ring thread from a long distance which is extremely troublesome in the hilly area and costly as well. Local NGO can introduce a mobile ring thread building crew to do that at the site for the people or some of the community members can be trained, who can do it on payment for the people who will own that.
4. There is a language barrier and therefore attempt should continue to recruit NGO workers from the Tripura community. Even if any worker leaves the project the member of the Tripura community should replace the same. It needs to be recorded here that the project workers of Tripura community is also the beneficiary, not only the service provider. However, it may create more social inequality and in the long run power inequality among the Tripura community itself but it will also work as a process of empowerment of the community as the workers would get chance to have access to the local government and government power structure. The power and economic inequality is already there in the Tripura community. What perhaps can add to that is the prowess of the community as a whole. There are evidences of their powerlessness and empowerment—both.
5. The teachers engaged in teaching children should be given some training on teaching techniques and other related issues so that they can perform better as a teacher. Teachers should be preferably recruited from the Tripura community, wherever available and possible as that removes the language barrier.
6. CBO leaders should be formally introduced to the local government authority including to Sub-district Executive Officer (UNO), Assistant Commissioner (Land) and officer-in-charge of police. On some occasions they should be invited to attend the functions of the CBO like annual day, sports day of the school and so on. Presently local NGO is practising that, which should be strengthened further as the CBO leaders do not consider it adequate.
7. Donor agency can give grant fund instead of loan fund to make Tripuras' development activity a sustainable one, as the local NGO has to develop its capacity.

8. Bengali-Tripura relation has improved due to implementation of a development project and it can be improved further by continuing implementation of the same type of project. But it needs to be noted here that with the increased strength of the Tripura community revenge attract may also increase in future for which a community-relation building (CRB) work should continue and a solidarity maintaining approach should also get an institutional shape. A solidarity forum can be created (which seems to exist in a form) taking members from both Bengali and Tripura community so that all disputes, conflict and atrocity can be solved or removed through their intervention. Local NGO should monitor whether any kind of domination of the Bengali people is there or not.
9. Trainings have been given from the local NGO to all members of the group but all could not utilize that as they were lacking resources and entrepreneurship quality to make use of training and fund. It will take time for such an excluded community but a continuous effort from the local NGO side would bring success. External help is necessary for internal development. Local NGO needs to pay attention to that problem by doing some kind of demonstration works. A fair can be arranged for them where the NGO can show the community members about other community members' achievements. They can also use a cultural team to compose lyrics in Tripura language to make a clarion call for waking up of the slow-going community members. Tripura community has good cultural teams who can do that. Donor agency can give technical assistance in this connection if the NGO does not have that technical or financial capacity.
10. More schools are needed in the community area as these days Tripuras are showing more interest in sending their children to the school. Even some Bengali poor people are also showing interest to send their children to local NGO school. Local NGO can do some advocacy work to reactivate or establish new government school.
11. Separate project for Bengali and Tripura and alternative livelihood for Bengali and Tripura may be undertaken by the local NGO in that remote area. It has several consequences where if the project is operated for both the communities it would reduce the tension between the two groups as poor Bengali people would not have any sense of deprivation as they would see now that project is there only for Tripura. On the other hand, such approach can cause a development-induced in-migration, which again can aggravate the situation in that land-hungry area. Any development of such kind should be planned very carefully which otherwise may create tension among the poor people of both the communities.
12. Local NGO can take necessary initiative to ensure land for living and farming on lease from the government as to ensuring safe living of the Tripura community. For that they can organize a national level advocacy programme.
13. Provisions for secondary education of the Tripura students should be created. For that a local level initiative should be there, where local NGO can facilitate the process.

Notes

1. For detail please see S.M. Mahfuzur Rahman—*Tripuras, Dhaka, Banglapedia*, p. 220.
2. Ibid., p. 220.
3. Ibid., p. 220.
4. Ibid., p. 220 and Satter, 2000.
5. Earlier married women were topless to show that they are married and unmarried women were wearing some cloths. But now both the groups are wearing some cloth.
6. One goat is given to one household for rearing. After getting the first time calf from the goat the grown up calf have to be distributed among other households and the mother goat and subsequent calf would be of that households.

References

OPCA, (2005), Progress Report.

Rahman, S.M. Mahfuzur, (2003), "The Tripura", *Banglapedia*, Dhaka, Asiatic Society of Bangladesh.

Sattar, Abdus and Araney, (2000), Janapad, (2nd edition), Nowraj Shahitta Sombar.

4 'Salwa Judum' and Loss of Cultural Practices among Tribes of Bastar

An Anthropological Concern

DEVESH K. SAHU AND ANKITA ARYA

Tribes of Bastar as in the Writings of Verrier Elwin

The Muria ghotul, the village dormitory, the bachelor's hall of the Muria of Bastar. Similar, in-situations are widely distributed among communities of the Austro-Asiatic cultures, but it is probable that the Bastar ghotul is one of the most highly developed and carefully organized in the world and is for the Muria boys and girls learn to live together, 'the centre of their social and religious life'.

The tribal people, inhabitants of Bastar region are the least influenced by the outside world and have retained most of their religious and cultural institutions. They live in the Abujhmar mountains and they are both shy and friendly, an attractive people, cultivating their desolate and lonely hills with axe and fire. Their characteristic is music, dance and aesthetics like the marriage dance with a splendid bison-horn head-dress. A megalithic culture survives among them, and there are traces of a ghotul system long since moribund.

Emergence of Naxalism in Bastar

The word 'Naxalism' is loaded with nameless fears and aspirations, stirring hopes or despair and strong passion. At least nine out of 16 districts of Chhattisgarh, where Naxalism seems to have its deep root may not explain the ideology but does undoubtedly give an indication of the revolutionary change that it seeks to bring about. The Naxalites take their name from an uprising of workers in the tea garden in the north Bengal countryside near Naxalbari Thana in early 1967. Yet, the fact remains that Naxalites do have their impact on the political scene and moral constitution of the Indian sensibility. It is a group that most Indians are aware of, though without clarity as to what they stand for.

Bastar offers geographical advantages, surrounded by three states of Andhra Pradesh, Maharashtra and Orissa. The division is infested with deep forest and difficult terrain where police access is not easy. The majority of population is tribal. The geographical condition and socio-economic situation in the region is still poor. Naxalism entered Bastar from Andhra Pradesh. The anti-Bhanjdeo activities of the Government of Madhya Pradesh was propagated by them as anti-tribal and anti-Bastar. The government policy of containing the influence of Maharaja Praveen Chand Bhanjdeo helped the Naxalites in gaining the support of the tribals and the brutal killing of the Maharaja, whom the tribals worshipped, alienated them from the government completely.

In 1980s, the Naxalites, the ultra-left wing armed opposition group, made inroads into Bastar region from neighbouring Andhra Pradesh. Then Madhya Pradesh government had little semblance of presence in the Bastar region. The plight of the dispossessed and exploited Adivasis provided the classical situation for starting a communist revolution. As the Naxalites took over the tasks meant to be done by the state and provided protection to the Adivasis against exploitation by the corrupt officials, police, forest department officials, timber mafia, moneylenders etc., it was not difficult for the Adivasis to relate to the ideology of the Naxalites. The Naxalites gradually increased their influence day by day. The fact construe to inform that Naxalism might have emerged as a reaction to the mismanagement poverty alleviation programmes and developmental schemes launched which have but marginally helped the poor especially tribals. The real beneficiaries are those who oppose the Naxalites in the area.

Naxalites has not only raised their voices against all these issues even they started to appoint judges and then regularly hold Jan Adalats in the villages. The traders, contractors and even officers are summoned to appear before the Jan Adalat. They are made to accept the guilt. If necessary, physical force is also used. The judgement takes place in the same Adalat before the people gathered. This process, howsoever defective it may be, has popularized the Jan Adalat in the region. "Let the Naxalites be the enemy of corrupt officials, traders and contractors who are dishonest, but they are our friends in need as well as indeed." This is the expression of one of the tribals of the region during my fieldwork in Bastar area some seven years ago. Even it was quite often to hear the incidents of looting in the bazaars and distribution of looted food grains among the tribals.

Present Situation and Salwa Judum

But at present, there are certain conflicts of interest in the present context of contact, which is mainly due to change in the ideology of the Naxalites movement in the area. Even though majority of the cadres of the Naxalites are Adivasis but they do not have the decision-making powers. Most of the leading positions of every Dalam are occupied by the outsiders only which leads to keep local tribals in isolation within the Dalam. This change in the ideology has created separation between local tribals and Naxalites.

In order to protect their rights, exactly four years ago, in June 2005, a movement arose by the local tribals in Dantewara named 'Salwa Judum', whose aim was to throw the Naxalites out of the district. It apparently arose spontaneously, the handiwork of villagers fed up with having grain taken away to feed guerillas wandering in the forest. However, Salwa Judum was soon adopted and reshaped by the leading politician of Dantewara, Mahendra Karma, who is currently the Leader of the Opposition in the Chattisgarh Assembly. The state government was persuaded to throw its weight behind the movement. As many as three thousand Salwa Judum supporters were given the title of 'Special Police Officer', paid a monthly salary by the state, and presented with a rifle each. They were asked to monitor the movements of civilians, and to assist the police and paramilitary in taking on the revolutionaries.

Mahendra Karma christened it as Salwa Judum, peace initiative. It soon received the state sanction and became part of Chhattisgarh government's experiment with counter-insurgency operations to tackle the Naxalites. The civil war began in earnest. Now the Salwa Judum campaign has been taken over by the state as a full-pledged counter-insurgency programme. Involvement of state as well as Central government, the Salwa Judum has become far from a peaceful campaign with hundreds of the cadre being given full military training as special police officers. It has created a civil war where one is either with the Naxalites or with the Salwa Judum. As the Naxalites followed the policy of forcibly recruiting one cadre from each family, in numerous cases, members of the same family have been pitted against each other. The Adivasis, who wanted their plight to improve and bring an end to exploitation by the corrupt government officials, police, moneylenders, contractors etc., instead, they find themselves in the midst of a civil war.

By creating these 'Special Police Officers', the state had created a culture of machismo among the unemployed youth of the district. Educated just enough to have a certain disenchantment for labouring in field and forest, but not enough to be absorbed with honour in the modern economy, these boys were enticed into a job which paid them a salary (albeit a meagre one—Rs 1,500 a month), and gave them a certain status in society. With a gun in hand they now strutted around the countryside, forcing those without weapons to fall in line. Ironically, by arming civilians the state were merely reproducing the methods of the other side. For these boys were joining Salwa Judum for much the same reason as other boys had previously joined the Naxalites. There, too, those less than enthusiastic about farming or hunting were attracted by the prospect of a quasi-formal position and the weapon that went with it. Call them Sangam Organizer or Special Police Officer, the young men of Bastar were seduced by their new-found—and essentially unearned—authority. In this manner, the machismo of revolution was being answered by the machismo of counter-revolution. On both sides, there were now several thousand young males are being killed.

The Naxalites responded with violence against the Salwa Judum cadres irrespective of whether they are joining on their own volition or by force. Between 5 June 2005 and 6 March 2006, at least 138 Salwa Judum activists have been allegedly killed by the Naxalites. In the Darbhaguda massacre of 28 February 2006 in which 27 persons were killed and 32 others were injured, the Naxalites allegedly killed many injured by stabbing and clubbing. Even the children of the Salwa Judum cadres were not spared.

Though it has not been confirmed, but through some unofficial sources it was known that the state government in Chhattisgarh plans to set up 580 new tribal villages in Dantewada. Apparently tribals from 644 villages who have abandoned their homes to live in the camps on the roadside will be settled in these new villages. The new villages will also be set-up by the roadside and requests to the Centre for compensation are already in place. Each tribal shall be sanctioned between Rs 12,000 for building a new home in the new village. It may be a part of planned displacement of the local tribal families from this region for the set-up of big industries for groups like Tata and/or Essar? But very few are concerned about the livelihoods of these tribals in the future. Once the compensation grant has been used up to build the dwelling etc., what will be the source of income for the tribals? This is a question that does not seem to warrant any attention at this time.

Further, it was also reported that the Naxalites have been harassing the tribals who were living in villages off the roadside. When they are living by the roadside, their troubles shall end. Do they want to develop this region as Naxal base? Are government and Naxalites working with more or less same aspirations? Do tribes will loose everything?

Loss of Cultural Practices

Naxalites took over this area practically unoccupied by the state. The political handling of the issue and efforts to suppress by brute force making situation more difficult. The government may also be running with the idea that all the inhabitants of the jungle, who are basically tribal people, will relocate to the refugee camps which will further developed as colonies. By doing this, Naxalites will be deprived from all kind of support from their tribal friends and this isolation will be forced them to surrender or leave the area or engage in suicidal battle with paramilitary force. Officially there are thousands of people relocated in different camps located on road sides spread over Konta, Geedam, Bairamgarh, Bijapur and Usoor blocks. There is absolutely no way to get the exact figure of total number of affected people in the region or which may be deliberately done for aim of further manipulation.

The Adivasis became victims of gross violations of human rights such as "violence to life and person, in particular murder of all kinds, mutilation, cruel treatment and torture; taking of hostages; outrages upon personal dignity, in particular, humiliating and degrading treatment; and passing of sentences and the carrying out of executions without previous judgment pronounced by a regularly constituted court affording all the judicial guarantees which are recognized as indispensable by civilized peoples", at the hands of the Naxalites. Some of those who were injured in the landmine blast on 28 February 2006 at Darbhaguda village were allegedly stabbed and clubbed to death by the Naxalites. The policy of the Naxalites of forcibly recruiting one cadre from each Adivasi family compelled many families to give the female members to the Naxals. Hence, traditional Adivasi social taboos were challenged and destroyed by the Naxalites and resentment against the Naxalites grew.

The tribes of Bastar region are socialist. The idea of property and ownership of land was never strong in them and even today it is not strong. Communal ownership of property is still in practice in this region. But due to frequent insurgencies making difficult due to either temporary migration or living in the refugee camps.

The habit of drinking among tribes of Bastar region has also increased due to the government excise policy. The government became the seller of liquor and that is at the root cause of all mischief. Left to themselves they were drinking *Mand* or beverages or the juice of the *Salphi* tree. This makes them tipsy but never drunkards. But since government made it illegal for them to prepare their Mand or Salphi and introduced bottle drinks of wine, without knowing the fact that they offer this drink to their gods very often in very rituals.

Role of Media

The first press reports on Salwa Judum were complimentary. It was presented as a people's movement, autonomous of party politics that had successfully combated the Naxalites and thus proved itself worthy of emulation by other districts and states. Its presentation was made more attractive by the fact that while Karma is a Congressman, his enthusiasm for Salwa Judum is shared by the BJP Chief Minister of Chattisgarh, Dr Raman Singh.

Later reports about Salwa Judum were more ambiguous. Elements in the movement were said to have gone astray, and taken to harassing ordinary villagers in much the same manner as some Naxalites had done before.

Conclusion

According to some estimates there are more than 20,000 Adivasis from Chhattisgarh camping in Andhra Pradesh in fear of Salwa Judum militias. Adivasis from Chhattisgarh are also camping in Orissa and Maharashtra. They also fear attacks from Naxals. Tribals have felt the wrath of the Salwa Judum in far greater measure. In several villages there are many tribals whose homes had been looted and burnt by them. But there are some other tribals who had been attacked by the Naxalites also.

On the basis of above mentioned facts, we reached to our most worrisome conclusion—that the creation and consolidation of Salwa Judum had greatly increased the level of violence in this region. Tribals who were very much confined to their rituals and practices only are now being forced to choose one side or the other. Those who hesitated were savagely set upon. In the past year, several hundred people had died as a consequence of the conflict. Since 'Salwa Judum' translates as 'Peace Initiative', its literal meaning has to be understood in Orwellian terms alone.

Recommended Solution

It would be a gross mistake to regard it merely as a law and order problem which can be tackled by the law and order machinery, the existing machinery which itself requires a lot of reorientation and training in dealing with sensitive matters of this kind. It needs to be realized that Naxalism is not a problem: it is symptoms of serious social diseases.

What particularly requires greater and serious attention is to take up the old issues of land reform, education, health, employment and reduction in poverty as well as large disparity in income and wealth and above all the vulgar exhibition of richness which remain the romance of feudal and colonial heritage. The reform themselves should have an explicit redistributive content. It needs to be realized and recognized that a reform strategy which aims to withdraw the state from investment, liberalize finance and diver finances form the state to the private sector, liberalize agricultural trade and thus enrich the rich at the direct cost of the poor and seeks to control inflation and balance of trade problems through deflation and devaluation, is at its root a fundamentally iniquitous adventure.

Select References

ACHR Report, (2007), *Naxal Conflict in 2006*, New Delhi: Asian Centre for Human Rights.

Balagopal, K., (2006), "Chhattisgarh: Physiognomy of Violence", *Economic and Political Weekly*, June 3, Vol. 41, No. 22, Mumbai.

Bastar Development Plan, (1984), Bastar, Bhopal: State Planning Board Madhya Pradesh, Government of Madhya Pradesh.

Elwin, Verrier, (1947), *The Muria and their Ghotul*, Bombay: Oxford University Press.

———, (1949), *Myths of Middle India*, London: Oxford University Press.

Grigson, W.V., (1949), *The Maria Gonds of Bastar*, (Reissued with supplement), London: Oxford University Press.

Kurup, A.M., (1964), *People of the Unknown Hills: The Abujhmadias*, Vanyajati, Vol. 12, No. 2, April.

Naik, T.B. (ed.), (1963), *The Abujhmarias*, Chhindwara: Tribal Research Institute.

Russell, R.V. and Hiralal, R.B., (1916), *The Tribes and Castes of the Central Provinces of India*, Vol. III, London: Macmilan and Co. Ltd.

Sahu, Devesh Kumar and Mukherjee, B.M., (In Press), Cultural Aspect of Health and Illness: The Tribal Chhattisgarh" in *Bio-Social Issues in Health*, (edited by) Prof R.K. Pathak, Dr A.K. Sinha, Prof B.G. Banerjee, Prof R.N. Vasishta and Dr C.J. Edwin, New Delhi: Northern Book Centre.

———, (2007), "The Knowledge that Helps Indigenous People: An Anthropological Exploration" in *Traditional Knowledge in Contemporary Societies: Challenges and Opportunities". Intangible Cultural Heritage of India–5*, (edited) K.K. Misra and K.K. Basa (Bhopal). Indira Gandhi Rashtriya Manav Sangrahalaya (National Museum of Mankind), and Delhi: Pratibha Prakashan.

Sahu, S.L., (1955), *Bastar-Land and its People*, Modern Review.

Shukla, H.L., (1986), *Tribal Heritage of Madhya Pradesh*, Delhi: B.R. Publishing Corporation.

———, (1999), *Chhattisgarh in Making*, Delhi: B.R. Publishing Corporation.

5 Scientific and Cultural Gap in Explaining Health

An Ethnographic Analysis of Reproductive Morbidity among Tribal Women in Kerala

O.G. SAJITHA

Various conceptualizations of reproductive health consider reproductive morbidity as inclusive of conditions of physical ill-health related to 'successful childbearing' and 'freedom from gynecological disease and risk' (Zurayk et al., 1993). The reproductive morbidity related to childbearing hence encompasses the morbidity during pregnancy (antenatal), childbirth (natal), abortion, post-abortion or post-natal. Gynecological morbidity covers any condition, disease or dysfunction of the reproductive system that is not related to pregnancy, abortion or childbirth, but may be related to sexual behaviour (Fortney, 1995). Gynecological morbidity can further be divided into reproductive tract infections, endocrine disorders, infertility, gynecological cancers, congenital malformations or birth defects, injuries, sexual dysfunction, menopausal symptoms etc.

Various surveys showed that abortions are responsible for 10–20 per cent of all maternal deaths in India (Phanindra et al., 1998). Untreated incomplete miscarriages are a source of serious reproductive tract infection and undetected foetal death in uterus can endanger the mother's life (Sundari, 1993). The culture and environment of the individuals would generally determine the health behaviour and this would vary from individual to individual in accordance with the variation in the determining factors. In a study (Mutharayappa, 1994) conducted among two different endogamous tribal populations living in similar ecological settings, namely Jenu Kurubas and Kadu Kurubas of Karnataka showed that while 20.5 per cent of Jenu Kuruba women experienced deliberate or spontaneous abortion, only 5 per cent of Kadu Kuruba women experienced it; showing the effect of tribal culture in determining health behaviour. High rates of fetal wastages and infant mortality were also reported among the scheduled tribes in India compared to others (IIPS and ORC Macro, 2000). The rates of foetal death were 140.55 and 130.09 per 1,000 pregnancies among Gujars and Bazigars of Punjab, respectively (Sidhu, 1994). Pregnancy wastage was one of the reasons cited for the low birth rate among the diminutive tribal community Aranadan tribe of Kerala (Kakkoth, 2004). Another study (Joseph and Mathew, 2005) done among the Irulars and Mudugars of Palakkad district of Kerala state found that consanguinity between the couples had a significant risk effect in the prenatal and post-natal mortality. However limited attempts to depict the difference in explaining the causes or approaches to reproductive morbidity in tribal context in par with existing biomedical approaches would restrict health seeking.

Hence the present paper aimed to analyse and compare the explanatory models suggested as the cause of abortion, gynecological morbidity and antenatal, natal and post-natal morbidity by three different tribal groups in Kerala.

Objective

The objective of the paper is to study and compare the explanatory models suggested for various reproductive morbidities by three different tribal groups in Kerala.

Data and Methodology

Characteristics of Tribes Selected

The first twelve major tribal groups in Kerala were classified on the basis of education and occupation and three tribal groups were selected as follows.

1. Kani/Kanikkaran—High per cent of cultivators and high literacy.
2. Adiyan—High per cent of agricultural labourers and medium literacy.
3. Kattunayakan/Kattunaikkan—High per cent of population engaged in forestry or related works and low level of literacy.

The habitat of Kani tribe was Southern Western Ghat region of Kerala state, and it comes mostly under the boundary of Trivandrum district. The other two tribal groups selected (Adiya and Kattunayakan) were inhabitants of Wayanadu district of north Kerala. Kanikkaran had a nomadic life in the past and now they lead a settled life with usual contacts with non-tribes. There is a tremendous change in the life of Kani tribe including the shift of settlement level collective decisions in all the matters of life to household decisions. In the past, people depended on the traditional medical practitioner named 'Plathi' for treatment but now most of them are using modern allopathic medicines. Monogamy was strictly followed in the settlements and there were punishments to those who offend it in the past. Even after the abolition of punishment system, premarital and extramarital relations and resulting pregnancies were viewed as offense in the society.

The Adiya of Wayanadu district was one of the slave tribes in Kerala. They mainly depend on agriculture labouring for their living. As the cultivation became non-profitable, the earnings they had from agricultural labouring reduced and nowadays, they struggle very much for their livelihood. Polygamy within the tribal groups was permitted but so with persons from outside their community was considered as an offence and they are allowed to undergo purification ceremony known as 'Kalachu Veypu' and then they can join back their group.

Kattunayakan was one of the five primitive tribal groups in Kerala. They lived very much in tune with the nature. Collection of forest produce and hunting were the means of living of Kattunayakn tribe. But the restrictions to enter and find the means for life from the nature, in the name of protecting forest and wildlife now forced them to find work outside the forests. Even after their willingness to work for very low wages, unemployment and poverty was very severe among them. Another important factor was the medicinal system and its close association with the culture. They use traditional medicines for common ailments and use modern medicines at the time of emergency but only after seeking consent from 'God' through the chieftain or priest (generally both roles are taken by the same person) through a well-defined set of traditional *poojas*.

Data Collection Method

The focus group discussions (FGDs) were utilized to collect information for preparing culturally defined explanatory models for the reproductive morbidities. The participants of each FGD was fixed as the traditional birth attendant, wife of chieftain, wife of traditional healer and some educated women in the settlement (if present in the settlement) with some other women having at least one pregnancy for the last five years as participants in the focus group discussions: a group not more than twelve members. Even though the list of participants gives an impression that they are a heterogeneous group, there is homogeneity in the group that they are from same tribal group in the same or near settlement. But among Kani tribe it seems very difficult to get such a group. So Kani women in Kudumba Shree Unit (organized women units for the upliftment of family in all the parts of Kerala) situated in the tribal area, wife of medicinal man and women having at least one pregnancy for the last five years were grouped and focus group discussions were conducted. Number of FGDs done was six, two each from each tribal group. The discussions were taped and written notes also supplemented the tape.

Terms Used

Abortion

Abortion is the termination of pregnancy both spontaneous and induced before five months of gestation (Induced abortion is very low in the entire studied group and it is observed that it is done only at the time of very high medical emergency).

Antenatal Morbidity

Any swelling of hands and feet, paleness, weakness/tiredness, dizziness, visual disturbances, bleeding, convulsions, no movement of foetus and abnormal presentation.

Explanatory Model

It is a framework showing the reproductive health challenges in terms of their belief system, or in terms of the etiology, time and mode of onset of symptoms, or course of sickness.

Gynecological Morbidity

Any of white or coloured discharge from the vagina with bad odour, itching or irritation, lower abdominal pain and fever with vaginal discharge, abnormal frequency of urination with burning sensation while passing urine, ulcers or rashes in private parts and pain during intercourse.

Natal Morbidity

Any of haemorrhage, tear, stillbirth, and infant death. Stillbirth and infant death at the time of delivery were included in the tribal context as the success of the natal health they measures in the successful outcome of live birth.

Post-natal Morbidity

Any of high fever, lower abdominal pain, and foul smelling vaginal discharge and excessive bleeding any time after one week of delivery to two months of delivery.

Ethical Considerations

To give due consideration to the sensitivity of tribal population towards various issues, no attempt was done to take written consent from the participants as signing in paper is viewed with suspicion. They are also given an assurance that each respondent would be coded to a number and no data or no publication should be done which will identify their name and settlement or any other individual identification. They provided with all essential information before they participated in it and only those who wished to participate were included. Before starting the data collection the concerned Tribal Extension Officer of the settlements, Panchayat President or member and chieftain of the group were informed about the study but the individual consent was the ultimate criteria to include as the participant.

Analysis

Explanatory Models for Reproductive Morbidities

Focus group discussions facilitated the preparation of culturally defined explanatory models for selected reproductive morbidities. The symptoms of morbidities associated with pregnancy (antenatal), childbirth (natal), immediately after child birth (post-natal), abortion, and gynecological morbidity were discussed and the their beliefs for the occurrence of the morbidity were observed. Morbidity during childbirth included the condition resulting from stillbirth or infant death. The coded reasons cited by all groups are given in Table 1. The reasons cited by different groups depict how they connect the time and mode of onset of various morbidities with the culture and traditions they hold together with biomedical or socio-economical causes.

The symptoms of major reasons cited for the occurrence of various challenges were described separately for each tribal group and are pictured in Figures 1, 2 and 3. In each figure there are three components showing the models for:

Figure 1 *Explanatory Models by Adiya Women for Reproductive Morbidities, Kerala, 2002–03*

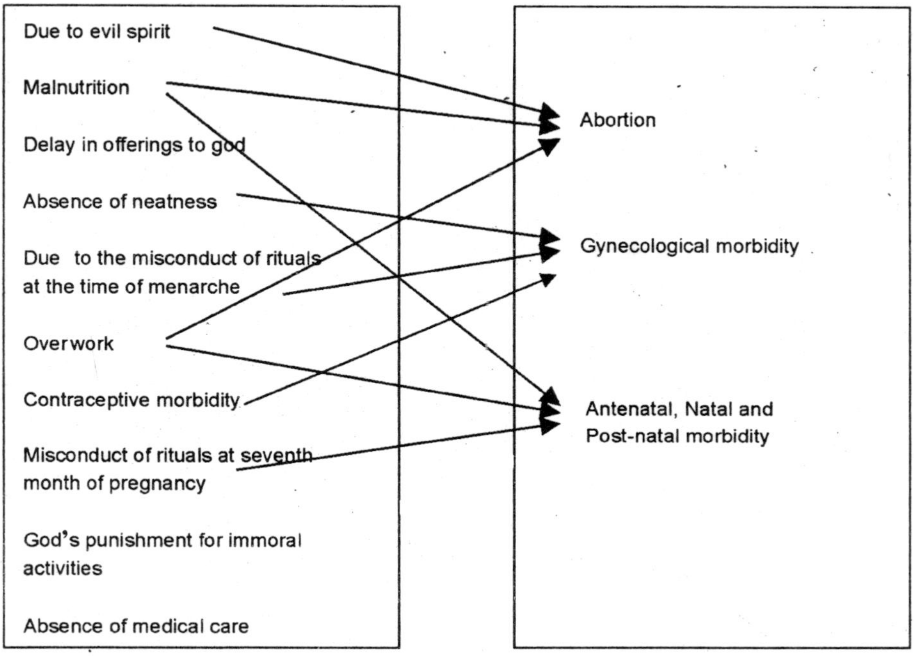

Figure 2 *Explanatory Models by Kanikkaran Women for Reproductive Morbidities, Kerala, 2002–03*

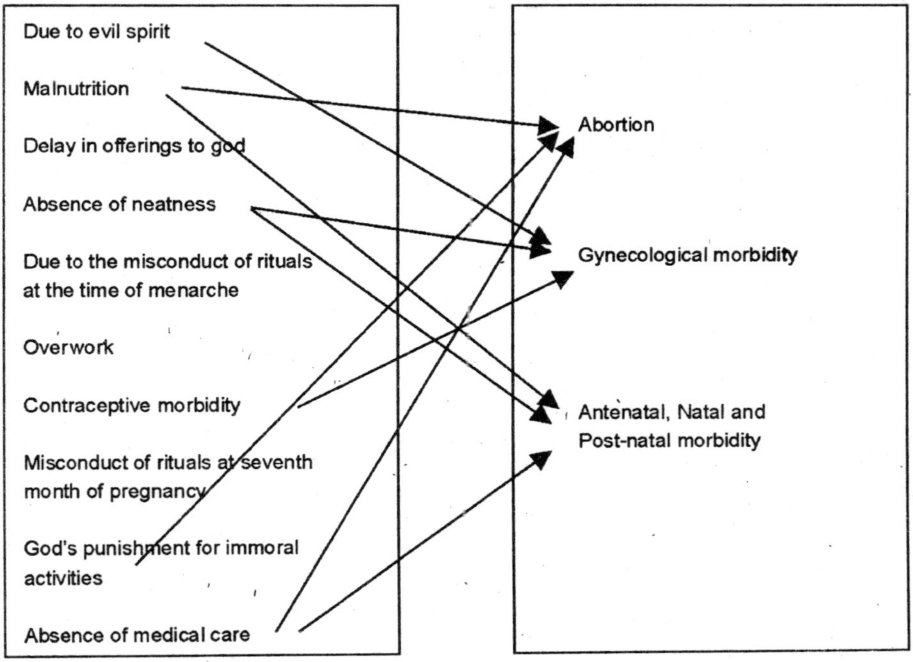

Figure 3 *Explanatory Models by Kattunayakan Women for Reproductive Morbidities, Kerala, 2002–03*

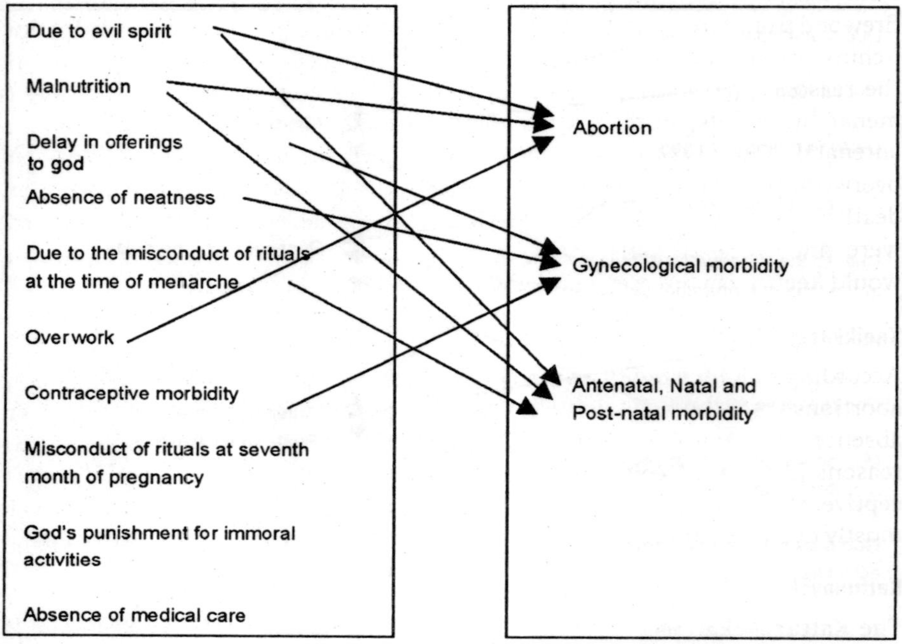

1. Abortion,
2. Gynecological morbidity and
3. Antenatal, natal (including stillbirth and infant death) and post-natal morbidity.

Table 1 *Reasons for Various Reproductive Morbidities according to Adiyan, Kanikkaran and Kattunayakan Women in Kerala, 2002–2003*

Reason Number	*Reason*
1.	Due to evil spirit
2.	Malnutrition
3.	Delay in giving offerings to god
4.	Absence of neatness
5.	Due to the misconduct of rituals at the time of menarche
6.	Overwork
7.	Contraceptive morbidity
8.	Misconduct of rituals at seventh month of pregnancy
9.	God's punishment for immoral activities
10.	Absence of medical care

Adiyan

The Adiya women responded that the major reasons for the occurrence of spontaneous abortion were the mischief of evil spirit, malnutrition and overwork. By 'overwork' they mean activities like the bringing of drinking water from far places, going for agricultural labour during pregnancy, collecting firewood from forest etc. For gynecological morbidity like pain during urination, itching, irritation, blood visible after sexual intercourse etc., they pointed out the reasons like absence of neatness, the misconduct of rituals at the time of menarche, and use of contraceptive methods like Copper-T. They believed that antenatal and post-natal problems were mostly due to malnutrition and overwork. However, the chances of breech presentation, stillbirth and infant deaths would be high if the rituals at the time of seventh month of pregnancy were not doing properly. Because they strongly believe that such practices would keep away the pregnant lady from the harms of 'pisachu' (evil spirit).

Kanikkaran (Kani)

According to Kani women, the major reasons for the occurrence of spontaneous abortions were the malnutrition, God's punishment for immoral activities and absence of medical care. For gynecological morbidity, they suggested the reasons like the mischief of evil spirit, absence of neatness and use of contraceptive methods. They believe that antenatal and post-natal problems were mostly due to malnutrition, absence of both neatness and proper medical care.

Kattunayakan

The Kattunayakan women were of the opinion that the major reasons for the occurrence of spontaneous abortion were the mischief of evil spirit, malnutrition and overwork. By overwork, they mean activities like bringing of drinking water from far places, walking far distances to buy things for day-to-day life, collecting firewood from forest etc. For gynecological morbidity, they concluded that the reasons were delay in giving offerings to god, absence of neatness and use of contraceptive methods like Copper-T. They believed that antenatal and post-natal problems were mostly due to the evil spirits and malnutrition. However, the chances of death of mother and infants would be high if the ritual practices at the time of seventh month pf pregnancy were not done properly. Because it was practising to keep away the pregnant lady from the harms of *pretham* (evil spirit). They said that the soul of person who died in adolescent or adulthood would make more problem if the practices were done not properly or at time. They also added that they would not report the infant deaths under the suspicion that, it's soul would make much more problems to other children and would burn or leave the living hurt if somebody dies in adolescence or youth. It showed the depth of the tradition and believes they had.

Comparative Analysis of Causes of Reproductive Morbidity among Three Tribal Groups in Kerala, 2002–03

All the three studied tribal groups narrate malnutrition as a cause of abortion. The conceptualization of malnutrition arouse from their argument that severe hunger arising from poverty is a cause of spontaneous abortion particularly during the initial periods of pregnancy. FGDs in Kattunayakan and Adiya cited examples of surrounding women who experienced repeated abortions due to the absence of food or severe poverty in the house. However, both FGDs in Kanikkaran arrived at the conclusion that not only hunger but also the absence of nutritious food like fruits, milk and vegetables would cause abortion. The Kanikkaran tribe also believes in medical care during pregnancy to avoid abortion as well as antenatal, natal and post-natal morbidities. The other two reasons cited by Kanikkaran for antenatal, natal and post-natal morbidities (including causes of stillbirth and infant deaths) are malnutrition and absence of neatness.

The role of evil spirits in creating reproductive morbidity is deep rooted in the beliefs of tribes studied. Kattunayakan and Adiyan believe that the abortion can be caused by evil spirit; but Kani believes that itching, irritation and ulcers in and around private parts (symptoms of gynecological morbidity) is caused by it. Kanikkaran is a monogamous group and they believe that abortion would occur as a punishment to immoral activities like sex outside the marriage.

It is repugnant to note that all the groups treat use of artificial contraceptive methods as a major reason for gynecological morbidity. Kattunayakans linked the symptoms of gynecological morbidity also to a back history of misconduct of rituals at the time of starting menses that is menarche. And Adiyans connected the symptoms of antenatal, natal and post-natal morbidity as a result of misconduct of rituals at the seventh month pf pregnancy.

Conclusion

Only socio-economically better tribe (Kani) compared to backward (Adiya) and primitive (Kattunayakan) considers the absence of medical care as cause of reproductive morbidity. Backward and primitive linked the morbidity to a back history of misconduct as well as non-practice of rituals at the time of menarche or pregnancy, which is not the case with Kanikkaran. However all the three tribal groups studied believe evil sprits as cause of reproductive morbidity. Hence the study suggests that knowledge regarding the pathophysiology of reproductive morbidity varies among tribal groups and is combination of cultural and scientific causes. Socio-economically advantage group tend to scientific but inclusive of cultural and primitive or backward group tend more to cultural and hardly inclusive of scientific while explaining the causes of reproductive morbidity.

References

Fortney, J., 1995. "Reproductive Morbidity: A Conceptual Framework". Family Health International Working Paper No. WP95–02.

IIPS and ORC Macro, (2000), National Family Health Survey Report, India, 1998–99, Mumbai.

Joseph, Stephen and Mathew, P.M., (2005), "Effects of Inbreeding in the Mudugar and Irular Tribal Populations in Kerala", *Journal of Human Ecology*, 17 (4).

Kakkoth, Seetha, (2004), "Demographic Profile of an Autochthonous Tribe: The Aranandan of Kerala", *Anthropologist*, 6 (3), 163–167.

Mutharayappa, R., 1998. "Fertility and Family Planning Among Jenu Kuruba and Kadu Kuruba Tribes of Karnataka". *Man in India*. 78(1–2): 119–126.

Phanindra Babu, N., Verma Nidhi and Ravi, K., "Abortion in India: What Does the National Family Health Survey Tell Us", *The Journal of Family Welfare*, 44 (4), December, (1998), 45–54.

Sundari, T.K., (1993), "Can Health Education Improve Pregnancy Outcome", Report of a Grassroots Action-Education Campaign, *The Journal of Family Welfare*, 39 (1).

Zurayk, H. et al., 1993. A Community Study of Gynecological and Related Morbidities in Rural Egypt. Study in Family Planning. V. 24, No. 03. pp. 175–85. http://linksjstor.org./sici.

Zurayk, H., Khattab, H., Younis, N., El-Mouelhy, M. and Fadle, M. 1993. "Concepts and Measures of Reproductive Morbidity", *Health Transition Review*, 3, 17–40.

6 The Ethnographic Imagination

MOHAN RAMANAN

This is an opinion that the division of academic disciplines into humanities and social sciences is artificial and perhaps the time has come for us to see the necessary ways in which (our) two schools must interrelate. A process of symbiosis must be set in motion and I believe that a good opportunity has been afforded to us to begin this process. Anthropology and the ethnological dimensions of the subject are of great importance in our present times. This is because we do not live in a world of easily held beliefs and certainly any essential formulations like Man, Justice or Love are looked upon with a degree of scepticism. In our post-world where we have even denied the human it is crucial for us to focus on collectivities and sectors and groups, each divided from the other because of the specific histories and cultures embedded in them. This is where the anthropological and ethnographic imagination can have free play because these activities allow us to focus on particularities and individual categories in all their quiddity and substantiveness. In literary criticism after the work of Amitav Ghosh we can speak about the ethnographic novel or ethnographic novelist. Ghosh indeed is one such novelist. In his researches he is able to fictionalize the specific histories of people of dissimilar backgrounds. Nowhere is this more clearly evident than in his novel *In An Antique Land*. This is a novel which goes beyond national boundaries, to far off Egypt and shows through a brisk narration the way in which, even when people are separated by language, religion, and ethnicity, they can still speak to one another. Ethnography thus has the ability to connect people and cultures apparently dissimilar. The important point to note, of course, is that it does this without essentializing, without obliterating difference and plurality. The relevance of such an intellectual procedure cannot be overemphasized in our country and I am mainly interested in the ramifications of the ethnographic imagination for India. Ours is a nation only so to speak. Certainly no hard or solidified notion of nationhood can be attributed to this land mass, so-called India, because of its sheer diversity of linguistic communities, castes, classes, religions, ethnicities and many other things. To reduce India to a formulation and to leave that formulation wriggling against a wall is to do disservice to the great and varied history of the land and its people and to the truth itself. The truth is that we have never had a nation except in some amorphous cultural terms. Nationhood was thrust on us because of historical developments and had much to do with the modernizing forces of British rule and colonialism. We moved towards modernity because of the Imperial connection and one aspect of that modernity, of course was, the idea of India, a new nation. I do not wish to obliterate that history either and surely no one can deny that after independence we have the makings of a modern nation state. But note—it is only in a manner of speaking. To solidify the idea of India and to cut corners and to erase the local and specific cultural histories of our myriad people would be to do harm to the fragile unity in diversity our new nation enjoys. We must, of course, strengthen that unity but it must only be with a genuflection, the direction of our diversity and our plural existence. Any other way is neither pragmatic nor morally correct.

Thus in the context of India, to discuss the human practices of our tribes, subaltern communities and our caste-based society is to recognize the regenerative power of the discipline of anthropology and its important branch-ethnography. The way our forests are being destroyed in the name of development, the exploitation of the tribal people and the forest dwellers, the various aspects of tribal developments—these are the legitimate areas of concern, not only of the anthropologist but of the other disciplines too. I speak mainly as a literary scholar. My reading of tribal literatures not only from India but from other parts of the world, notably the Amerindian writers of the USA, tells me that there is a rich mine of information about people in a particular stage of development. This should not be mistaken for a location of tribes in an axis of development which is accepted by the nation's ruling establishment. I respect the particularities of the tribes and without attempting to judge their level of development I must say that they can be no overarching idea of progress and perhaps we might learn a great deal about values of honesty, sacrifice, love and community from people who are not urban like us or 'developed' like us. I am not romanticizing tribal life but if Verrier Elwin is a good guide, which I think he was, then we must be very careful to judge the tribes by our standards of living and development.

Ethnographic discourse is again not a monolith and we must understand that within it there is a great deal of specificity. I shall note only one collectivity or specific sector—woman. In many of the Amerindian works I have become familiar that woman is at the centre, either as the author of the work, usually autobiographical, or the centre of focus. This suggests that woman had an important role to play in tribal life. In fact, I would suggest that woman is the power behind the throne, the inspirer of the deeds of the warriors and while the external manifestation of the woman as a squaw or as chatter is nonetheless, there it is only a small aspect of the real condition of existence of the tribes. Woman was not marginalized at all. It is with the spread of progress and the cultural encounter of the tribes with the exploiting 'other' that woman's position becomes problematic. I am suggesting that a proper ethnographic analysis of the role of woman in tribal culture might reveal startling facts about tribes and provide modern society with a recuperative model. An emancipatory discourse, not just for man but also for woman.

Literary culture revels in discussion of the self and the other. These binaries have caused harm and we have tended to see the colonizer-colonized, male-female, white-black as exclusive and rigid categories. Ethnographic work, like Ghosh's, allows us to blur these distinctions and to see the interpenetrating aspect of these relationships. There is, as Gandhiji, knew, something of the man in every woman and certainly something often woman in every man. His pleas for an androgynous imagination are probably the most significant value in his long and distinguished career. Ethnography then allows us to see that the colonized is possible only because of the colonized and that the reverse is true. Thus it should lad to a way old collapsing such distinctions and insisting on the virtue of inters subjectivity. Thus the hegemonic structures, which are part of the established discourse, can be deconstructed and a profound humanism can take its place. The value of ethnography surely is that it enables a greater human franchise.

Hopefully with these intellectual initiatives, both humanities and social sciences can come together to forge a new society free of hegemonic and exploitative tendencies. Finally let me say that we can speak of the Self only when we recognize in the Self the mirror image of the 'other'. To 'other' is to exclude but ethnographically speaking what is required is not exclusion but inclusion, not separation but community, not power but with love.

Further Readings

Benjamin, Walter, (1968), *Illuminations*. New York: Harcourt Brace.

Clifford, James and George Marcus, (1986), *Writing Culture*. Berkeley: University of California Press.

Foucault, Michel, (1970), *The Order of Things: An Archaeology of Human Sciences*. New York: Pantheon.

Goldman, Lucien, (1975),*Towards a Sociology of the Novel*. London: Tavistock.

Lukacs, Georg, (1971), *The Theory of the Novel*. London: Merlin.

Trinh, Minh-ha, (1977), *Woman, Native, Other*. Bloomington: Indiana University Press.

7 Ethnography Training for Translators

RAMESH C. MALIK

Literature is the product of cultural process and practices which decoded through language. "Literature can help in interpreting the existing ethnographic and sociological sources" (Oscar Lewis, 1959: 27).

"Translation is no longer something anyone with a smattering of a foreign language and a dictionary can sit down and do. It is today a highly sophisticated activity requiring an agile intellect and multi-disciplinary training" (Harris, 1997: Preface). In the context of Bible translation, Nida has suggested the relevance of translator training and also he pointed out the three basic pre-field preparations such as biblical, anthropological, and linguistic training are absolutely very crucial to the translator. Further, he states that anthropological and ethnological both types of studies, which, of course, are supplementary to each other, are necessary for the translators. And he claims that the most important type of study in cultural anthropology which a translator should undertake concerns the problems of acculturation.

1. the problems of acculturation in the language community to which he goes;
2. the adaptations which he himself as foreigner must make the culture which he is entering, and
3. the adaptations which the people are to make in accordance with the teaching of the text (Bible). Without an understanding of these three problems and a decision about policy, much of the translators energies will be spent beating the air (1947: 56–59). It clearly indicates that the translators should aware of the ethnography training for communicating the message faithfully embedded in source texts. It is fact that when a translator is engaged with the process of translating, he/she is mainly facing how to bridge the gap between two texts and mostly, ethnographic materials are creating more problems to search closest natural equivalent into target language culture (TLC). So, ethnography training is an absolute importance to the translators, because they are always dealing with the texts which are constructed in the process of ethnographic techniques.

Linguistic anthropologist Alessandro Duranti remarks that "ethnography is the written description of the social organization, social activities, symbolic and material resources, and interpretive practices characteristics of particular group of the people" (1997: 85). It conveys that the functional properties of ethnography can helps to study human race, society, language, culture and their cognitive processes related with their socialization. In another point, it means that ethnography as a translational process of verbal society which axis with different issues related in language, culture and its social process. On the other hand, James Clifford suggested that ethnography is actively situated between powerful systems of meaning. It poses its questions at the boundaries of civilizations, cultures, classes, races, and genders. Ethnography decodes and recodes, telling the ground of collective order and diversity, inclusion and exclusion. It describes process of innovation and structuration, and is itself a part of these processes. To apply above theoretical notions of ethnography, I want to make a comparative analysis between two texts and build up a theoretical notion that how original ethnography of Paraja is condensed in English translation of Paraja what the original writer, Gopinath Mohanty has mentioned in the acknowledgement of English translation like: "Dr Das prepared a condensed version which was then scrutinized and edited by Oliver Stallybrass" (Mohanty, 1987).

Paraja is a primitive tribe that lives in the district of Koraput, South Orissa region. Secondly, *Paraja* is an ethnographic Oriya novel, which is written by Janapith awardee Gopinath Mohanty, and it was first published in 1946.This novel is based on the life of the primitive Paraja tribe living in a village called 'Sarasupadara' and the adjacent areas. The author has tried to document the life of the Paraja tribe and their food habits, shelter, clothing, marriage, hunting, festivals, spiritual beliefs and superstition etc., in detail. The fictional theme of the novel shows how the moneylenders, forest guards, revenue officers have exploited the Sukru Jani's family and that is why eventually Sukru Jani and his two sons have taken revenge on Sahukar (moneylender). It has been rendered into English in 1987 by Bikram K. Das who was a professor of English in the SEAMO regional language centre, Singapore. The original Paraja encompasses specific cultural references of the tribal group, but the translated text, being an abridged version, has deviated from the original in some cases. Thus there are difference between the SLT and TLT, which are the focal point of this discussion.

Ethnographic Translation and Problems

In his paper "The End of Translation", Joseph B. Casagrande laid down the ideas on ethnographic translation and stated that ethnographic translation is concerned primarily with the explication, either in annotation or in the translation itself, of the cultural context of the message in the source language. A secondary goal is the specification and explanation of differences in meaning between apparently equivalent elements of messages in the two languages, particularly with those differences that may be masked by other forms of translation. It may be noted that the overall purpose of ethnographic translation is closely akin to that of ethno-linguistics. He also states that ethnographic translation is not limited to placing a message within its broader cultural context; it also figures in a finer-grained approach. In the process of transcoding one is frequently called upon to supply supposedly equivalent terms for traits that are analogous rather than identical in the two cultures. While in most contexts the meaning will not be materially affected by this translator's fiction, in others the difference between, say, poison (potassium cyanide) and 'poison' (a compound of human exuviae and innocuous herbs) may be crucial, and its specification becomes important (1954: 336). Because language is part of culture, but translation from one language into another involves, in addition to the other cultural problems, special characteristics of the respective languages (Nida, 1964: 94). His experiences of translating elevated that problems, which are essentially problems of equivalence, may be conveniently treated under (1) ecology, (2) material culture, (3) social culture, (4) religious culture, and (5) linguistic culture (ibid.). The question is here to mention that how all these ethnography materials are deviated from the original novel Paraja in its English translation.

Cultural Deviation

In translation studies, cultural deviation is a phenomenon which compares equivalences between two texts and evaluates the translators' emotive notions in the translation product. What the translators "faced with an element of the source culture which is absent from the target culture, the translator relies on different procedures that enable him to convey to member of the target culture the content of that particular elements. When the target culture lacks a given element (object, concept, social institution, pattern of behaviour, etc.), its language will normally lack an expression for it, and it is the translator's task to find an expressions in the target language that will adequately convey the missing elements to speaker of that language" (Ivir, 1987: 36). This statement by Vladmir Ivir proposes that the translators should find the closest natural equivalent in target language with particular reference to culture specific materials. But the translator of *Paraja* has been silent and he has deleted, summarized and also misrepresented the cultural taboos and expressions such as food items, spiritual belief, geographical locations and personal names, place names in the TLT. These materials are highly charged with cultural connotations and are closely linked with the Oriya as well as the Paraja socio-cultural realities.

While discussing the translation of cultural expressions, Aaltonen (1993: 53) and Schulze (1991: 94) have considered the following theoretical assets.

1. Living and livelihood
2. Spiritual world
3. The home and its environment
4. Names and their translation

Schulze (1991, 91–92) and Aaltonen (1993, 54) have found that the following strategies are followed in the translators' socio-cultural concepts;

1. Omission
2. Addition
3. Direct transfer: the item is not translated, but transferred to the TLT in its original form.
4. Adaptation: The item is adjusted to the target culture's spelling and pronunciation rules.
5. Semantic translation: the denotative meaning and perhaps aspects of the connotative meaning are rendered in the target language forms.

6. Replacement: Because of linguistic, social and other asymmetries, the source text item is replaced by a completely different target text item.
7. Transfer of an artistic device.
8. Substitution of the target language item with and equivalent of the source language item.

Let us now see how these strategies have been used in the English version of Paraja.

Living and Livelihood

Living and livelihood helps to identify the cultural authenticity of a society. Especially, food items, clothes, ornaments, household and the concept of the spiritual belief of the tribe reflect a general observation on their ecology. If all these parameters are subjected to change in the target text definitely it will reduce the cultural right as well as encourage cultural deviation. How these deviations are located in context of 'Paraja' are discussed below.

Food Items

First, let us take the name of various food items used in the novel.

Example 1

SLT

pahili andha:re sa:hira a:lua jete beLe juku juku disila: sukruja:nira piNDha:re culi jaLila: a:mba koilra sasa sa:ngare ma:NDia:cuna: gaNDie paDi ha:nDire sijhila:, gurdi sa:ga sijhila: (p. 10).

TLT

As the little fires began to flicker in the dark all along the streets, the hearth in Sukrujani's house was also lit for the evening meal (p. 16).

My Translation

As the tiny fire began to flicker in the dark village, the hearth was lit in Sukrujani's veranda. Mango kernel mixed with a little ragi (ma:NDia:) powder was boiled in an earthen pot, gurdi leaves were also boiled.

Example 2

SLT

sijha: kandamuLa, maka:, khai a:u baNara phaLa ba:Taja:ka kha:i kha:i sema:ne bakara bakara hoi a:santi. ba:Ta badhe na:hiM kete bheTa bheTi hue, kete mana ulusa: miLe, e ra:ije o se ra:ijara katha, puNi sema:ne (p. 65).

TLT

The market is the place for meeting friends, new and old, exchanging gossip.

And the market is also, often the place where lovers meet (p. 84).

My Translation

They come talking endlessly and eating boiled sweet potato, maize, fried paddy and wild fruits all the way.

In the above examples, the underlined words are deleted without equivalents. E.g./a:mba koilira sasa/(mango kernel),/ma:NDia: cuna:/(ragi powder) and/gurdi:saga/(gurdi leaves),/sijha:/kandamuLa/(boiled sweet ,potato),/ makka:/(maize)/khai/(paddy fried with sugar),/baNara phaLa/(wild fruits) which denote information about food items, food habits and food preparation of the Paraja tribe has been dropped in TLT.

Spiritual World

The spiritual belief or totemic system of tribals is usually based upon natural objects such as tree and stone, animals along with gods, ancestors, spirits, etc. All these have been dealt with in details in the SLT. However, the translator has deleted some portions which contain these in the TLT.

The following examples are illustrative

SLT

ga:M majhire na:ca la:githa:e "bhera:maNa''na:Ta nisa:pa pangata basiba:ra ja:ga.

eiThi pitru purusa pathara, mala purusa smruti sakase goja: pathara:, strimananka paiM caTa pathara (p. 145).

TLT

The dance was on (p. 153).

My Translation

The dance was going on in the village. bhera:man is the place for court, cultural functions and assemblies. Here pointed stones for the memory of the male ancestors and flat ones for female ancestors are these.

The word bherama:N is used by the Paraja speakers to refer a particular place in the middle of the village used for the above activities. The word goja:pathara and caTa: pathara refer to the pointed stones for male ancestors and flat stones female ancestors respectively.

The Home and its Environment

The home and its environment represent an ethno-cultural reality of the concern tribe. In the SLT, the author has elaborated the Paraja's indigenous house building design and method whereas in the translated version the translator has ignored all these.

SLT

sei Pra:china paddhatira ghara. majhi ghara, ta:ra da:NDa kaba:Ta achi, ekare bhaNDa:ra ghara, sekare roseighara, dui ghara kha:li bhitara kaba:Ta achi da:NDa gharaku la:gi se a:tu,sangha:, adha:ka:nthi ha:NDi rakhi ba:ku pa:ha:ca, da:NDa ghara caTa:Nare ma:NDia: sua:M pesiba:ku ga:ta sabu puruNa ritira kintu nua: (p. 184).

My Translation

The houses are of the same old type. The middle house has a front door, on this side is the store, and on the other side is the kitchen. The two rooms have only inside doors. That ceiling and sangha (platform for keeping things on) and shelves for keeping pots, a hole on the floor in the courtyard for pounding ragi grains.

This instance shows the architectural skills of the Paraja tribe and how they build their house on hill sides. It also describes the methods of their house construction.

The above examples in this section show differences between SLT and TLT. Many such aspects of the Paraja cultural identity and livelihood have been dropped in TLT.

Names and their Translation

Proper names can be defined or discussed under various disciplines particular references to the translation studies, translation of proper names Zabeeh (1968: 59), states that proper names are pragmatically used to identify, refer to, or distinguish a single person or object, or they may have all three functions at the same time. To say that a proper name is used to identify, not to signify, however, not entirely valid. In Saussurean terms, proper names may have connotations when applied to persons and places, which are well known to both the speakers and the hearers, but in themselves, turn out of context, they often mean nothing at all (Ullman, 1972:74). In the use of ordinary language, however, we cannot tacitly choose any particular connotation for our audiences (Aaltonen, 1993: 64). Perri (1978: 291–292) has accurately described proper names as abbreviations or cluster of conjunctive or disjunctive descriptions, which denote or refer to unique individuals or objects. Martinet (1980: 59–62) divides proper names used in a novel into non-fictional and fictional proper names. Non-fictional names place the action of the novel in a given culture, time and place, they are indicators of the cultural setting, and the information conveyed by them is of a socio-cultural, historical and geographical nature (quoted in Aaltonen, 1993: 64).

In the context, of the Paraja novel the author has used all those proper names, all being well known in that geographical area. But the translator has transferred some of those proper names directly into target text where as some others have been translated into English. For example—/bilei jholla:/ (p. 170), has been translated as 'Cat's Ravine' (p. 173), but kania: jholla: (p. 177) (bride ravine) has been retained as it is.

A comparison of the use of proper names of the SLT with the TLT reveals that there is no consistency in the treatment of personal names, place names, month names and flora and fauna of the former are in the latter. The inconsistency can be represented as shown in Table 1.

Table 1

C PN	TSL T	TTT	D	A	EF
PNM	57	44	13	1	1
PNF	26	16	8	—	2
PNV	43	23	18	—	2
M/T	3/3	1/4	2/–	—	—
G/M/R	4/5/3	2/3/3	2/2–	—	–/–/1
FL	28	20	6	—	2
FA	18	10	6	—	2

Note: CPN = Classification of proper names
TSLT=Total in source language text
TTT = Total in target text
D = Deletion
A = Addition
EF = Equivalence effect

Personal Names

The SLT contains 57 male personal names and 26 female names. The translator has deleted 13 male and 8 female names in the TLT text. Consider the following examples:

Example 1

SLT

ehipari kete sa:huka:ranka aktia:raru kandhama:nanka jami ca:ligala.:, campia: gopi suNDhi,dumbripadaria:sona:si sunDhi, paTaNia: surina:ra:ya:Na:, samastanku dakhala cyuta kari mesreT pa:ika ratana ma:jhi, dinabandhu ma:Li a:si, eke eke jamisabu phiTa:edei gale (p. 195).

My Translation

In this way, acres of the Kondh's land went out of the hands of the sahukars like Gopi Sundhi of Champi, Sonasi Sundhi of Dumbri Padar and Patania Suryanarayana and taking the lead the magistrate's soldiers Ratan Majhi and Dinabandhu Mali returned the land to them (Kondh's).

Names not only reflect the cultural connotation but also indicate the traditional naming system of a society. Those deleted names have mythological connotations. For example: Gopi according to our mythology literally denotes a woman of mythological kingdom named Gopa. These Gopis were working as mediators between Lord Krishna and his beloved Radha.

1. Dinabandhu is one of the names of Lord Vishnu which means 'friend of the poor'.
2. Suryanarayana is a compound denoting the sun and Lord Narayana.
3. Ratan means gem.

Example 2

SLT

budra:ja:ni a:sichi, kakna;mudulim, TenDa paraja:, gora:, citam, o keja:Ni kete goTi (p. 72).

TLT

Budra jani had come back from his work and so had Kakna Paraja and Tendaw, Gora and Cheetum (p. 88).

A more serious error occurs at the place where Kakana Muduli is replaced by Kakana 'paraja'. The surname 'Muduli' denotes 'leader of a group' in Dravidian whereas 'paraja' refers to a subjects or common men in Oriya. Some female names also show the same kind of deviation. For example: benia:maNi (p. 112), namramati (p. 168), ra:mei (p. 297) are dropped in TLT.

Place Names

The story of Paraja is set in the village Sarasupadara and the nearby hilly areas ghats, and ravines. For a good introduction to the readers, the author has started the novel with a description of the Koraput and Lakshimpur of South Orissa. He has portrayed in an elaborated manner how the village stands in the hilly tribal region and also how the tribal people have adopted themselves to food gathering, hunting, cultivating and have developed their unique administrative system.

The author has stated that 43 villages are closely related with three markets and two towns. But in the TLT only 23 villages with one market and three towns are found. The translator has added a town named Rayagada (p. 1) which is not mentioned in the SLT. He has left out names of many villages, markets, ghats, ravines, mountains which are closely linked to ancestral names, achievements of forefathers. The following examples are illustrative:

SLT

ba:ghara na: manusa:re kete ga:M ra na:M dia: hoichi, kouTa: ba:ghalmati, la:mti la:mti (menca:, menca:) ba:ghoi, dasa,pandaraata: 'ba:gri' na:M, kouTa ba:ghuipadara, kouTi ba:ghara guDa:, bhayara na:m sanka:' 'baDa sanka:' 'Cili sanka:' (p. 287).

My Translation

Several villages have been named after the tiger, like where many tigers are found (ba:ghalamati), and a host of baghris, ba:gha padara, ba:gharaguda and for the fear of the Tiger they are named like fear (sanka:), great fear (baDa sanka:) and small fear (cili sanka:).

The translator has deleted all these names though these are related with their forefathers' fear for the tiger.

Flora and Fauna

Flora and fauna constitutes the local identity of a particular village. Gopinath Mohanty has used names of many flora and fauna located in the forests of South Orissa in SLT whereas many of those are misrepresented in the TLT.

Example 1

SLT

dipa:kha bha:ri baNa candana, bija:, sarigaka:Thara (p. 145).

TLT

Through thick jungles of sandalwood, sal and bija trees (p. 145).

Here the translator has replaced a word for 'sariga' as 'sal'.

Some times the translator has translated the names of certain fruits in such a manner that they denote very different things. For example, giruDi a:mba gacha (p. 3) has been translated into English as 'old mango tree' (p. 6) giruDi is a type of mango that is small in size with a good flavour and not sweet taste.

The other important point to be mentioned here is that the TLT contains more than one equivalent for the same word in SLT.

Bell (1991: 6) has cited the definition of translation by Hartmann and Stork (1972: 713): "Translation is the replacement of a representation of a text in one language by a representation of an equivalent text in second language". However, they have elaborated on the equivalent matching from source language competence into target language competence. Such a linguistic approach tends to stress that translation involves the replacement of meaning as well as grammatical categories contained in one set of linguistic competence into anther set of linguistic competence.

A translator may face many difficulties of linguistic transfer, difficulties which sometimes almost in surmountable. Let us look at the following examples in SL T and TLT.

The word/kukuDa:/has been rendered in English in three different ways, i.e., chicken, fowl and hen in three different places in the translated text.

Example 1

SLT

kukuDa: a:sila:, ta:ra Dimba bi a:sila: (p. 7).

TLT

Brought him offering of chickens and eggs (p. 11).

Example 2

SLT

dina di pahare joDie kukuDa: tinoTi paNasa dhari jangal jama:n pa:khe ja:I sukruja:ni upa:dhia: paDila: (p. 7).

TLT

At midday, Sukru Jani went to the forest guard with two fat hens and three big jack fruits (p. 12).

Example 3

SLT

barasaku barasa kete kukuDa: kete pa:ra: baLi dei dei khetaku ta:ra se besi urbara karichi (p. 193).

TLT

He had scarified pigeons and fowl to the Earth goddess before each harvest (p. 193).

Example 4

SLT

kha:li kukuDa: haNa:, parua: haNa:, kha:li menDha: haNa: (p. 388).

TLT

Sacrifices of goats and pigeons (p. 332).

In Oriya the word,/kukuDa:/refers to 'hen' On the other hand, Oriya has a word such as *ganja:* (cock) which is the male counterpart of the/kukuDa:/. In a context both cover different meanings in Oriya. KukuDa is a domestic bird commonly kept in house for eggs and meat. Its English equivalent cannot be fowl. In the last example the two words kukuDa: and meNDha: (sheep) do not have equivalents in the TLT.

Conclusion

Thus, it is clear that the TLT has deviated in many places at various levels from SLT. Therefore, the translation is not good especially because the SLT is ethnographic in nature dealing with primitive tribe called Paraja. And above discussed observations can make a clear support to raise the question on translator training because that will help to prepare a faithful translation rather that gloss or bad translation.

Note

SLT: Source language text.
TLT: Target language text.

Bibliography

Aaltonen, Sirkku, (1993), *Gallous Stories: Two Transplants into Finish of the Play of the Western World,* Vaasan: Yliopisto University of Vaasa.

Barala, K.C., (2005), "Ethnography and Fiction: Verrier Elwins' World", (edited by) T.B. Subba and Sujit Som, *Between Ethnography and Fiction: Verrier Elwin and the Tribal Question in India,* Hyderabad: Orient Longmans.

Bassnett McGuire, S., (1996), *Translation Studies,* (Revised), London: Routledge.

Bell, Roger T., (1991), *Translation and Translating: Theory and Practice,* London: Longman.

Caminade, Moniouqe and Anthony, Pym, (2004), "Translator-Training Institutions" (ed. by Mona Baker), *Routledge Encylclopedia of Translation Studies,* London: Routledge.

Casagrande, Joseph B., (1954), "The Ends of Translation", *International Journal of American Linguistics*, Vol. 20, No. 4, October, 335–340, Chicago: The University of Chicago Press.

Clifford, James and George E. Marcus, (1990), *Writing Culture*, Delhi: Oxford University Press.

Das, Bikram K., (Trans.), (1987), *Paraja*, Delhi: Oxford University Press.

Duranti, A., (1997), *Linguistic Anthropology*, New York: Cambridge University Press.

Harris, B., (1997), *Translation and Interpreting Schools*, Amsterdam: John Benjamins Publishing Company.

Hervey, S. and Higgins, (1992), *Thinking Translation: A Course in Translation Methods*, London: Routledge.

Ivir, Vladimir, (1987), "Procedures and Strategies for Translation of Culture" (ed.), Gideon Toury, *Translation Across Cultures*, New Delhi: Bahari Publications Pvt. Ltd.

Lewis, Oscar, (1959), *Five Families*, New York: Basic Books.

Lotman, J. and Aupensky, B., (1978), *On the Semiotic Mechanism of Culture*, New Literary History, IX (2).

Martinet, H., (1979), "What about Proper Name in Translation". In S. Hanon and V. A. Pedersen (ed), Paper from the 10th Annual Conference on Computational Linguistics, Odense Universitet, Odense.

Mohanty, Gopinath, (1997), *Paraja*, (8th edition in Oriya) Cuttack Vidyapuri: Balubazar.

Nida, Eugene A., (1961), *Bible Translating*, (Revised), London: United Bible Societies.

—, (1964), "Linguistics and Ethnology in Translation-Problems" (ed.) Dell Hymes, *Language in Culture and Society: A Reader in Linguistics and Anthropology*, Bombay: Allied Publishers Pvt. Ltd.

Perri, C., (1978), On Alluding, Poetics 7.

Schule, B., (1991), "Problems of Cultural Transfer and Cultural Identity: Personal Names and Titles in Drama Translation". In H. Kittel and A.P. Frank (eds.), *Interculturality and the Historical Study of Literary Translations*, Enrich Schmidt, Gottingen.

Snell Hornby, M., (1988), *Translation Studies: An Integrated Approach*, Amsterdam, Philadelphia: John Benjamin Publishing Company.

Ullaman, S., (1972), *Semantics*, Oxford: Basil Blackwell.

Zabeeh, F., (1968), *What is in a Name?*, The Hague: Martinus Nijhoff.

II

Language, Literature and Culture: An Enthnographic Appraisal

8 How did the Oriya Language Catch 'Fire'?

PANCHANAN MOHANTY

In his discussion on the strained relationship between modern linguistics and etymology, Malkiel has raised the following questions: "How could such almost violent separation of two erstwhile close allies have occurred at all? How could the split have materialized in such a distressingly short period of time? What is etymology bereft of linguistics likely to become? In what direction is linguistics deprived of its etymological roots most likely to stray? Can etymology be at all expected to acquire a much-needed touch of modernity? And, above all, are there any prospects of eventual reconciliation between the two disciplines now so visibly at loggerheads?" (1983: 497). Before delving into the answers of all these questions, he has tried to determine the causes that led etymology to such a catastrophe. According to him, the following are the five main causes:

"1. The general demand for constant innovation—the recoil from the *déjà vu*—tends to discredit any emphasis that enjoyed heightened prestige as late as half a century ago; in other words, the former strength of etymology is in itself a heavy liability".

2. The passionate, not to say occasionally morbid, interest in theory places any intellectual pursuit that hinges on chance discoveries, flashes of imagination, and irremediably lacunary records in a vulnerable position.

3. The diligent amassing of data that some early-20th century etymologists practiced, as if to compensate for the element of arbitrariness or caprice at the moment of decision-making, has grated on the nerves of those younger linguists who have been spoiled or, if you prefer, immunized, as regards any excessive commitment to data-gathering, by structuralism and related movements.

4. Etymology is unavoidably, incurably historical and explicative, not descriptive. This circumstance, which in other cultures or at other junctures might have been a major asset, has turned out to be a liability in our Age of Cross-Disciplinary Militant Ahistoricism.

5. The style in which etymological discoveries are ideally announced caters to the experts' or laymen's leisurely reading habits. Where reading as the principal vehicle of intellectual experience is itself in full retreat, the sub-disciplines geared to its vigorous growth are apt to be weakened" (1983: 499).

The above remarks of Malkiel (1983) are very crucial in the context of the present paper because of two reasons. First, it is absolutely necessary to possess a sound knowledge of phonology and morphology in order to decipher the etymological history of a word. Second, the Oriya word for fire /niã:/ has a Dravidian source and it is indicative of the importance of Dravidian substratum in the Oriya language and culture.

Words for Fire in NIA and Oriya/niã:/

Among all the words for 'fire' in Old Indo-Aryan (henceforth OIA), /agni/ is the most commonly used one and most of the Neo-Indo-Aryan (henceforth NIA) languages use words derived from it. Let us take the following examples from Turner (1966: 3): Sindhi/ a:g, a:gi, a:go/, Punjabi /agg, a:g/, Nepali /a:go/, Bengali /a:g/ (MSB./a:gun/)/, Maithili /a:gi/, Bhojpuri /a:gi/, Awadhi /a:gi/, Hindi /a:g, a:gi/, Marathi and Konkani /a:g/. It is quite interesting that Oriya uses altogether a phonetically unrelated word /niã:/ for 'fire'. Let us first discuss the views of Oriya scholars about it.

Scholars hold divergent views regarding the biography of this word. These views can broadly be categorized into two groups. The first one is that its source is in Sanskrit and most scholars favour it. The second one is that it is derived from a native source, i.e., its source is not determined. So let us consider the first view in detail.

There are also differences of opinion among those who believe that /niã:/ has been derived from a Sanskritic source. According to Praharaj (1934: 4261), its etymological history is as follows:

agni → gnia → niã → niã:

Needless to say that this derivation is a concocted one, because metathesis of/agni/to/gnia/and elision of/g/are highly unmotivated and unnatural. In metathesis, normally two phonemes replace each other, e.g. /æks/ for /æsk/ 'ask' in English or /buD/ for /Dub-/ 'to sink' in Oriya. Then dropping of/g/from/gn/is unacceptable as it is stronger than /n/. As per the rule, it is the weaker phoneme that gets dropped, not the stronger one. Consider the following examples:

Source Word	*Oriya Word*	*Gloss*
šmaša:na (Skt.)	masa:Ni	'cremation ground'
sthira (Skt.)	thira	'still'
station (Eng.)	Tesan	'station'
driver (Eng.)	Da:ibhar	'driver'

Notice that in the first three source words, sibilants/š, s/are weaker than/m,th,T/and that is why they are dropped in Oriya, but in the fourth source word /r/ being weaker than /D/ gets elided. Again, nasalization of the final vowel also does not conform to the genius of the Oriya language. We will not dwell upon it, because it will be taken up later.

Realizing the awkwardness in Praharaj's (1934) derivation, Mohapatra (1976: 105) has derived it from/agnika:/in the following way

agnika: (Skt.) → annia: (Pkt.) → niã: (Or.)

It should be noted here that */annia:/is not attested in Prakrit. As/g/is stronger than/n/, /gn/, in fact, has become/gg/in the assimilation process, not */nn/. Nasalization of the final /a:/ is alsc extremely doubtful.

Though Turner (1966) identified Skt. /nida:gha/ as the source of Oriya /niã:/, no Oriya scholar has taken note of it with the lone exception of Dash (1982: 411), who fully supports this view. In fact, Turner (1966: 411) has given the following derivational history for this Oriya word:

Skt. /nida:gha/→ Pali /nida:gha/→Pkt. /Nida:ha, Nia:ha:/ →Oriya /niã:/

While endorsing Turner's (1966) view, Dash (1982: 170) has stated the details regarding the change of Pkt. /nia:ha/ to /niã:/ in Oriya. His argument is that there are two steps involved in it, i.e. drop of the final /ha/ and then nasalization of /a:/. Though the first one is possible in Oriya the second one is not. His statement "If there is a nasal consonant in a word, then there is no dearth of examples in which the word final vowel gets nasalized." (my translation) must not hold for a word derived from Skt. /nida:gha/. Turner was very right when he made the following statement long ago: "... etymologists have been led astray by not holding firmly to their lifeline, the regularity of sound change" (1960: 50). Now in order to make the point clear, let us discuss the Oriya nasalization rule.

Unlike some other NIA languages like Hindi and Bengali, vowels do not get nasalized in the environment of a nasal in Oriya. For example, in contrast with /mã:/ 'mother' in Hindi and Bengali, Oriya has /ma:/ from Skt. /ma:ta:/. Notice that when the former two languages show nasalization on /a:/, there is no nasalization in Oriya. Oriya follows a rule very consistently that can be formulated like the following:

Oriya Nasalization Rule

If the source word has a non-nasal consonant in a syllable and it is deleted in the derived word in Oriya, the remaining vowel need not be nasalized even though the preceding syllable contains a nasal.

The following examples will drive home the point:

Sanskrit	*Oriya*	*Gloss*
nagara	naara	'town'
nava	naa	'nine'
nadi:	nai	'river'
na:va	na:a:	'boat'
ma:tṛ	ma:i	'female:'
ma:tula	mauLa:	'maternal uncle:'

Or the other hand, when a nasal in the source word is deleted in the derivational process, the Oriya word shows nasalization. For example:

Sanskrit	*Oriya*	*Gloss*
na:ma	nã:	'name'
gra:ma	gã:	'village'
va:ma	bã:	'left'
dhu:ma	dhuã:	'smoke'
bhu:mi	bhũĩ	'earth'
a:miSa	ã:isa	'non-vegetarian food'
bhramara	bhããra	'a big black bee'

Therefore, after the elision of /d/ in the second syllable of Skt. /nida:gha/, the vowel /a:/ cannot be nasalized even though /ni/ precedes it.

Not only this, there is also another reason which creates difficulty in accepting Skt. /nida:gha/ as the source of Oriya /niã:/. It is interesting to note that Oriya seems quite sensitive to the morpheme boundaries. This can be illustrated by taking the example of sonorization of /D,Dh/ in this language. While rejecting the earlier view of Oriya scholars regarding the Oriya phonological rule that D → R/V-V and Dh → Rh/V-V, I have shown that this rule does not work if/D, Dh/are preceded by a morpheme boundary (Mohanty, 2000). The following examples are illustrative:

ni + Dara	→	niDara/*niRara	'fearless'
be + Dhanga	→	beDhanga/*beRhanga	'lack of manners'
su + DhaLa	→	suDhaLa/*suRhaLa	'beautifully proportioned'

It is clear from these examples that this boundary blocks sonorization of /D,Dh/. In other words, this boundary blocks the process of weakening of /D, Dh/ in Oriya.

The word /nida:gha/ is derived by adding the prefix /ni-/ to the stem/da:gha/(<dah-) (Monier-Williams, 1976: 548). If we extend the argument that the above said boundary does not allow weakening of the initial consonant of the stem, then /d/ of /da:gha/ cannot elide. So it has to remain as /nida:gha/ in Oriya. In fact, the extant Oriya literature testifies it. This word has been used by various poets and writers of this language.

The other point to be mentioned here is that *Carya:gi:ti*, which contains the earliest specimen of Oriya and was written between 9th and 12th centuries, has /a:gi/; not /niã:/.

> Da:hai Dombi: ghare la:geli a:gi
> sasahara lai sincatu pa:Ni (Poem No. 47)

It has been translated as: "The Dombi burns—fire has been applied to the house. Taking the Moon, I sprinkle water." (Kvaerne, 1986: 255).

Not only that, the first major Oriya poet Sa:raLa: Da:sa's *Sa:raLa: Maha:bharata* (15th century) attests different words for 'fire' like /agni/, /anaLa/, /jui/, /bahni/; but never /niã:/. Another 15th century prose-writer Na:ra:yaNa Da:sa has used /agni/ and /anaLa/ in *Rudrasudha:nidhi*, but /niã:/ is not there. If we accept Turner's (1966) and Dash's (1982) contention that Prakrit /nia:ha/ (/Nia:ha/) has become /niã:/ in Oriya then it should have found a place in *Carya:giti*, as well as in the earliest Oriya compositions like *Sa:raLa Maha:bharata* and *Rudrasudha:nidhi*. Most probably the first occurrence of this word is found in the narration of GauDia: Gobindadeba's reign in *Ma:daLa:pa:nji*, a text that was written towards the end of 16th century or in early 17th century. GauDia: Gobindadeba ascended the throne of Orissa after the death of King Mukundadeba of Chalukya dynasty in 1568; but it has not been supported by the historians of Orissa. However, it is interesting to note that after just one sentence of the one that contains /niã/, we find the use of /agni/. It clearly indicates a transition between /agni/ and /niã:/.

The Source of Oriya /niã:/

Now the question is: Where does /niã:/ come from and why did it replace other existing words for fire, to be specific /agni/? Let us discuss the second part of the question first as it has caused the introduction of /niã:/.

Besides /niã:/ there are two other Oriya words, i.e., /agi/ (<Skt./agni/) and /jui/ (Skt./jyoti/) which refer to 'fire'. But both of these are used predominantly in the context of funeral pyre. After the cremation of a dead body is over, when people go to extinguish the pyre, it is called /agi sitaLa:iba/' cooling of fire'. Even in the *MusaLiparba* of *Sa:raLa: Maha:bha:rata,* /agni/ has been used in the description of cremating Lord Krishna's dead body /jui/ refers to either funeral pyre or the pit on which cremation takes place. It can be argued here that because of this reason /agi/ and /jui/ became taboos in Oriya and therefore a new word was required to replace them. In Mohanty (1998), I have shown that the non-human plural marker /-guRa:/ has been introduced in Oriya only after *Sa:raLa: Maha:bha:rata* was written because its occurrence is extremely rare, which I consider to be a later interpolation. Likewise, /niã:/ has most probably been taken from the Dravidian source though Dash (1982: 170) has categorically rejected such a possibility by stating that "Words like /nerippu/ (Tamil), /nerippu/ (Malayalam), /nippu/ (Telugu), /niyur/ (Kurux), etc., are found to be used for fire in Dravidian languages. But it cannot be decided from these that Oriya /niã:/ has been derived from them." (tr. by me). But it is worth mentioning here that the South Central, Central and North Dravidian languages, which are spoken mainly in Orissa, West Bengal, and Bihar, use many words that are very close to /niã:/ in both meaning and form. For example, Malto uses /niru/' sunshine, heat' (DEDR, 2910, Burrow and Emeneau, 1984: 252), Parji /nir-/' to blaze', Kurux /niyu:r/ embers, live coals, wood glowing with fire', Malto /nare/ 'flame' (DEDR, 2929, ibid., 255). What is significant is that all these words are listed under the palatal nasal/ñ/which is referred to as /niã/ in Oriya. There is also another source which is the word for ashes in these languages, e.g., Parji /ni:d/, Gadaba/ni:r/, Gondi /ni:r/, Konda /ni:ru/, Pengo /ni:z, ni:s/. But the most crucial evidence comes from Manda which has /ni:y-darambu/ (DEDR, 3693, ibid., 329). It is a compound and /darambu/ refers to 'ashes' in the South Central Dravidian languages like Pengo, Manda, and Kuwi (DEDR, 3092, ibid., 268–269).

It is, therefore, obvious that /ni:y-darambu/ cannot mean 'ashes-ashes'. Since/darambu/refers to ashes in Manda, /ni:y/ has to have some other referent and the most probable option is fire. The evidence in support of this claim comes from the fact that such doublets are very common in Oriya (along with other Eastern NIA languages) and we find a blend of Dravidian and non-Dravidian words in some of them, e.g., /luga: paTa:/ 'clothes', /kaNTa: jhaTa:/ 'dried weeds', /ghara ba:Ri/ 'house and the space behind', /ka:ntha ba:Ra/ 'wall and fence'. In these examples, /pa:Ta/ and /jhaTa:/ are related to Tamil /paTTai/, Telugu /paTTa/ (DEDR, 3876, Burrow and Emeneu, 1984: 346); Tamil /ceTi/, Telugu /ceTTu/ (DEDR, 1941, ibid., 176), Tamil /vari/, Kannada /bari/, (DEDR, 4112, ibid., 365) and Parji /par/, Konda /paru/ (DEDR, 4030, ibid., 359); Tamil /varai/, Kannada /bara/, Telugu /varaju/ (DEDR, 5261, ibid., 475) respectively. Likewise /niã: pã:usa/' fire and ash' is also a doublet that is used quite frequently in Oriya. So my contention is that Oriya /niã: pã:usa/ is a reflection of Manda /ni:y-darambu/ and Oriya /niã:/ has come from Dravidian and related to Manda /ni:y/.

Conclusion

To sum up, this paper shows that many scholars have determined wrong sources for the Oriya word /niã:/ because they have not fully understood certain phonological and morphological rules of the Oriya language. Thus, it is evident that sound grammatical knowledge is required for etymological studies. Then it has been argued that the source of Oriya /niã:/ is not in Indo-Aryan as some scholars have claimed; but in Dravidian. It gives a clear indication regarding the presence of a very strong Dravidian substratum in the Oriya language and culture.

Bibliography

Burrow, T. and Emeneau, M.B., (1984), (2nd edition), *A Dravidian Etymological Dictionary (DEDR)*, Oxford: Clarendon Press.

Da:sa, Sa:raLa:, (1965–72), *Sa:raLa: Maha:bha:rata,* (Saralas' Maha:bha:rata), Bhubaneswar: Department of Cultural Affairs, Government of India.

Dash, Kulamani, (1996), *SaraLa utkaLa abhidha:na,* (A Simple Oriya Dictionary), Cuttack: Grantha Mandir.

Dash, Siniruddha, (1982), ORia: 'niã:' sabdara utpatti, (Development of the Oriya word/niã:/), *ESaNa*: 4, 167–171.

Krishnamurti, Bhadriraju, (2001), *Comparative Dravidian Studies: Current Perspectives,* Oxford: Oxford University Press.

Kvaerne, Per, (1986), *An Anthology of Buddhist Tantnic Songs: A Study of the Carya:gi:ti,* Bangkok: White Orchid Press, (first published in 1977).

Malkiel, Yakov, (1983), *From Particulars to General Linguistics*, Amsterdam, Philadelphia: John Benjamin Publishing Company.

Mohanty, Artaballabha (ed.), (1940), *Ma:daLa:pa:nji,* (The Chronicle of Jagannath Temple), Cuttack: Prachi Samity.

Mohanty, Panchanan, (1998), Number-agreement in Oriya, Paper presented in International Seminar on Agreement Organized by Department of Linguistics, Delhi University from January 9 to 11.

Mohanty, Panchanan, (2000), "On Sonorization in Oriya", *Indian Journal of Linguistics*, 19, 12–22.

Mohapatra, Dhaneshwar, (1976), *ORia: dhwanitattwa o sabda-sambha:ra*, (Oriya Phonetics and Lexicon), Cuttack: Grantha Mandir.

Monier Williams, Monier, (1976), *Sanskrit-English Dictionary*, New Delhi: Munshiram Manoharlal, (first published in 1899).

Nandasharma, Gopinath, (1995), (5th revised edition), *Sabdattwabodha abhidha:na*, Cuttack: New Students' Store, (first published in 1916).

Praharaj, Gopala Chandra, (Compiler), (1934), *PurNacandra oRia: bha:sa:kosa*, Vol. IV, Cuttack: The Utkal Sahitya Press.

Sen, Sukumar, (1971), *An Etymological Dictionary of Bengali: C, 1000–1800 A.D.*, Calcutta: Eastern Publishers.

Sheth, Hargovind Das T., (1986), *Paia-sadda-maha:NNavo*, (A Comprehensive Prakrit Hindi Dictionary), Delhi: Motilal Banarsidass, (Reprint).

Turner, R.L., (1960), *Some Problems of Sound Change in Indo-Aryan*, Poona: University of Poona.

Turner, R.L., (1966), *A Comparative Dictionary of the Indo-Aryan Languages*, London: Oxford University Press.

Zvelebil, Kamil V., (1990), *Dravidian Linguistics: An Introduction*, Pondicherry: Pondicherry Institute of Linguistics and Culture.

9 Question-Words and its Morpho-Syntactic Study of Rongmei Language

HAIREISIM NEWME

Rongmei is the name of the language spoken by a particular group of people as a means of communication. There is no script, hence no written record of their history. Their ethics and social values are being passed on to younger generations orally. They believe that they had a script written on the animal skin long ago (probably in the form of scroll), but they had eaten it up (Rev. Pamei, 1996: 103).

Questions are the universal structures with at least one universal function. In all natural languages it can be classified into a number of types—two most common question sentences are *wh-question* and *yes/no question*. Questions have the function in eliciting information or response and define sometimes on grammatical and either on semantic or socio-linguistic ground. To turn a declarative sentence into a yes/no question the main verb contains a modal 'have' or copular verb 'be' is moved to front.

To understand the question sentence structures and question-words one must be equipped with the structures of noun phrases, verb phrases, adjectives, clauses and larger units, i.e., the simple sentences. In a sentence the agreement features such as number, person, gender, case, tense, etc., must exhibit co-occurrence harmoniously. The modifiers, complementizers, classifiers should have agreement with the heads, i.e., noun, verb, etc.

Brief discussion of word order in Rongmei: The unmarked word order in Rongmei is SOV. It is a verb final language. To verify this information we shall look at the following examples:

1. ĵialu ĵon - ta nĵian ne
   S O V
   ĵIalu john ACC love Vprt
   'Jialu loves John'

2. ai naŋ khaŋ banra ti—puni
   S O V
   1PS you for doll give TnM
   'I will give you a doll'

This paper is based on my dissertation submitted to the Department of Linguistics, North Eastern Hill University, Shillong, July, 2006.

Alternative word order of SOV, according to Greenberg's universal 7 is OSV. Rongmei has rarely exhibits.

3. heo ĵao tu we
O S V
banana monkey eat Vprt
'Monkey eats banana'

Postposition: Like many other TB languages Rongmei do have postposition.

4. goi khaŋ
good for
'for good'

5. ai lɛŋ khau lau kan the
1PS bed Pos cloth keep TnM Vprt
'I kept a cloth on the bed'

6. hai lairik ka–khaŋ ye
Det book 1PS Pos Vprt
'This book is for him'

In Rongmei direct object and indirect object can precedes and follow each other.

7. Direct object precedes indirect object
kamai čithi ka—khau nsin—lau the
3PS letter 3PS Acc hand TnM Vprt
'he handed a letter to hi/her'

8. Indirect object precedes the direct object
kamai ka—khau čithi nsin -lau the
3PS 3PS Acc letter hand TnM Vrpt
'He handed her a letter'

Genetive case marker precedes the governing noun

9. mosi-tuaŋ riakdin
Moses Gen law
'Moses' law'

10. hai a—tuaŋ phurit ye
Det 1PS Gen shirt Vprt
'This is my shirt'

The maker of comparison follows the standard of comparison

11. adaina nĵiangoŋ khaŋsuaŋ tan ran ye
adaina njiangong than strong ComD Vprt
'Adaina is stronger than Njiangong'

12. nkhuai-dui čini khaŋsuaŋ ndai ran ye
bee water sugar than sweet ComD Vprt
'Honey is sweeter than sugar'

Time adverbial precedes place adverbial in descending order in Rongmei

13. a—niu daulanai ĵiŋbaŋ siti tat re
1PS Plu yesterday night city go TnM
'we wenr to city last night'

14. ai nthuan laothuan thuanĵiŋ khau:a bam puni
1PS tomorrow morning early there stay TnM
'I will be there tomorrow early morning'

Adjective follows the head noun

15. hai thu hai subak khaŋ kuŋ ye
Det nut Det crack to hard Vprt
'this nut is hard to crack'

Complementizer (quotative verb 'to say') follows the embedded sentences.

16. damei so ye kamei mi-ta tan puni
Damei said Vprt 3PS it Acc do TnM
'Damei said that she would do it'

Modifiers: Adjective can precedes as well as follows the head noun (in the form of noun phrase but not so in the form of simple sentences).

17. a. naila—mai tuna
happy Nom girl
'happy girl'

b. tuna naila- mai
girl happy Nom
'happy girl'

18. ka—mai naila ye
1PS Nom happy Vprt
'He/she in happy'

Some adjective in this language precede the head noun and can never follow.

19. luŋsi-mai pu
poor Nom man
'A poor man'

Adjective do not exhibit any agreement features with the modifying noun and verb.

20. ka—mai nailo hak ye
1PS Nom happy very Vprt
'he/she is very happy'

In Rongmei there is no overt determiner (definite and indefinite articles). Also determiner does not have agreement feature with the head noun. We rarely found the split determiner like other TB languages (Mizo does have).

21. hai ros
this rose
'this rose'

hai ros nun
this rose plu
'these rose'

Negative marker occurs in the final position in the sentences.

22. ai ĵaŋ mak ge
1PS drink Neg Vprt
'I do not drink'

hai tan rio
this do Neg
'Do not do this'

In Romngei we find the relative clauses without the relative pronoun overtly. There is no relative pronoun like in English, e.g., who, whom, where, etc.

23. tunapui atuŋ čithi ti—lau- mai aziana napui ye
girl Atung letter give Prf Nom Aziana daughter Vprt
'the girl whom Atung gave a letter to is Aziana's daughter'

In most of the language families found reduplication, and echo features. Here in Rongmei reduplication exhibits uniquely.

24. lum lum-mai čobuaŋ khat a—ta ti yo
hot Nom cup (tea) one 1PS Acc give Vprt
'Give me on hot cup of tea'

25. kaniu nču-nĵæŋ–mai loni ye
3PP peace Nom want Vprt
'They want peace'

Tone is another essential character which plays a grammatical and lexical feature in conveying an intended meaning in full. In phonology tone is referred to as the distinctive pitch levels of syllable. Rongmei exhibits two types of tone, i.e., register tone and contour tone; there are six types of tone but we shall see the example of register tone.

26. High/rising tone 55
tiŋ33-puk55 'sky'
mi55-tei33 'that'

27. Middle tone 33
Mek11-ge33 'not available'

28. low tone 11
hi11-yo33 'write' (*yo* is an imperative marker)

Questions: Like many other natural languages of the world Rongmei has the question words mainly on the basis of 'information seeking question' or 'confirmation seeking question' and other type of questions such as yes/no, alternative, tag, echo and rhetoric questions. The information seeking questions (or popularly known as wh-questions), the basic question word is *tabui* 'what'. For all these types of questions are derived from the word *tabui* and convey their meaning by suffixing particular morph or morpheme. Therefore, in Rongmei *tabui* is the root word for the information seeking questions. However, the question word *thao* 'who/whom' is exceptional by condition of the type of questions.

29. tabui 'what'
tabui-thaŋ 'where to'
tabui-khau 'where in/on'
tabui-suna 'why'
tabui-kuma 'how'
tabui-ta 'which'

30. naŋ-ĵan tabui čo
2PS name what Qprt
'What is your name?'

31. naŋ tabui su bam čo 2PS what do Prog Qprt 'What are you doing?'

32. ka—mai tabui-thaŋ tat ni čo 3PS Nom where (to) go TnM Qprt 'Where is he/she going?'

33. a—tuaŋ kolam tabui-khau naŋ lau—kan čo 1PS Gen pen where Loc you keep TnM Qprt 'Where did you keep my pen?'

34. ka—mai naŋ-ta tabui-suna mphut-kan tu čo 3PS Nom you Acc why (reason) scold TnM Emp Qprt 'Why did he/she scold you?'

35. naŋ tabui-kuma koikham lanpat čo 2PS how door open Qprt 'How do you open the door?'

36. tabui-ta tan rAn čo Which strong ComD Qprt 'Which one is stronger?'

A term often used within the framework of transformational grammar to refer to a basic kind of transformational operation. Movement transformational have the effect of moving a constituent (usually on at a time) from one part of phrase-marker to another (landing site). It is also found that all the question words are occurring in the scope position in the sentences. Therefore, movement is a redundant process as both the deep and surface structures exhibit the same (example given below):

37.	Deep Structure (DS)	Surface Structure (SS)
	John tabui tu čo	John tabui tu čo
	John what eat Qprt	John what eat Qprt
	S O V	S O V
	'What did John eat?'	

Rongmei does not have auxiliary inversion for the information of yes or no in so call yes/no question type. But Rongmei do have yes/no question markers such as *dai, hau, nih, buh, ngau* followed by question particle *čo.*

38. ka—mai nɛila dai—čo
3PS Nom happy Qprt
'I he/she happy?'

39. Mac ĵau ĵaŋ buh- čo
Mac wine drink Qprt
'Does Mac drink wine?'

Example: wh-movement in English is given below:

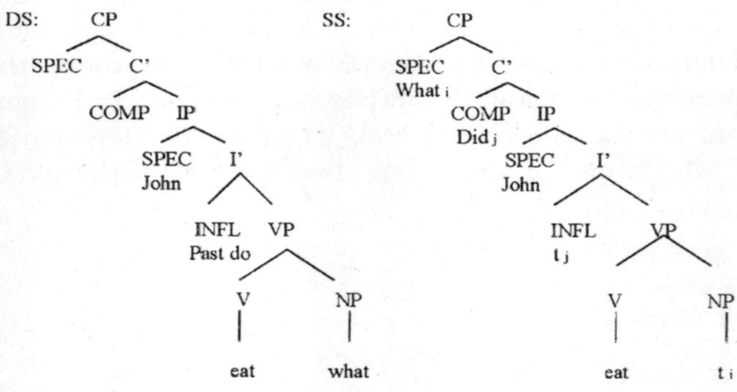

tabui-movement in Rongmei: No movement is required.

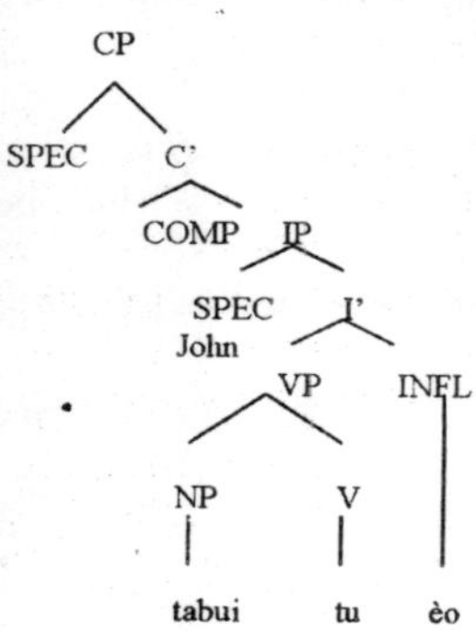

Alternative question is another type of yes/no question that expect the answer by providing alternative either yes or no in question itself.

40. peter komla-dui ĵaŋ the nih, ĵaŋ mak gai čo
Peter orange water drink TnM Alt drink not Alt Qprt
'Has Peter drank orange juice or not?'

Tag type of questions have three forms—*ŋau, tha* and *dai* which occur in the final position of tag sentences and their use are base on the type of alternative questions. But *ŋau* is the basic tag question word whereas the other two are optional (or depend on the choice of speaker).

41. lovely zai ĵæk thai de, thai mak ŋau
Lovely pond swim know Vprt know not TgM
'Lovely knows how to swim, doesn't she?'

Echo questions are mostly used in conversation between two or more people. *yai* is the basic form for echo question construction which occurs in the final position. Besides, tone plays a very crucial role, i.e., when it is a mere repetition of the first speaker and *čo* in the final position whereas emphatic marker preceded.

42. Speaker A. ĵill a—ta ĵian ye
Jill 1PS Acc love Vprt
'Jill loves me'

Speaker B. ĵill naŋ—ta ĵian ye yai Or Thau naŋ—ta ĵian ye yai
Jill 2PS Acc love Vprt EcM who 2PS Acc love Vprt EcM
'Jill loves you?' 'Who loves you?'

Rhetoric question is also another type of yes/no question but the answer is predetermined and expected 'no' (Crystal, 1991).

43. ai mbo-mai de na naŋ niŋ nau
1PS mad Nom Vprt Conj 2PS think RhM
'Do you think that I am mad?'

44. thau khaò-khau kačak lau ni čo
who cliff Pos jump Prf like Qprt
'Who will jump in the cliff?'

There are sentences which resemble question sentences but they are actually used in exclamations. This kind of sentence expresses strong feeling and emotion of speaker and asks the hearer to agree. Despite the presence of a negative element they are strongly positive in meaning.

45. ka—mai dai—pat mak gai
3PS Nom big out not Qprt
'Hasn't he/she grown!'

Conclusion

In both simple and complex sentences and assertive and questions sentences the word order is SOV—the verb final language at the level of deep structure and surface structures. Morphemes, with clear-cut boundary between them, carrying grammatical functions such as tense, number, person, gender, and genitive etc., with their meaning. Like, many other Tibeto-Burman languages, Rongmei does not have relative pronouns in the relative clauses. We can observe from the above-mentioned examples that those morphemes agglutinate to construct a larger unit of words and in some cases we also found that most morphemes do stand alone (isolating).

Tabui 'what' is the root word for all the *wh*–questions on which affixes are attached to convey other different *wh*-questions with their meaning. In almost all the cases (formal) the question particle *čo* is an inevitable element that occurs in the final position of question sentences. Always *tabui* (question words) occupied the scope position. Therefore, no movement is required. But it is optional in yes/no question types because these type of question have their own specific question markers.

In some cases, tense markers are coverted in the surface structure and cannot be identified. The tense marker *kan* is special because it has a grammatical function of both perfective and past tense in this language. Phonologically, the verb particle that occurs in final position is strongly assimilating by the preceding word final phoneme but no distant assimilation.

The best efforts have been made to bring it into conclusion. Yet, the data given above are not transcribed to the satisfaction of the native speaker. But I am sure this work would open the pathway for further linguistic investigation in this language.

List of Abbreviations

Acc	Accusative Case Marker
Aqm	Alternative Question Marker
ComD	Comparative Degree
Conj	Conjunction
Det	Determiner
EcM	Echo Question Marker
Emp	Emphatic Marker
Gen	Genitive Case Marker
1PS	First Person Singular
2PS	Second Person Singular/Plural
3PS	Third Person Singular
3PP	3rd Person Plural
LOC	Locative Case Marker
NCM	Nominative Case Marker
Neg	Negative Marker
Plu	Plural
Pos	Postposition
Prf	Perfective
PTM	Progressive Tense Marker
Qprt	Question Particle
TQM	Tag Question Marker
TnM	Tense Marker
Vprt	Verb Particle

Select References

Bright, W., (Chief editor), (1992), *International Encyclopedia of Linguistics*, Oxford: Oxford University Press.

Clark, V.P., Paul A. Eschholz and Alfred F. Rso., (1986), (5th edition), *Language Introductory Reading*, USA: St. Martins' Press Inc.

Crystal, D., (1991), *A Dictionary of Linguistics and Phonology*, London: Blackwell.

Dryer, M.S. and Suny, (2000), Word Order in Tibeto-Burman Languages, April Draft, Canberra, Australian National University Press. Buffalo, New York.

Freidin, R., (1992), *Foundation of Generative Syntax*, (3rd print 1994), Massachusetts: MIT Press.

Greenberg, J.H., (1966), (2nd edition), "Some Universals of Grammar with Particular Reference to the Order of Meaningful Elements", in J.H. Greenberg (ed.), *Universal of Language*, Cambridge University: Mass, MIT Press.

Grierson, G.A., (1903), (Reprint), *Linguistics Survey of India*, Vol. III, Part II, Delhi: Motilal Banarsidas.

Keyser, S.J., (Editor in Chief), Spring (2005), *Linguistic Inquiry*, Vol. 36, No. 2, Cambridge: MIT Press.

Morenberg, M., (1997), (2nd edition), *Doing Grammar*, London: Oxford University Press.

O'grady, W., Michael Dodrovolsk and Mark, Aronoff, (1979), *Contemporary Linguistics: An Introduction*, New York: St. Martins' Press.

Pamei, Ramkhun, (1996), *The Zeliangrong Nagas: A Study of Tribal Christianity*, New Delhi: Uppal Publishing House.

Radford, A., (1988), *Transformational Grammar: A First Course*, Cambridge: Cambridge University Press.

Subbarao, K.V., Mimi, Kevichusa and Kumar, Rajesh, *Typological Characteristics of Tibeto-Burman Languages*, New Delhi: University of Delhi.

Wurmbrand, S., (2001), *Infinitive: Restructuring and Clause Structure*, New York: Mouton de Gruyter Berlin.

10 Trajectory of Extinction

Forgotten Spirit of Arabic-Malayalam

YASSER ARAFATH P.K.

Language and Identity

Constructed and entrenched conscience of identity and conflicts, based upon varied linguistically distinguishable identities has had a very long standing in the history of violence and resentments. No language confines itself to the mere mode of expression and conviction. On the other hand, it would stand as concrete personification of a macro-identity with its own micro and sometimes conflicting identities. Language in its varied forms is expressed as the personification of individual/group identity and the spirit of nationality and, sub-nationality. Language also formularize the basic structure of regionalism and religious belief in local geographical space and pays tributaries for racial and caste identities. Sometimes the tone, accent and pronunciation of one's language can explicitly show a person's economic status and capacities in the social hierarchy. The dichotomy of superior and inferior is constructed by the way language is spoken. It is often said that a person with better accent or with an 'anglicized' or neutralized accent would belong to better ladder of social hierarchy. Classification of 'classic' and 'colloquial' are defined in the same manner with regard to who speaks language.

The history and development of any ancient or modern language show that language can not have an existence without undergoing a process of lending and borrowing. By deliberately transcending the boundaries of 'originality' and 'purity', language evolves itself as an expression of self assertion and mode of information. Recent history shows that the reluctance in accepting ideas and expression from 'foreign' language forms nullify the growth and popularity of any spoken or written language. Borrowing can be from a neighbouring language or a different dialect or a specified form of expression and sometimes from one accent itself. When the trade of Malabar coast passed into the hands of Arab traders, the rich recourses they brought with them were directly accepted by the then existing *Manipravala Malayalam* which is a hybrid linguistic form of Malayalam, Tamil, and Sanskrit languages. This process of linguistic convergence became a very decisive in the growth of the hybrid Malayalam from the 17th century onwards.

Land of Others: Need for a New Language

From AD 8th century onwards the interaction between local population and the emigrant Arab traders paved way for a multi-carpeted socio-cultural format. It is understood that every walk of life in this specified geographical situation, representation and reflection of many and varied cultural traits are very much explicit. It in this background that this paper tries to reproduce how this inter-religious reciprocal form resulted in the emergence of Arabic-Malayalam or *Mappila Malayalam* as it is defectively called, as a language form in Malabar.

Before we go into the details of the evolution of the Arabic-Malayalam, it should be noted that, since its origin, Malayalam as a language has passed through many stages. It was the last among Dravidian language to take its shape and cultivated a distinct identity. It has had a long and intimate association with Tamil. Early Malayalam prose appeared to have originated in the beginning of the 13th century AD. One of the most striking features of Malayalam language is its power of assimilation to the other language forms.[1] It had borrowed many words, usages, proverbs, terms and concepts, from many neighbouring languages like Tamil, Kannada, Telugu, and Sanskrit before the establishment of the Arab settlements on the coastal areas of Malabar. Generally a speaker of any language considers his/her mother tongue as the most logical or the best for all sorts of interactions or the oldest, or the most highly developed and scientific.[2] Surprisingly this sense of superiority did not occur in linguistic psyche of the Malayalee population in the pre-modern times.

It is in this backdrop that I would like to examine the origin, evolution and virtual extinction of the Arabic-Malayalam as language form in the linguistic consciousness of the Malayalees. Arabic-Malayalam remains as the everlasting legacy of the cultural synthesis between the Arab traders and the indigenous converts of Kerala. When two communities are associated with a common religion but alienated by two different languages, they would have felt the necessity for a link language which resulted in the emergence of the Arabic-Malayalam. The whole process of mutual cultural exchange can be seen in the development of Arabic-Malayalam, a unique language form of Malabar. This language form has had a long process of historical evolution of its own. It had taken its own route of development in the time span of three to four centuries. This unique mixture and form of language evolved as a critical way of communication and an accepted lingua franca of mercantile sectors of sea merchants and ancillary commercial groups in Kerala, especially Malabar. Even though the credit of spreading the language goes to all communities involved in the then existing trade and economic transactions, the primary contributions were given by the newly converted religious identity of the Mappila community on the coastal belt of Malabar in the Arabian Sea.

Early Muslim settlers from Arabia, who had a distinct cultural identity from the society in which they chose to live in, gradually adapted and accommodated despite negating the assimilating functions on reciprocal dealings. They could lead a peaceful life in a different cultural geography with their own distinctive practices. As far as the early settlers were concerned, language became the biggest barrier in order to carry out their work. Arabic-Malayalam was born out of this compulsion in order to have meaningful communication necessitated by the socio-economic condition of the given context.

Arabic-Malayalam became a deliberate attempt to overcome the problems of interaction between the Arab merchants and their local relations.[3]

During the period under study, Malayalam as a language did not have the sophisticated script for writing. Therefore, it was necessary for existence on the part of Muslim settlers to invent a new method in order to facilitate their economic activities. On the other hand, as the age reflects, Arab merchants who were staunch supporters of Islamic faith, seemingly thought that certain elements of belief systems and practices were not accurately expressed in the vernacular language. In order to overcome this problem they adopted a new script which was fitting in to the local language form. This facilitated the birth of Arabic-Malayalam script by using Arabic alphabetical orders with its own Malayalam sounds. But it should be noted that this language retained all the basic and essential aspects of the then existing Malayalam and put on the beautiful garb of the Arabic script.

Any form of the society or organized existence cannot take shape without means of proper communication. Progress and evolution in human societies depend on the development, adaptability and efficiency of the communications. The long history of human civilization witnessed diverse cultural variants, receiving inspiration from one another and making innumerable mutual borrowings. Linguistically people who lose their language would also lose their history, modes of thought and living and their social equilibrium and inevitably become a shapeless, useless and dangerous parasite that finally reacts injuriously against culture of their conqueror.

Arab settlers have never faced the problem of losing their exclusive identity. They adapted the cultural elements of their receivers and kept their cultural identity elements intact. Mappilas with the help of their foreign patrons developed this script by adopting the Arabic script of Malayalam making necessary additional alphabets. A study of the relation between Arabic and Malayalam scripts and cultural background of its emergence will lead us to an understanding of the cognitive process of interaction between Mappila Muslims and the rest of the society. Since the development of language depends on communicative practices, Arabic-Malayalam was shaped and reshaped and during the course of the time and as a result, Malayalam language became the beneficiary in this process. Subsequently this particular form of language essentially became the collective consciousness of all communities in Malabar.

As it is understood, task or object of the scientific study of languages is possible only to a very limited extent and for very few languages.[4] Interestingly, unlike most of early languages, scientific study of Arabic-Malayalam is possible as its history has its specific beginning, development and signs of decadence as well. The comment in *Muhiyuddheen Mala,* "O, people, I have strung this *Muhiyuddheen Mala,* by joining together pearls and rubies"(Arabic and Malayalam respectively) rightly shows the relation between the two languages in the development of a common language.[5]

Largely, Arabic-Malayalam literature, which emerged on the scene in 9th century onwards, has a unique blend of Malayalam grammar, Arabic script, Arabic, Tamil, Urdu, Persian vocabulary and a few additional orthographic symbols being utilized according to the needs.[6] Arabic-Malayalam was enriched with different signs of communication and forms borrowed from different communitarian practices and cultural elements. Signs are repeated in successive discourses in social interaction. The language in the due course of time became quite independent of the single identity as it cannot be a creation of a few grouped individuals. It became essentially social and presupposed the collectivity as a social product.[7] The development of Arabic-Malayalam tradition thus represents the greatest area of the cultural assimilation and accommodation in pre-colonial Malabar between the Muslims and the others.

A shift in the language of a community can have many effects on the identity of the speaker. Language shift of the Arab traders and their local progeny was accompanied by a shift in ethnic identification coupled with the full cooperation of the group into the local language system. Language shift can take place without lose of identity as well. It is also possible that cultural and ethnic assimilation would take place in the absence of the language as well. The reasons behind the rise and development of the Arab-Malayalam language must be sought both in voluntary acts of linguistic creativity on the part of the Arab settlers and in the differential impact of social factors upon the Arab Muslims.[8] It is obvious that either people of alien speech must learn language of hosts or the hosts should learn guest's language.[9] This dimension of the 'hosts' and 'guests' can be seen in the development of Arabic-Malayalam as in the formation of 'pidgin' or 'trade languages' such as *Coast English* or *Creole French* due to the compromise of the external and internal parties.[10]

Arabic is considered to be the most widely used language in the Semitic group. It is derived from the *Nashki* script.[11] Arabic language was the lingua franca of Prophet Muhammad and in turn *Quran* is also written in this language. Muslims also consider Arabic language as the language of the paradise. Non-Arabic languages are insufficient in conveying the full significance of Islamic terms and ideas. It was observed in the due course of time that certain terms, trends and concepts in the Malayalam language, which had the dominant influence of the native spirituality and belief systems, was in conflict with the religious belief, ethical concept and moral values close to Muslims.[12] Therefore, apart from commercial interest, strong religious beliefs would also have played a crucial role in the development of this language. There could have been a feeling that religious instruction could effectively be conveyed only through the mother tongue, though script was to be in Arabic due to the fear of mutilation of the originality. Another important reason could be the concern for women. Muslim women could only speak Malayalam but not read and write it. Their familiarity with *Quran* would have definitely eased their learning the spoken language in Arabic script.[13]

Usage of Arabic Terms in Malayalam

Once the Arabic-Malayalam took root in the soil of Kerala, it became the part and parcel of the existing literature and spoken language. Arabic-Malayalam literature enriched the Malayalam vocabulary immensely with many number of words and terms in due course of time. Interestingly, Arabic-Malayalam literature gave adequate representation to the words from Tamil, Urdu, Persian and local dialects. These literatures deal with many different subjects like architecture, arithmetic, astronomy, biographies, dictionary, eulogy, etymology, fiction, history, medicine, satire, sexology, sports, jurisprudence, and trade both religious and secular in nature.

Some of the common words absorbed into the present day Malayalam are listed below. These words are categorized in four groups in terms of their origin.

Those Emanated from Commercial Transactions of the Commodities

Words like: *anamath, enam* (reward), *kitab* (book), *haluwa* (haluwwa), *jilebi* (a sweet eatable), *malik* (king, rich man), *kabool* (acceptance), *bwaathil* (void, rejected), etc. These words are not only commonly used in Malayalam but also in other modern Indian languages.

Words Particular to the Missionary Activities

E.g., words like: *thaakheed* (warning), *dulm, khabar*(news), *kabar* (crematorium), *janathul firdous* (paradise), *khalb* (heart), *mayyith* (corpse), *safar* (journey), *fasad* (miscreant activities), *shakku* (doubt), *duniyav* (world), *akhir* (other world) *salamath* (peace), *khair* (well being), *thwalaqh* (divorce), *nikah* (engagement-marriage), *mahshara* (other word), *niyyath* (believe), *shaitan* (demon), *dawath* (preaching), *khibr* (imperious), *qiyamath* (judgment day), *miskeen* (poor), *fakheer*(destitute), *jahil* (ignorant), *balal* (cursed), *baith* (songs).

Words of Jurisprudence, Law and Order

Words like: *qarar,* (agreement), *harji* (petition), *tahasildar* (tahsildar), *khasba* (town), *amin* (amin), *jephti, vasool* (acquisition), *mamool* (local tradition), *raddu* (cancel), *munsif* (local town).

Miscellaneous

Fourth category has the benefit of the words like *shipoy, kaneshmari, shikari* and *karpooram* etc.[14] In the opinion of Hermaan Gundert, the first lexicographer of Kerala, there are three thousand Arabic words in the regular use in Kerala irrespective of religion and class. Numbers are many when it comes to the common Mappila dialect. It is quite interesting to see that local dialects did not have any disinclination in absorbing a foreign language into their fold.

Arabic-Malayalam Literature: Representing Many

A wrong perception prevails that Arabic-Malayalam literature represents only the socio–cultural and religious attitude of Mappilas. This literary stream became the part of the collective consciousness of the Malabari population. Though some portions of this literature exclusively deals at the macro- and micro-level religious and cultural identity of the Muslims of Malabar, an equal attention has been paid to the socio-cultural landscape of the larger society, which is not by any possibility only Islamic.[15]

Initially, as the Mappilas started expressing themselves in this script Arabic-Malayalam, it had acquired a literary dimension. The literature can be divided into prose and verse in which latter occupies the foremost importance. Generally termed as Mappila songs or *Mappila pattu,* this verse tradition includes hymns that enclose the holy figures (*madhu pattukal*), martial songs, (*pada pattukal*), songs of praise (*malapattukal*), love lyrics (*katthu pattukal*) and so on.

In the devotional genre works like *badar mala, nafeesath mala, mambram mala, malapppuram mala* can be included.[16] But the most important this sort remains to be the first one, *muhiyiddin mala,* written by Qhazi Muhammad of Calicut in 1607 AD. It renders in a devotional tone, the miraculous deeds and devotion of Sheik Muhiyuddhin of Jilan, the eminent Sufi.[17] *Muhiyuddhin mala* as a devotional song has had a profound influence by the ongoing Bhakti and Sufi tradition in south India. Devotion and prayer to the personified gods can be seen from Bhakti tradition in many verses of this work. Sufi concepts of 'Anal *Haq*'('I am the truth') and *Wahdathul Wujud* ('Unity of being') are very much explicit in its content. This *mala* is a reflection and adoption of the *Addhyathma Ramayana* recital tradition of the local Hindu population. *Muhiyuddhin mala* adopted the style and dialect of the common population, a tradition embraced from *Addhyathma Ramayana* authored by Thunchath Ezhuthachan in the 17th century. He induced the vernacular and popular usage and terms in his version of *Ramayana.*[18] *Muhyuddhin mala,* apart from its rich religious spirit also enriched itself with generous use of Urdu, Sanskrit, Persian, Tamil, Kannada, Thulu, Konkani and so on. *Kodi, khutubu, bahja, bhashibhumi, balle, vedam, pashu, majlis, kasham* are some of many words borrowed from different languages.

There are over fifty martial songs (*padappattukal*) in Arabic-Malayalam. The most prominent ones being *Bador patappattu* (Battle of Badr), *Uhdu patappattu* (Battle of Uhdu), *Makkam fathhu* (Victory of Makkah) and so on.[19] If one go by the Islamic terms alone denoted here it would be sure that he/she would miss to understand the real motive behind the emergence of this kind of literature. As we stated in the beginning, Arabs and the indigenous converts had a dominant position in the Arabian Sea. When the Portuguese appeared in the peaceful and serine water of Arabian Sea, Muslims had started using both the pen and sword simultaneously. *Tuhfathul mujahideen* of Sheikh Sainuddheen Makhdum[20] *Fathhul Mubeen* of Quasi Muhammad are some deliberate attempt from the Muslim scholars who enjoyed the favour and protection from the local rulers to influence and encourage the Malabar population particularly Mappilas to wage the war against the colonial powers.

When Moin Kutty Vaidyar, the most famous writer in Arabic-Malayalam wrote *Badar Padappattu* (1876), the colonial dominance in Kerala was of ten years in age. After the death of Tipu Sultan, there was no formidable enemy for the British in the area and they became the masters of the Arabian Sea. Mappilas, who were the original traders of the Arabian coast could not stand the large scale merchandise of the colonial power and were outnumbered by the British in all terms. As a part of ongoing brutal suppression of Muslims at all India level after the war of 1857, they adopted the same policy in Malabar. They associated with some of the prominent *Janmis* (Zamindars) who were Hindus by religion and projected Muslim peasants and the traders as their biggest enemy. It is in this backdrop Vaidyar made his magnum opus *Badar Padappattu.* Vaidyar had drawn parallels from the history of Islamic civilization. He brought in the historical experience of prophet Muhammad, who won the famous 'Battle of Badar' against fully prepared army of non-Muslims who were three times more in number than Muslims. This particular work became the rallying point against the British supremacy and brutality on the Malabar Coast. He induces energy in the fighting warriors of the Malabar against foreign domination. The crux of his war songs was to "Defend and attack any power who takes away your respect and freedom".[21] Many war songs were composed in the later years by taking inspiration from Vaidyar's works. Later, British administration understood the strength and the depth of these work and banned carrying and singing of these songs by law, especially *malappuram padappattu*.[22]

Even though most of the *Mappilappattus* reflect the Islamic culture and format, it reflect the sensibilities of the larger Malayalee culture. *Kallyanappattu* (marriage songs), *Vettilappattu* (bettle leaf songs), *Talolappattu* (lullabies), *Mailanchippattu* (henna song), and many of these genre astonishingly reflecting the cultural realities of the total populace. These songs, which had medieval origin are still sung in marriages, social gatherings, and festivals of all religions of Malabar. The tunes rhymes and alliterations used in *Mappilappattus* are taken from Arabian musical tradition and rich materials of local folk songs. Tamil Bhakti songs also have had very strong influence in the development of many *Mappilappattus*. In the due course of time Arabic-Malayalam language fashioned parallel songs to the *Koithupattu* (harvest songs), *Njattupattu* (sowing songs), *Pulluvar pattu* and so on which were generally circulated among the lower strata of the local population. With the passage of time, many Arabic words started travelling to the rich and widespread tradition of *Vadakkan Pattukal* (northern ballads) of Malabar. With many years of interaction with Arabic-Malayalam literatures, *Vadakkan Pattukal* now have very profound glimpses of Mappila social and cultural life.

Though deeply influenced by the local tradition, Arabic-Malayalam literature did not totally abandon the original tradition of incorporating the Arabian musical tradition into it. Dramatic representations of uncertainties and surprises are imbibed from the rich tradition of Arabian poetry. Thematic adaptations of Imru'l Qaise[23] can be seen in the works of Moinkutty Vaidyar especially in the songs related to love and lust. It is explicit in the epic work of *Badrul muneer* and *Husnul Jamal* in which he depicts the pain and vulnerability of lovers and their longing for each other. Though most of the *padappattus* (war songs) deal with the events in the Islamic history, the motive and the contexts are always entrenched in the socio-economic settings of Kerala. Even the metaphors and examples used in the poetic lines are directly taken from indigenous traditions of Kerala. These particular aspects can be seen in many of the Vaidyar's works where he talks about local musical instruments, dressing pattern, food, mode of transport, war equipments, pattern of war etc.

Arabic-Malayalam and its Identity

Arabic-Malayalam is now considered the oldest known dialect of Malayalam language. This particular language form has had a very broad geographical boundary and readership. It has the characteristics of the Dravidian languages of South India, Indo-Aryan language of Persian and rich tradition and characteristics of Semitic Arabic. Though originated through the native converts it had undergone drastic changes in the due course of time. Some argue that Arabic-Malayalam is not a language in itself because the whole construction of the language is Malayalam and only the script is Arabic. But it is notable that pure Arabic and Persian words and sentences are used in most of the Arabic-Malayalam literature. In *Muhiyuddheen Mala* and many works of Moinkutty Vaidyar we would see that many of the sentences written in Arabic with Tamil mixture.[24] Likewise there are many stanzas which used only Malayalam language and Tamil.[25] It is important to note that importantly this language has its own history, tradition, growth and development and script.[26] Besides, other words or terms found in Malayalam are mostly of Malayalam dialect spoken exclusively by Malabar Muslims and their lower caste brethren. This particularity can not be seen in the geographical areas of southern Kerala. Above all, Arabic-Malayalam is a language developed and established far before the establishment of present day Malayalam as the lingua franca of the total geographical extant of Kerala.

Now Arabic-Malayalam has become an integral part of Kerala culture irrespective of regional boundaries. Earlier it used to be confined to the northern districts of Kerala where large number of Muslims and lower caste Hindus reside. In southern parts this language form has little currency due to various reasons. Most important one is the lack of meaningful cultural exchanges between Muslims and the majority Christian population in the southern districts. *Mappilappattu*, the biggest legacy of Arab-Malayam language has now become the experience and common heritage of Kerala. Many used this language and experience and it reflects in their masterpieces. Names of M.T. Vasudevan Nair, P. Bhaskaran, Vaikkam Muhammad Basheer are some of the very prominent in this regard. There are also many films made with predominant usage of Arabic-Malayalam. Films like *Kuttikkuppayam*, reflect the Muslim social life expressed in their own language and surprisingly made by mainstream film-makers.

Language Losing its Soul and Spirit and Way to Extinction

Now Arabic-Malayalam almost lost its presence in the literary sphere of Kerala. Though it is still spoken widely in the Malabar region, textual form of the language has become extinct. Mainstream realm of the society does not want to use this language as it is considered to be 'polluted'. Following paragraphs will examine the historical and socio-economic reasons behind the gradual disappearance of this language from the common cultural and linguistic consciousness of Malayalee.

With the collapse of erstwhile local *naduwazhis* (chieftains) and the establishment of imperial state with the help of local elites, the state patronage to the scholars was considerably lost. The legitimacy established by the state through the association with religious leaders and priests permanently disappeared. When the above mentioned categories lost their patronage, the imaginative and creative spirit of the scholars reduced. Simultaneously, the writers patronized by the local elites have also lost the mobility due to the dissociation from the state. Khasi Ahmmad, the author of *Muhyuddhin Mala*, Sainiddhin Makhdum,[27] the author of *Thuhfathul'l—Mujahideen* and many prominent litterateurs enjoyed the patronage and privileges of local power centres. After the establishment of colonial settlements on the coastal areas, the local chieftains and kings lost their economic prosperity on a considerable scale and the peaceful ambience of the creative setting had also been lost. After independence and emergence of many a movement in Kerala, the interest and growth of the Arabic-Malayalam suffered a setback. As a result of these phenomena, the classical Arabic-Malayalam became endangered and in the way of extinction. When a language goes to die or died its speakers' culture, art and history also die. Once that happens, almost no chance of reviving those remains.

Apart from the above mentioned reasons, vanishing process of Arabic-Malayalam is resulted by large scale internal and external migration, emphasis on market-oriented education, raising importance of common/national languages and assimilation into the dominant cultures. The particulars of Arabic-Malayalam encapsulate the history of Malayalees in general and Mappilas in particular, by sparkling on their ways of living and thinking. It reflects people's perception of the world, examine their history and shape thinking process and imagination itself.

One major reason for the disappearance of this language is that it is not taught anymore by parents to their children and used actively in everyday matters. It is understood that the fewer the children learn the language, the lesser it develops. As an obvious consequence of the globalization and liberalization policies, the vernacular languages become the ultimate sufferer. Parents and educational institutions insist students to go for English and some foreign languages like French and Spanish. Also some people say that they do not want to bring children into a world where their society, language, and people have no place. One of the most common factors that lead a community to shift from one language to another is that the acquired language is thought to be economically beneficial by its speakers. Like their counterparts around the world, Malabar parents want their children to prosper, to access material wealth and social prestige specific to their cultural setting.

Conditions like those of number of speakers, communication with peer groups, use of other languages regularly in various cultural settings, feelings of ethnic identity and attitudes about their language in general contribute to the process of disappearance.[28] The drift in the urban and rural categories, especially among the younger population, government policies, medium in the education as well as economic intrusion are also some of the factors in this regard.

When speakers move to other areas where different languages or dialects are spoken, general interest and scope of retaining the original spoken language could be lost. As the situation in the Malabar reminds us, most of the internal and external migrations in Malabar happens among the Mappilas and low caste Hindu population who are the real promoters of this language. After the oil boom in the Middle East from early 1970s, coincidently, not a major work is produced in Arabic-Malayalam. Similarly, internal migration from the interiors of Malabar to the metros also has a large impact on the language.[29] Arabic-Malayalam as script as well as a language form has been disappearing from the emerging middle and upper class. Using this 'antique' or 'polluted' or sometimes 'corrupted' Malayalam will bring 'bad impression' or image according to them. In urban areas, even people with pure dialect would be seen burning their tongue to catch the 'real Malayalam'.

Government policy of promoting the use of a specific language in school and other educational institutions in the form of 'standardize' language, virtually took away the main root of Arabic-Malayalam. Earlier, even after the independence, students had their religious and secular education from the institutions called *Othupalli* (place of reading). Textbooks were written in Arabic and

Arabic-Malayalam alike. But once government schools and aided educational centres emerged in the educational scenario of Kerala, this Othupalli institutions lost its importance and space. This encouraged people to learn the wider-known languages like English and Hindi by giving negligible importance to Malayalam itself. Often those speaking Arabic-Malayalam chose to learn a more prestigious language with the hope of greater economic opportunities.[30]

Arabic-Malayalam and Revitalization Movements in Kerala

Arabic-Malayalam literature witnessed a heavy setback from Islamic revivalist movements in Kerala, especially in Malabar area. The language in due course of time was reduced in the hands of Muslim priests and scholars, who had little world experience and broader outlook. Most of them represented the priestly hierarchy and scholarly supremacy. Emergence of radical revivalist movements especially *Islahi-movement* (*Kerala Nadwatul Mujahideen*) in the first half of 20th century is considered to be the biggest setback in the development of Arabic-Malayalam. This organization wanted to liberate Muslims from all 'unislamic' and 'non-textual' practices. By assigning themselves the duty of purifying Islamic practices, they dragged then existing religious scholarship into the controversies and verbal abuses. By portraying Muslims in the 19th and early 20th centuries as people of bid'ah (innovators in belief and rituals), they unleashed a large-scale campaigning for purified monotheism (*Tawheed*). Ongoing Islamic practices with its local elements, as we can see in any part of the world, whether in Iran, African countries and South East Asian countries and many parts of India itself, are projected to be blasphemous. *Islahi* movements promoted pure Arabian form of Islam which has Arab nationalism as its integral part, and vehemently opposed the absorbing and accepting indigenous traditions and customs. Even though the superstitious and harmful elements were to be denounced, the heterogeneous and plurality of the regional culture which was represented in Arabic-Malayalam also lost on this way.

Identifying educational reforms as one of the basic requirements of the Muslim community during those days, Islahi movements started setting up many institutions for elementary, secondary and higher education under an education board. Under this board, Madrasas, or religious schools, were started in various parts of the state in a meticulous way with modern amenities. They concentrated on religious education of the 'misguided' *Umma* (community). The newly constructed Madrassas adopted Malayalam in the original script unlike in the *Sunni* (then existing Islamic tradition)-Madrassas, run by so-called 'orthodox' and people of *shirq* (polytheism). By dominating the religious educational system of Malabar, and using Malayalam or Arabic in their study material, Islahi movements gave a major blow to the development of Arabic-Malayalam literature and its scriptural form. Though the original and early Arabic-Malayalam books are still available in limited number, creative writing in this language is virtually lost.

There was some stated reason apart from the simplification of the language used till then in madrassas. One of them was that Arabi-Malayalam literature became the tool of the orthodox scholars of the Muslim community. Most of the literary and scholarly writings contained the elements of superstitions and anti-Islamic traits. Some works, which were influenced by the Bhakti and Sufi tradition as we pointed out earlier, were shown as anti-Islamic and hence the very medium of the expression bore the burnt of the accusation. This biographical/hagiographical literature was full of exaggerations and extra human capacities of saint leaders[31] as these are the outcome of their imaginative capacity. Their attribution of godliness and divine power[32] were taken as anti-Islamic and blasphemy. Some of these verses became very popular and the characters cited in those became the household names of the Muslims of Malabar. Sometimes these saints were lifted to the position of the 'Gods' or 'Semi-Gods'. Puritan elements in the community could not see it happily and they cultivated feelings of the resentment against the language itself. *Jamathe-Islami-Kerala,* another revivalistic Islamic organization claims that it could liberate the Madrassa education system of Kerala Muslims from the draconian clutches of Arabic-Malayalam which promoted meaninglessness and superstitions.

Though some of the arguments put forward by the so-called progressive organizations can be considered, it is surprising to see that the language form in itself is the culprit of the spreading of the superstition and polytheism. By denouncing the usage of Arabic-Malayalam, above mentioned revivalistic movements made irreversible damage to the long tradition of this literature. In the disguise of promoting 'modern outlook', these ideologically radical organizations which call upon the Muslims for homogeneity and 'the establishment of the Islamic state' made a death call to the large-scale literary potential of this unique literary form.

Most of the Islamic organizations in Kerala have long-standing problem with the localization of the Islamic community. They do not welcome Mappilas who still accept and practice some of the belief system and customs of the native land. They equalled the Islamic identity with unfamiliar Arab nationalism for a 'pan-Islamic' identity which does not have any thing in common with local conditions.

When the wind of modernity and vernacularization sweeping across the communities in Kerala, centuries old traditions are on the deathbed. This work is not a cry for the continuation of superstitions and man made gods. But, here the question is that, if we should allow a language form which represented the gamut of literature, economy, polity, customs, traditions, way of living for many centuries to have an untimely death. With the disappearance of Arabic-Malayalam language the existing chunk of literary tradition; *Mappila Pattukal, Oppana Pattukal, Mailanchi Pattukal, Katthu Pattukal, Madhu Pattukal, Baithukal, Malakal,* all rich ingredients of the cultural fabric of Malabar; also would lose their soul and spirit.

When a language dies it means that a unique creation of human beings is gone from the world. Each language has grown up with its society and is an expression of the facets of that society's culture. Each is an intricate system of words, phrases, clauses, and discourse patterns showing contrasts and agreements that its speakers use to describe their world and the customs they use in relating to each other. They use the language to tell their stories, recount their past, express their plans for the future, recite their poetry, and pass on their way of life.

Linguists are aware that the extinction of a language does not necessarily mean that the people who spoke it have all died. Instead, the speakers may shift to a different language, over one or more generations. Sometimes parents decide not to speak in their mother tongue to their children, because they perceive an economic or educational advantage for their children with a second language. They do not want their children to repeat the 'mistake' of theirs by not having fluency in second language. They have a mistaken notion that children can learn to speak only one language well. That is not true. Children can learn several languages well, as long as they know when to speak each one. Childhood is the best time to learn languages well.

The Mappilas, who patronized Arabic-Malayalam in a peaceful ambiance later, acquired an inferiority complex about their culture and language through contact with the outside world.[33] Scholars of language studies and cultures declined to have noted that certain social-political or religious functions of those societies must cease when there are not enough people left to handle the tradition of their language.[34] Arabic-Malayalam literature is endangered, or has even become extinct, while many dialects of Malayalam remain intact. To keep its life moving, this language needs the linguistic description, and its speakers need literacy and other help.

Notes

1. Malik Muhammad, *Role of Arabic, Persian, Urdu and Hindi in the Development of Malayalam*, in Commemoration Volume, The Cochin Synagogue 400th Anniversary Celebration, Kerala History Associations' Silver Jubilee Years Publication, Cochin, 1971, p. 159.
2. Joshua A. Fishman, *Reading in the Sociology of Language*, Mount on Publications, The Hague, 1968, p. 376.
3. P.K. Muhammad Kunnhi, *Muslingalum Kerala Samskaravum*, Kerala Sahithya Academy, Trichur, 1982, p. 209.
4. Ferdinand de Saussure, *Third Course of Lectures on General Linguistics*, Pergamon Press, 1993, http://www.marxists.org/reference/subject/ philosophy/works/fr/ saussure.htm.
5. Quazi Muhammad Bin Abdul Azeez, *Muhiyuddheen Mala*, (Trans.), Otta Maliyekkal Muthukoya Thangal, Ashrafi Book Centre, Tirurangadi, 2000. He says *mutthum manikkavum onnai korthapol Muhiyuddheen malaye korthe nan malore*, line 142.
6. Roland Miller, *Mappila Muslims of Kerala: A Study in Islamic Trends*, Orient Longmans, Madras, 1992, p. 289.
7. Ferdinand de Saussure, http://www.marxists.org/reference/subject/ philosophy/works/fr/saussure.htm.
8. Paul Wexler, "Jewish Inter Linguistics: Facts and Conceptual Frame Work", *Language*, Vol. 57, No. 1, March 1981, p. 103.
9. A. Werner, "The Languages of Africa", *Journal of the Royal African Society*, Vol. 12, No. 46, 1913, p. 121.
10. Ibid., p. 121.
11. Das Aqarwalla, *A Common Script System*, Calcutta, 1960, p. 8.
12. Tayka Shu'Aib Alim, *Arabic, Arawi, and Persian in Sarandhib and Tamilnadu*, Colonial Press, San Rafael, 1993, pp. 73–75.

13. Ibid., p. 89.
14. Suranat Kunjan Pillai, "Mappila Pattukal", *Chandrika Weekely*, Republic Day Issue, Kozhikode, 1970, p. 12.
15. Balakrishnan Vallikkunnu, *Mappila Charithrninte Kanaapurangal* (Malayalam) Capital International, Calicut, 1999, p. 101. He says that Mappila songs are the collective and creative compilations of the Arabian musical consciousness and Malabari consciousness of the diverse, p. 100.
16. M.N. Karasserry, "Mappilappattu", in *Thapasam*, A Quarterly Journal for Kerala Studies, Vol. 1, issued on 4, April 2006, p. 786.
17. Ibid., p. 786.
18. P.K. Muhammad Kunnhi, *Muslingalum Kerala Samskaravum*, Kerala Sahithya Academy, Trichur, 1982, (Malayalam), p. 216.
19. M.N. Karassery, op. cit., p. 786.
20. Originally his book is known as *Thuhfathul Mujahideeen Fee Basi Akhbaril Burthukhaliyyeen* (A Presentation to the Warriors with the Information about Portuguese).
21. K. Aboobacker, *Mahakavi Moinkutty Vaidhyar Samboornna Krithikal*, Kondotti, 2005, pp. 23–24.
22. Ibid., p. 25.
23. He was a pre-Islamic poet of Arabia. Among the seven immortal poets, he was the most famous and considered to be the undisputed 'king' or the legend of Arabic poetry, the other being Zuhair, Trafah, Amru ibn Kulsum, al-Haris, Antarah and Labid.
24. Second, Fortieth, Sixty Fourth stanzas of *Muhiyuddheen Mala* has only Tamil and Arabic mixture.
25. Stanza 72, *Muhiyuddheen Mala*.
26. Tayka shu Ayb Alim, op. cit., p. 90.
27. He had a very close association with Sultan Ali Adil Shah of Bijapur. He hails sultan as the protector and savior of Muslims from the murdering Portuguese traders on the Coromondal and Malabar. Sainudhhen spent a considerable portion of his work to glorify the deeds of the sultan. He presented his work to the sultan as a *thirumulkhazhcha. Tuhfathul Mujahideen*, (Trans. Malayalam), C. Hamsa, Al Huda Book Stall, Kozhikode, 1999, pp. 35–37.
28. Gloria Kindell, http://www.sil.org/sociolx/ndg-lg-faq.html.
29. B.F. Grimes, *Languages of the World*, Dallas: SIL International, 2000, p. 502.
30. http://www.sil.org/sociolx/ndg-lg-vitality.html.
31. Stanzas 36, 61, 74, *Muhiyuddheen Mala*.
32. Stanzas, 105, 107, 112, 113, 114.
33. B.F. Grims, op. cit., p. 303.
34. Ibid.

11 Narrating the Voice of the Voiceless

A Critical Interrogation of Marginality in Modern Indian Fiction

K. VENUGOPAL REDDY

I take this moment of international forum to ponder on the theme of marginality as articulated in Mulk Raj Anand's *Untouchable* (1935) and Kamala Markandaya's *Nectar in a Sieve* (1954). I make an attempt to look at the texts for the ideas about the way certain sections get marginalized in the course of rapid economic transformation or have been historically oppressed in Indian society. I seek to articulate on the trauma of that experience or transformation as portrayed in these novels. I choose to focus on these narratives of Mulk Raj Anand and Markandaya for two principal reasons. First, because I think these narratives are wondrous testaments on fictional representation of marginality in Indian society. Second, because they have effectively communicated the most agonizing process of marginalization as gone through by the individuals in the society. The reading of these narratives acquire critical significance particularly in the context of the ongoing process of displacement of the people from their native lands in the name of industrialization and economic development in the Nandhigram, Singhur, (West Bengal) Raigad (Maharashtra) and the yet undiminished and persisting practice of manual scavenging and the curse of untouchability in the contemporary Indian society.

The fiction writers in colonial or post-colonial India have conscientiously and critically responded to the innumerable forms of extant debilitating and putrefied social practices and traditions. By their critical interrogation, they constantly attempted to demystify the hegemonic social or cultural values and thus unravel the nature of exploitative economic and social relationships between the exploited and the exploiters. So, the multiple forms of social, cultural, religious or economic forms of marginality form the critical themes of their social fiction.

It is, therefore, that the relationship between novel and the existing social context is an exciting area for critical analysis. Novels delineate the social environment by illuminating the darkened spheres of society and attempting realistic portrayals of the experiences of an individual or a social group. They document contemporary social iniquities. Hence, they have come to be regarded as the expansive markers of the social reality or social phenomenon. A novelist as a social commentator articulates on the contemporary social practices or social milieu that may be repressive or exploitative, humane or egalitarian. Novels of such genre provide very valuable information for historians to critically analyze the extant social processes and thus justify their position in the literary canon as indispensable texts to perceive the social reality. Therefore, a critical analysis of a contemporary novel as a crucial source of social knowledge helps in the project of constructing social history of any community or a nation.

Text as Discourse of Context: Narrating Marginality through Fiction

The early years of twentieth century witnessed the emergence of creative fiction. The decades of the 1920s, 1930s, and 1940s particularly witnessed cataclysmic changes as discourses of nationalism and colonialism collided, even as India was thrust into modern conditions of living and thinking.[1] Indian fiction during the era witnessed the widening of the base of literary attention. The transference of literary focus from the upper classes to the masses was very striking.[2] With the dawn of the twentieth century, the novels of social protest began to emerge and focus more forcefully on the concerns of contemporary social relevance. The novel has become an effective instrument for social change in the hands of at least a few novelists. These novelists made bold attempts in the creative rendering of the contemporary social reality. They used the novel as a form of social protest for a vigorous delineation of the reality of contemporary life.[3] Of the novelists succeeding Bankim Chandra Chatterjee and Rabindranath Tagore in the early decades of the twentieth century, Sarat Chandra Chatterjee (1876–1938) was one novelist, who stands prominent in the world of creative social fiction. His works focused on the world of 'down-and-outs' and have fearlessly portrayed the "the tears and sweat of the lower middle and have-not classes".[4] His literary creations in Bengali language and those of Munshi Premchand in Urdu and Hindi may be understood to have anticipated the best social fiction of Mulk Raj Anand in English.[5]

The politics of colonial India seemed to have exercised a perceptible impact on the expression of creative literary endeavours. As a consequence, there was a notable upsurge in the release of the creative energies, which was authentically reflected in the growth of literature both in English and the 'vernacular' languages.[6] In the regional languages too, the similar trend of reflecting the themes of social concern was visible. The realist novels in the regional languages deal with themes that can be called 'pan-Indian'—landlord-tenant relationship, economic exploitation of the peasant/bonded labourer, untouchability, natural calamities and urban capitalism and their intrusion into rural life, Gandhian and revolutionary pre-independence political activities.[7] Writers resorted to fancy no more; they did not invent incredible situations to dupe or entertain their readers. Instead, they rendered the familiar in familiar terms, closely, intensely, and faithfully.[8]

Exploring Marginality in *Untouchable* by Mulk Raj Anand (1935)

Mulk Raj Anand (1905–2004) belonged to that group of socially conscious novelists who explored the life of the oppressed and marginalized social classes through their novels. With the appearance of the novels *Untouchable* (1935) and *Coolie* (1936), Anand achieved a wide recognition. About *Untouchable*, reflecting after three decades, he wrote "The book poured out like hot lava from the volcano of my crazed imagination, during a long week-end".[9] *Untouchable* narrates a day in the life of Bakha, an unfortunate outcaste, who suffers a number of humiliations in the course of his day. So, it was this social oppression of "the poorest of the poor human beings"[10] that pricked the social conscience of Anand and awakened his humanist spirit. Reminiscing why he created a character like Bakha, he evocatively explains: "Superficially, it seems that a rare human being, whom I had known from my childhood and adored as a hero because he was physically like a god, played all the games superbly and could recite whole cantos from the epic poem *Heer Ranjah* of Waris Shah, was knocking at the gates of my awareness".[11] Therefore, that an individual like Bakha, who, due to his low birth, destined to work as a latrine sweeper had tremendously impacted his consciousness. He writes:

> Even at the level of common sense reality, I was aware of his tragedy. That this otherwise near-perfect human being was a sweeper who was always being humiliated by most of our elders on account of his low caste, was not allowed to go to school even if his father had sent him (which he would not have), flawed his excellence, for no fault of his ... . The contradiction between the inborn qualities of this youth and the down and out status to which he was condemned, may certainly have been the obvious cause for my broodings about him.[12]

Anand's success as a creator of social fiction representing "even the so-called lowest dregs of humanity, living in utmost poverty, squalor and degradation"[13] unquestionably stemmed from his accurate depiction of their social reality in his works. His was a voice protesting against all kinds of oppression and exploitation[14] (62). His inexhaustible concern for the underprivileged and the downtrodden had been amply demonstrated through his works.[15] Thus, *Untouchable* is the perfect example of Anand's deep involvement with social realism as the novel is centred on the harsh world of oppression and endurance of the subaltern class.

Mulk Raj Anand for the first time through his inspired texts in English portrayed contextually the travails of the socially oppressed and marginalized in colonial India. This trend of realistically representing the subalternity of the untouchable community continued throughout the twentieth century and in post-colonial India. It is, therefore, quite significant to note that Mulk Raj Anand's masterpiece *Untouchable* presaged the upsurge of genre of critical works on the various dimensions of subalternity of untouchables in India.[16] Literary texts at once reflect and enact history.[17] The text acquires a definite historical significance, as it can be located in a contemporary context of social conventions.[18] Thus, Anand's fictions mirrored the contemporary social environment in colonial India.[19]

E.M. Forster aptly remarks with reference to the job of scavenging and the life of those traditionally engaged in it in colonial India: "What a strange business has been made of this business of the human body relieving itself!" (14). The remark pithily encapsulates the overwhelming significance of Mulk Raj Anand's influential masterpiece *Untouchable* on the pernicious social system prevalent during the third decade of the twentieth century colonial India.

The Hindu society has been organized around the principles of Varna system as articulated in the religious scriptures of ancient India.[20] Though the origins of untouchability as practised in recent times are unknown, the "untouchables" normally consist of those castes, which are placed at the bottom of the caste hierarchies. They have the lowest ritual standing and usually the lowest economic position and are traditionally subjected to several arduous social and civic disabilities.[21] Though the disabilities experienced by the untouchable communities varied from location to location in their intensity, there was, however, certain similarity in their prevalence and practice in colonial India.[22] These communities were denied access to public facilities such as wells, schools, roads, etc. They were restricted from entering the temples, shrines connected to temples, and drawing water from temple tanks. They were forbidden to learn the Vedas, the holy scriptures of Hinduism. They carried out dirty and menial work. Their residences were segregated typically in more extreme form, which required them to remain outside the village. They were denied of access to the services, such as those provided by other castes namely, barbers, laundrymen. They were required to use separate utensils in shops and theatres. They were prohibited from possessing and the use of goods indicating comfort or luxury. They were required to maintain deference in forms of address, language, sitting, and standing in presence of higher castes. Their movement was also restricted and they were not allowed on roads and streets within prescribed distance of the houses or persons of higher castes.[23] Thus, the untouchables experienced a kind of perpetual slavery with little hope of betterment in this world.[24] It is this social life of untouchables that has been well documented in the novel *Untouchable* by Mulk Raj Anand.

However, the colony of the untouchable community, which is invariably located on the periphery of the village, is portrayed as a striking signpost of wretchedness,[25] which was in fact a true picture of the social landscape in colonial India.[26] Its location and appearance is also a stark pointer to the miserable living conditions of the untouchables and the insensitive treatment of these people by the caste Hindus. Writing on the habitation of untouchables in Bengal in 1949, Nirmal Kumar Bose, a social anthropologist, observes: "Hindu society has always despised this agricultural caste (*Namashudras*), and has gone to the extent of treating its members as untouchables and making them live in separate hamlets on the fringes of the villages."[27] Even in 1950s, an identical condition is encountered glaringly in the context of Khalapur village in the district of Saharanpur of Uttar Pradesh. It is remarked that a legacy of the past is still evident in Khalapur in the spatial isolation of the untouchables' residential quarters, which are scattered about the periphery of the village settlement.[28]

It is this inhumanness and segregation[29] perpetrated within the Hindu society, which has been captured, recorded and evoked through the description of the outcastes' colony in Bulashah town in the novel. Mulk Raj Anand portrays their colony thus:

> The outcastes' colony was a group of mud-walled houses. There lived the Scavengers, the leather workers, the washermen, the barbers, the water-carriers, the grass-cutters and other outcastes from Hindu society .... And altogether the ramparts of human and animal refuse that lay on the outskirts of this little colony, and the ugliness, the squalor and the misery, which lay within it, made it an 'uncongenial' place to live in.[30]

Elsewhere he presents its distinctiveness of form in even more revealing mode:

> ... the outcaste colony, where there are no drains, no light, no water; of the marshland where people live among the latrines of the townsmen, and in the stink of their own dung scattered about here, there and everywhere; of the world where the day is dark as the night and night pitch-dark.[31]

And in this colony, 'the twelve feet by five, dark, dingy, one-roomed mud-house' is all that the untouchables could boast of as their house, which is a grim repository of their shocking poverty and social existence.[32] Moreover a critical observation of the 'material possessions' of these people as portrayed in the house of Lakha as the items of the daily use, i.e., a couple of brooms, an empty refuse-basket, a can, an earthen pan, two earthen pitchers, a chipped enamelled jug, the broken cane chair, a broken string bed, the clay utensils, and an oven of two-bricks or fireplace evidently testify to the enormity of the misery and meagre conditions of these socially marginalized and disadvantaged people.[33] The 'brush and basket' the tools of their occupation and the symbols of their social mortification and existence adorned the façade of their house.[34]

It was customary among the members of this community to obtain their food by going around each house and solicit the caste Hindus for a morsel of it,[35] an aspect that has been brought out in a clear but moving manner in the novel. It is related through the hesitation of Bakha in accepting the food from Rakha, his younger brother, who returns home after his 'successful endeavour' (in begging the food) in which he himself was almost a 'failure'[36] on the day. The predicament of Bakha is presented by the novelist thus:

> Bakha dipped his hands in the basket. There was a heap of food there, broken pieces of chapattis, some whole ones and lentil curry in a bowl. But his hand touched a piece of sticky, wet bread ... . The picture of a sepoy washing his hands in his round tray, over the leavings of bread and salad, and then throwing them in Rakha's basket appeared before him. He had himself gone so often to beg for food and the only thing he hated about it was the sight of those bits of bread softened by the water poured upon them.[37]

This dependence of the untouchables on the caste Hindus for their livelihood and sustenance highlights the stark reality of their social marginalization. The social disabilities reinforce their social exclusion, which they had lived through in the matter of their accessibility to the necessities of daily existence. Their touch was held to pollute such things as cooked food, water, and sacred places.[38] Consequently they were not allowed near upper caste hearths, or wells.[39] Mulk Raj Anand has realistically portrayed it thus:

> The outcastes were not allowed to mount the platform surrounding the well, because if they were ever to draw water from it, the Hindus of the three upper castes would consider the water polluted. Nor were they allowed access to the near-by brook as their use of it would contaminate the stream.[40]

Scavenging or the removal of filth is the characteristic duty traditionally assigned to them.[41] What Bakha inherited as occupation from his father included the job of cleaning "from one doorless latrine to another, cleaning, brushing, pouring phenoil". [42] The ancient traditions, including the transmission of craft skills within the caste, and restrictions on the use of wells and temples, also served to keep the untouchables in their place.[43] The miserable plight of the people, who were denied of direct access to the most vital source of life, has been most objectively portrayed here thus:

> So the outcastes had to wait for chance to bring some caste Hindu to the well, for luck to decide that he was kind, for Fate to ordain that he had time—to get their pitchers filled with water. They crowed round the well, congested the space below it high brick platform, morning, noon and night, joining their hands with servile humility to every passer-by, cursing their fate, and bemoaning their lot, if they were refused the help they wanted, praying, beseeching and blessing, if some generous soul condescended to listen to them, or to help them.[44]

That the members of the untouchable community were prohibited from entering the village temple[45] was one of the agonizing social experiences undergone by these people in the colonial India.[46] Anand has brilliantly demonstrated this aspect through Bakha's fervent desire to enter the village temple, which was, however, not fulfilled as he "realized that an untouchable going into a temple polluted it past purification".[47] Similarly, the anguish of being denied access to education has resonated in the deeply felt yearnings of Bakha for education, who later "realized that there was no school, which would admit him because the parents of the other children would not allow their sons to be contaminated by the touch of the low-caste man's sons".[48]

The adherence to the ossified social practices was a norm, and not an exception. And their enforcement was often cruel. Any deviance from established social pattern was met with brutal action from the caste Hindus. So, it is difficult to say how much physical violence accompanied the transgression of caste mores in the Hindu community across the country through the centuries. Here was a glimpse of the physical violence inflicted on an individual belonging to the untouchable community because he drank water from the temple well in a village of south India.

> In May, some forty years ago (about 1927), when I was ten years old ... we saw an unruly crowd of about fifty or sixty people. My father had the driver of the carriage stop and we saw to our horror a thin, middle-aged man being beaten and chased by the crowd from a Hindu temple on the river bank below. A little inquiry revealed that the man was an Untouchable who had committed the unforgivable crime of drawing water from the temple well to quench his thirst on that hot day. He was 'caught by the act' the temple priest who raised an alarm, attracting the crowd that was belabouring the man. We got down from the carriage and my father shouted to the people below on the sands to leave the man alone which—because my father, who was a civil servant in the Madras Government, and looked like an obviously important citizen—they did, at least for the time.[49]

The novel portrays a similar experience undergone by Bakha but in a different context. The mere touch or presence of the untouchables was polluting to the caste Hindus or the highborn.[50] So, when Bakha inadvertently bumped into a person of high caste Hindu, he was abused and slapped by him. He was also abused by 'the cruel crowd'.[51] Bakha's agonizing and mortifying experience that underline the long-established social existence of untouchables has been brilliantly narrated in the novel. Anand writes on the humiliation of Bakha thus:

> 'You swine, you dog, why didn't you shout and warn me of your approach!' he shouted as he met Bakha's eyes, 'Don't you know, you brute, that you must not touch me!'. 'Dirty dog! Son of a bitch! The offspring of a pig!' he shouted. Bakha 'felt like collapsing'. But the crowd, which pressed round him, staring, pulling grimaces, jeering and leering, was without a shadow of pity for his remorse. It stood unmoved, without heeding his apologies, and taking a sort of sadistic delight in watching him cower under the abuses and curses of its spokesman. To Bakha every second seemed an endless age of woe and suffering. His whole demeanour was concentrated in humility ... . Well, take this for your damned irresponsibility, you son of a swine! And tonga-wallah heard a sharp, clear slap through the air ... .[52]

It is appropriate to observe that the practice of social exclusion and oppression through adherence to the notion of pollution continued to prevail even in the post-colonial India.[53] J. Michael Mahar, a social anthropologist, researching on the untouchables of Khalapur village in the district of Saharanpur in Uttar Pradesh in 1950s and 1960s writes thus:

> A man of the Shoemaker caste was observed as he was about to enter Khalapur with a load of tanned cow hides on his head. An elderly Rajput rose from his porch, brandished a stick, and threatened to thrash the shoemaker if he did not reverse his course and proceed around the outskirts of the village.[54]

Similarly, social segregation was so transparent that the members of the untouchable community were not allowed to sit in the presence of social superiors. Any lapse on the part of these untouchables would invite the wrath of the caste Hindus. Here is a typical incident narrated by the social anthropologist on this aspect. He writes thus:

> On one occasion, for example, an elderly Chamar was invited into the anthropologist's room and asked to be seated on a chair. At first the Chamar declined, but after much urging, he sat down. Shortly thereafter a middle-aged Rajput happened to glance into the room. He immediately cursed the Chamar and told him to remove himself from the chair or he would be beaten for his impertinence.[55]

Not very dissimilar to the context cited above, a caste Hindu lady witnessing Bakha resting on the steps at the entrance of the house began to abuse him thus, "May you perish and die! You have defiled my house! Go! Get up, get up! You eater of your masters! Why didn't you shout if wanted food? Is this your father's house that you come and rest here?"[56] It is this realistic representation of the extant social reality that establishes the 'untouchable' as an important critical literary source on the social history of the untouchability in colonial India.

The language used in social discourse reflects social reality.[57] It also reveals the nature of social relations that is embedded in the social discourse among the social classes. The use of the vocabulary by the caste Hindus in the social discourse is one of dominance and condescension. The mode of address and the tone of voice in issuing instructions to the members of the untouchable community is a mode of asserting their social superiority.[58] And the language used in the daily discourse also served as a medium to reinforce this objective. It was highly abusive and derogatory. When critically understood in the context of the contemporary social circumstances, its use in the text acquires definite social significance. Hence, a critical look into the 'idioms and commonplaces of culture and discourse' related in the narrative positions the point clear that the text was written in the context of prevailing traditions of discourse, available languages and vocabularies of legitimation.[59] The social discourse underlined the social subordination of these hapless people. Accordingly, the reassertion of the attitudes of social arrogance of caste Hindus was seen in the every day experience of these untouchables.

Anand has quite typically brought out this important social aspect of the manner of addressing the untouchables by the caste Hindus and the tenor of their arrogance as expressed in their daily social discourse. Havildar Charat Singh's shouting at Bakha using swear words thus "Oh, Bakhya! Oh, Bakhya! Oh, you scoundrel of a sweeper's son! Come and clear a latrine for me!",[60] Lalla, the caste Hindu and the tormentor of Bakha, cursing him with rage, "you rogue of a Bahke!. You swine, you dog, why didn't you shout and warn me of your approach! Dirty dog! Son of a bitch! The offspring of a pig!",[61] Panditji (Priest of the village temple, who attempted to molest Sohini) shouting at the untouchables gathered around the well, "Get away, you noisy curs, get out of the way!",[62] a shopkeeper throwing a warning at Bakha, "You be sure to shout now, you illegally begotton! If you have learnt a lesson!"[63] and the cursing of Bakha by a caste Hindu lady thus, "may the vessel of your life never float in the sea of existence! May you perish and die! You have defiled my house! Go! Get up, get up! You eater of your masters! Why didn't you shout if wanted food? Is this your father's house that you come and rest here?"[64] were all characteristic of the depths of the verbal humiliation to which the members of this community were subjected. Here the discourse of social discrimination, the atmosphere of social subordination, and the language and tenor of upper caste arrogance, which underscore the social life of untouchables in colonial India, were clearly presented.[65]

The life of the untouchables was one of deprivation. They were denied equal access to the services. Thus the denial of service to the untouchables has also served to define their lowly place in the caste hierarchy,[66] an aspect that has been narrated in the text quite movingly through Lakha's pleading the village doctor to save his son (Bakha) from a persistent fever. The wretchedness and the vulnerability of untouchables in such crucial movements imploring when being denied the most essential service is reverberated through the words of Lakha thus: " Hakim ji, I shall be your slave all my life. The meaning of my life is my child. Your shoe on my head".[67]

Like the food, the clothing used by these people was also scanty. While the patched, greasy, discoloured and inadequate blanket used in the Lakha's family, a simple tunic and pair of baggy trousers worn by Bakha's mother, Sohini's trousers and a transparent muslin shirt with no bodice, and the borrowed clothing of Bakha reveal their wretchedness that of the caste Hindus, i.e., Havildar Charat Singh's wearing of lion-cloth, and money-lender Ramanand's wearing of a transparent muslin cloth and a shirt indicates the characteristic patterns of traditional wear.[68]

The oppressive social milieu as expressed in the incidents of humiliation that has been experienced by Bakha in a single day set him to ponder and interrogate himself thus "Why was all this?"[69] Finding no answer, he recoils himself and begins to shout signifying his adherence to the repressive and iniquitous social order thus "*Posh* Keep away, *posh*, sweeper coming, *posh*, *posh*, sweeper coming, *posh*, *posh*, sweeper coming!".[70] This social mortification of Bakha, a representative of a socially excluded community and a victim of an unjust social structure, has been well depicted textually by the narrator thus: "I am an Untouchable!" he said to himself, an "Untouchable!" he used to announce his approach: '*posh*, *posh*, sweeper coming.' The undertone, Untouchable, Untouchable, was in his heart; the warning shout, *posh*, *posh*, sweeper coming was in his mouth.[71]

To conclude, Mulk Raj Anand for the first time through his inspired text in English portrayed contextually the travails of the socially oppressed and marginalized untouchable caste in colonial India. He exposed the inhumanness that in fact characterized the traditional social relations embedded in Hindu society. He conveyed to the world much more effectively through the medium of his highly authentic and influential social fiction that a section of humanity has been kept under the conditions of degradation for such a long period in Indian history.

This trend of realistically representing the subalternity of the untouchable community continued throughout the twentieth century and in post-colonial India. In the late 1960s and 1970s, the state of Maharashtra had witnessed an explosion of literature by Dalit writers constituting thus a remarkable phase in the development of social fiction in post-colonial India. These writers drew from a shared experience of caste subordination and their accounts are marked by anger and agony that embody the subalternity of Dalit community. Shalini Ramachandran writes thus: "The writers identified themselves as Dalit, an old Marathi word meaning 'ground' or 'reduced to pieces', thus calling attention to the continuing oppression of untouchables in Indian society. Since the 1970s, the term Dalit has gained currency as a self-chosen name of political and cultural identity for untouchable communities throughout the country".[72] It is, therefore, quite significant to note that Mulk Raj Anand's masterpiece *Untouchable* presaged the upsurge of genre of critical works on the various dimensions of subalternity of untouchables in India.[73]

Moreover, through exploring the diverse aspects of subalternity of the untouchables in the text *Untouchable*, an attempt has been made to establish relationship between the novel and social history. Literary texts at once reflect and enact history.[74] The text acquires a definite historical significance, as it can be located in a contemporary context of social conventions.[75] The *Untouchable* thus quite realistically depicts the several social disabilities experienced by the members of untouchable community.[76] Though the text sensitively focuses only on a single day's experiences of an untouchable in Bulashah, it unmasks the oppressive social milieu that was in existence and a social process that has been continuing with little change in India. Thus, Anand's text mirrored the contemporary social environment in colonial India.[77] So, due to its realistic representation of social conditions, it can be certainly regarded as a critical text for the study of social life of the untouchables in the first half of twentieth century. And it can also be constructively used as an important source for construction or reconstruction of the social history of untouchability in particular, and the caste system in general, in colonial India.

Telling the saga of suffering; a critical exploration of marginality in *Nectar in a Sieve* (1954) by Kamala Markandaya:

> Hope, and fear. Twin forces that tugged at us first in one direction and then in another, and which was the stronger no one could say. Of the latter we never spoke, but it was always with us. Fear, constant companion of the peasant. Hunger, ever at hand to jog his elbow should he relax. Despair, ready to engulf him should he falter. Fear; fear of the dark future; fear of the sharpness of hunger; fear of the blackness of death.[78]

The disastrous consequences of British colonial rule continued to confront the life of Indian peasants and had not subsided in rocking their existence even after India's independence in 1947. Therefore, the post-colonial India still witnessed the spectre of poverty, unemployment, population growth, malnutrition and other wretched conditions of life and was still the site of sheer deprivation in 1950s. It was during this epoch that Kamala Markandaya sizzled out the most pathetic narrative, i.e., *Nectar in a Sieve* in 1954 on the travail of a tenant family in located in time and space in colonial south India. It was a narrative of a south Indian peasant family, which had undergone most traumatic experiences in their life. The unrelieved fading of their happiness and their slow slithering into the vicious trap of poverty and degradation on account of failure of crops and onset of famine conditions forms the central theme of the novel. Furthermore, the two sons left them in search of work and never to return to their parents, and the other two sons died in the course of their struggle for survival confronting the poverty and malnutrition. The tale never ends there. Driven by the fate or heartless of the landlord, the peasant family had to relinquish the land, which they had been cultivating for decades and to which they were deeply attached and migrated to the city, where they became quarry workers. The long deprivation and the exhaustion of struggle for survival culminated in the death of Nathan, the quintessence of love and life for Rukmani. Thus, for the hapless peasant family, the nectar of life was lost in the sieve of relentless poverty and deprivation.

Nectar in a Sieve is Kamala Markhandaya's first novel to be published and it became a best-seller around the world. The novel was published in 1954, less than a decade after India won its independence from Britain. It is evidently influenced by this event, depicting some of the difficulties encountered by the Indian people as they negotiated with the changing epoch. The narrative does not refer to a specific time or place, however, which gives the story universality.

Some of the troubles that the main character, Rukmani, encounters are not only the consequences of the changing times, but they are the kinds of problems such as destitution, deprivation, death, loss of tradition that are experienced by many people for many reasons in contemporary India.

"'I shall have a grand wedding" I would say. "Such that everybody will remember when all else is a dream forgotten." This was the imagination of Rukmani as girl child about her forthcoming marriage. But her imaged world came crashing, when her parents married her to a "tenant farmer who was poor in everything but in love and care" for her. She was even further depressed and wanted to cry when she came to know that the home she was going to live was "nothing but mud and thatch".[79] However, she got reconciled to the life of being the wife of the farmer Nathan.

Living for the peasant family in the initial phase of their married life was not hard as it was, it was to present itself in the later days. As the size of the family was large with eight members, it was difficult for the family to feed all the children properly. The fortunes of the family began to decline and the under-nourishment was yet to become a fact of their daily life. "A dowry of one hundred rupees", which they had to pay for getting their only daughter, Irawaddy (Ira) married, was a big drain on their meagre and dwindling resources. Placed as they were in such delicate situation, they agreed to go for the match. Else, "One hundred rupees will not win such a husband, we have no more."

In India, the world of the peasants was very much dependent on the vagaries of nature. Their very existence was dictated by the twists and turns of the nature. Rukmani, Nathan's wife best summarizes the perception of how the peasants look at the nature and how their lives are intertwined with its munificence or ferociousness. Nature has been perceived not only as a regenerative force but as one with an infinite power of destruction. It is conceptualized as a trained 'wild animal', which, if not treated sensitively or disregarded, has the ability to be more destructive in its disposition. Untamed nature is represented to be treacherous and ruthless. The author explicates it in the musings of the narrator, Rukmani, the wife of Nathan: "Nature is like a wild animal that you have trained to work for you. So long as you are vigilant and walk with thought and care, so long will it give you its aid; but look away for an instant, be heedless or forgetful, and it has you by the throat".[80] She also communicates movingly the picture of the fury of the nature through incessant rains dislocating the lives of the peasants, washing out the paddy in the corn fields and rendering several people homeless. The devastation was visible in the uprooted trees, dead dogs, cats and rats cluttering the roadside. The storm had left in the entire village 'disaster and desolation'. And now their life was one of struggle for survival.

What could perhaps be a common sight in even contemporary rural India is strikingly communicated by the novelist in the narrative and the ruthless rupturing of life and rural landscape is eloquently portrayed thus:

> In the village the storm had left disaster and desolation worse than on our own doorstep. Uprooted trees sprawled their branches in ghastly fashion over streets and houses, flattening them and the bodies of men and women indiscriminately. Sticks and stones lay scattered wildly in angry confusion. The tannery stood, its bricks and cement had held it together despite the raging winds; but the workers' huts, of more flimsy construction, had been demolished. The thatch had been ripped from some, where others stood there was now only a heap of mud with their owners' possessions studding them in a kind of pitiless decoration. The corrugated iron shacks in which some of the men lived were on more: here and there we could see the iron sheets in unexpected places—suspended from tree tops, or blown and embedded on to the walls of houses still left standing. There was water everywhere, the gutters were overflowing into the streets. Dead dogs, cats and rats cluttered the roadside, or floated starkly on the waters with blown distended bellies.[81]

The novelist also demonstrates that the occurrence of a severe famine is another instance of the inestimable destructive power of nature. Famines are not uncommon phenomenon in colonial India. The failure of rains, which can disorganize the world of peasants, is touchingly conveyed by the novelist through the bewailing of Rukmani that "Each day the level of the water dropped and the heads of the paddy hung lower. The river had shrunk to a trickle, the well was dry as a bone".[82] Rukmani complains that "the earth is parched to dust and all that I grew is dead".[83] She moves on lamenting on the unrelenting impact of the drought:

> The drought continued until we lost count of the time. Day after day the pitiless sun blazed down, scorching whatever, still struggled to grow and baking the earth hard until at last it split and great irregular fissures gasped in the land. Plants died and the grasses rotted, cattle and sheep crept to the river that was no more and perished there for lack of water, lizards and squirrels lay prone and gasping in the blistering sunlight.[84]

As the scorching heat endured for days and days, the hopes of the family for a better harvest got evaporated.

Starvation had become a stark reality and a constant companion of their life, as almost all that was grown on the land had been sold to pay the rent of the land. It had begun to unfold its debilitating power and the tentacles among the poor and the hapless peasants in the village. It pushed the sons of the peasant family to become workers in the tannery. It also stirred the rise of the militant temper among the hitherto docile individuals. It awakened them to redefine their attitude to the life and occupation. One of the sons of Nathan and Rukmani had this to underline the life of exploitation, to which they were subjected: "If it were your land, or mine, I would work with you gladly. But what profit to labour for another and get so little in return? Far better to turn away from such injustice" (p. 74).

The two elder sons, Arjun and Thambi, growing conscious of the exploitation in the tanning factory, become involved in the labour dispute and subsequently lost their jobs. They were also discontented and thought of those like his father Nathan, "who have sold themselves cheaper than dirt" as tenants. However, forced by the unemployment and the prospect of starvation, the two sons migrate to Ceylon to work in the tea plantations and they never returned.

Man's emotional attachment to the land is the other dimension, which is remarkably communicated in the text. It may be possible "for a year perhaps" but "not forever".[85] The grievous questions such as "Where can we go?", "Where are we to go?", and "What shall we do?" reflect the dilemma of the peasants and their emotional and existential attachment to the land. They also express the excruciating trauma of those who find themselves suddenly displaced from the land on which they have been living for decades. It is particularly relevant in the present context of the struggles being launched by the Indian peasants to protect their land through forcible acquisitions by the state governments or the private individuals. This aspect can be grasped from the lament of Rukmani:

> This hut with all its memories was to be taken from us, for it stood on land that belonged to another. And the land itself by which we lived. It is a cruel thing, I thought. They do not know what they do to us.[86]

The bond between the land and humans is demonstrated to be eternal. The idea that those who work on the land 'cannot live except by the land' asserts the belief of the novelist in the unbreakable tie between the people living in the countryside and the land. Rukmani and Nathan, who, when displaced of their land, migrated to the town, had always thought of returning to the land. The ruminations of Rukmani display the deep attachment of the people to their land.

> With each passing day the longing for the land grew; our plans were forged against a background of brown earth and green fields and the ripe rustling paddy, not, curiously, as they were, but as we had first known them ... fresh, open and unspoilt, with their delicate scents and sounds untainted, with the skies clear above them and the birds finding sanctuary amid the grasses.[87]

The declaration of Selvam to his father that he "can always return to the land" and "... live as we did." reasserts the writer's faith in infinite and indissoluble association between the land and the people. The brown earth that is part of us needs to be cared. She reminds us to be attentive not only to harness the land but also to replenish its sapped energies.[88]

To the novelist, nature is a vital sustaining force of human life. It is therefore important to preserve and protect it from rapacity of humans. So, the narrator forcefully articulates her concern for preservation of the nature's serenity. She expresses her views strongly against the industrialization and its harmful bearing on the natural environment. She considers that the insensitive industrialization not only pollutes the natural landscape but also dislocates the lives of the people in rural India. A critical interrogation of the text reveals the writer's implicit ideas on this aspect.

Markandaya discreetly displays her unhappiness over the dislocation consequent to the beginning of industry on the lives of the villagers. She is distrustful of its advantage. The change it brings is rapid, violent and disorganizing.

> Change I had known before, and it had been gradual. My father had been headman once, a person of consequence in our village: I had lived to see him relinquish this importance, but the alteration was so slow that we hardly knew when it came. I had seen both my—parents sink into old age and death, and here too there was no violence. But the change that now came into my life, into our lives, blasting its way into our village, seemed wrought in the twinkling of an eye. Arjun came with the news that "Hundreds of men," he gasped. "They are pulling down houses around the maidan and there is a long line of bullock carts carrying bricks." ... "It is the new tannery they are building," he said.[89]

Markandaya believes that the change ushered in by the growth of industry marginalizes the subalterns by displacing them from their lands and ruining their very livelihoods. And she is strongly convinced that growth of industry is not a signpost of everlasting happiness for majority of people eking out their livelihoods in the rural areas:

> It was a great sprawling growth, this tannery. It grew and flourished and spread. Not a month went by but somebody's land was swallowed up, another building appeared. Night and day the tanning went on. A never-ending line of carts brought the raw material in—thousands of skins, goat, calf, lizard and snake skins—and took them away again tanned, dyed and finished. It seemed impossible that markets could be found for such quantities—or that so many animals existed—but so it was, incredibly.

> Somehow I had always felt the tannery would eventually be our undoing. I had known it since the day the carts had come with their loads of bricks and noisy dusty men, staining the clear soft greens that had once coloured our village and cleaving its cool silences with clamour. Since then it had spread like weeds in an untended garden, strangling whatever life grew in its way. It had changed the face of our village beyond recognition and altered the lives of its inhabitants in myriad ways. Some—a few—had been raised up; many others cast down, lost in its clutches. And because it grew and flourished it got the power that money brings, so that to attempt to withstand it was like trying to stop the onward rush of the great juggernaut.
>
> But for us as we were now, and others like us, there could be only resignation and resentment. ... but we had lost more than we had gained or could ever regain. Ira had ruined herself at the hands of the throngs that the tannery attracted ... . My sons had left because it frowned on them; one of them had been destroyed by its ruthlessness. And there were others its touch had scathed. Janaki and her family, the hapless chakkli Kannan, Kunti even ... .[90]

The beginning of the industry meant invading their village with clatter and din, taking away from them the maidan where their children played, and making the bazaar prices so high for them. In the distressing voice of Rukmani, the novelist sharply brings out the impact of the rising prices on the life of the rural folks thus: "what could I buy with the money prices so high everywhere? No sugar or dhal or ghee have tasted since they came, and should have had none so long as they remained".[91] She is sharply critical of the other consequences such as the industrial pollution and the disruption to the tranquility of the rural landscape. Answering to Kunti's query that "Are you not glad that our village is no longer a clump of huts but a small town ... . Soon there will be shops and tea stall, and even a bioscope,"[92] Rukmani said:

> No doubt I will," I said. "It will not gladden me. Already my children hold their noses when they go by, and all is shouting and disturbance and crowds wherever you go. Even the birds have forgotten to sing, or else their calls are lost to us.[93]

Markandaya is also highly critical of the effects of the industrialization and urbanization on the natural environment and inestimable damage to the purity of nature. She also sharply conveys how the humans become insensitive to the aesthetics of nature. The ill effects of the urbanization are seen in the growth of unhygienic conditions and the disoriented life of humans. The final outcome of this process in the towns is the loss of man's connection with the aesthetics of nature, the ultimate benefactor of humanity. This view is extraordinarily communicated by the novelist thus:

> Not in the town, where all that was natural had long been sacrificed, but on its outskirts, one could still see the passing of the seasons. For in the town there were the crowds, and the streets battened down upon the earth, and the filth that men had put upon it; one walked with care for what might lie beneath one's feet or threaten from before or behind; and in this preoccupation forgot to look at the sun or the stars, or even to observe they had changed their setting in the sky: and knew nothing of the passage of time save in dry frenzy, by looking at a clock. But for us, who lived by the green, quiet fields, perilously close though these were to the town, nature still gave its muted message. Each passing day, each week, each month, left its sign, clear and unmistakable.[94]

Markandaya voices her sharp protest against the demoralizing impact of the industrialization. She also endeavoured to highlight the disorganizing effects of urbanization spurred on by the progress of industrialization. Her representation of unhygienic conditions in the towns and her distaste for highly urbanized cities conspicuously reflect her intense anguish at the catastrophic environmental impact of colonial and post-colonial industrialization. Her fictionalized narrative of the changing landscape on account of the growth of industry does indicate not only the rapid pace of the process of marginalization of the rural communities but also the emerging consciousness for the protection of the natural environment. Her narrative becomes all the more significant in the context of rising environmental awareness in different locations of the world. The novelist has been able to portray through her fictional representation not only the marginalization of a peasant family but also the incalculable damage done to the nature rupturing its broad contours in the name of development. She forcefully communicates her ideas on how man and the nature are interlocked in a symbiotic relationship. She also brilliantly demonstrates that the survival of humanity depends on the sensitive treatment of nature. Certainly, she expresses her concern for careful husbanding of resources. Any thoughtless approach or any disregard to the dynamics of nature and its functioning, or any move to alter or redesign its contours would only lead to the consequences, which would be quite unimaginable to the human mind or which would put the survival of humanity in jeopardy. So, Markandaya's *Nectar in a Sieve* can rightly be considered a critical text for comprehending the process of marginalization of rural communities in post-colonial India.

Similarly Mulk Raj Anand's *Untouchable* is a significant literary text of early twentieth-century Indian writing in English representing the resentment and helplessness of an individual in the face of a dreadful and decadent social practice of scavenging that often meant carrying containers of human faeces on the head to the place of disposal. Through the poignant portrayal of the lives of the untouchables in the hilly town of Bulashah, the novel describes their depressing poverty and vulnerability in disturbing detail. Nonetheless, it is not just the conditions of living of the untouchables that delineate the grim ethos of this social fiction; the exceptional quality of *Untouchable* lies in the realistic portrayal of the social oppression that persisted in colonial India. Anand's work thus becomes truly a project of liberating the marginalized and oppressed outcastes from the tyrannical traditional Hindu social system. Though the text ranges over various literary terrains, it retains its own complex connection to the historical context of agonizing social oppression, denial of equal opportunity and the stirring of resolved resistance in an individual. It connects the inexpressible social and psychological agony of an individual to broader historical context of social oppression. It also brilliantly depicts the yearnings of an individual to attain and maintain a semblance of social, cultural, psychological and creative freedom. The book ends with an avid anticipation for change. Therefore, the narrative becomes the discursive means for the emancipation of the marginalized community.

It can be concluded that while Mulk Raj Anand explored the theme of social marginality, which an individual representing a social community had intensely experienced, Kamala Markandaya brilliantly demonstrated the depths of economic marginalization to which a peasant family was forced to sink and suffer its consequences. Both the narratives are enduring and outstanding illustrations of social and economic marginality not only in the era during which they have been articulated but they also retain a critical relevance and bearing to the contemporary socio-economic conditions in India. It may be apt to end by quoting the Cuban leader Fidel Castro's words of forewarning to the mankind that political development as well as limitless and irrational technological creations in the world are putting mankind's survival at risk. He said: "Extermination wars, climate changes, hunger, thirst and inequality surround us everywhere." He add that mankind is threatened as never before "by the combinations of society's political underdevelopment and the technological creations, apparently limitless and beyond all rationality in their self-destruction capability".[95]

Notes

1. Alpana Sharma Knippling, "Twentieth-Century Indian Literature in English", in Nalini Natarajan et al. (eds.), *Handbook of Twentieth-Century Literature of India*, London, 1996, p. 89.
2. Rajan, P.K. (ed.), *The Growth of the Novel in India 1950–1980*, New Delhi, 1989, p. X.
3. Srinivasa Iyengar, K.R., *Indian Writing in English;* New Delhi, 2001, p. 325. Romesh Chunder Dutts' *The Lake of Palms;* (1909), T. Ramakrishnas' *The Dive for Death;* (1912), S.K. Ghoshs' *The Prince of Destiny: The New Krishna;* (1909), Sir Jogendra Singhs' *Nasrin;* (1915) and *Kamni;* (1931), Firoz Khan Noons' *Scented Dust*, Hari Singhs' Gours' *His only Love*, Ahmed Alis' *Twilight in Delhi;* (1940) and Kumara Gurus' *Lifes' Shadows* and *A Daughters' Shadow* were all interesting works of social fiction on diverse aspects of colonial Indian society.

   Note: The Lake of Palms by R.C. Dutt is a study of social life in Bengal towards the close of the 19th century. It portrays the action climaxes in the marriage of the young widow Sudha to Sarat, *The Dive for Death* by T. Ramakrishna is knit around the certain superstitions which make cowards of the characters, Sir Jogendra Singhs' *Nasrin* presents the self-indulgence of the Nawabs and Taluqdars of yearster years. And his *Kamni* is about the pathetic life of a barbers' daughter, Hari Singh Gours' *His only Love* is a study of the consequences of the emancipation of Indian women, Ahmed Alis' *Twilight in Delhi* is a narrative of Muslim life in modern Delhi. The theme of Kumara Gurus' narratives unusual psychological studies set against the backdrop of a changing Hindu society-changing but not necessarily for the better.
4. Srinivasa Iyengar, K.R., op. cit., p. 318.
5. Ibid.

   Note: The best works of Sarat Chandra Chatterjee are *Srikanta, Grihadaha, Pather Dabi, Bipradas* and *Ses Prasna. Srikanta* have been translated into English by K.C. Sen and Theodosia Thompson and some others.
6. To mention a few remarkable texts of the period: Mulk Raj Anands' *The Sword and the Sickle*; K.A. Abbass' *Inquilab*; K.S. Venkataramanis' *Kandan the Patriot*; Raja

Raos' *Kanthapura*; N.S. Phadkes' *Leaves in the August Wind*; Bhabani Bhattacharyas' *So Many Hungers*. These were outstanding commentaries on the extent political and social environment of colonial India. See Kesavanarayana, B., 'Social Reform and Telugu Literature, 1920–1947, Presidential Address, Socio-Economic History Section, *Proceedings of South Indian History Congress*, Kalady, 1998, p. 137.

Note: In Telugu language, the works of social relevance were: Doma Venkataswamy Guptas' *Malapilla, The Mala Girl*, 1936, Karlapalem Krishna Raos' *Mallepuvu*, 1935, Madduri Annapuranayyas' *Mala*, 1936, Somanchi Suryanarayana Sarmas' *Malavadu*, 1938. See also Srinivasa Iyengar, K.R., op. cit., pp. 323–324.

7. Nalini Natarajan et al. (eds.), *Handbook of Twentieth-Century Literature of India*, London, 1996, p. 11. For instance in Hindi, Munshi Prem Chand in *Godan* delved deep into the soul of peasants. He explored the complexity of village life, while presenting the characterization of authentic individuals. In Telugu, Unnava Lakshminarayana's *Malapalli*, The Hamlet of Untouchables, in 1921 was the first novel in Telugu to present the social evil of untouchability in a fictionally compulsive manner. In the novel, the writer depicted the emerging social forces urging immediate correcting of imbalances with remorseless objectivity. *Malapalli* is a trendsetter in a number of ways. For the first time, the social underdog becomes the subject of a literary work in the regional expressions. The life of the inhabitants of a Harijan hamlet is rendered in the local dialect used by those people. It was a work of fiction that has been turned into a powerful forum for foregrounding social tension and ideological conflicts. See also Kesavanarayana, B., op. cit., p. 137; and Subbarayudu, G.K., and Vijayasree, C., "Twentieth-Century Telugu Literature", in Nalini Natarajan et al. (eds.), op. cit., p. 321; In Oriya, Gopinath Mohanty's *Harijan*, 1948, deals with the sufferings of the untouchables and dramatizes the contrast between two ways of life: the life of the rich and the life of the poor untouchables. The novel is full of bitterness, of direct social criticism but it ends in the defeat of the untouchables; See Jatindra Kumar Nayak, 'Oriya,' in Rajan, P.K. (ed.), op. cit., pp. 51–53; In Kannada, the literature turned its eyes and heart towards marginalized groups such as the factory worker, the farmer, the compositor in the printing press, the prostitute and the beggar.

   Note: A.N. Krishna Rao believed "Only humanist values can save the world from exploding and the writer is the prophet of humanism". When he wrote *Nagna Satya, Shani Santaana* and *Sanje Gaththalu*, that threw light on the issues of prostitution, the conservative writers were shaken and called him a 'vulgar writer' for writing such a subject. "If telling the truth is vulgar, then I am a vulgar; if the act of covering with a cloth, a downtrodden, helpless, naked woman on the street is vulgar, then I am a vulgar writer" was Anakru's reply (A.N. Krishna Rao was popularly known as 'Anakru'), See Seshagiri Rao, L.S., 'Kannada' in Rajan, P.K. (ed.), op. cit., pp. 111–113.

8. Sharma, I.K., 'Hindi', in Rajan, P.K. (ed.), *The Growth of the Novel in India*, New Delhi, 1982, pp. 32–33.
9. Mulk Raj Anand, "The Story of My Experiment with a White Lie", in M.K. Naik et al. (eds.), *Critical Essays on Indian Writing in English*. p. 5.
10. Ibid., p. 13.
11. Ibid., p. 5.

12. Ibid., pp. 5–6.
13. Ibid.
14. Khan, A.G., "Mulk Raj Anand: Crusader for the Downtrodden", *The Journal of Indian Writing in English* (hereafter *JIWE*), Vol. 33. No. 1, January 2005, p. 6.
15. Ibid., p. 7.
16. See also for a critical analysis of the emergence of Dalit literature in Tamil Nadu; GJV. Prasad, "Tamil Dalit Literature: A Brief Overview", in I. Thirumali (ed.), *South India: Regions, Cultures and Sagas*, (New Delhi, 2004), pp. 157–162; For Andhra region see, P. Kesava Kumar, "Emergence of Dalit Novel in Telugu: An Overview", Thirumali, *South India*, pp. 163–170; Also see, A. Satyanarayana, "Dalit Protest Literature in Telugu: A Historical Perspective", *EPW*, January 21, 1995, pp. 171–175; Also see, Veena Deo, "Dalit Literature in Marathi", in Nalini Natarajan et al. (eds.), op. cit., pp. 363–380.
17. Steven N. Zwicker, *Politics and English Literary Culture, 1649–1689*, (Ithaca and London, 1993), p. 1.
18. Henry James, *The Art of Fiction*.

    Note: Referring to the analogy between the art of painter and the art of novelist, he writes thus: "As the picture is reality, so the novel is history. That is the only general description (which does it justice) that we may give the novel. But history also is allowed to compete with life, as I say; it is not, any more any more than painting, expected to apologize. The subject-matter of fiction is stored up likewise in documents and records, and if it will not give itself away, as they say in California, it must speak with assurance, with the tone of the historian".
19. Brunton, T.D., "India in Fiction: The Heritage of Indianness", in M.K. Naik et al. (eds.), op. cit., p. 219.

    Note: The caste system is here shown not as a static structure, but as a system of social intercourse. Its cruelty is harshly apparent.... In this book, it seems to me, we learn something both about ourselves as human beings and, more generally, about the quality of social life in India. Dr Anand has stuck to the novelists' prime task of depicting the limited, the specific, and the concrete.
20. Srinivas, M.N., *Caste in Modern India and Other Essays*, (Bombay, 1962), pp. 63–64; Also see, Kate L. Mitchell, *India without Fable: A 1942 Survey*, (New York, 1942), p. 22.
21. Marc Galanter, *Competing Equalities: Law and the Backward Classes in India*, (London, 1984) p. 13; Also see, Sir George Schuster, *India & Democracy*, (London, 1941) p. 43; Gail Omvedt, *Reinventing Revolution: New Social Movements and the Socialist Tradition in India*, (New York, 1993), p. 8.
22. Kumar Goshal, *The People of India*, (New York, 1944), p. 44.
23. Marc Galanter, op. cit., p. 15; See also for a detailed account of the social disabilities suffered by the untouchables in India, Dhananjay Keer, *Dr. Ambedkar: Life and Mission*, (Bombay, 1962), pp. 1–2.
24. Rajshekar, V.T., *Dalit: The Black Untouchables of India*, (Atlanta, 1987), p. 16.
25. Joan P. Mencher., "Continuity and Change in an Ex-Untouchable Community of South India", in J. Michael Mahar (ed.), *The Untouchables in Contemporary India*, New Delhi, p. 39.
26. Kate L. Mitchell, *India without Fable: A 1942 Survey*, New York, 1942, p. 23.

27. N.K. Bose, *The Structure of Hindu Society,* (New Delhi, 1975), p. 157; Also see Dhananjay Keer, op. cit., pp. 1–2.
28. Michael Mahar, J., "Agents of Dharma in a North Indian Village", in J. Michael Mahar (ed.) op. cit., p. 18.
29. Kate L. Mitchell, op. cit., p. 23.
30. Mulk Raj Anand, *Untouchable,* p. 1; Also see Dhananjay Keer, op. cit., pp. 1–2.
31. Mulk Raj Anand, *Untouchable,* p. 75.
32. Ibid., p. 2 and 6.
33. Ibid., p. 6, 13, 14 and 67.
34. Ibid., p. 7.
35. Michael Mahar, J., "Agents of Dharma", op. cit., p. 23.
36. Mulk Raj Anand, *Untouchable,* p. 59, 65, and 68.
37. Ibid., pp. 75–76.
38. Marc Galanter, op. cit., pp. 14–16; Also see Kate L. Mitchell, op. cit., p. 23.
39. Michael Mahar, J., "Agents of Dharma", op. cit., p. 18.
40. Mulk Raj Anand, *Untouchable,* p. 14.
41. Gardner Murphy, (1953), *In the Minds of Men: The Study of Human Behaviour and Social Tensions in India,* New York, p. 35.
42. Mulk Raj Anand, *Untouchable,* p. 8.
43. Michael Mahar, J., "Agents of Dharma", op. cit., p. 25.
44. Mulk Raj Anand, *Untouchable,* p. 15; Also see, Marc Galanter, op. cit., p. 16.
45. Michael Mahar, J., "Agents of Dharma", op. cit., p. 18 and 26; Also see, Adrian C. Mayer, (1960), *Caste and Kinship in Central India: A Village and its Region,* Berkeley, p. 57.
46. Marc Galanter, "The Abolition of Disabilities-Untouchability and the Law", in J. Michael Mahar (ed.), op. cit., p. 229.
47. Mulk Raj Anad, *Untouchable,* p. 49.
48. Mulk Raj Anand, *Untouchable,* pp. 30–31; Also see Marc Galanter, *Competing Equalities,* op. cit., pp. 14–15; Also see Sir George Schuster (1941), *India and Democracy,* London, p. 43; Also see Dhananjay Keer, op. cit., pp. 1–2; Also see Rajshekar, V.T., op. cit., p. 54.
49. Chandrasekhar, S., "Personal Perspectives on Untouchability", in J. Michael Mahar (ed.), op. cit., XI; Also see J. Michael Mahar, "Agents of Dharma", op. cit., p. 22 and 26.
50. Morris E. Opler, "North Indian Themes-Caste and Untouchability", in J. Michael Mahar (ed.), p. 5; Also see Marc Galanter, *Competing Equalities,* p. 14.
51. Mulk Raj Anand, *Untouchable,* pp. 38–42.
52. Ibid.
53. Judith M. Brown, (1994), *Modern India: The Origins of an Asian Democracy,* Oxford, p. 395; Also see for the persistence of untouchability in Jugundla village of Thimapur mandal of Karimnagar district of Andhra Pradesh, where some school children and also their parents refused to eat food that was prepared and served by a Dalit woman in the government school, *The Hindu,* 15 April 2005, Hyderabad.
54. Michael Mahar, J., "Agents of Dharma", p. 22.

55. Ibid., p. 23.
56. Mulk Raj Anand, *Untouchable*, p. 63.
57. See for a critical analysis of the concept of language, Raymond Williams, (1977), *Marxism and Literature*, Oxford, pp. 20–43.
58. Michael Mahar, J., "Agents of Dharma", p. 23.

    Note: Ironically, the swear words used by Englishman in Hindustani such as *kala log zamin par hagne wala* (black man, you who relieve yourself on the ground), *sur ka bacha* (son of a pig) and *kute ka bacha* (son of a dog) signify the racial arrogance of colonizer as against the colonized'; See Mulk Raj Anand, *Untouchable*, pp. 10–11 and p. 114.
59. Pasi Ihalainen, "Language and Literature in Intellectual History", in David Robertson, (1994), (ed.), *English Studies and History*, Tampere English Studies 4, Tampere, p. 226.
60. Mulk Raj Anand, *Untouchable*, p. 7.
61. Ibid., p. 38 and 39.
62. Ibid., p. 21.
63. Ibid., p. 42.
64. Ibid., p. 63.
65. Ibid.
66. Michael Mahar, J., "Agents of Dharma", p. 22; Also see Marc Galanter, *Competing Equalities*, p.15.
67. Mulk Raj Anand, *Untouchable*, pp. 72–73.
68. Ibid., p. 5, 6, 9, 11 and 14.
69. Ibid., p. 42.
70. Ibid.
71. Ibid., p. 44.
72. Shalini Ramachandran, "'Poisoned Bread': Protest in Dalit Short Stories," *Race and Class*, Vol. 45. No. 4, 2004, p. 27; Also see Sathianathan Clarke, "Dalits Overcoming Violation and Violence: A Contest between Overpowering and Empowering Identities in Changing India", *The Ecumenical Review*, Vol. 54, No. 3, 2002, p. 278; To find both articles, visit www.questia.com.
73. See also for a critical analysis of the emergence of Dalit literature in Tamil Nadu; GJV. Prasad, "Tamil Dalit Literature: A Brief Overview", in I. Thirumali (ed.), *South India: Regions, Cultures and Sagas*, (New Delhi, 2004), pp. 157–162; For Andhra region see, P. Kesava Kumar, "Emergence of Dalit Novel in Telugu: An Overview", Thirumali, *South India'*, pp. 163–170; Also see A. Satyanarayana, "Dalit Protest Literature in Telugu: A Historical Perspective", *EPW*, January 21, 1995, pp. 171–175; Also see, Veena Deo, "Dalit Literature in Marathi", in Nalini Natarajan et al. (eds.), op. cit., pp. 363–380.
74. Steven N. Zwicker, (1993), *Politics and English Literary Culture, 1649–1689*, Ithaca and London, p. 1.
75. Henry James, *The Art of Fiction*.

    Note: Referring to the analogy between the art of painter and the art of novelist, he writes thus: "As the picture is reality, so the novel is history. That is the only general description (which does it justice) that we may give the novel. But history also is allowed to compete with life, as I say; it is not, any more any more than painting, expected to apologize. The subject-matter of fiction is stored up likewise in documents and records, and if it will not give itself away, as they say in California, it must speak with assurance, with the tone of the historian."

76. Judith M. Brown, *Modern India*, p. 20.

    Note: It is difficult for contemporaries to grasp the power of caste conventions in the past, although they operated well into this century. A novel such as M.R. Anands' *Untouchable*, the *Outcaste's Autobiography* by Hazari or a village study can best bring the social order to life.

77. Brunton, T.D., "India in Fiction: The Heritage of Indianness", in M.K. Naik et al. (eds.), op. cit., p. 219.
78. Kamala Markandaya, (1954), *Nectar in a Sieve*, p. 110.
79. Ibid., p. 13.
80. Ibid., p. 57.
81. Ibid., pp. 60–61.
82. Ibid., p. 101.
83. Ibid., p. 104.
84. Ibid., p. 108.
85. Ibid., p. 69.
86. Ibid., p. 182.
87. Ibid., p. 225.
88. Ibid., p. 48.
89. Ibid., p. 39.
90. Ibid., pp. 67–68, 180–181.
91. Ibid., p. 43.
92. Ibid., p. 44.
93. Ibid., p. 44.
94. Ibid., p. 156.
95. *The Hindu*, 27–06–2007.

12 The 'Other' Amidst 'Us'

The Narrative of the Domestic Worker

TUTUN MUKHERJEE

In these times when we valorize independence and self-sufficiency, rarely do we consider how service-dependant we actually are in our daily lives, or spare a thought for those people whose labour ensures our personal comfort and the smooth running of our homes. In fact, in the hierarchical Indian society, these are the people who constitute a class of their own: that of the 'domestic worker', a silent ubiquitous presence in all upper and middle class homes across India.

A 'domestic worker' is generally understood to be a servant who often lives in the employer's household. They are distinguished from 'serfs' and 'slaves' because they receive payment for the work they do. They also have the freedom to leave their job if they wish to. Typically, a domestic worker in an Indian home takes care of the house; runs errands and purchases vegetables and other food items; performs sundry odd jobs and household chores like cooking, cleaning and washing utensils and clothes; takes care of the very young or the elderly and/or the disabled. On the whole, they comprise a vast unorganized labour force that has as yet no laws or rules to either assist or govern it. There is no specific age suitability or limit for the domestic worker—one can be anything between the age of 7 or 80 of either sex—child labour being rampant in India. There is no job description commensurate with age or sex, other than perhaps for a driver or a watchman (jobs generally confined to adult male workers till date) nor designated hours of work; no wage specifications or rights and/or privileges that one can demand or claim; no norms to monitor the employer-employee relationship. The best deal that a domestic worker can get is through careful negotiation with the employer. The payment they receive, often too paltry to be called 'salary', could be a combination of cash and food and for the very abject and needy, only food. Their future out of employment is uncertain, often bleak, and to cope with sudden adversities of life like illness or

---

Literary texts can claim to be sources of ethnography. In her paper, "The 'Other' Amidst 'Us': The Narrative of the Domestic Worker" Tutun Mukherjee explores ethnographic motivations in literary texts. Her study focuses on two literary texts: *The Diary of a Maidservant*, a translation of Krishna Baldev Vaid's Hindi novel *Ek Naukrani ki Diary* and *A Life Less Ordinary* by Baby Halder translated into English from Bengali original *Alo Andhari*.

senility, any form of help or compensation they may expect depends entirely on the temperament and generosity of the employer.

It is not surprising, therefore, that the domestic workers are vulnerable to exploitation and oppression. With shocking regularity the media report stories of cruelty and abuse meted out to the domestic workers employed in India or abroad.[1] In response to the persistent need to address the problems of the domestic workers, few organizations sprang up in Mumbai with the mandate to make a difference in their working conditions but till date there is no noticeable change in their status.[2]

Theirs is also the voice that has remained unheard—mainly because there is really no one they can communicate with beyond their own immediate community and certainly because of the lack of literacy among them. After all, in our capitalist-consumerist societies with the 'use-and-throw' culture, not many of us care to respond to the call of the distressed, especially the poor working class. If and when they choose to speak, one can only wonder how fascinating or horrifying (to go by the reports of the cruelty they often endure) their articulations could be, considering their role as witnesses to the interplay of human relations and the web of complex motivations within the family and the human escapades of various kinds that occur in the domestic sphere.

Yet, one recalls that this was not always the way the domestic workers were treated in India. In the joint family system which is fast disintegrating, a servant was regarded as a member of the family and identified affectionately by kinship-signifying honorifics like 'chacha/ kaka/ mama' (uncle) or 'bhaiya' (elder brother) in the case of a male servant; and 'didi', 'mousi/bua' (aunt) or 'dhai ma' (foster mother) in the case of a female servant. They enjoyed many liberties and could even influence individual or family decisions. They were trusted completely. In return, they gave their lifelong service and unswerving loyalty. Stories about the loyal retainer are galore in our annals and become the *rohstuff* of legends. The history of the Rajputs, for instance, carries the tale of Panna Bai who sacrificed her son to save her master's son. It is said that the Moghul emperor Akbar honoured his 'dhai ma' (nurse) as much as his mother and listened to her advice even on administrative matters. The Indian entry for the 2007 Oscars was one such story of a royal guard Ekalavya who would not hesitate to lay down his life to protect his master from all dangers. A well-remembered poem "Puratan Vritya" (the old servant) by Rabindranath Tagore describes the way a servant selflessly nurses his master afflicted by the feared small-pox and dies consequently of the contagious disease.

One cannot be sure when the disjunction really happened to sour the employer-employee relationship and estrange the domestic worker within the family. Gradually however, the domestic servant became commodified as an anonymous service provider and began to be identified by the work they performed as 'cook', 'driver', 'watchman', 'ayah', or 'bai'. Their identity and individuality were effaced and their intimate bonding with the family they served, ceased. The relationship became a matter of expediency for the two parties, governed purely by monetary concerns. Thus, with the disappearance of the old values of mutual trust which used to perpetuate human understanding and mutual help, the domestic servant gradually became the 'other' in our midst.

This paper discusses two texts that articulate the inner life of the domestic worker in contemporary times and the changed social contexts when s/he figures as the 'other' in a household. The relationship with the family s/he works for is also extremely fragile. The first text is called *The Diary of a Maidservant*, a translation of Krishna Baldev Vaid's Hindi novel *Ek Naukrani ki Diary*. It is an imagined and fictional account of the daily activities of Shanti or Shano, a young girl who earns her livelihood by working as a maid in few households in a Delhi suburb. The second text titled *A Life Less Ordinary* by Baby Halder is a translation from its Bengali original *Alo Andhari*. It is an exciting text which claims to be an authentic autobiography of a domestic servant—perhaps the very first to have ever been written in India.[3]

The Diary of a Maidservant (2007)

Shanti, the protagonist of Vaid's novel, is a semi-literate teenager who has left school—as children of many impoverished families often do—to help her mother earn their upkeep by working as a domestic help in several households. As Shanti dusts and cleans, she also turns the pages of the newspapers and books that lie around on the tables. Noticing Shanti's interest in books and other reading material, an educated and kindly Mrs Varma gives her a notebook to write in. Shanti is thrilled with the gift and starts to write down her thoughts and daily experiences (9–10). Thus begins Shanti's documentation of the activities that fill her days, the experiences which were at once diverse and monotonous, her thoughts and feelings about the people she interacts with, and her tentative reflections upon the 'rightness' and 'wrongness' of things. Begun merely as an exercise in curiosity, these daily jottings in her notebook become almost an obsession as she fills notebook after notebook with comments about her employers, their families, attitudes and personalities. The sahibs and the memsahibs, the good-for-nothing brother who turns up only when he needs money, the lecherous shopkeepers and her friends in the community of maidservants, are all perceived with the curiosity of a young mind and budding maturity and portrayed with their idiosyncrasies.

Shanti copes with a family struggling to survive, predatory males, demanding mem-sahibs, and a multitude of her own desires. By writing her thoughts in the diary she educates herself about the ways of the world and understands her relationship with others around her. Even the kindness of her middle-aged employers, 'Biji' and 'Newspaper Sahib'—two people who idealistically set out to improve Shanti's lot in life—brings problems with it especially because not all the employers are generous like them. Some of them nag and complain endlessly:

> Fatty Mem began yakking again while I was dusting today. What is it you people eat that gives you so much energy? You'll break everything to bits! How many times do I have to tell you that you've got to handle my things gently! The way she throws them around! And such expensive things, too! God only knows if there are any brains in that head of hers or just bhoosa! (2)

Shanti follows her mother's advice of not retaliating to such shrewishness. It is better to get another job and leave, she is told. Her mother also shares with her the worldly knowledge about employers:

> Ma says all mistresses are alike. They're all as mistrustful and miserly as you can get. And the masters are all lecherous and lustful. But this Fatty is the worst! Fatty is jealous of me. She knows I'm prettier than her. Her husband knows it too .... All mistresses are jealous of their young maidservants. They see them as potential co-wives. They are afraid the maidservants will steal their husbands. Ma says some maidservants do just that .... (2)

The people Shanti meets are given nick-names which reveal their nature and her own attitude towards them. Some get her respect while others are treated with scorn. She thinks that she understands her employers very well and can manipulate them easily. For instance, while she respects Newspaper Saab who treats her with affection, she does not hesitate to take advantage of his good nature and credulity:

> I didn't even feel like going over to Newspaper Saab's. I'd have to make up a lie to tell him tomorrow, so what? Newspaper Saab is an innocent man. Any lie at all would work with him. I've noticed that elderly men are often innocent. Sometimes they're a bit stupid too. But not all of them! Some old men are real rascals, such as our hakeem. The Newspaper Saab is very well-educated, but completely simple. He never sees through my lies. He believes whatever I tell him. (18)

It is inevitable that the servants get to know all about the domestic upheavals and problems of the families they work for. Such knowledge, as is well known, is often the source of neighbourhood gossip and feeds the network that circulates information about the residents of an area. Shanti, for example, discusses the 'rumpus' in the Bengali family she works for when the family learns of the elder daughter Jharna's relationship with a Muslim boy. Shanti records the twists and turns of the story till Jharna's suicide.

Woven into the many strands of the stories that her work as domestic help brings to her notice, is Shanti's own narrative of initiation into adulthood. She tests her knowledge on human interaction with the budding maturation which accompanies puberty and experiments with sexuality with the men she meets, whether it is the adolescent son of the Fatty Mem, the odd-jobs man Electric Suresh, or the young vendor she awaits every evening. She also learns to weigh the options that life has to offer through her own experiences and those of her friends and acquaintances and the consequences thereof which could be sweet or bitter. The diary becomes her confidante to record her struggles and disappointments, her dreams and desires, and the gradual maturing of her body and mind. It becomes a means of self-discovery as Shanti explores her feelings through her writing. Sometimes she writes in despair:

> Ma says masters and mistresses are by nature mean, you can't trust them, they don't have any sympathy for our kind, so you should never trust what they say. Ma has gotten old scrubbing other people's pots and pans. Just like Ma, I will grow old slogging as a servant. My children too. (1)

Or, in a spirited resistance of the inevitability of fate, she declares: "I'll never marry. I'll never have children. I'm a maidservant of the new age. I feel like laughing and crying at the same time" (1). There is also regret: "I shouldn't have quit school. By now I'd have passed tenth. But then what? I'd still be a maidservant who'd managed to pass her tenth" (1). It novelist seems to be interested in creating the impression of the uncertainties and ambiguities of the immediate situation, an effect that is heightened during moments of Shanti's insights into various situations. As Ashok Vajpayi writes in the "Introduction" to the volume, "Vaid explores the multiple layers of modern Indian individual—his [her] well of phantasy and interiority" (xiv). It is evident, however, that Shanti feels empowered by her ability to write down her thoughts. She describes herself as a rare case: the 'story-writing maidservant' which, she conjectures, may make her appear arrogant or the 'hung-up' in others' eyes (25).

The fascination and appeal of Shanti's diary is retained till the end, though there is no story line as such, nor a conclusion. When the novel closes, Shanti is alone at home. She enjoys her solitude, feeling as though she is "soaring like a black rain cloud" full of promise. She announces with confidence, "I'll start a new notebook tomorrow" (258).

A Life Less Ordinary (2006)

The second text, translated as *A Life Less Ordinary* is claimed to be an autobiography of Baby Halder, a domestic servant who is encouraged by her employer Prabodh Kumar, a retired anthropology professor living in Gurgaon, to write the story of her life.

The narrative of the self begins with the pleasant recollection of Jammu & Kashmir where Baby's father initially works and the family lives till she is four-years-old. They visit Murshidabad in West Bengal briefly where their relatives live before travelling to the father's new place of work at Dalhousie. After a year, the family returns to live permanently at Murshidabad near their uncle's home while the father rejoins his job. For the next few months the father writes and sends money quite regularly. But soon both letters and money stop coming. With four children to feed, their mother finds it very difficult to manage even with the help of their relatives and neighbours who are not well off themselves. Her mother struggles to keep the household going but finally exhausted by her husband's extended absences and his failure to provide for the family, goes to the market one day and does not return ... till twenty years later when Baby is already a mother of three. Yet Baby does not seem to bear any grudge towards her mother for her desertion of the children, perhaps because subsequently, she herself feels the agony and despair of bearing alone the burden of rearing children and losing the fight for survival and dignity. When her mother does return, she seems estranged and detached and Baby's feelings towards her are closer to pity than resentment. Her feelings towards her father are more ambivalent although she describes him without any apparent trace of anger. The father comes across as a complex character. He is not a typically loving father or a provider; he beats her for telling her school friends that there was no food at home; begins to bring home one 'new mother' after another and does not stop his 'wife' from ill-treating the children and making them do all the housework. Yet his is the home where the children return when they need a shelter. Perhaps Baby feels that the pulverizing impact of poverty makes him self-centred, unscrupulous and uncaring about his children.

The intermittent spells of schooling of the children finally stop as there is no money to spare and soon, because their father can no longer afford to keep her, the elder daughter Sushila is married off. Baby is too young to understand the significance of the preparations for her own marriage when she reaches puberty. She writes about her excitement with the new things being bought for her wedding:

> ... before I knew it I was twelve years and eleven months old. One day I saw Baba and my Mami coming back from the bazaar with bags full of vegetables ... I noticed a suitcase lying nearby. I asked Baba about it and he told me it had things for my wedding. My stepmother and Mami opened the suitcase and showed me what was inside. I was so happy to see all those wonderful things! The next day Baba bought me a new quilt, mattress and a pillow and I was beside my self with joy! (33–34)

She recalls that she "laughed a lot that day" (34). But later, thinking back,

> Baby wonders how she spent that day of sorrow in such merriment. Little did Baby know that this was the beginning of her days of grief and pain, little sis she known what the future held for her ... . (34)

She is married off to a much older and an abusive husband and the horrifying realization about her new married life follows soon after. She becomes pregnant but a thirteen year-old can hardly be expected to understand how to cope with the changes in her body or how to take care of herself. Shankar, her husband neither looks after her nor gives her money to buy food and other provisions. There are daily quarrels at home. Barely understanding what is happening to her, she is rebuked by the doctor for 'choosing' at so young an age to have a child. The childbirth itself is excruciatingly painful for her ill-treated underfed body. Her first son is born, making Baby a mother at the age of thirteen.

Baby's suffering continues and two more children are born to her. One day the news comes that her sister Sushila is dead, beaten and strangled by her husband. There are similar stories of oppression and cruelty suffered by the women in her neighbourhood. It seems to be women's lot to be beaten and burnt. Baby's own troubles become aggravated when a neighbour Ajit bothers her with his unwelcome attentions. As she fears, her husband holds her responsible and beats her repeatedly and mercilessly:

> Finally I decided I would not stay silent any more and I began to answer back when my husband threw accusations at me. We spent nights fighting and screaming at each other. I hated the language he used; I hated being beaten; I simply wanted to pick up my things and run away. (81)

She goes away to her father's place several times but "after two or three days, Baba would bring me back and leave me there" (81). Matters come to a crisis when during a fierce altercation, Shankar picks up a "stone from the ground and hit me on the head with it. My forehead split apart, and blood gushed out ... . All I asked my husband was what I had done to be beaten like this. The words were barely out of my mouth when he picked up a sturdy piece of wood and began hitting me on my back" (84). Being pregnant at the time, Baby feels a piercing pain in her stomach that steadily exacerbates, making her thresh about in agony. Her suffering finally ends in an abortion a couple of days later.

Unable to bear more violence, Baby Halder decides to live separately from her husband:

> I'm not going there any more. Only I know what I have had to bear living with him, now I've had enough. If I go back, the same will start all over again and my life will not only be living hell but also a sideshow for any one who wants to watch. (118)

For her livelihood she begins to work as a domestic servant. But apprehensive that she may not be allowed to live alone for long, she decides to go away to her elder brother and boards a train to Delhi, where she searches for and finds work as a domestic servant. She manages to eke out a living and initially even sends out her small son to work. Her experience with her various employers is unpleasant in general. Some of them even insist that she lock her children in the attic while she worked. It is back breaking work from six thirty in the morning till late at night for the meagre amount of money and two meals that she gets. Unable to bear it for long, she decides to leave one day:

> One day I took my children and left. I did not ask Memsahib or wait for her permission, or take my things. I just left. (144)

Her desperation is apparent in her writing. A single parent at twenty-five, struggling to feed her three children by working as a maid for a series of exploitative employers, Baby Halder has hardly any time to even contemplate upon the harsh reality of her existence until she starts working in the home of a sympathetic retired academic, who finds her browsing through his books when she was meant to be dusting the shelves. He discovers her interest in literature and that she has attended school till class seven. When he learns that she can read and write well, knows about the works of Rabindranath Tagore, Kazi Nasrul Islam, Sharatchandra, Satyendranath Dutt, Sukumar Rai, he is amazed. He gives her more books to read, notably Taslima Nasreen's *Amar Meyebela* (My Girlhood). He also gives her a notebook and pen, and encourages her to start writing whatever she wished:

> If you want, you can write your life story in this. Whatever has happened in your life ever since you can remember and you became aware of yourself. Whatever you remember up to now, write it down. Try to write a little bit every day. (152)

Her employer makes her feel as though she is a part of his family and encourages her to call him 'Tatush' as his sons and their friends do. He offers her a home when their tenement gets bulldozed. Baby feels secure and happy again. Tatush helps her eldest son find a job where could also study. She is encouraged to take her children to the nearby park in the evening where she meets other maidservants and can talk with them as friends.

Perhaps seeking an outlet to express her suffering, Baby Halder decides to write the story of her life. She writes at night after her chores are done. Left alone with her memories, she pours the narrative of loss, deprivation and pain of her early life into the notebooks. Prabodh Kumar, who is also her mentor is impressed with what she has written and tells her to continue her narrative. After several months, he sits down with her and helps edit her text to give it a chronological shape of a book. He then sends the manuscript to a few of his friends for their feedback. They compliment Baby profusely saying that her writing reminds them of Ashapurna Devi and Anne Frank. One day, a parcel comes for her containing a magazine which has published her "Alo Andhari".

Baby Halder recounts her life story in plain language and style. The narrative is rough, devoid of any literary embelishment and conveys without a trace of sentimentality or self-pity the grim depiction of the typical life of a poor Indian woman. There is raw emotion but no rage. She rarely blames her father or husband for the cruelty she has experienced. But the facts stand out powerful and clear.

Baby Halder is now 32-years-old and despite her book's success, has no plans to change careers. She has a vocation, however. "I want to be a writer and I will continue to write," she says. When asked to talk about her book during an interview, she says:

> Where should I start? Should I begin with how when I was seven-years-old my mother suddenly left us by thrusting a coin each in our hands, or tell you about how my nephew told my Baba that he saw his father strangling his mother, my Didi, to death, or how my Baba used to suddenly vanish from our life and then resurface. Or should I tell you about my husband to whom I was married to when I was 12 and why I left him and came to Delhi with my three children? (np)

What she considers most significant is that her book talks about the life of women like her: "Many girls back home go through a similar life and yet nobody looks at it as anything different." She hopes that the story of her life would sensitize the society about impoverished women, many of whom eke out their living as domestic workers.

Summing Up

Vaid's text is a 'novel-diary' or a fictional diary—comprising features of both the literary forms. The 'diary' is a 'private' kind of writing that has a specific and an identifiable point-of-view and a single 'voice'. At its purest, diary writing is a form of self-reflection, a therapeutic mediation of one's life that is not intended for others' knowledge. It would also seem, as in the case of Anne Frank, that the depth of emotions expressed in the diary reflects the degree of stress and trauma suffered by the writer. Hence, the habit of keeping a diary, of creating a narrative of events, thoughts, hopes and emotions, may be considered at one level intensely private. Yet, as the history of the form makes evident, diaries, like letters/epistles, may also be seen as following certain widespread cultural conventions of expression and topic and for this reason diaries have also been written by public figures such as Swift, Evelyn and Pepys to analyze contemporary society, politics and culture with the future readership in mind. Clearly, a diary can be a valuable document of individual life as well as of historical and social circumstances. Literary critics therefore prefer to regard diaries as *personal* rather than *private* texts. Diaries are shaped by moments of inspiration and the writing of them tends to evolve gradually as a habit. The writer of the diary reveals the play of tension—between concealing and revealing—which vies with the pleasure of self expression. Whereas letters are written to a certain addressee as the 'other', diaries are ostensibly written for oneself or an 'imagined other' addressed sometimes as 'Dear Diary' or by a fictitious name like Anne Frank's "Kitty".

Fictional diaries or novels employing the diary form represent a significant literary genre used by eminent writers like Dostoevsky (*Notes from the Underground* and *Diary of a Writer*), Gogol (*Diary of a Mad Man*), George and Weedon Grossmith (*Diary of a Nobody*), Sue Townsend (*The Secret Diary of Adrian Mole*), William Butler (*The Butterfly Revolution*), Helen Fielding (*Bridget Jones's Diary*). None of these can be called a 'fake' diary. Each is a piece of writing purporting to combine a personal and intimate tone with social rhetoric. Michal Glowinski describes the form as occupying the in-between space between the two literary genres.

Diary of a Maidservant manifests the basic characteristics of the novel-diary discussed above. Shanti's point-of view becomes the writer's lens for examining middle class life from 'below'[4] and from a female perspective. It is also a social commentary on the life of the working class, their daily struggles and travails and exploitation at their workplace. The writer shows a tendency to typify the characters and situations which are obviously fictitious, yet they are not too far from the real. Though a teenager, Shanti's insights into the characters are remarkably valid showing her to be mature beyond her years. This too is a cruel reality of the children of poor parents who are forced into adulthood before their adolescence is over. Inevitably at the same time Shanti reveals the vulnerabilities of her age. It is commendable that Vaid succeeds in conveying an authenticity in his protagonist's 'voice' and her style of articulation.

Amelia Gentleman compares Halder's *A Life Less Ordinary* to Frank McCourt's *Angela's Ashes*, the Pulitzer Prize winning account of his unhappy childhood in Ireland. Both the texts present the sedimentation of the experiences of pain and loss expressed with sadness and resigned acceptance. Since one function of the past is to explain the present, each autobiographical recovery of the past makes some claims about the subjectivity of the writing 'self' in the present circumstance, the person's family, social background, and history. As the eminent philosopher-psychologist Sir Frederick C. Bartlett explains in his book *Remembering* (1932), memory is not a thing labeled by a noun, but rather an activity labelled by a verb. Memories are things people may have, but remembering is something people do to reconstruct them in accordance with ideas of the self and the views about who one is and how s/he got that way. Such 'construction' of the past is within the accepted 'grammar' of the literary form of autobiography or the procedure of 'writing the self'.

Baby Halder's autobiography excavates the past to explain her present position as a domestic servant. Her writing becomes an enabling process which, by recollecting the past, leads her towards the realization of her selfhood and subjectivity. Although there is in the book the description of the typical life of a domestic servant, the focus here is more on the personal growth of a confident individual who finds respectability in her chores as a domestic worker and dignity in being able to write about her life.

Halder's book has scored many 'firsts'. Reviews of Halder's book have hailed it as breaking the 'tradition of silence' (Kapur) about the little known lives of 'Others' who live amongst us. Responding to an interviewer's question whether the writing of her autobiography has brought any change, Halder answers (2007):

> The 'Baby' who existed earlier, that Baby has gone. She does not exist. There are so many women like her, who have their own stories, their own thoughts. But to know what they think, you must take time, like Tatush did with me. There is a second Baby now, and this Baby is yours (She gestures at the journalists gathered around). She is your creation. As for me, my story is still incomplete.

It also attempts to restore the long-forgotten bonds of friendship and understanding between the employer and the employee within the domestic sphere. A little help from a kind and sympathetic employer made the emergence of a confident 'Baby Halder' possible. A sensitive community of employers might urge more such 'silenced voices' to speak up and share their unique stories to change social perception about human interaction.

It must also be acknowledged that the transmission of the two fascinating texts into English is successfully achieved without incurring any loss of style or cultural specificities. The self effacement of the translators must therefore be appreciated. The translations make it possible for the texts to reach the wide readership they richly deserve.

Notes

1. Equally horrifying are stories of murderous attacks on employers by the domestic workers. Such incidents underline the distrust that has vitiated the relationship.
2. Exemplifying some solidarity, women servants working in big apartment complexes in Delhi, Mumbai and Kolkata have tried to itemize the types of work to be done with the payment to be received. Due to this kind of solidarity, if a servant is fired for no reason, the employer finds it difficult to get a replacement.
3. Such a document would be first of its kind in India though there are several such accounts, both fictional and real, available in Europe and Australia. A recent film, *A Maid in Manhattan* is of course a typical Hollywood fantasy.
4. Here 'below' indicates the subaltern perspective.

References

Baker, Russell and William Zinsser, 1987. *Inventing the Truth: The Art and Craft of Memoir*. (Ed by William Zinsser). Boston: Houghton Mifflin

Conway, Jill K. 1998. *When Memory Speaks: Reflections on Autobiography*. New York: Alfred A. Knopf.

Field, Trevor. 1998. *Form and Fiction in The Diary Novel*. Basingstoke: Macmillan,

Glowinski, Michal. *New Literary History*. Vol. 9, No. 1 (Autumn) 103–114.

Halder, Baby. 2006. *A Life Less Ordinary*. Tr. Urvashi Butalia. New Delhi: Zubaan, (Published as *Alo Andhari* in Hindi in 2002; in Bengali in 2004).

———. 2007. Interview published in *Business Standard* of January 26.

Heilbrun, Carolyn G. 1988.*Writing a Woman's Life*. New York: W.W. Norton & Co.

Hill, Bridget. 1996. *Servants: English Domestics in the Eighteenth Century*. New York. Clarendon Press of Oxford UP.

Kapur, Mita. 2007. "Writing has to be Classless," *The Hindu Magazine* Sunday, Apr 15.

Morson, Gary Saul.1981. *The Boundaries of Genre: Dostoevsky's 'Dairy of a Writer' and the Traditions of Literary Utopia.* Austin: Texas University Press.

Sprengemann, William C.1980. *The Forms of Autobiography: Episodes in the History of a Literary Genre.* New Haven/ London: Princeton University Press.

Vaid, Krishna Baldev. 2007.*The Diary of a Maidservant.* Tr. Sagaree Sengupta. New Delhi. Oxford University Press, (Published as *Ek Naukrani ki Diary* in Hindi).

Vellacott, Helen. 1995. *Diary of a Lady's Maid.* (Ed). Melbourne: Melbourne U. Publishing.

13 Depiction of Women in Ao-Naga Folk Tales

RESENMENLA LONGCHAR AND J. LIMAINLA AO

The central focus of this paper is drawn from the rich repository of folk tales and folk beliefs that are part of the Ao-Naga world view. In these oral sources, one finds many sets of actors who are constantly negotiating different role and status. In addition to human beings' we also find superhuman being characters like animal, spirit and mystical beings. Since the focus is on a woman which is under the research theme, and it tries to argue in the set of folk tales where women play a significant role as transmitters of the cultural traditions. They also leave a story which is at a considerable distance from the other folk and textual representation of the Ao-Naga. The point which is emphasized here is that, since the stories were authored (in most cases) by women and circulated in certain spaces where women have relative autonomy, a different picture emerges. In some places, the women are seen as other, the predicaments of women, power and moral authority. The last two are represented by using magical devices of transforming one's physical personality into a spirit as dispute arbitrator in both parties would listen to the moral authority of an elderly woman.

Though many of them do not fall within the standard accounts of the Ao-Nagas, where men are shown as brave and do the hunting and central figures in the art of bravery. Here we find the inversion of roles, status, and the power structures which is a considerable asymmetry between the other sources on the Naga history like the colonial records, church records, performing arts, ethnographical records etc. The fact is that these sources speak about different sets of themes and different order of things in itself shows that there is no singular process of uttering.

Folk tales and folklores are not only the primary source of recreation for the bulk of the people, but are inseparable also from ritual and work. Thus, the tradition of folklore is an important and living part of the socio-cultural milieu and deserves serious attention. The historians may see in folklore the common person's version of a sequence of grant events already charted, the anthropologists sees the oral expression of social systems and cultural meaning, the literary scholars look for genres of oral literature, the psychologists for universal imprints and so on. Most of the scholars have concentrated on certain kinds of genres, centred their attention on traditional grouping of people looking upon their ethnicity, religiosity and occupation. Thus, they concentrated on the question of how the lores and tales might show forth the dynamics of the group itself.[1]

In the 19th century, the term 'Folk' was inevitably defined as a dependent rather than an independent entity. Folk was defined in contrast, on the one hand, with 'civilization' and on the other hand with the so-called 'savage or primitive society'. In this way, the discipline of folklore did not have any strong interface with the discipline of history and, therefore, anthropological methods from folklore were suspended and de-legitimized by contemporary historians of the 19th and 20th century. The folk were understood to be 'the illiterate in a literate society' as opposed to the primitive people, who were ethnocentrically labeled 'pre-literate'.[2]

The immediate bearing of these practices on the historiography of the Nagas can be easily discerned; primacy of published administrative, ethnographic and church records which extension privileged one's set of themes and understanding and at the same time blocked out significant facets of society that have been lost. An example is in the near total absence of any major works on the role of bamboo in everyday life of the Naga and Mizo people. In a few years, the process of modernization, changing production process, compounded by linkages with market economy will erase completely the role of bamboo which is already being marginalized. The picture was diametrically opposite a century or half a century ago when around 65 species of bamboo with multiple uses found a favoured place in the socio-economic and cultural matrix of the Nagas.[3] Thus the marginalization of bamboo from the Naga historiography has in a way rendered the history of the Nagas incomplete. The reason this is grounded is due to the reluctance of historians to incorporate methods from folklore.

Folklore represents a tremendous spectrum of human expressions that can be studied in a number of ways and for a number of reasons. Its primary characteristic is that, its ingredients seem to come directly from dynamic interactions among human beings in communal-traditional performance contexts rather than through the more rigid likes and fossilized structure of technical instructions or bureaucratized education, or through the relatively stable channels of the classical traditions.

One of the main arenas for the study of folklore and folk culture was rural environment. It was focused primarily on lower classes, peasants, simple folks, backward cultures and primitive people, for it was believed that these kinds of people had avoided or resisted longest the sophisticating influence of the so-called advanced culture. Conversely, urban dwellers immersed in literature and sophistication, were thought to be immune to folklore. Thus, the 19th century view of folk and folklore was defined as dealing with peasants, lower class and lacking the benefits of education and progress.

Accordingly, the assumption seems to have been that, only away from the influence of technology and modern civilization would one find those antique remnants of tradition that might reveal to us the early stages of our cultural existence. This basic assumption for the normal habitant of folklore still exists today where folklore is understood to be, by definition, the traditions of the rural people. There have been skirmishes over the widespread view that folklore is simply, pagan detritus, stuff leftover from previous barbaric times, passed along by ignorant and illiterate peasants who didn't know any better or degenerated material from once courtly sources.[4]

If the 19th century's definitions of the folk as illiterate, rural and backward peasants are to be accepted then the study of the lore of such folk might well be strictly a salvage operation and the folk culture will tend to disappear in those places where a high degree of industrialization develops. It can also be said that folk cultures can hardly be said to exist in the developed countries.

Thus, Alan Dundes in his book; *Interpreting Folklores* defined folk as 'the term *Folk* can refer to any group of people whatsoever who share at least one common factor. It does not matter what the linking factor is—it could be a common occupation, language or religion—but what is important is that a group formed for whatever reason will have some traditions which it calls its own. In theory a group must consist of at least two persons, but generally most groups consist of many individuals. A member of the group may not know all other members, but he will probably know the common core of traditions belonging to the group, traditions which help the group have a sense of group identity.[5] One of the most common external criterions used to define folklore or folk tale is the way in which folklore is transmitted.

Having highlighted some of the glaring problems in the historical writings, one of the methods to retrieve some lost ground would be the adoption of methods from folklore and thereby use folk tales as a source. Advances in historical linguistics like study of loan words, phonological structures etc., had led many scholars to take a re-look at folklore in general and the folk traditions of the Nagas in particular.[6] The problem of primary and secondary orality is so beautifully tackled by Walter. J. Ong in his work on, 'Orality and Literacy' and has helped restore the legitimacy of oral traditions. Relating this to the Ao-Naga history, all forms of folklore and folk tales are transmitted through oral tradition or passed orally from generation to generation. Thus, oral tradition is one of the most common methods used to review the past.

Temsula Ao, in her book *The Ao-Naga Oral Tradition* describes N. Scott Momaday's definition of oral tradition. It says "the oral tradition is that process by which the myths, legends, tales and the lores of people are formulated, communicated and preserved in language by word of mouth, as opposed to writing, or it is a collection of such things".[7]

Jan Vansina, describing about oral tradition states that "memories can be faithful repositories which contain the sum total of the past human experience and explain how and why of present day conditions. Through memory the mind carries culture from generation to generation. How it is possible for the mind to remember and to spin out of nothing, complex ideas, messages and institutions for living, which manifest continuity over time, is one of the greatest wonders one can study. Oral tradition should be of central importance, central to a student's culture, ideology, sociology, psychology, art and finally history".[8]

Among the Naga tribes, there exists a legend which revolves in different versions about how the written records of the Nagas were lost and how they were doomed to be without literacy. It goes on to say that, in the beginning God gave the knowledge of writing and reading both to the Nagas in the hills and the plainsmen, but, whereas the plainsmen were given stone or paper on which to record their writings, the Nagas were given a book of skin which came to an end owing to its edible quality. Consequently, while the plainsmen preserved their records permanently, the Nagas lost their scripts. Thus, the folk literature, be it the fiction and stories or songs were simply stored in memory and passed on from generation to generation orally and the orally transmitted stories and tales of the ancestor's social and cultural lives, customs, religions practices and political organization were reviewed in reconstructing the Naga history.

We may divide the whole narrative tradition into two broad categories. On the one hand are those tales, which are generally believed by the folk to be based on actual happenings, and on the other are those, which are told primarily for amusements. The Naga folk tales have distinctive features of their own. They reflect the mind, the character, the background, the belief system and taboos, the superstition, the tradition, the culture and everything that makes the Nagas distinct from others.

There are stories based on various animals and birds that help in locating the ecology of the Nagas. These, besides offering morals of ethical value, reflect an amazing affinity between human beings and the animals. There are also stories based on the ill behaviours of stepmothers to their children. There are stories relating to the creation of the earth, origin of the Nagas, transformation tales, some tales of the supernatural forces and how headhunting began as well. On the whole, however, the tales portray a large variety of men and women with local colour.

Most of the Naga tribes have more or less the same story about the creation of the earth and they credited to the Supreme Being, how he works and reveals his mysteries through creation.[9] Tales relating to the Ao-Naga tribe, mention of a God named Lijaba and of all the gods or Tsungrems, Lijaba is considered to be the Almighty and all powerful one and also the creator of the universe and all the creatures inhabitating it. It is also believed that the earth is balanced on *Lijaba's* head.[10]

W.C. Smith in his book, *The Ao-Naga Tribes of Assam*, narrated the myth relating Lijaba the creator of the world. He writes, "the outlook of the Ao's is very limited and to them the world contains their own little territory and that of a few others of the neighbouring hill tribes, together with the portion of the Assam Valley that is visible to them from their hills. When he had smoothed out the present valley, and was ready to begin operations on the hills, a cockroach came and told him that war demanded his immediate attention. He discontinued his work, never to take it up again. Consequently we have the rugged hills where the Ao's live".[11]

Similar to what Smith describes, we also find in the book of J.P. Mills, *The Ao-Nagas*, where he even attributes to Lijaba the creation of the world. He worked quietly and steadily at first, and had time to make the plains smooth and neat. But just as he began work on the area where the Naga Hills are now, a water beetle called out "Enemies are upon you. So he had to work in a desperate hurry and only had time to make a jumble of hills".[12] Thus, through this illustration, one can say that, Nagas too believed in the Supreme Being, that is God of the creator and attributes them with sacrifices of animals and foods.

In the Naga folk tales, there are many stories, which have animals as their principal characters. Those animals portrayed in the tales generally do not act as animals but behave and speak like human beings making the animal more anthropomorphic in nature. Reviewing those animal tales, we can find that it was the animals who decided to have day and night alternatively, it was the cock who persuaded the sun to return or to rise when, only the cock crows. The monkey showed the way of making fire, the birds pointed out the place where the water was available, the rat brought and gave the rice to humans and the squirrel, cock, buffalo and pig helped humans in the process by their search for the land and so on. There are tales, which tell us how and why elephant's eyes became small.[13]

According to the tales, during this period man and animals lived together in amity and understanding because each spoke and understood each other's language. The bond of relationship between human beings and animals were so close that there are tales reflecting on instances, of a girl falling in love with a tiger. All these tales clearly reflects the close inter-dependence of man and other species of life. And in due course of time as man's lifestyle began to undergo changes, animal left areas inhabited by human beings and sought dwellings in the thickness of the forest and high mountains.

Thus, by closely looking at the tales related to the animals, it portrays the limitation of human beings who are views as a source of all the problems. It was not the animals who were not true in their words by agreement but it was the human who failed in keeping their promise to the rat[14] and also cheated the monkey by stealing away the fire.

Man's quest to understand the phenomenon of nature is reflected in many of the Naga tales in which the natural forces appear in every being, tree, rocks, flowers. Accordingly, the nature is supernatural in quality and the supernatural is nature itself. For an illustration we may refer to the story of a girl falling in love with a handsome man who, in reality, was only a tree.[15] There is also another tale, which tells us about the marriages of female angels and human beings.[16] In most of the Naga folk tales, angels were referred to as females and were believed to be so. Regarding the marriage between human beings and female angels, people nostalgically sing about them with a sense of fantasy.

Ao-Naga folk tales and folklore provide interesting information about the life and status of women in society. The woman has an interesting status in contrast to textual depictions of later period. Though her role is important, it is always subservient to that of the man in certain aspects. But this had never been viewed as giving the woman an inferior status in society. Rather there seems to be a well-defined and well-protected role given to her. Her domain is the home and the children and all the allied activities that are associated with this role. In the tales of the Ao-Nagas, women were given a role as equal or in parallel to men folk. She executed the power not directly but more often indirectly in social as well as in administrative set-up through her husband at home.

The past decades had seen a remarkable growth in the awareness of women's contribution to society and culture and of the fact that women, whose significance in art, science and the very functioning of society itself has commonly been ignored or wrongly assessed.[17] Thus, there is a crucial need to investigate the images of women that have been projected down through the centuries, to understand stereotypes of women is to understand how women have been perceived and misperceived and how perceptions have bolstered injustices and falsehood.

Before analyzing the folk tales the point regarding the themes and representations would help to set the context in a proper historical perspective. With regard to the theme, we find that unlike the focus on any singular aspect like battle, administration etc., the folk tales portrays a wide variety of tales ranging from origin, migration, magic and quick nature of women, family life and animals. Surprisingly, folk stories do not deal much with romantic episodes which shows that the order of preferences is different from other sources on the history of Nagas. In Ao-Naga folk tales, one-finds woman portrayed as heroine of a migration legend and is about the *Legend of Akangla* where it protracted state of warfare between Longkhum and another village called Nokrang which was famous for its fierce warriors.[18] The villagers of Longkhum were the aggressors. As the distance between the two villages was great, the attacker sought a midway base in a friendly village called Waromong and Akangla, the legendary queen belonged to this village. Her house was one of those houses, which were selected as temporary lodges for the assault party.

Though the villagers of Longkhum were excellent warriors, they were constantly beaten back by the Nokranger's because they had a pack of fierce hunting dogs that fought along side their masters and created havoc among the attackers. Thus, the Longkhum villagers turned to this woman called Akangla for advice. Therefore, Akangla asked all her village women to wash their hair on the same day and to collect all the hair that fell out of their heads and bring the same to her. She then had huge pots of a special rice cooked and instructed the rice to be rolled into many fistfuls, in each of which a few strands of the women's hair be mixed. She distributed these balls of rice to the Longkhum warriors during their next assault with the instruction that as soon as the dog came near them, these were to be thrown to them. The next day the warrior did as she had instructed them and, as the battle progressed, the dogs were so busy untangling the hairs and sticky rice from their mouth that they could be killed easily by the attackers and the Longkhum warriors overcome the Nokrangers and they were victorious and took many heads as trophies. Owing their victory to the clever device designed by Akangla, the villagers of Longkhum acknowledged her as a wise women and their benefactress and immortalized her in many ballads and folk songs.

The tale relating to the heroine of the origin myth dates back to the first village established by the Aos called Chungliyimti.[19] Longkongla is the name of the heroine of the origin myth who is supposed to be the foster-mother of the progenitor of an Ao clan called the Ozukumer.[20] Longkongla's tale contains the elements of transformation and magic, she, as the heroine remains human in form till the end.

Yajangla's story in Ao folk tale is a story of a woman who possesses supernatural powers, which find actual physical manifestation.[21] In this tale, her magical powers can transform her into another form and can subsume the human form and instincts for a certain spell of time. Yajangla's power was such that she could turn herself into a tigress and she also could cast magic spells which could clear her paddies of all weeds and other unwanted growth. But apparently she led a normal life, was married and even had a son.

There are categories of tales where women's inherent cunning nature is portrayed. This is about a woman who, in spite of her husband's strict injunction, used his best Dao during his absence and damaged it. She was very much afraid by his ire but cleverly waited for the right moment to confer her crime. When her husband returned home, he found that his favourite curry had been cooked and his wife was in a very flirtatious mood. At night, she blurted out her misdeed but the husband being in a state of intense passion and the love of his wife, he dismissed the damaged weapon as of no account and assured his wife not to worry. In the morning however, he realized that his wife had very cunningly escaped from his wrath and he could do nothing but chuckle to himself in chagrin.

This tale reflects the undeniable power that a woman possesses over man. And even today, when an Ao man is observed to be hopelessly enamoured of a woman, in spite of her lack of virtue, people smile knowingly and say "oh it's the broken Dao all over again".[22]

There are also tales which can be considered as the Cinderella equivalent in which the persecuted heroine, inevitably an orphan girl encounters the cruel stepmother and the marriage of the orphan girl with the chief or the rich man's son is the culmination. But there is a departure from the stock Cinderella syndrome as there is no magic involved and there is a revenge motive where the story does not end with the happily-ever-after, but a sworn revenge for the ill-treatment during her childhood by her stepmother.

Thus, women in Naga folk tales along with their inclination of fulfilling their social obligations are mostly portrayed as an unequivocal and vigorous in their protests against injustice and discrimination. The role of woman was played such that she saves the life of her husband or the life of her siblings in many tales. She played her role in such a way that her dignity had been maintained and also respected by the entire village. In contrast to this, there are tales, which portrays a woman's ill treatment by her husband and discrimination.[23]

Folk tales and oral historical traditions has been the best and most effective means of transmitting events of the past to the present. Often, one finds by the fireside, an elder telling folk stories to a group of children. It appears that in the early days storytelling at the boys' *(Morung)* were more organized, the elder or priest would come prepared and the events of the past were recited. Folk stories contain less romantic episodes, they tell more about customs and traditions of the past, they also tell about the nature and spirit worship, and so on. In the absence of any written document, folk tales and oral historical traditions remain the sole links between the past and the present. One acquired the skills of learning folk tales by the most assiduous cultivation of the memory.

But, in the present days as the *Morung* around which much of the Naga folklore had originated and flourished in its height has ceased to exist now. As a result, storytelling as an amusement and moral rendering has almost become a forgotten aspect of the Naga life. There also occurs the lack of correspondence between the tales and other aspects of culture where traditional tales have lost much of their vitality.

The real value of folk tales as a source of recovering Naga history lies not in its concern with particular incident but in its typical portrayal of situations, relationships and attitudes. In folk tales and folklores, situations and descriptions are in written or 'literary' literature. One who has been in contact with a living folk tradition cannot fail to mark how quickly stories based on real happenings get modified in the course of oral transmission so as to conform to the stereotyped pattern of popular legends.[24]

In spite of its limitations, folk tales and folk culture remains a valuable source of recovering one's history. Naga society with its vast body of beliefs, customs and institutions, which have been growing and accumulating for several millennia, presents such a formidable field where one can hardly afford to neglect folk tales as a rich source of information about its device aspects.

In conclusion, we may say that the process of recovering history from the folklore is complex, but not impossible task and here a rich diversity of sources with their multiple representations can be highlighted. In the Ao-Naga women's context, the different strategy can reveal a set of ideas, desires, imagination in which some facet of society are given in different treatment which is not consonant with regular narratives. It is this aspect which reveal the process of 'Othering' within the Ao-Naga society, which helps to understand the past in a more wholesome and objective manner.

Notes

1. Toelken, *The Dynamics of Folklore*, USA: Houghton Mifflin Company, 1979, p. 27.
2. Alan Dundes, *Interpreting Folklore*, Bloomington Indiana University Press, 1980, p. 2.
3. A. Wati Walling, "Community and Conservation of Bio-diversity: A Study of Bamboo in Nagaland", 2005, An unpublished Dissertation, Department of Sociology, University of Hyderabad.
4. Toelken, op. cit., 1979, p. 5.
5. Alan Dundes, op. cit., 1980, pp. 6–7.
6. Vesier Sanyu, *A History of Nagas in Nagaland (Dynamic of Oral Tradition in Village Formation)*, New Delhi: Commonwealth Publishers, 1996.
7. Temsula Ao, *The Ao-Naga Oral Tradition*, Guwahati: Bhasha Publications, 1999, p. 7.
8. Jan Vansina, *Oral Tradition as History*, Wisconsin, 1985, p. xi.
9. In almost all the tales Supreme Being is personified as male being accept in the case of the Angamis whom they referred to as kepenophu female being. See J.H. Hulton, *The Angami Nagas*, Kohima: Government of Nagaland, (Reprint), 2003, p. 181.
10. Temsula Ao, op. cit., 1999, p. 78.

11. W.C. Smith, *The Ao-Naga Tribes of Assam*, New Delhi: Mittal Publications, (Reprint), 2002, pp. 79–80.
12. J.P. Mills, *The Ao Nagas*, Kohima: Directorate of Art and Culture, (Reprint), 2003, p. 220.
13. *Folk Tales from Nagaland*, Directorate of Art and Culture, Government of Nagaland, Kohima, 1989, p. 209.
14. A. Wati Longchar, *The Traditional Tribal Worldview and Modernity*, Jorhat: Barkataki Publications, 1995, p. 31.
15. J.P. Mills, op. cit., 2003, p. 317.
16. *Folk Tales from Nagaland*, op. cit., 1989, p. 103.
17. Francis A. Decaro, *Women and Folklore: A Bibliographic Survey*, Greenwood Press, 1983, p. ix.
18. Temsula Ao, op. cit., 1999, p. 156.
19. Ibid., p. 86.
20. *Folk Tales from Nagaland*, op. cit., p. 1.
21. Temsula Ao, op. cit., p. 109.
22. Ibid., p. 158.
23. *Folk Tales from Nagaland*, op. cit., 1989, p. 17.
24. Indra Deva, *Folk Culture and Peasant Society in India*, Rawat Publications, 1989, p. 6.

References

Ao, Temsula, (1999), *The Ao-Naga Oral Tradition*, Bhasha Publications: Guwahati.

Decaro, Francis A., (1983), *Women and Folklore*, A Bibliographic Survey, Westport, Connecticut: Greenwood Press.

Deva, Indra, (1989), *Folk Culture and Peasant Society in India*, Jaipur: Rawat Publications.

Dundes, Alan, (1980), *Interpreting Folklore*, Bloomington: Indiana University Press.

———, (1989), *Folk Tales from Nagaland*, Directorate of Art and Culture, Kohima: Government of Nagaland.

Longchar, A. Wati, (1995), *The Traditional Tribal Worldview and Modernity*, Jorhat: Barkataki Publications.

Mills, J.P., (2003), (Reprint), *The Ao Nagas*, Kohima: Directorate of Art and Culture.

Sanyu, Vesier, (1996), A *History of Nagas in Nagaland, (Dynamic of Oral Tradition in Village Formation)*, New Delhi: Commonwealth Publishers,

Smith, W.C., (2002), (Reprint), *The Ao-Naga Tribes of Assam*, New Delhi: Mittal Publications.

Toelken, (1979), *The Dynamics of Folklore*, USA: Houghton Mifflin Company.

Vanisina, Jan, (1985). *Oral Tradition as History*. Madison: University of Wisconsin Press.

III

Rethinking History and Deconstruction of Ethnographic Realism

14 Under Surveying Eyes

Ethnographical Profiling and the Construction of 'Identities' in the Colonial Writings in the Garo Hills

BABITHA JUSTIN

The British colonization of India and the subsequent representation of Indians in the colonial documents had been of academic and scholarly interest for quite a long time. But the colonial representation of the communities in the periphery had been quite a neglected realm of study. This paper is about the study of the ethnological profiling conducted in the Garo Hills on the Garo tribe during the colonial times.[1] In this study, my primary aim is to look at the ways in which the Garo tribe has been represented in selected colonial texts.

To begin with, it is necessary to look at the history of British occupancy of the Garo Hills. The British governance over the Garo Hills was not that easy and effortless a task. It took around half a century after 1765, after the accession of Dewany of Bengal from the Mughal emperor, Shah Alam, that the 'Regulation X of 1822' was passed in order to bring the inaccessible areas in and around Assam under the direct rule of the British government. This became a reality after the expulsion of the Burmese from Assam after compelling them to accept the treaty of Yandabu[2] in 1826. Though the control of the foothills of Assam was feasible, the penetration of the interior areas, especially the Garo Hills, was virtually impossible due to geographical reasons as well as the due the incipient resistance of the natives towards the British. The most opportune administrative tool for reaching out towards interiors of the hills was through knowledge. It was necessary to systematically study, then illustrate the characteristics of the tribe and then manipulate on the one hand and to control through education and proselytizing, on the other. According to Barpujari, who worked extensively on the American missionaries in the Northeast, the ostensible objective of the British administration as well as the Baptist missionaries was, "To humanize the Garos who were always at feuds and at times carried their raids into the British districts ... (The British administration) sought to establish a school in their midst to instruct religious teachings apart from some useful arts".[3]

For the British, the most practicable administrative tools ready at hand were that of gauging knowledge of the tribe and the subsequent initiation of the tribe into new systems of knowledge were In this study, I would like to look at how these strategies worked at the narrative level in colonial texts. I am taking up two texts on the Garos written by the British: *The Garos (TG)* (1909) by Major Playfair and *The Garo Jungle Book* (*GJB*) (1919) by William Carey. Major Playfair's book is a monograph on the Garos as he had been assigned by the British government to compile ethnographical information about the Garos. William Carey narrates the story of conversion of the natives of the Garo Hills into Christianity. Both these books, besides being examples of travel narratives, also add to the construction or the making of the 'other'. They are also excellent examples of how the ethnological representations of the Garos as a tribe took place during the colonial times. Here, besides the study of ethnography, I shall also be looking into the construction of the Garos as a 'tribe'.

These texts are chosen for my study because they contain one of the earliest documented narratives of the Garo tribe. There were travellers and deputed British government officials who had talked about the tribe, earlier. The recorded lithographs and monographs of J. Eliot (1792), E.H. Dalton (1872), Horatio Bickerstaffe Rowney (1882), etc., are examples of studies conducted on the Garos. What makes Major Playfair and William Carey's books different is that they provide exclusive, documented information about the Garo tribe. For the first time, in these texts, the specific tribe and their location get a kind of valuable and assiduous attention. The first text I have chosen for study, *The Garos*, published in 1909, was one of the first ethnographic works which concentrated the focus on the Garos. In 1903, Bamphylde Fuller, the Commissioner of Assam, initiated a project of compiling information on the important tribes and castes of the Northeast by preparing a series of monographs. He assigned this duty to the then Deputy Commissioner, Major A. Playfair. He seems to have been in close contact the people, studied the language and even made comparative studies of the tribe in general for compiling the monograph.

The Garo Jungle Book (1919) by William Carey, interestingly, tells us about the conversion of the Garos into Christianity, thus opening up multifarious debates on conversion among the tribes of the Northeast India. Both the texts are complemented with photographs of the Garos. These books provide one of the first instances of contouring the Garos as a tribe, both in print and in the visual media. This also gives us a glimpse into the role of the media, the visual and the print, in the construction of the 'tribe'.

Hence, in this paper I shall be looking into two major issues:

1. The linguistic, rhetoric and related devices which go into the making of the 'tribal identity' of the Garos and the definition of the tribe as a generalized category in the Northeast as well as the rest of India, and
2. How these cultural constructions were closely related to the new discourse of ethnography which emerged during the colonial times.

The Rhetoric of the Construction of a Tribe: The Patterns

In the author's "Preface", Playfair begins the monograph by stating his acute awareness of his function as the custodian of a culture that is fast losing its pristine nature. "(The Garos) are a people who are little known to the outside world, and, though living in the midst of a civilized province, have remained free from foreign influence in a remarkable degree. This is due partly to the supposed unhealthiness and inaccessibility of their hills, and partly to their natural conservatism" (*TG*: xxiii). He also paints the tribe as quite arcane and closed to the outside world (read 'civilization'). So, not only does Playfair assume the redeemer-role of the Garo tribe which is isolated and alienated, he also bestows the tribe with the implicit 'savage' appendage, while striking a stark contrast with the 'civilization' which prevailed outside the reaches of the Garo Hills. Meanwhile, he tells us the amount of suspicion and distrust that persisted among the Garos whose life and sustenance were under the intrusive scanner of academic profiling. Here, he proffers them with the tag of hostility, which is again associated with their supposedly closed nature (read 'savage').

The pattern that Playfair follows in the description of the Garos as a tribe is quite interesting. In the beginning itself, he proffers information about the geographical contours of the Garo Hills and he goes on to quote Dalton's description of the Garo physiognomy in comparison with their next door neighbours, the Khasis. These comparisons and contrasts with the other tribes are also part of the schemata of ethnographic profiling as a strict hierarchy is set within the gradation of the newly encountered tribes. Gradations were necessary devices to control through organized knowledge. Organization of the knowledge of 'other' cultures offered a systematic methodology. And trying to systematize whatever little or more could be gauged was one of the marked ways of manipulation and mastery over the community and region.

Here we can see that, not only does Playfair assume the redeemer-title of a particular culture which is isolated and alienated, he also bestows the tribe with the implicit 'savage' appendage. There are characteristics in the ethnographic study which typecast Garos as naïve, uncorrupted, straight-forward people who were dirty and filthy till their conversion to Christianity. There is also the underlying assumption that the converted Garos are malleable to the sophistications of civilization and the mannerisms that ensue it. He says:

> There is much that is very pleasing in the character of the Garos, when their manners have not been corrupted, as is sometimes the case, by a veneer of civilization or by contact with foreigners. They are friendly and pleasant in manner, and usually exhibit very little trace of shyness. They are neither subservient in demeanour nor unduly forward in their advances they are honest and fairly truthful … . (*TG*: 3)

After making the most generalized comments on the tribe, when Playfair tries to gather information about the religion of the indigenous Garos, he is at once confronted with resistance and bewilderment from the part of the natives as well as his own inability to comprehend the complexities and intricacies of an alien religion which he terms as pagan or heathen. Playfair tells us thus that "On the subject of their religious belief, it's not easy to receive information, and I have often been hopelessly baffled by the characteristic reply 'Uija'—'I do not know'" (*TG*: 3). The role of superstition on the tribal imagination is also particularly stressed by Carey. He says, "The logic that works in their (the Garos) day to day life overlaps into their belief systems, thus making those beliefs rather inane and simplistic … . The imagination of the Garos is constantly darkened and terrorized by the presence of the evil spirits, malignant and powerful superstition and religion" (*GJB*: 22). By positing the indigenous religion as illogical, superstitious and simplistic, Carey provides an anticipatory defence against all the endeavours at conversions in the Garo Hills.

After commenting on the belief systems, we can also see generalized observations on the Garos regarding their hygiene, cleanliness and day-to-day activities. By stereotyping the tribe as unhygienic, in accordance with the Western notions of what cleanliness is all about, the readers (mostly the Western readers at home and those who read these books for administrative purposes) are given generous hints on savagery *ad nauseam*. Playfair remarks, "The Garos are not noted for their love of washing and leave much to be desired in the way of personal cleanliness: this applies especially to eastern Garos, who are much dirtier than the western" (*TG*: 3). He also speaks about the effect of modernity on personal hygiene and cleanliness. He makes it a point to tell us that only through conversion a simultaneous physical and spiritual cleanliness can be achieved by the community. "This remark applies to uncivilized Garos only … . Christian villages show a considerable improvement, and both men and women have learned to clothe themselves and to take pride in personal cleanliness" (*TG*: 3). We can see an echo of the same sentiment in Carey too where he equates physical cleanliness with that of the spiritual hygiene as he tries to draw parallels between conversion and hygiene in an interesting anecdote. In the text *The Garo Jungle Book*, Carey uses the 'soap' as a device of modernity which conflates the two disparate realms of materiality and spirituality. He uses it as a metaphor to delineate the process of spiritual and physical cleansing of a community which was at the threshold of being ushered into spiritual modernity as well.

> Naturally one of the first and best remedies for such a people as a whole was soap. From early days to the present soap has been imported in large quantities by the missionaries. Mr Mason, telling of an interesting case of soap treatment, says: "In one village I noticed a lad in his early teens sitting abjectly by himself in the corner of the young men's house. I went to him and inquired concerning his condition, when the people said, "He is dying: he cannot live long … . I could see that he first of all needed a washing, but he might not able endure so a drastic remedy. So I gave particular directions that water be warmed and brought, and that soap be well applied …". (*GJB*: 258)

The Construction of the Northeast

As we look at the text, it undulates with overt hints of savagery of the tribe—the rude, uncouth, barbarous, wild, bloody and licentious tribal behaviour is foregrounded vigorously in the book. Geographically, the Northeast is always construed as remote, far and inaccessible. It is portrayed as far away from the civilization, canopied by a lair of savagery, wilderness (read 'wildness') and mystery. This image of the untamable wilderness concealed under an unbridled virginal appeal strikes the key note of the book. Carey assumes the role of the White traveller as well as the herald of the civilized world, at the same time his narratives exude a sensuality which borders on the pleasures of voyeurism.

In the beginning itself, Carey scans the landscape of the Garo Hills with the eye of a conqueror, looking for a kind of cultural, geographical and political annexation, as though the 'savagery' and 'recklessness' of the region necessitated it. He calls the Garo Hills a 'jungle lair' by laying bare the wild sexuality wrapped up in the region. The evil nature ensconced in the darkness and the inaccessibility of the place is equated with an untapped sexuality and an untamable nature. Here, Carey takes on the role of a male custodian whose gaze desires to possess and control.

Carey begins the book by describing the Garo Hills as a 'mine of interest'/the jungle 'lair', which is the secret dwelling of a wild animal. The sexual imagery in the term 'jungle lair' and the voyeuristic gaze latent in Carey's narration are reminiscent of a kind of initiation which borders on the tell tale signs of the sexual intrusion of a virgin land by a male traveller. In Carey's language itself, there are lots of terms connotative, especially when he tells us about the Garo Hills as an impenetrable, virgin terrain.

The Construction of the Terror Narratives

After sizing up the materialistic possibilities of the geographical area, Carey scans the human beings there. He emphasizes the homicidal instincts of the Garos and he narrates that this nature is suffused with vindictiveness. The author's interest in the hills can be figured out from the obvious voyeuristic and entrepreneurial gaze with which he looks at the tribe. The tribe in itself is seen as an excellent species that is amenable to a kind of lucrative spiritual trade.

The merchant's gaze is one such feature that can be easily detected in this narrative of spiritual sojourn. Carey remarks thus, "Instead of barren rocks and unprofitable wastes, a wealth of timber, coal and cultivation was discovered" (*GJB*: 49). These instances sum up the gaze of an imperial traveller who discovers first and then intends to possess. And the urge to possess is a holistic one which covers the physical, geographical, economical and social realms not to mention the spiritual one.

Playfair and Carey simultaneously uses devices to record—like documentations, memoirs and photographs to render a scientific credibility to the ethnographic narrative that they depict. Even the sample collection of the tribe is embedded with racism. The delineation of the physical terrain (hostile terrains and the labyrinthine dimensions of the land), reinforces the subtle and the insidious sexual metaphors which directly or indirectly refer to the sleepy hollow. The verbal construction of the picturesque landscape and the caricaturing of the human bodies become a device to represent the 'other'. These constructed terror narratives gave credibility and reinforcement to the bloodless victories of the British government.

The exposition to the book discloses a kind of an excitement in the dissemination of the new kind of knowledge which comes from the discovery of a new place and tribe. Carey tells us in the exposition that the hills are "luring to conquest, haunted by devotees, a fine field for proselytizing priests, passing rich in natural sources, and maintaining a large commerce ... with its wealth only half exploited" (*GJB*: 1). This successful yoking together of evangelization, commerce and the illusion of civilizing the natives is one characteristic feature of this book. Carey also adds that Assam is one of the strategic outlets to Northern Asia. "Assam is not only India's backdoor to Burma and China, but the most natural pass through the Himalayan range into Tibet and Northern Asia. Towards this the roads are being rapidly constructed, over which are to move evangelization, civilization and commerce for those great Mongolian races" (*GJB*: 1). Thus the locale itself becomes the vantage point where trade and spirituality could be conveniently linked.

Ethnographic Discourse in the Garo Hills

If we look at the documented narratives on the Garos, we can see that the most productive period of exclusive ethnography was from 1870s to 1920s. There are various reasons for the late entry of this scientific discourse into the region. One reason must have been the late arrival of the British to the Garo Hills. The geographical inaccessibility and the initial hostility of the native tribe towards the outsiders can be stated as the possible reasons for this. One can also say that the focus of the British administration was also concentrated on the other parts of India, rather than the northeastern region. A glimpse into the material resources of the region must have possibly initiated a methodical study of the region. This instance of the roving consumerist eyes can be detected in almost all the colonial narratives of the Northeast: from ethnographical surveys to travel books to missionary writings.

The major problem faced by the ethnographers of the Garo Hills was the major dilemma of the categorization. Primarily, the Garos did not fit into the mainstream Hindu Aryan stock. Racially they were mostly Mongoloids, and ample Aryan–Dravidian–Mongoloid inter-racial mingling had also taken place down the line. To complicate matters further there were innumerable oral narratives of migration which confounded the British sense of history. The most difficult of all was that the race fitted into the category of the pagan/heathen/animistic slot, like the Hindus to a certain extent, but there was no trace of a caste system which characterized Hinduism in the plains. Though they dwelt in the hilly forest cover their different race, culture and oral histories of recent migration were also unlike that of the indigenous aboriginals in the plains. The only striking similarity between them was their proximity to nature. This proximity bestowed an image of the hill men, in this context the Garos, as the pristine children of nature, which constructed them as naïve and barbarous at the same time. They were represented as unsophisticated and fierce, lacking the cunning of the so-called 'civilized' world outside. It is here the strategy of imposing a double edged imperialism manifests itself. Both Playfair and Carey explicitly describes the tribe as rude, uncouth, wild, bloody and licentious is indicative of the verbal evocation of the narratives of terror.

The Double Imperialism

The representation of the Garos as a fierce black clan, in fact, brings into our notice a bleak picture of a double imperialism that worked in the narratives of the travel writers, ethnographers and missionaries of the time. Double imperialism is that phenomenon where an unconscious oppression from two quarters, from the British as well as the mainstream Hindu level, is perpetrated. The community in the periphery, here, the Garos, used to be at the receiving end of both physical and psychological oppression from both the quarters. The verbal enunciation of the cult of the masculine and its association with the Garo tribe are pointers to the fact that among the British subjects there was a conscious subdivision between the mainland Hindus and the animistic hill men. The hill men, especially the Garos, are portrayed as examples of strong and honest men compared to the plainsmen who are Hindus. The Hindus or the plainsmen are represented as effeminate, cunning and dishonest. In the same manner, the

Garos are also represented as lascivious in nature, hedonistic and Epicurean. Carey also makes it a point to give details of their inebriated ribaldry.

> Wild as these savages are, their normal temper is not ferocious, nor are they morose. They are human and interesting withal, practicing a domestic economy in advance of some modern ideas, grateful for their kindness, and with this righteousness about them—fidelity to their spoken word. "They possess", says Dalton, "that pearl of great price so rare among the eastern races, a love for truth" (*GJB*: 9).

This is an example to demonstrate that such representations accommodate the idea of savagery that co-exists with the simple, the child-like nature of the tribal who naturally possesses the inviolate and untapped natural instincts of an animal.

The depiction of an obvious dichotomy between the Garo and the plainsman Hindu marks the beginning of the oppositional stereotyping of the tribal versus Hindu. The Garo man is set in deep contrast with that of the plainsman. Their descriptions verbally promulgate an imaginary virility of the Garo male. He is always associated with his weapons, however scanty and unsophisticated they are; he also symbolizes a kind of fecund masculinity. Their lascivious nature and other Epicurean excesses are also emphasized strongly by both Playfair and Carey. Furthermore they stress on the bloodthirsty, homicidal nature of the Garos as representing them as ruthless and uncouth headhunters. Playfair, in his book, refers to this tendency as a thing of past. He says that, "Less than half a century ago, the Garos were looked upon as cruel and blood-thirsty savages, who inhabited a tract of hills covered with almost impenetrable jungle, the climate of which was considered so deadly .... The Garos were notorious as perpetrators of numerous raids into the plains at the foot of their hills in the districts of Goalpara and Mymensingh. On each occasion a number of defenceless *ryots* were killed ..." (*TG*: 66–7). Both the narratives speak about of 'head hunting' instincts of the Garos. If we analyze these accounts we find that these authors have never witnessed one directly nor have they heard of a first-hand narrative. Their sources are either the versions of the British officers who have previously written about the Garos or from the upper caste Bengali traders who had an unequal and highly exploitative relationship with the Garos. However, it has to be noted that virility, cruelty, ruthlessness and savagery were the characteristic markers of the Garo men in comparison to the effete, subtle and cunning plainsmen Hindus.

The so-called democratic nature of the Garo society, the status of the Garo women, the matrilineal heritage among them, etc., are also closely studied and delineated in both the books. These authors also bring in a subtle comparison with the rigidity of gender divisions within mainstream Hindu society. Here, both Playfair and Carey speak moralistically about the 'sexual licentiousness' of the women of the Garo society. The licentiousness endowed to the women of the society and the sexual wantonness verging on nymphomania is also rather etched out rather with an erotic interest. The inaccessibility of the region, myths of savagery and the Garo societal norms which escaped the Western sense of comprehension were the base on which the construction of the identity of the tribe as such is built.

Conclusion

Though both the texts deal with different subjects' altogether, the agreement on the 'savagery' of the Garos is remarkable. Surprisingly both the authors belong to different backgrounds; one was a British official and the other was on a religious mission. Playfair makes a positivistic ethnographical study on the Garos based on epistemological collection of available data. He follows the study from socio-cultural perspective by verifying the data with a cross-cultural milieu in mind. He compares and contrasts the cultural mannerisms and behaviour of the Garos in comparison with the other tribes of the Northeast. Carey also etches out the cultural biography of the race on almost the same lines before getting into the details of the story of conversion and the progress of missionary work in the Garo Hills. Though their purposes are different, the manner in which their narratives converge to conjure up a definite tribal identity is worth research. In this paper, mine is a limited endeavour in laying bare the patterns and formations of cultural stereotypes that these books share in the early attempts at classifying the Garo tribe. These early attempts at ethnography have a long lasting effect in the sense that these books are used as source texts for information on the Garo culture before written Garo was introduced. These books also contain definitions helped create a different 'identity', completely antithetical to the localized and parochial identity, which was gradually forged into the larger concept of 'nationhood'.

Notes

1. The Garos are a tribe living in the state of Meghalaya, and they are of Tibeto-Burmese origin. They speak the Garo language.
2. M.L. Bose, *Social History of Assam*, New Delhi: Concept Publishing Company,. 1989, p. 21.
3. H.K. Barpujari, *The American Missionaries and Northeast India (1836–1900)*, Guwahati: Spectrum Publications, 1986, p. 13.

References

Bal, Ellen, (2000), *They Ask if We Eat Frogs: Social Boundaries and Ethnic Categorization and the Garo People of Bangladesh*, Deft: Eburon.

Barpujari, H.K. (1986), *The American Missionaries and Northeast India (1836–1900)*, Guwahati: Spectrum Publications.

Bose, M.L. (1989), *Social History of Assam*, New Delhi: Concept Publishing Company.

Carey, William, (1919), *A Garo Jungle Book or The Mission to the Garos of Assam*, Philadelphia: Judson Press.

———, *The Garo Jungle Book*, (1966), New Delhi: Horizon Printers, 1993.

Dalton, Edward T. (1872), *Descriptive Ethnology of Bengal*, Office of the Superintendent of Government Printing, Calcutta.

Denzin, Norman Kent, (1997), *Interpretive Ethnography: Ethnographic Practices for the 21st Century*, New Delhi: Sage Publications.

Dewanji, Malay, (1996), *William Carey and the Indian Renaissance*, Delhi: ISPCK.

Dube, Saurabh, (2004), "Colonial Registers of a Vernacular Christianity: Conversion to Translation", *Economic and Political Weekly*, January, 10–16.

Eliot, John, (1792), "Observations on the Inhabitants of the Garrow Hills made during a Publick Deputation in the Years 1788 and 1789", *Asiatick Researches*, iii, Calcutta, 17–37.

Gammell, William, (1854), *A History of American Baptist Mission in Asia, Europe and North America*, New York: Boston Gould and Lincoln.

Hammersley, Martyn and Paul Atkinson, (1994), (2nd edition), *Ethnography: Principles in Practice*, London: Routledge.

Leask, Nigel, (2002), *Curiosity and the Aesthetics of Travel Writing, 1770–1840*, Oxford: University Press.

Playfair, Major, (1909), *The Garos*, Guwahati: Spectrum Publishers, 1998.

Rowney, Horatio Bickerstaffe, (1882), *The Wild Tribes of India*, Delhi: Low Price Publications, 1993.

Rubies, Joan–Pau, (2000), *Travel and Ethnology in the Renaissance: South India through European Eyes*, Cambridge: Cambridge University Press.

Sangma, Milton S., (1987), *History of American Baptist Mission in North-East India (1836–1950)*, Vol. 1 and 2, New Delhi: Mittal Publications.

Sword, Victor Hugo, (1992), (Rev.), *Baptists in Assam: A Century of Missionary Service*, Delhi: Spectrum.

Viswanathan, Gauri, (2002), *Outside the Fold*, New Delhi: Oxford University Press.

15 Creating Identities

British Rule and the Hos of Singhbhum, 1820–1932

SANJUKTA DASGUPTA

One of the features of political life in contemporary India is the increasing visibility and articulation of hitherto marginalized, and indeed silenced groups, such as *adivasis* and Dalits, testified, for instance, by the recent creation of the state of Jharkhand as the homeland of the tribals of Middle India. Implicit in this is the development of the concept of a tribal or *adivasi* as given and unproblematic, leading to the formation of a new, unified and distinct identity for the tribals of a region, concentrating on their perceived similarities. For long, historians tended to view individual tribal groups as being undifferentiated, united and geographically concentrated[1] and it is only recently that research has begun to highlight the differentiations and tensions existing within particular groups.[2] A new angle to the debate on the 'tribal question' has been provided by recent scholars who question the very validity of the concept of tribe in the Indian context. It has been argued that tribes are essentially a colonial construct, a part of the 'colonial project'.[3] Non-existent in the pre-colonial period, this category was created and formalized by the colonial state part of its legitimizing ideology and operated as a device to catalogue conquered populations, formulate imperial policies and to facilitate the incorporation of these populations into the colonial system.[4] The concept of 'tribe' was therefore one of the elements through which Europe constructed part of the Indian reality. It was further argued that after independence, India retained the myth of the tribe as it served the interests of certain dominant socio-economic groups and that post-colonial essentialising through special constitutional provisions for Scheduled Tribes thus came to perpetuate the concept of tribe.

Such objections, however, do not take into consideration the perceptions of difference that existed between *adivasi* and non-*adivasi* Hindu communities, separating and distancing them from one another.[5] The colonial discourse on tribes was largely informed by the prevailing concepts that represented tribals as 'the other'. It has to be stressed that while characterizing the *adivasi*, particularly during early colonial rule, the state evidently appropriated some categories of Hindu representation of *adivasi*.[6] In this sense, tribes may justifiably, be considered to be more a Brahmanical construct than a colonial one.[7] The question then is whether it will be valid to view the descriptions of tribes under colonial rule only as a specific 'invention of tradition'[8] a deliberate collaboration of European officers and their Indian informants? The concept of 'the invention of tradition' has given rise to the assumption that that which is 'invented' is not 'real'. Scholars have argued that traditions were invented in order to impose colonial hegemony upon the colonized. However, this paper suggests that British rule appropriated and restructured certain pre-existing social norms and thereby introduced new attributes in communities identified as 'tribes'. If by invention of tradition is meant the introduction of new meanings and applications, colonial rule did do so. It needs to be asserted that these considerations were not invariably part of a larger deliberate colonial project. Secondly, the notion of tribes as a colonial construct tends to deny the colonized people any agency and shows them as being manipulated by colonial policies. The impetus for reinventing the identities of the tribal people did not always predominantly rise from colonial agency. Like other social groups, tribal groups were, and are, constantly evolving and defining themselves in the context of specific political and socio-economic situations leading to changes in their self-perception.

This paper shows, with reference to the Ho tribe of Singhbhum, the changes in the perceptions of the colonial rulers and the gradual evolving of a colonial policy concerning the Hos. It argues that under colonial rule, there existed a multiplicity of opinions regarding tribes, generated either by the colonial power itself or arising out of a process of interaction and adaptation. Thus, several, often contradictory policies towards the indigenous people emerged in course of the 19th and 20th centuries.[9] The second section of the paper attempts to locate the agency of the colonized subjects in the making of their own history and discusses how the Hos accommodated themselves to such changes under colonial rule and, in the process, carved out for themselves a new identity. This is studied with reference to four social-religious movements among the Hos which greatly influenced the contours of the identity that Hos were attempting to create for themselves.

Changing British Perceptions of the Hos

Western Singhbhum[10] in the early 19th century was a rugged country, protected by hill ranges and watered by numerous rivers, fertile and productive in some places, stony and barren in others. Many diverse ethnic communities inhabited this space, the Oraons, the Mundas, the Gonds, the Bhuiyas, the Bhumijes, the Tamarias and the Hos, the latter being the most populous. The open, undulating tract in the southwestern part of Singhbhum district popularly known as Kolhan was almost exclusively peopled by the Hos, whose allegiance was claimed by the rulers of Singhbhum, that is, the Porahat raja, his vassals, the *kumars* of Seraikela and Kharsawan and in the south, the raja of Mayurbhanj. Colonial records of the early 19th century, a period of general unrest and turbulence in Singhbhum, reveal that the apparatus of state power of was very much in existence in the countryside, even though this may have lost much of its potency over the years. Like the Nagbanshi Raj of the neighbouring Chota Nagpur, the state system of the Singhbhum Raj had entrenched itself in the countryside over time and thus had a well-organized bureaucracy which was chiefly associated with collection of tributes and impositions of various kinds. However, unlike the Nagbanshi Raj, the authority of the Singhbhum royal family had weakened over the years due to a continuous struggle for power among the junior members of the ruling class and their vassals and also due to the challenge of the Mayurbhanj rulers in the southern part of the district. Nevertheless, several links connected the Hos with the supra village authorities. These links were not merely economic in nature, being associated with the revenue collecting mechanism. Other ties of loyalty and cultural factors also cemented the hold of the state power over the tribal population. These included the land tax or *pancha* collected from individual villages and sundry other payments associated with religious and social practices.[11] Significantly, the Porahat Raja also claimed military service of the Hos partly through the ritual status they had gained, and partly through promises of booty. Thanks to their serving as the Raja's militia, the Hos came to acquire the popular epithet Larka Kol or the warrior Kol.

The British was first drawn to the region by the recurring law and order problem there. Economic insecurity often forced the tribal people, who depended principally on subsistence agriculture, to raid the neighbouring settled peasant tracts. Although such uprisings did not threaten the political stability of the colonial empire, these were interpreted as a law and order problem and as an improper defiance of the state's legitimate authority. The tribal world, therefore, figured in official perceptions as the backdrop for the counter-insurgency measures of the colonial state. In the early 19th century, a period when British political authority began to impinge on the Chota Nagpur region, the Singhbhum rulers sought British assistance in quelling their turbulent subjects who increasingly displayed a tendency to repudiate their obligations to the ruling class. In Singhbhum, as in other parts of Chota Nagpur, the early 19th century British administration came to regard the local feudatory chiefs as the lawful rulers and the tribal population there as being subject to their authority. The former were considered to be local controllers with a long-standing anchorage in indigenous society. As in England, the 'respectable' inhabitants and men of property were recognized as the protectors of the locality. It was with the support of this group of local collaborators that the British intended to maintain a system of loose control over the tribal regions which then lay at the outskirts of the empire.

Since British intervention in Singhbhum in the early 19th century occurred at the request of the Singhbhum raja, the image of the tribal population that they formed at this initial point of contact was therefore entirely based on the prevailing notions that existed among the local Hinduized ruling groups. In fact, the term Kol which early British military officers and administrators applied to much of the tribal population of Chota Nagpur was derived from the Hindus of the region. Whether the term Kol was derived from the Sanskrit *kola* meaning pig,[12] or from the word *horo* (meaning man in the Ho language), is difficult to decide, but it is certain that in popular usage, Kol was, and remains, a contemptuous epithet of abuse that the Hindu population of the region used for the tribals. As stated earlier, in the case of the Hos the term was further qualified and they were referred to as the Larka Kols rather than as Ho, a term by which the Singhbhum tribal would normally identify himself. The Larkas were perceived to be "dreadful pests to the civilized part of Singboom",[13] who terrorized the adjacent country through their depredations. Thus British officialdom in the early 19th century portrayed the *adivasi* population as a 'savage race' whose 'atrocious crimes' challenged the legitimate political authority of the 'civilized' 'reputable castes'. The Ramgarh Magistrate described the Hos in 1817 as "the lowest kind of Hindoos and in their manners and customs are little removed from savages".[14] The Hos were also characterized as a fiercely exclusive community who would not permit the entry of any outsiders in their territory. Commenting on their famed propensity for exclusiveness Major Roughsedge, who led the British forces into Singhbhum in 1821, wrote, "A traveller would as soon think of venturing into a tiger's den as of traversing any point of Larka Cole."[15]

In was only in the wake of tribal rebellions, such as the Kol rebellion of 1831–32, that the British began to put in place a tribal policy in Singhbhum. The state no longer regarded the tribals as 'predatory raiders' and 'savages' prone to violence, but rather came to see them as a community grievously wronged by alien intruders and therefore goaded into violence. Enquiries into the recurring tribal rebellions convinced the government of the distinctiveness of the tribal regions which made them particularly vulnerable to powerful adversaries and this changed perception was reflected in administrative innovation. The British government reassessed their policy of befriending the indigenous ruling classes in Singhbhum and questions were raised about the utility of a political alliance with the discredited chiefs of the region who could barely keep their overmighty subjects in check. Such considerations finally prompted the British to assume direct control over the Ho of Singhbhum. Declaring their intention of extending *pax Britannica* over Singhbhum, it was decided in 1837 to separate the Ho villages of the region from the control of the indigenous rajas and to form with these the Government Estate of Kolhan, incorporated within the South West Frontier Agency, under the direct control and management of the British government.[16] Later, under Act XX of 1854 Singhbhum became a non-regulation district under the jurisdiction of the Lieutenant Governor of Bengal.

The Larka Kols were now seen as isolates and from the 'savage' the British elevated the tribals to 'noble savage' living a life of Arcadian simplicity, unable to cope with exploitation of the non-tribal outsiders.[17] This myth served to justify the presence of the Raj and the role of the missionaries as the protectors of the 'wild' yet 'innocent' tribals against 'rapacious' outsiders and even from their own 'self-destructive' customs.[18] While force was advocated to quell the outbursts against law and order, the British also claimed to provide for protection of the tribals from the exigencies of the outside world. Thus, the twin features of the new government policy were paternalism and isolationism. The paternalist rule of district officers was designed to protect the tribals against the machinations and designs of the non-tribal population, projected by the British as the chief enemy of the tribals. As Ashis Nandy observed, the dominant imagery of 19th century British governance was that of an adult caring for and chastising an innocent yet wayward child.[19] In tribal India this paternalism was taken to extremes. For instance, Tickell, the first Assistant Political Agent of the Kolhan Government Estate (whose duty was to conduct the administration and enforce law and order in the country) was provided with a set of 'Instructions' by the Political Agent Wilkinson designed to assist him in the administration of the district. These instructions spelt out his duties: the administrative functions and social reforms he was expected to undertake and also provided him with a brief outline of the nature of the country and the customs of the people he was expected to govern. Above all, Tickell was exhorted to be at all times in direct touch with the tribals and to be meticulous in the discharge of his duties. Wilkinson admonished,

> You should at all times be accessible to the people under your charge, except at your hours for meal and recreation and take particular care not to transact business with them through the agency of any of your establishment, which will be the surest means of checking anything in the shape of exaction and oppression; your patience and temper will often be tried but I have every faith in your exercising both in the work for which you have been selected.[20]

The mid-19th century saw the emergence of anthropologically-inclined British administrators such as E.T. Dalton in the tribal areas of Chota Nagpur. Unlike earlier British officials, they were not limited to narrow considerations of the need to maintain law and order. Although commissioned by the Government of Bengal, in collaboration with the Asiatic Society of Bengal to prepare an "ethnographic handbook" since, in course of his long service in Assam and Bengal he had more opportunities of "observing the various races and tribes than other officers in the service", Dalton's *Descriptive Ethnology of Bengal* (1872) was not limited to governmental imperatives. His was a comparative study of the ethnic peculiarities of different tribes, an analysis of the inner world of the tribes, their social organizations, magico-religious beliefs, customs and superstitions. His classification of different groups of tribals was based on two principles, namely, language and the influence of Hinduism on the tribes.

Dalton portrayed the Hos as, "A people who till recently, had no notion what it was to pay rent to anyone, or even to give pecuniary support to their chiefs. They had their *Mankis* and *Mundas*; but no one exercised any right arising from a title in the land except the cultivators".[21] Thus a notion of the total isolation came to be perpetrated. This was in fact one of the myths that was being popularized by the colonial administration since the annexation of Kolhan 1837. Although in the early 19th century, the British had recognized the claims of the indigenous rulers over the Hos, gradually the assumption that the Hos had never been fully under the control of the ruling families of the region and were virtually a 'stateless' people found acceptance among the colonial authorities in their endeavour to legitimize their authority as the protectors and the guardians of the Hos.

Dalton believed that the endemic restiveness of the tribals of Chota Nagpur was explainable partly in terms of the enforcement by the government of its laws and regulations, which had not taken into account the historical specificities of the local tribal society.,

> The same law for all is a very high sounding and popular cry, and it is much favoured in the legislature of recent years; but I think in this craving for homogeneity, the heterogenous character of the component parts of the population of India should always be borne in mind.[22]

Nonetheless, the hegemonizing colonial will was very much present in Dalton, even if was not confined to the mere pursuit of governmental ends. Dalton had no doubt that the British rule as protectors of the Hos had proved to be beneficial for the Hos. Thus he wrote:

> They have been directly under our Government for about 37 years, and coming to us as unsophisticated savages, we have endeavoured to civilize without allowing them to be contaminated, and whilst they still retain those traits which favourably distinguish the aborigines of India from Asiatics of higher civilization, a manner free from servility, but never rude, a love or at least the practice, of truth, a feeling of self respect rendering them keenly sensitive under rebuke, they have become less suspicious, less revengeful, less blood thirsty, less contumacious, and in respects more amenable to the laws of the realm and the advice of their officers.[23]

It was also from the mid-19th century that we find the increasing use of the term Ho to designate the tribe rather than Kol or Larka Kol in both official and non-official accounts. The switch over to Ho was evident by the time of the census operations. Since 1872, the census came to used as tool of social control to gather knowledge of the colonized which would thereby strengthen the Raj. The census provided data on the questions of religion, ethnicity, the nature of demographic movements, emigration and immigration and the circumstances necessitating these shifts. Conceived originally as a statistical operation to quantify the subject population, the census also proposed a new classification of Indian society. The Census Report of 1872, for instance, divided the indigenous population into five broad groups: aboriginal tribes, semi-Hinduized aboriginals, Hindus proper, persons enumerated by nationality only and Hindus not recognizing caste. The criteria adopted in this classification were those of racial origin and occupation. Race however was not just a biological category here, but also referred to religious groups. The census tended to represent the Hos as a homogenized community and portrayed them as belonging to the first category and largely professing animism with a small minority of Christians.

The census data therefore tended to categorize different communities as specific 'tribes', with their own inherent specific attributes. Yet, simultaneously with the census operations, official data was being collected for yet another purpose: standardization of revenue assessment through land settlement operations. Since the mid-19th century down to the 20th century, settlement operations took place throughout Chota Nagpur. In contrast to the census reports, settlement reports were more concerned about tenants rather than tribes, about revenue payment rather than with determining degrees of primitivism associated with tribes. Thus, a wide disparity in contemporaneous official colonial attitudes becomes evident.

Ho Attempts at Reinventing Tradition in the 20th Century

The previous section discussed the evolution of colonial policies concerning the Hos and argues that there was no single concerted tribal policy and that multiple, often contradictory practices tended to co-exist. This section shows that the tribal people did not simply react passively to colonial attempts at categorization but actively attempted to forge a new identity for themselves through socio-cultural reform movements. The primary intention behind these attempts on the part of the Hos to reinvent themselves was to gain in self-respect vis-à-vis the non-Hos. These were thus intended to strengthen their tribal identity so that they could better deal with their enemies. Such movements reveal that an ethnic communitarian consciousness, transcending village and kin ties, had developed in course of the 20th century, as the interaction of the Hos with outsiders groups increased. These also reflected the changing perceptions of the Hos regarding themselves and their enemies. This section will explore four such instances which occurred in the early years of the 20th century.

Under colonial rule, the traditional village structure of the Hos faced new onslaughts particularly as a result of the influx of alien outsiders. The colonial state proved incapable of providing adequate safeguards to protect the interests of the tribal community. Under these circumstances, it became imperative for the tribal people to devise a new social order which would enable them to effectively cope with the new realities. This required a re-evaluation of tradition, particularly of their old religious beliefs, which seemed inadequate in the changed times. Increasingly, since the beginning of the 20th century, new religious reformist movements spread among the Hos which aimed at strengthening the community through reforming their customs. Reforms entailed both, a rejection of certain traditional beliefs and practices and borrowing from Hindu cultural life. Yet, it would be misleading to characterize such reform movements as assimilation with the Hindu cultural world since only certain aspects of the Hindu traditions were selectively introduced within the belief structure of the tribals.

In 1907, a religious reform movement spread among a section of the Hos. Believed to have been started by one Singrai Ho of Bhuta village in Barkela *pir* (district subdivision), the Satya Dharam or the Punya Dharam movement was looked upon as a 'new religion'[24] by contemporary British officialdom. After the death of the founder, the religion was propagated by four gurus or teachers, namely Bamiya Ho of Garahatu, Hari Ho, Dula Ho and Birjo Ho of Guira.[25] The movement aimed at the purification of the Ho religion through reform of some customary practices and the adoption of certain Hindu mores. For instance, they put on sacred threads like the Hindu Brahmans. However, it is not clear whether this signified a claim for a higher ritual status. At the same time, many other popular beliefs and practices associated with Hinduism were sought to be challenged. The notable feature of the new religion was that its adherents worshipped only one God, who was omnipotent and invisible and was addressed as Sat Malik or True Lord.[26] Denouncing the idolatry of the Hindus, the Satya Dharamis did not have any image or representation of their God. The True Lord was an abstract concept who was to be worshipped through *dhyan* and *jap*, that is meditation and devotion. While this went against the popular Hindu practice, it also reflected the influence of abstract metaphysical Hindu thought.

What was more significant was the break with the Ho tradition. The followers gave up the traditional dancing and other observances of the Hos. They also gave up the drinking of rice beer and became pure vegetarians.[27] Neither of these practices were traditionally opprobrious in Ho society. In fact, rice beer was traditionally associated with Ho religion as the Hos believed that the primeval pair of brother and sister could learn to procreate and thus give birth to the Ho people only after Sing Bonga offered them intoxicating rice beer. However, such customs were commonly looked down upon by the higher caste Hindus. Other articles of food were also proscribed, such as *ghee*, sugar and ordinary salt. Instead, they used oil, *gur* and rock salt. They did not eat sweets or food prepared by men of other religions. They observed many ceremonies and every aspect of their daily lives was governed by fixed rules 'even to the minutest details'. For instance they bathed daily and if they went out they could not re-enter their houses without taking a bath. They did not vaccinate their children nor did they use any medicine when they fell ill. They believed that prayers to their God would save them from sickness.

The Satya Dharam movement was however limited in scope and was confined to the villages around Chaibasa. Judging from the timing, the space and from the programme of religious reform, it may be presumed that the Satya Dharam movement was to an extent influenced by Birsa Munda's movement among the Munda tribe, which also had spread from the town of Chaibasa.

Social Reform Movement among the Hos

Attempts at reforming customary practises were not confined to the realm of religion alone. Their social customs were also sought to be changed as well. Such attempts at social regeneration were spearheaded by educated Hos who organized meetings at various places in Kolhan which, in the words of a contemporary observer, urged upon the Hos to "guard up their loins and save their society from rack and ruin".[28] The agenda of reform reveals the concern of the educated, Hos regarding the image of their community among their Hindu neighbours. Thus many of their traditions, which were immoral or degenerate in the eyes of the Hindus, came under attack. Chief among them were drinking rice beer, dancing and sexual 'licentiousness'.

The reformists argued that excessive drinking of rice beer had told upon the health of the people, as a result of which the men had become weak, lazy and worthless. Thus, it was argued that the burden of both domestic work and the task of earning a livelihood fell largely upon the women, because of which they had become sexually licentious. At a meeting in Lupungutu on 25 March, 1924 which was presided over by Dulu *Manki*, the tribal member of the Bihar and Orissa Legislative Council, reformist Hos adopted resolutions against the traditional dances *Dama Duma* and *Sisun* attested by seventy influential members of the Ho community. These customs were held responsible for causing ill health among the people on account of keeping late hours, for serving as an impediment to the progress of students, for being detrimental to the morals of young people who went from village to village to take part in the dances and for generally demoralizing the youth. It was also argued that such dances involved an unnecessary waste of time and energy. The most significant objection that the reformists raised was that the music and dances were looked down upon by 'cultured neighbours' as being 'very low and degrading'.[29]

At the same time, there were efforts to reinvigorate certain tribal customs which were facing destruction in the changed socio-economic circumstances of the time. A vital issue confronting Ho society related to growing liaisons between members of the same *killi* or clan group. Traditional Ho society was divided into several exogenous clan groups or *killis*. Members of the same *killi* were believed to have descended from a common ancestor and marriage within the *killi* was strictly proscribed. But gradually the laws governing such taboos became more lax particularly with the growth of industrial centres such as Jamshedpur and the coal mines which provided shelter to the runaway couples. Nonetheless, such conduct was generally considered deviant and the participants at the Lupungutu meeting urged the youth not to indulge in such liaisons and suggested that in case of transgression of tribal norms the offending members should forfeit protection from the society and be disinherited from their ancestral property.

The third major issue discussed at the Lupungutu conference related to the practice of bride price. Among the Hos the bride price that was asked had always been very high. Even in the mid-19th century, E.T. Dalton had noted the high incidence of unmarried girls of marriageable age, who were to be found in the Kolhan and attributed this to the high rate of bride price that prospective grooms were expected to pay to the brides' family.[30] In the early 20th century, the bride price often went up to thirty heads of cattle, forty to fifty silver coins and ornaments worth forty rupees, besides 200 to 300 pots of rice beer,[31] which was more than what an ordinary Ho could pay. According to Rev. A. Logsdail who was in charge of the Anglican Mission at Chaibasa, a *Manki* (a leader of a group of villages) in Kolhan had received forty heads of cattle as bride price before delivering his daughter over to her husband.[32] The meeting resolved to introduce a fixed rate of bride price in order to improve the social condition of the Hos. It was decided that for those who possessed land of their own for cultivation, the maximum bride price should not exceed Rs thirty, two bullocks and a cow, while for those without land, the maximum bride price should not exceed ten rupees.[33] These resolutions were corroborated at a subsequent meeting at Chainpur on 13 April, 1924.

The other issues touched upon at this meeting included female labour and sale of goods to *dikus*. With increased sale of goods from Kolhan at the numerous *hats* and *bazaars*, the spread of the Hindu influence became apparent so far as reforms related to female labour were concerned. Traditionally Ho women did not lead a life of seclusion and they could freely participate in the economic affairs of the village. However, at the meeting it was suggested that employment of female labour was incompatible with their ideal of social reform and it was resolved that in future no Ho women should carry straw, hay or grass to the market. Similarly, the practice of hawking fuel from house to house of the *dikus* had come to be considered demeaning to the dignity and self-respect of the Hos. It was decided that in future people should sit in some place to sell fuel. In case a *diku* required fuel to be carried to his house, an additional fee should be levied for the service.

Finally a resolution was passed condemning the habit that labourers particularly had developed of drinking *diang* or liquor in public godowns and liquor shops, over and above the country-made rice beer. It stated, "This meeting of the aborigines of Kolhan most emphatically condemn the practice of taking liquors in wine shops and urges upon the Ho labourers in the interests of the society to discontinue the practice".[34] This insistence on temperance as a measure of self-purification can be partly attributed to the influence of the Gandhian movement in the region. It became more apparent in 1931–32 in course of another religious movement, the Haribaba movement.

Another meeting of reformist Hos was organized on 6 April 1924, again at Lupungutu. The issues addressed were all concerned with the status of women. Because of the high bride price, forcible marrying of young girls by men who could not afford to pay for a regular marriage had become common. The meeting decided to introduce a fine of Rs fifty for offenders in order to discourage such a practice. In case of default the man was to be excommunicated. Another practice of keeping women of 'low social position' as mistresses by the Hos also came under fire. The phrase 'low social position' indicated Hos who ate beef. The reformists argued that Hos traditionally refused to eat with one who took beef and women who did so were looked down upon and regular marriage with them was normally proscribed. A resolution condemning the practice was passed by the reformists and Hos were called upon to purify their lives by not keeping women of low status as their mistresses.[35] This outlook of the reformists undoubtedly owed its origin to the spread of Hindu influence, reflecting as it did the usual Hindu aversion to the eating of beef. Contemporary anthropological accounts reveal that traditionally Hos did not have any taboos against the consumption of beef. However, it may be argued that though the reformers were influenced by Hindu social norms they did not aim at Hinduization of the tribe through assimilation within the Hindu social structure. Instead their aim was to strengthen Ho identity through effecting the regeneration of their social organization which was based partly on borrowing from Hindu cultural life. To do so they attempted to purge the Ho society of what was perceived by their neighbours as their negative attributes. The reformist Hos shared the belief that the *adivasi* society was less civilized than that of the Hindus. They did not, however, wish to become Hindu, but attempted to gain in self-respect through a programme of reform.

Haribaba Movement

In the early 1930s, there were two major religious reform movements among the Santals and the Hos, the former started by Silu Santal or Tarachand and the latter by Duka Ho, who took the name of Haribaba. Although these were apparently religious movements, they also had political overtones. What is interesting is the merging of the movements of the Hos and the Santals, a fact noted by British officers. R.P. Ward, the Deputy Commissioner stated that, "the fact that there is some sort of connection between Silu the Santal and Duka the Ho is rather curious as these two tribes usually keep strictly apart and the Hos have very little use for the Santals".[36]

In 1930, Silu Santal of Rajabasa in Dhalbhum or Tarachand as he came to be known by his followers claimed to have founded a new religion. Claiming divine inspiration through dreams, he set himself up as a healer with miraculous powers and called upon his people to give up drinking, eating crabs and snails.[37] Tarachand attempted to mobilize followers at Rajabasa by circulating mango leaves through villages in Dhalbhum, Mayurbhanj and south Kolhan with the message that the villages would be visited by an epidemic if they were not passed on. On 15 May, 1931, a large number of Santals collected at Rajabasa and proceeded to display their independence by pulling down telegraph wires,[38] the symbol of colonial power and authority. Tarachand threatened the local authorities that he would win *swaraj* because he had with him a "large number of soldiers without uniform", to whom "the British guns would cause no injury".[39] He was arrested but while on bail he next shifted his activities to Hurangda village in neighbouring Kharsawan. There he collected some 3,000 to 4,000 Kols, Bhumijes and Santals of Kharsawan, Seraikela and Tamar on 18 July

1931 and incited them to cut down timber and other trees from the State Reserved Forest and use them for erecting mandirs and other houses.[40]

The Haribaba movement spread at around the same time as Tarachand's movement, i.e., in 1931–32. It started in the northern parts of Singhbhum and from there it gradually spread to the whole of Ranchi district. Duka Ho, or Haribaba, was originally from Siriapos village in Seraikela estate. He set up his *ashram* in the forest at Jamrogara, near Chitpil which was located twelve miles north-west of Chakradharpur. Haribaba's fame spread through popular ceremonies from one village to another and people flocked from as far away as Manoharpur to see him and listen to his teachings. In the initial phase, the movement was largely concerned with religious reform as he preached the need to re-establish traditional purity. The programme of purification, which aimed at cleansing the unclean elements from Ho culture, was therefore linked with the assertion of Ho identity. Hence Haribaba also laid stress on racial isolation. His disciples were all *adivasi* and he exhorted them not to have to do anything with the *tantis* or the weaver caste and others whom he designated as inferior people. This anger against the *tantis* may be traced to the rapid change during the colonial period in the role of the latter within the Ho village economy. They could take advantage of the new system to acquire new sources of power in the village. An official report of 1897 stated that "The village accountants or tahsildars and *dakuas* or village watchmen are almost invariably of this caste. A *tanti* is the legal adviser of the villagers, no suit or litigation being entered on without his opinion being taken. Some had also acquired land in the tribal village.[41] In such circumstances the ire against *tantis* is understandable. The movement also aimed to drive out alien oppressors, particularly the Hindus. A Ho of Kera had informed the Kolhan Inspector that, "if ... the Hindu tried to oppress the Hos, the Hos could drive them out with bows and arrows".[42] Haribaba also advised his followers to give up the practice of witchcraft, a practice that was popularized by the village priests as it enhanced their authority.

In terms of purification, the Haribaba movement was essentially an anti *bonga* (spirit) movement. The faith of the people in the *bongas* had been eroded by the latter's inability to assist the Hos in their material concerns during a general time of economic and political instability.[43] This indicated the need for religious reformation. *Bongas* and *bhuts* were believed to hide themselves in the deep recesses of the houses and hence a hectic search for *bongas* was carried out amid deafening sounds of drums and gongs. New disciples would be initiated into the order through an elaborate ceremony to expel *bongas*. Those who wanted to join Haribaba's religion had to discard from his house all *agom tapan* objects, i.e., objects kept as outward signs of some promises to perform sacrifices on receiving favours from certain malevolent spirits. All the implements used for practising black magic kept in their houses, such as the *najams* or objects used for poisoning the enemy, the *chuka* or earthen vessels used for divination, the *padkis* or a measure for two seers of grain used for divination, had to be thrown out. Following the cleansing of the spirits in the houses, other purification rites had to be performed by the disciples. They had to bathe in the local rivers and visit the sacred grove or the jahira of the village.[44]

They also developed certain other customs of their own. Haribaba emphasized the need for absolute cleanliness. The followers of the cult bathed twice a day and women had to bathe before cooking. Old cooking pots and baskets were thrown out. They believed that Singbonga created oxen on Tuesday and so they did not work the oxen on Tuesdays. Similarly, since Lakshmi was created on Thursday and since the Harababites called the cow Lakshmi, they did not use cows for work on Thursdays. Haribaba preached that since they worked with cows and buffaloes, they should not eat them. Although it had traditionally been a common practice to sacrifice a buffalo to Marang Bonga and later partake of the meat, Haribabites gave up eating beef.[45] Vegetarianism was a rule and drinking was prohibited among them. These reforms bear a resemblance to the Gandhian temperance movement. As pointed out earlier, it may be argued that these practices were adopted by the *adivasi* reformers as they coincided with their own programme of reform.

Together with the purification of tribal usages and customs certain Hindu customs were also adopted. The Haribabites worshipped the tulsi plant and wore the sacred thread. They worshipped Hanuman and imitating him they danced with bows and arrows in their hand. Haribaba's wife Harima used to sprinkle holy water (*haripani*) on the followers on payment of a nominal amount.[46] Mathew Areeparampil argues that these reforms amounted to an attempt at sanskritization and emphasized the influence of the model of the Hindu caste system on the Haribabites.[47] However, as B.B. Chaudhuri points out, it is not certain that the emulation of such Hindu cultural traits amounted to the introduction of the caste hierarchy among the Haribabites.[48] Even the official report was not clear as to the implications in terms of any positional change in the caste system. The influence of Hindu cultural traits in the movement is unmistakeable, but this was utilized to strengthen the Ho identity by cleansing it of what was perceived to be evil within it. Similarly, there was no attempt to reject their tribal identity and adopt the traditions of the Hindus. There are no indications to show that the 'purified' Ho tended to be integrated into the Hindu caste system. In fact the movement aimed at strengthening the Hos against the *dikus*, most of whom were Hindus, by reforming and purifying those aspects of Ho society which were considered derogatory by the Hindus.

The Haribaba movement, however, did not remain confined to religious reformation but gradually developed into a political movement in its second phase.[49] However, the influence of the freedom struggle, the trends in the Haribaba movement were largely determined by the existing Ho culture. Gandhi's social and cultural programmes only marginally affected the 'purification' movement. On 19 July, 1931 Duka Ho, or Haribaba visited the Congress headquarters. Prior to this visit, the Congress had little connection with the *adivasi* population of the neighbourhood. The few volunteers who did enlist to the Congress included the *tantis* and non-*adivasi*. According to the police report, it was after this visit that Haribaba began to preach the non-payment of rents and the wearing of *khaddar*.[50] It was around this time that Haribaba established links with Tarachand and his disciple Jaichand or Jai Singh Santal who had set up their abode at Hurungda, about seven miles from Kharsawan. Haribaba visited Tarachand so as to 'exchange ideas'.[51] Haribaba declared to his followers that if they listened to his teachings and carried on the worship according to his instructions, he would arrange for a great meeting on some hill near Jamshedpur which would be attended by Haribaba himself, Tarachand and Gandhi[52] and he promised to restore the same set of things that existed before the coming of the British. Haribaba, in fact, told his followers that British Raj had come to an end and the reign of Gandhi had begun. The advent of the reign of Gandhi was celebrated with dances and feasts[53] and exuberant disciples danced and shouted *Haribol, Haribaba ki jai, Gandhi ki jai.*[54] As the Haribabites increasingly displayed a 'seditious attitude' the three most influential leaders were arrested. The Kharsawan police arrested Tarachand on 25 July, 1931, his disciple Jaichand was arrested on 27 July on the charge of assaulting the police and Haribaba himself was arrested on the evening of 27 July for disturbing peace.

With the arrest of the three leaders, the political phase of the movement gradually came to an end. However, the aspect of spiritual purification persisted for some time. Haribaba's disciples refused to accept the news of his imprisonment. Several miraculous tales circulated regarding his whereabouts. There were rumours that he had gone out to fight the British[55] and that he lived at an unknown spot on the banks of the Kanchi river, his body had turned to stone chest downwards, but was flesh and blood upwards and through his long hair flowed milk and water which were endowed with supernatural powers.[56] Several lesser 'Haribabas' came up to propagate the new religion. One Jojo Tamaria, called himself a disciple of 'god Hari' in Chota Nagpur and preached on the lines of Duka Ho.[57] After Duka Ho's arrest his wife Nani Kui set up her akhara at Nandpur near Manoharpur and preached Haribaba's religion. To avoid imprisonment herself, she restricted the movement to its purely religious form and took written engagements from her followers that they would not disobey the government. Nonetheless, the local government authorities decided to stop the movement, as they were not certain what it would lead to eventually. Some *Mundas* (headmen) who had been removed from office for their participation in Congress activities in 1924 in Kolhan called upon the people to flout the authority of the *Mankis* and *Mundas* (the traditional leadership) loyal to the British. They were arrested and the Haribaba movement was declared illegal.[58] Although the *Mundas* and *Mankis* were ordered to stop it, there were furtive attempts to continue it at Kasira. The Deputy Commissioner of Singhbhum visited six villages in the area on 18 January 1932 and broke up the bamboo fences and huts.[59] A few Hos in Manoharpur instigated the people not to pay the rent and they were arrested as were Hari Ma along with Jojo Tamaria.[60] What is interesting is that even Christian *adivasi* were forced to join the movement, while a missionary records that many Christian *adivasi* willingly joined the movement.[61] However, ultimately the government's repressive measures succeeded in subduing the movement and the new religion of Haribaba gradually subsided.

Pan-Tribal Identity Movement: Sarna Dharam Movement

Around the same time as the Haribaba movement, there were attempts to forge a distinctive pan tribal identity for the *adivasi* of Chota Nagpur based on the ancient ritual practices of the *sarna* or the sacred grove, which was associated with almost all the Chota Nagpur tribals. The sarna, or the *jahira* as it was known among the Hos, referred to cluster of *sal* trees located at the outskirts of a tribal village in which lived Dessauli or the village deities. Traditionally, there was a strict taboo against cutting trees in the jahira. However, in course of the 19th century, as the village community structure weakened because of the new pressures brought about by the colonial government, the communal laws upholding this taboo had also weakened. In the changed circumstances, the Hos had come to lose much of their old reverence for their sacred traditions and institutions. Although, formerly no Ho would dare to cut even a branch or use the wood for his household and other domestic purposes, a report on Ho society and culture in the second decade of the 20th century noted that this respect due to the abode of the *bongas* was gradually dying out.[62] This change in the cultural values could be explained partly in terms of economic needs, as was indicated by the report. It stated that during the settlement operations of 1913–1918, "it was noticed that the trees had been skinned off, so that the trees may die and the villagers be able to appropriate the dry wood without being accused by the local authorities of having felled live trees".[63]

In the early 20th century, an attempt was made to unite the tribal groups of Chota Nagpur on the basis of the practices centring on the sacred grove. To create a common platform for the *adivasi*, a conference was held at Chaibasa in 1932, which was attended by *adivasi* delegates from Bihar, Orissa and Bengal. The conference agreed on a common name, Sarna Dharam, to denote the ancient religion of the tribals of Chota Nagpur. Each of the *adivasi* communities developed its own organization for the propagation of the religion. Thus, the *Mundas* called it Munda Sarna Sangh, the Santals called it Sarna Dharam Semlet and the Oraons called it Sarna Nav Yuvak Sangh.[64] The Hos did not have any organization on the lines of the Sarna Dharam, but they formed an association known as the Dupup Samaj which urged its members to follow the Dupup Dharam. While the Hos accepted the tenets of the Sarna Dharam, they did not use the term, preferring use their own nomenclature of Dupup Dharam.[65]

Conclusion

In conclusion we may make two observations. In the first place, this essay demonstrates that British policies were seldom motivated solely by ideological considerations. This is not to deny the role of ideology in policy-making, but to stress the fact that often ground realities and the exigencies of the time played the determining role. Thus, it would not be correct to talk of colonial tribal policies as a well thought-out project as some recent scholars have done. Secondly, while British rule undoubtedly created categories and policies that impacted in a major way on indigenous identities, we should remember that tribal people were not simply passive participants in the making of their destinies. In fact, as this essay shows, they too sought to actively recreate their self-identity in keeping with the socio-economic and political culture of the time.

Notes

1. Such a point of view is expressed in diverse writings ranging from articles in Bengali literary journals, such as those of Asit Kumar Haldar ("Ho der Katha", *Prabashi*, 1322 B.S., Part 15, Vol. 2, No. 1, pp. 27–32), to the output of nationalist historians like Kali Kinkar Datta (*Santal Insurrection*, Calcutta, 1940), Dhirendranath Baske (*Saotal Ganasangramer Itihas*, Calcutta, 1976) and anthropologists and political scientists professing a 'Sons of the Soil' approach, such as Myron Weiner (*Sons of the Soil, Migration and Ethnic Conflict in India*, Delhi, 1988).
2. See for instance, Sangeeta Dasgupta, "Reordering a World: The Tanabhagat Movement, 1914—1919", *Studies in History* (New Series), Vol. 15, 1, 1999; Sanjukta Dasgupta, "A Middle Indian Tribe in Transition: the Ho of Singhbhum, 1821–1932", unpublished Ph. D. Thesis, Calcutta University, 2007.
3. Jagannath Pathy, *Anthropology of Development: Demystifications and Relevance*, New Delhi, 1987, p. 46.
4. Susana B.C. Devalle, *Discourses of Ethnicity: Culture and Protest in Jharkhand*, New Delhi, 1992, p. 50.
5. In Gujarat, for instance, the terms 'jangli jati' (literally forest people) and 'kaliparaj' (the black people) were commonly used to indicate *adivasis* of South Gujarat. David Hardiman, *The Coming of the Devi: Adivasi Assertion in Western India*, New Delhi, 1987, pp. 13–14.
6. An instance of such appropriation is the use of the designation *chuar* by which the colonial administration described the rebel tribals of South West Bengal during the period 1783–1832. The term was borrowed from the Hindus. *Chuar* in Bengali meant 'wild, ferocious and ill-mannered'.
7. I borrow this concept from B.B. Chaudhuri. See B.B. Chaudhuri, "The Myth of the Tribe? The Question Reconsidered", *The Calcutta Historical Journal*, Vol. 16, No. 1, p. 152.
8. For a discussion on 'invention of tradition', See Terence Ranger, "Invention of Tradition in Colonial Africa" in Eric Hobsbawm and Terence Ranger (eds.), *The Invention of Tradition*, Cambridge, 1983; Leroy Vail, *The Creation of Tribalism in Southern Africa*, London, 1989.
9. For instance, at a time when a section of colonial administrators glorified the Hos as noble savages, other groups such as the Koravas of South India, the Bhils of Western India and Lodhs of Western Midnapur were classified as 'criminal tribes'. In fact the idea of the criminal tribe germinated and developed over a long period of time, as Stewart Gordon shows with reference to the Bhils of Western India. Stewart Gordon, "Bhils and the Idea of a Criminal Tribe in Nineteenth Century India", in Stewart Gordon, *Marathas, Marauders and State Formation in 18th Century India*, New Delhi, 1994, pp. 151–162.
10. A part of the Chota Nagpur Division of the Bengal Presidency till 1911, Singhbhum today falls in the newly created state of Jharkhand, i.e. Erstwhile South Bihar. It lies between 22°E and 23°E north latitude and 86°53'E and 85°2' E of east longitude and forms an important part of the lower plateau of Chota Nagpur.
11. T.S. Macpherson, *Final Report on the Operations for the Preparation of Record-of-Rights in Pargana Porahat in District Singhbhum, 1905–07*, Calcutta: Bengal Secretariat Press, 1908, pp. 78–79.
12. E.T. Dalton, *Descriptive Ethnology of Bengal*, Calcutta, 1872, (Reprint), Delhi, 1974.

13. Ramgarh Magistrate to Bayly, 30 June, 1817, Bengal Judicial Criminal Proceedings, No. 39, 29 July, 1817, West Bengal State Archives, hereafter WBSA.
14. Ibid.
15. E.T. Dalton, op. cit., p. 192.
16. At the time of its formation, the Kolhan Government Estate comprised of 620 Ho villages in 26 *pirs* of Singhbhum and Mayurbhanj. Bengal Judicial Criminal Proceedings, No. 15, 6 June 1837, WBSA.
17. S.R. Tickell, "The Memoir on the Hodesum", *Journal of the Asiatic Society of Bengal*, Vol. IX, Part II, 1840, p. 806.
18. The most significant of such customs that the British considered 'self-destructive' related to witchcraft.
19. Ashis Nandy, *The Intimate Enemy, Loss and Recovery of Self Under Colonialism*, Delhi, 1983, pp. 11–18.
20. Wilkinson to Tickell, 5 May, 1837, Paras., 1–2, Bengal Judicial Criminal Proceedings, No. 15, 6 June, 1837, WBSA.
21. E.T. Dalton, op. cit., p. 10.
22. E.T. Dalton, *Descriptive Ethnology of Bengal*, Calcutta, 1872, (Reprint), Delhi, 1974.
23. Ibid.
24. D.M. Panna, "Note on the Hos", in A.D. Tuckey, *Final Report on the Resettlement of the Kolhan Government Estate in the District of Singhbhum*, Patna, 1920, p. 128.
25. Ibid.
26. Ibid.
27. Ibid.
28. D.N. Majumdar, "The Cry of Social Reform among the Aborigines", *Modern Review*, March, 1925, p. 287.
29. Ibid., p. 287.
30. E.T. Dalton, op. cit., p. 200.
31. D.N. Majumdar, 1925, op. cit., p. 288.
32. Eyre Chatterton, *The Story of Fifty Years' Mission Work in Chota Nagpur*, London, 1901, p. 127.
33. Ibid., p. 288.
34. Translation provided by D.N. Majumdar, 1925, op. cit., p. 289.
35. Ibid., p. 289.
36. Extract from A.D. Tuckey's fortnightly D.O. No. 287, TC, 27 July, 1931, Government of Bihar and Orissa, Political (Special) Department, File No. 57, 1931, Bihar State Archives.
37. A. Majid to A.D. Tuckey, (Comm.), CND, 27 March, 1931, cited in K.S. Singh, "The Haribaba Movement in Chota Nagpur, 1931–32", *Journal of the Bihar Research Society*, Vol. XLIX, Parts 1–4, p. 285.
38. Ibid.
39. Extract from confidential diary of Superintendent of Police, Singhbhum for the period ending 27 May, 1931, cited in ibid.
40. Raja Sriram Chandra Singh Deo, Ruling Chief of Kharswan Feudatory State to the Deputy Commissioner of Singhbhum, 26 July 1931, Government of Bihar and Orissa, Political (Special) Department, File No. 57, 1931, BSA.

41. J.A. Craven, *Final Report on the Settlement of the Kolhan Estate in District Singhbhum in the year 1897*, Calcutta, 1898, p. 21, Para. 73.
42. Extract from A.D. Tuckey's fortnightly D.O. No. 287, TC, 27 July, 1931, Government of Bihar and Orissa, Political (Special) Department, File No. 57, 1931, BSA.
43. R.P. Ward to Tuckey, Confidential D.O. No. 132/C, 30 July, 1931, Para. 8, Government of Bihar and Orissa, Political (Special) Department, File No. 57, 1931, BSA.
44. Ibid., p. 400.
45. Ibid.
46. F.E.A. Taylor, *Final Report on the Revisional Settlement of Porahat Estate, District Singhbhum, 1928–32*, Patna, 1938, p. 31.
47. Mathew Areeparampil, "Socio-Cultural and Religious Movements among the Ho Tribals of Singhbhum District of Bihar", in Mrinal Miri (ed.), *Continuity and Change in Tribal Society*, Simla, 1993, p. 402.
48. B.B. Chaudhuri, "Society and Culture of the Tribal World in Colonial Eastern India: Reconsidering the Notion of Hinduization of Tribes", in Hetukar Jha (ed.), *Perspectives on Indian Society and History: A Critique*, Delhi, 2002, p. 65.
49. For a detailed discussion see K.S. Singh, "The Haribaba Movement in Chota Nagpur, 1931–32", *Journal of the Bihar Research Society*, Vol. XLIX, Parts 1–4, 1963.
50. R.P. Ward to Tuckey, op. cit., p. 4.
51. Ibid., p. 5.
52. Extract from A.D. Tuckey's fortnightly D.O. No. 287, TC, 27 July, 1931, op. cit.
53. G. Vanhoutta, 'Haribaba', *Chotonagpur Mission Letter*, No 11, November 1931, pp. 236–239.
54. Ibid.
55. W.G. Dickson, 'The Haribaba Movement, what it is', *Chota Nagpur Diocesan Paper No. 40* (New series) cited in K.S. Singh, 'The Haribaba Movement in Chota Nagpur', op. cit., p. 288.
56. G. Vanhoutta, op. cit., pp. 236–39.
57. K.S. Singh, op. cit., p. 292.
58. Ibid.
59. Ibid., p. 293.
60. Ibid.
61. C. Vanhoutta, op. cit. pp. 238–39.
62. Dhan Mashi Panna, Assistance Settlement Officer, Kolhan Government Estate, 'Notes on the Hos', op. cit., Appendix E, p. 128.
63. Ibid.
64. P.C. Hembram, "Return to the Sacred Grove", in K.S. Singh (ed.), *Tribal Movements in India*, Vol. 2 (Delhi, 1982), p. 87.
65. Ibid.

16 Challenging the Sanskritic Order

Emergence of the Sudra to Subaltern Consciousness in Pre-Colonial Orissa

BASANTA KUMAR MALLIK

Pre-colonial Indian society was broadly characterized as an unequal and hierarchical society. A specific form of economic, social and cultural hierarchy and inequitable growth of power in India were based upon the varna system. Proliferation of castes also enriched the age old varna system and strengthened the system of social hierarchy. This growth of inequitable power structure was legitimized by the religious concept that led to development of the cultural hegemony of a few over the masses. Following such a system of privileges for some and deprivation for many on the basis of birth, thus characterized to be the Sanskritic (Brahmanic) order was challenged at all times and in all places, though in an uneven manner, over the entire region.

The present paper analyzes various aspects of the social protest and cultural revolt that took place in pre-colonial Orissa beginning with the fifteenth century AD. The movement developed particularly in the coastal Orissa and in course of time its impact was seen in other parts of Eastern India. The medieval Oriya subaltern saints popularly known as *Sudramunis* endeavoured to transform the socio-cultural life by giving an alternative ideology of 'social equality' against the Brahmanical orthodoxy. Their discontent against the contemporary society, priests, ruling class and their sincere efforts for scholarly enquiry are clearly discernible in their writings. They protested against the authority of the 'four pillars' of the contemporary society.

First of all, they protested against the discriminatory social structure (i.e., caste, untouchability, low status of the Sudras and women and their deprivation of knowledge).

Secondly, they opposed the intellectual hegemony of the Sanskrit language and as a mark of protest they created parallel regional literature.

Thirdly, they criticized the religious impositions and various externalities like priesthood, rituals, pilgrimage and idol worship.

Fourthly, they raised their voice against the political authority and dominance of the ruling class. They, however, worked for the common people and wrote in the people's language and advocated equality between the raja and praja and propagated bhakti for worshipping personal deities.

The nature of their 'dissent and protest' and their transformation from the Sudrahood to subaltern consciousness can be understood better with a look at the socio-cultural background of the period. The contemporary society, religion and culture remained completely under the spell of Brahmanism with the growth of gigantic temples, establishment of Brahman *sasanas*, land grants to Brahmans, temples and other officials and the patronization of Sanskrit literature in Orissa during the period tenth-eleventh century. The scriptures remained entirely under the domination of Sanskrit, which served the official and professional language of a minority group in society that had monopolized education. Sanskrit enjoyed absolute primacy in the hierarchy of languages. For a long time, it was the only written language, but even when its monopoly had been challenged and literary vernaculars developed along side it, Sanskrit maintained a privileged position. It was seen as the sacred language guaranteeing unity of faith and salvation. It was believed that God could specifically be addressed in the medium of the *devabhasa*, i.e., Sanskrit. The layman did not know Sanskrit and to be literate one had to know Sanskrit. Accordingly the division of the people into literate and unlettered or semi-educated, a notion of late antiquity remained decisive.

The Brahmans, besides performing religious ceremonies, acted as the foci of culture. It was they who taught the people the immense benefits of listening to the *puranas*. Since the common people were not allowed to read the *puranas*, *Purana Pandas* read out and explained to them the contents of the *puranas* which were all written in Sanskrit. Apart from scriptural elements the *puranas* emphasized social norms as well as social sanctions or penalties for violating them. Over and above, the *Mukta Mandap* was an assembly of orthodox Brahman pundits within the premises of the Jagannatha temple. This was the highest authority in socio-religious matters and its verdict was enforced, if necessary under the authority of the King. *Mukta Mandap* (changed to be *Mukti Mandap* sometimes after sixteenth century) was also a place of religious and metaphysical discourse which only the Brahmans could carry on and their brethren and the King could listen to.[1]

The Sudramunis of medieval Orissa played the most vital role in generating the spirit of equality and human dignity. They undermined the established tradition of writing scriptures and *puranas* in Sanskrit and started composing them in the language of the common people, i.e., Oriya. They endeavoured to abolish the superstition preached by the orthodox priests and propagated that God could also be prayed to in their colloquial language and worshipped in their heart and mind filled in with bhakti. Sudramuni Sarala Dasa, a cultivator and poet composed the Oriya *Mahabharata* (late fifteenth century) in Jhankad village of the present Jagatsinghpur district, Sudramuni Balaram Dasa wrote the *Ramayana, Lakshmi Purana* and other treatises, *Bipra* Jagannatha Dasa composed the *Bhagavata* in Puri (both in sixteenth century) and another Sudramuni Achyutananda Dasa (in sixteenth century) composed the *Harivamsa* in his Nembal village of Cuttuck district, quiet far away from the royal court and without any royal patronage.[2]

The anti-caste pronouncements are very much conspicuous in their writings. Renouncing all original caste surnames they used *Dasa* after their names meaning servant or *sevaka* to God and Godesses. By doing this, they in a measure protested against different caste surnames, the discriminative character and the concept of high and low of the Brahmanical order.[3] The munis did not remain satisfied only by rendering the Sanskrit works in Oriya, they also attempted to participate in the Vedanta discussions held at the Mukti Mandap of the Jagannatha temple at Puri. Amongst them the most outspoken and revolutionary, namely, Balarama Dasa and Achyutananda Dasa challenged the Brahman pundits as regards the rights of the Sudras to study Vedas and Dharmasastras, which were a complex and contradictory synthesis of two different levels of culture.

The Sudramunis did neither believe in idol worship, nor in fasting, pilgrimage and celebrating the sacred days. According to Balarama, the people worship idols, because they do not know that God is imageless. The poet wonders how the people worship the God who does not even speak a word. The tradition of idol worship, pilgrimage, fasting, sacrifice, rituals and even existence of Gods and Goddesses are superfluous he firmly confirmed.[4] The poet wondered how the people really understand the reality although they were guided by the munis to think that all religious externalities were meaningless and means of exploitation. According to Achyutananda, the innocent people were deceived to worship the spirits and Gods. They did not know that the *mantras*, *japas*, fasting, pilgrimage and meditations were not for the welfare of society.[5] The Sudramunis advised the people not to believe in idol worship or in fasting etc., because they wanted to protect the people from the clutches of priesthood and Brahmanism as well. They wanted to keep direct relations between the God and the devotees through bhakti and therefore, there was no need of the intermediary priestly class.

The philosophy of these saints cannot be categorized and limited to a particular sect or religious community. The five poets were above any sectarian zealotry. They did not as such condemn any particular way of sadhana and plead in favour of their own way; but they were against narrow and rigid adherence to any particular way. Their attitude behind all what they spoke and wrote was one of an all accepting inner-integrity and purity. They accepted the noble principles of many contemporary religious strands but never fell into any of the sectarian lines. The Sudramunis were Vaishnavas, yet they were much more than those who close themselves into a sect called Vaishanava. They spoke and wrote about the necessity of *kayasadhana*, but they were not only *kayasadhakas*. They were Buddhists in much of their avowals, yet not Buddhists as far as to be Buddhists meant following a particular sect. They sang of and adored to the supreme Brahma, yet were much more than the doctrinaire Advaitins. They made a synthesis between nirguna and saguna and between jnana and bhakti. They were bhaktas and jnanis at the same time, because the real bhakta and the real jnani do combine the two in the process of his becoming. They proclaimed that to remain engrossed with the transitory worldly living was to live buried in maya, but they were not mayabadins. They were on the side of life, its enhancement and in its excellence in the full spiritual liberation of the term. They were inextricably attached with the human situations and they were true bhaktas, sadhakas and social reformers.[6]

The Sudramunis endeavoured so much to elevate the status of the lowly-placed in society and wrote special books to make them feel equal to others and also indispensable for the total functioning of the society. It is not surprising that these poets who proclaimed the presence of God in everybody and did not find much justice in the contemporary caste society. So they had their own way of dealing with the problem in order to solve it. Traditionally when the caste structure has been looked upon as a divine dispensation and its whole ethics was built with clever insularity, the poets declared themselves to be Sudras.[7] In fact, they belonged by birth to different castes in society; at least one of them was a Brahman but became Sudra by choice. They had their own way of explaining the origins of caste as a system. Achyutananda, for example, rejected the definition of the origin of the varnas given in the *Purusasukta,* i.e., Brahmans from the mouth, Kshatriyas from the arms, Vaisyas from the eyes and Sudras from the feet of the God. He provided an alternative in his *Gupta Gita* that Vaisyas were the eyes, Kshatriyas the ears, Brahmans the breaths of the nose and the Sudras the face as a whole. These four varnas were created from a flame.[8] With this analysis the poet has tried to explain different components of society and their interdependence. At the height of feeling of high and low, caste and untouchability, his struggle thus was successful in raising the spirit of egalitarianism.

The Sudramunis explained different stages of bhakti in terms of experience and fulfilment. They, however, attributed the Sudrabhakti is bhakti at its summit, bhakti that can sustain itself without faltering and also sustain the adherent bhakta on his honoured path. It may also be pointed out that bhakti remains at the religious level and makes allowances for necessary religiousities but the level of Sudrabhakti it is elevated to the spiritual plain and the Brahmadarshin fulfils himself by becoming a dasa of the God.

Propounding the social connotation of the theory of the bhakti, Achyutananda and other saints have openly moved against all caste considerations and attributes of high and low in society with now qualm in their conscience they had voluntarily declared themselves to be the lowest in society. They had declared that they had the Sudra propensity as the determining propensity and thus they were nothing but Sudras. Doing this, the Sudramunis gave a new connotation to the very concept of Sudra as a symbol of the sudrabhava and suggested that every aspirant after God realization pursuing the highest attainment had also to be a possessor of this Sudrabhava. Through this kind of philosophical exposition Brahmanism was certainly challenged and as a result of the consciousness of the dignity of the common men, the Brahmanical order underwent significant modification.

The Sudramunis have warned that without the guru coming to help one cannot know the real truth in the world. But as in everything else, they revolted against the idea of hero worship, i.e., making an idol of the guru. The guru, who encourages helpless dependence and makes an idol of himself, will be more of a hindrance than help. The Sudramunis were determined to start a mass movement in society for a change in outlook and attitude. Having personified the system of worship, they said that one could not see God only in the temple; one could feel him inside one's heart also. In this regard said Achyutananda,

"The knowledge you seek for is stored in your heart. You have to find it there and realize it. The knowledge of the Brahma, Brahmajnana, is never far from you, it is inseparably contained in your own temple".[9]

Orissan society, culture and religion have developed and conglomerated together mainly concentrating with Lord Jagannatha. Lord Jagannatha became the nucleus of the Orissan polity and culture. In medieval times and particularly during sixteenth century the cult of Jagannatha reached its climax. It was completely by then sanskritized and had become an integral part of high Hinduism. But the striking feature of the period is that in course of the resurgence of the Sudramunis' movement Lord Jagannatha found a remarkable position in their literature and contemporary bhaktas and kavis tried to reform the society by creating the regional literature woven around the name and cult of Lord Jagannatha. In course of time of the Hinduization of the deity, Lord Jagannatha was considered an elite deity at least up to the period of Sarala Dasa (late fifteenth century) and since then from Sarala Dasa to the Panchasakhas all Bhaktakavis have challenged the high Hinduism and endeavoured to retrieve Lord Jagannatha with a view to reviving their submerged glorious past. They have however been, successful in establishing Lord Jagannatha as the Patita-pavana (the redeemer of the fallen or depressed) and peoples' deity. Thus Lord Jagannatha, His cult, His temple and His *kshetra* found admiring expressions in the devotional songs and other writings of those bhaktas, the Sudramunis, are considered to be the peoples' poets of Orissa. The holy town of Puri was exalted in the writings of the Sudramunis and other poets. It was believed to be the replica of the eternal Gokul. Jasovanta Dasa described in his *Premabhakti Brahma Gita* that Nilachala (Puri) is greater than the religious places like Dwarka, Mathura and Brundavan.[10] Balarama Dasa composed and dedicated his *Jagamohana Ramayana* in honour of Lord Jagannatha. Jagannatha Dasa in his *Darubrahma Gita* has lucidly described and reinforced the viewpoint of Sarala Dasa that the image of Lord Jagannatha was carved out of the corpse of Lord Krishna which became the sacred log.[11] Rai Ramananda composed his drama *Jagannatha Ballava Natakam* in order to narrate the eternal dalliance of Radha and Krishna. He conceives the idea that Subhadra as no other than Radha. Again in Balarama Dasa's *Vedantasara Gupta Gita*[12] and in Achyutananda Dasa's *Sunya Samhita*[13] Jagannatha has been described as the embodiment of all the incarnations of Lord Vishnu. By this time in Orissan Vaishnavism Jagannatha was conceived to be an avatari (source of all incarnations) and all other manifestations were his avatara (incarnation).

The features of social protest and the people's version of their glorious past and heritage are conspicuous in the writings of the Sudramunis and other like-minded poet reformers who spearheaded the social movement during fifteenth and sixteenth centuries. Sudramuni Sarala Dasa laid the foundation stone of this movement by opposing all sorts of formalities of life and religion. The poet had a deep sense of sympathy for the downtrodden classes like tribals, Sudras, women and other commoners. In his *Mahabharata* Jara Sabara who was offended and debarred from military training by the Kauravas, emerges later on, the victor. Again he (Jara) kills Krishna, conceals his body and becomes the first worshipper of Lord Jagannatha in the form of Nilamadhava. Sarala Dasa was the pioneer for propounding the theory of tribal origin of the Jagannatha cult.[14] The primary analysis of the very fact of Sarala Mahabharata bears bright testimony to the poets' onslaught on the Brahmanical superstructure. The Brahmanical monopoly placing them as the custodians of religion and religious texts received a great challenge. Not that the poet merely challenged the prevailing social norms for the sake of opposition, his works prominently breathed an air of freedom in the process of social regeneration of the popular classes, women and other marginalized groups. His *Vichitra Ramayana* and *Chandi Purana* present the benign aspects of womanhood. He presented through literature the view that women were not weak, but equal and powerful along with the men folks of society.[15]

The social movement inaugurated by Sarala Dasa was carried forward to its logical end by the Sudramunis of subsequent times. They launched the movement at a time when the Brahmanical pretensions were at their apex. The Sudramunis opposed the Brahmanical supremacy by following Lord Buddha in their definition of Brahmanhood that a Brahman was a Brahman by character and not by birth. Two outspoken revolutionary Sudramunis—Balarama Dasa and Achyutananda Dasa challenged the Brahmanical hegemony at the Mukti Mandap of Puri. Balarama Dasa, in his *Ramayana*, shows his appreciation of Sugriba, Hanumana and Bibhisana for their honesty, sincerity and truly helpful attitude to Rama, and has also established friendship between the King Rama and tribal chief Guhaka. In critical tone, Achyutananda, in his *Sabdabrahma Samhita* satires the supposed sacredness of Brahmans is that a Brahman considers himself polluted if he touched a dead body. But how come the same Brahman could take meat of goats after they were killed and dead?[16] Achyutananda questions this paradoxical hypocrisy. In his *Kaivarta Gita* he emphasizes that a Candala is no other than the Brahman (almighty) itself.[17] As regards the varna system, Balarama Dasa even says that the four orders like Brahmans, Kshyatriya, Vaisya and Sudra originated from a single flame of light and therefore all belonged to one caste in this world.[18] Achyutananda stipulates in his *Gurubhakti Gita* that before one gets blessings from the guru (preceptor) one has to invite four persons from four different varnas and entertain them equally as honoured guests,[19] which shows his attempt not only to blow the caste distinction but also to assist the process of social equality, stability and integration.

The Sudramunis protested against the authoritarian activities of both the priests and the King. Achyutananda wrote in his *Harivamsa*, *Gopalanka Ogal* and *Kaivarta Gita* to glorify the milkmen and fishermen communities who had hitherto shrunk to the position of Sudras. Jagannatha Dasa translated the Sanskrit *Bhagavata* into Oriya for the people especially for the common men and women, who had no access to learning and education in the Brahman dominated society. In the *Vedanatsara Gupta Gita*, Sudramuni Balarama Dasa openly declared before the King and the assembly of the learned Brahmans that access to the *sastras* was not the exclusive privilege of the Brahmans alone. He invited the wrath of Gajapati and the Brahman priests. He offered his *Brahmavidya* test in the royal court as revealed from his *Gita Avakasa*.[20]

In course of the social movement launched by the *Sudramunis* it is observed that they developed a protest ideology and departed from the religious orthodoxy of the Brahmanical order. They maintained their distinction as the followers of the concept of void or *sunya*. They were regarded as concealed Buddhists (*prachhana Buddha*) by the Brahmans and thus the situation led to inflicting of the political torture upon them. The dominant vested interests created certain situations in which the protagonists were made to go through different humiliating tests. Sometimes they were imprisoned and were exiled from Puri (the religious headquarter of Orissa) to different isolated places: Balarama Dasa to Samagara Pata, Jagannatha Dasa to Balibantara sea beach, Achyutananda Dasa to Banki muhana and the followers of these saints to the Dandakaranya forest region of Orissa.[21]

Lord Jagannatha was the linchpin of society and the Sudramunis struck against the different props of the said society. The question that arises is: why did they spare Lord Jagannatha? Most of them had prayed to Lord Jagannatha at the initial stages of their writings, very often they also claimed to have been born by the grace of Lord Jagannatha. Besides, a large number of devotees renounced their affiliation with different minor religious sects and they worshipped Lord Jagannatha as the supreme deity. Here we should not forget that originally Lord Jagannatha was a tribal deity and it was only from the twelfth century onwards that he underwent the process of Brahmanization. This must surely have been disliked by the Sudras or non-Brahmans who often tried to project Him as a God of the Little Tradition. It was proved by the version of Sarala Dasa in his *Mahabharata* that Jagannatha was being worshipped by the Sabara Jara in the form of Nilamadhava.[22] Balarama Dasa and his other comrades have also characterized Lord Jagannatha as a deity of the Little Tradition.[23] *Lakshmi Purana* of Balarama Dasa is another evidence in which Lakshmi got a declaration of 'social equality' and a casteless society by Lord Jagannatha himself.[24] So it appears that the tirade was not so much against Jagannatha as it was against the metamorphosis that they experienced in course of time. Apart from this, when Lord Jagannatha had been so popular and was already considered to be the Lord of the Universe, it was wise on the part of the Sudramunis to use His name to mould the rest of the society. One could well argue that had Jagannatha continued as a deity of the Great Tradition, the majority of the people in Oriya society, who were no doubt Sudras, would have been alienated from Him and possibly might have set up a deity of their own. But it is not so in case of Orissa and it's people. The cleavage thus ended in cohesion. Jagannatha, the central pivot in Oriya socio-religious life, who was considered to be a deity of the King and the priests, now occupied a place in mass consciousness because of the lofty efforts of the Sudramunis.[25]

The Sudramunis, through their numerous writings, widened the scope and dimensions of social protest. They were not merely iconoclasts. They had more enduring commitment to society. Whatever they did was prompted by a vision, the vision of new egalitarian society based on common humanism. Most striking aspect of the Oriya literature created by the Sudramunis was born, developed and thrived because of the masses of unknown, secluded and marginalized people. Their feelings, dreams and aspirations found expression through literature. There is no praise of the sovereigns: no glorification of their deeds finds a place in these literary works. The literature of this period remained a world by itself with its indigenous style and rhythm. It, therefore, fulfilled the psychological need of the people. It also met their mythological, religious, aesthetic norms and expectations. The Sudramunis brought the spiritual lore that was as yet a sealed book in Sanskrit to the doorsteps of the peasant's cottage. "Knowledge cannot be monopolized by a particular section of society nor it can be expressed in a particular language" was the lofty message of these Sudramunis. In the processes of this cultural revolt the vigorous expression of the subaltern consciousness is conspicuously discernible with the radical departure from the spheres of the community, language and theme of the literary discourse in medieval Orissa.

Notes

1. Balarama Dasa, *Vedantasar Gupta Gita*, Union Printing Works, Cuttuck, 1910, pp. 1–2; See also *Madalapanji*, (edited by) A.B. Mohanty, Prachi Samiti, Cuttuck, 1940, p. 64; Georg Pfeffer, "Puri's Vedic Brahmans: Continuity and Change in their Traditional Institutions" in Eschmann, Kulke and Tripathy (eds.), *The Cult of Jagannatha and the Regional Traditions of Orissa*, Manohar, New Delhi, 1978, p. 427; Harihara Kanungo, "Mukti Mandap O. Sri Jagannatha Mandirara Samparka", in *Jhankara*, 48th Year, No. 4, July 1996, pp. 406–13; Subhakanta Behera, *Construction of an Identity Discourse: Oriya Literature and the Jagannatha Cult*, Munshiram Manoharlal, New Delhi, 2002, pp. 151–55.
2. Mayadhar Mansingh, *A History of Oriya Literature*, Sahitya Akademi, New Delhi, 1962, Second Print, 2005, pp. 46–64, 82–101; See also Chittaranjan Das, *A Glimpse into Oriya Literature*, Orissa Sahitya Akademi, Bhubaneswar, 1982a, pp. 47–107; B.K. Mallik, *Paradigms of Dissent and Protest: Social Movements in Eastern India* (AD 1400–1700), Manohar, New Delhi, 2004, p. 17.
3. Surendra Mohanty hints at the view point that the pre-Aryans have been identified as *Dasas* in the Rig Veda. Since the *bhaktidharma* based on *Krishna bhakti* was prevalent mostly among the people of a non-sanskritized society, the poets and preceptors of the society identified themselves with the title *Dasa*, which appears to be correct from the standpoint of the process of Hinduization in Orissa. See Surendra Mohanty, *Oriya Sahityara Madhyaparva O. Uttara Madhyaparva*, Cuttuck Student Store, Cuttuck, (6th edition), 1995, p.19.
4. Balarama Dasa, *Chhatishi Gupta Gita*, Dasarathi Pustakalya, Cuttuck, n.d.
5. Achyutananda Dasa, *Brahmasankuli* (*Prathama Kalpa*), (ed.), A.B. Mohanty, Mukur Press, Cuttuck, 1926.
6. Chittaranjan Das, op. cit., 1982a, pp. 75–76.
7. K. Pathisharma, "Mahapurusa Achyutananda", in B. Mohanty (ed.), *Konark* (Panchasakha Special), Orissa Sahitya Akademi Bhubaneswar, 1971, p. 459.
8. Achyutananda Dasa, *Gupta Gita*, Siddheswari Pustakalaya, Cuttuck, n.d.
9. Chittaranjan Das, op. cit., 1982a, p. 77ff.
10. Jasovanta Dasa, *Premabhakti Brahma Gita*, Prachi Samiti, Bhubaneswar, n.d.

11. *Darubrahma Gita* of Jagannatha Dasa quoted in Chittaranjan Das, *Balarama Dasa*, Sahitya Akademi, New Delhi, 1982b, p. 21.
12. Balarama Dasa, op. cit., 1910.
13. Achyutananda Dasa, *Sunya Samhita*, Arunodya Press, Cuttuck, 1914, pp. 55–52.
14. A.B. Mohanty (ed.), *Sarala Mahabharata (Musali Parva)*, Department of Cultural Affairs, Orissa, Bhubaneswar, 1965, pp. 50–61, 78–86.
15. B.K. Mallik, op. cit., 2004, pp. 89–91.
16. K.C. Sahoo (ed.), *Charikhani Ba Sabdabrahma Samhita* of Achyutananda Dasa, Books and Books, Cuttuck, 1979, p. 15.
17. Achyutananda Dasa, *Kaivarta Gita*, Chap. XXIII.
18. Balarama Dasa, *Chatisi Gupta Gita*, Dasarathi Pustakalaya, Cuttuck, n.d., Chap. VI.
19. Chittaranjan Das, *Achyutananda O Panchasakha Dharma*, Viswa Bharati, Shanti Niketan, 1951, p. 187.
20. Balarama Dasa, *Gita Avakasa*, Prachi Samiti, Bhubaneswar, n.d.
21. Surendra Mohanty, op. cit., p. 215, 231, 269 and pp. 240–7.
22. A.B. Mohanty, *Sarala Mahabharata (Musali Parva)*, pp. 50–61, 78–86, 208–27.
23. Nilambara Dasa, *Deula Tola Suanga*, quoted in B.M. Padhy, "Panchasakha Sahityare Sri Jagannatha", in B. Mohanty (ed.) op. cit., pp. 85–93.
24. Balarama Dasa, *Lakshmi Purana*, Sanyasi Pustakalaya, Berhampur, n.d.
25. R.K. Das, "Social Protest in Medieval Orissa", in *Proceedings of Indian History Congress*, 41st Session Bombay, 1980, p. 345.

17 The 'Savage Other' in Naga Historiography

Condition and Paradigm

TEMJENWABANG

> If one were to trace in detail, the origin and radius of diffusion of a certain thought-model, one would discover the peculiar affinity it has to the social position of given groups and their manner of interpreting the world.[1]

That, human mind is susceptible to assumptions and conceptualizations, conscious or unconscious 'biases' often take place in the process of writing a society different from the writers. 'Othering', a worldwide phenomenon, can be located mostly within a negative psychological and perceptual framework. It does not mean that all its aspects are negative; the persistent and the accommodating nature and tolerance of humanity have made it possible for individuals and societies to 'co-exist', even under trying relationships. However, othering contributes to a larger question of history. And when othering becomes a process of portrayal or representation, either in literate tradition or hearsay, the received understanding becomes a historical symbolism that withstands the rage of time. More explicit, when literate traditions have the potency to frame events and narratives—they become sources for succeeding generations. Reading meaning out of these symbolisms is then a prerogative judgement of the later writers and commentators.

Before this paper proceeds, let us consider a note on post-colonial scholarship. Post-colonial studies as a distinct area of interest, as Hastings says, has become more prominent since the late 1970s, partly triggered by Edward Said's *Orientalism* (1978), which called attention to the way that Western literary discourse about the East tended to define non-European peoples and cultures as an alien 'other', not part of the universalist culture of the West.[2] In contrasting the so-called colonial literature, which has been often considered as the universal normative aspect of political power and culture associated with the 'self' in the metropolis and the 'other' in the periphery, Hastings notes that post-colonial literature, which specifically focuses on tensions between indigenous culture and the late colonizers should include:

- how Western style education and the imposition of Western culture affects the indigenous cultures of colonized states;
- the significance of linguistic choices in literary creation;

- the psychological expression of a speaker who has been culturally indoctrinated to see himself/herself as inferior, or to be alienated from his (socio-cultural) self;
- race, class, and gender relations as influenced by the colonial situation.

Post-colonial methodologies therefore insist on the importance of history, a history reconceived and refocused on previously marginal areas, an important aspect of post-colonial writing is a concern with history and historical perspectives. Post-colonial writing seeks to create a new connection to history, one that inverts the Eurocentric value system and looks at history and society from the perspective of those voices that have been silenced or ignored by the mainstream.[3]

According to Bell, in seeking to grapple intellectually and professionally with the world beyond Europe, it is difficult to discard ethnocentric and metropolitan standpoints.[4] Reinforcing this with Strauss' contention that every civilization tends to overestimate the objective orientation of its thought and this tendency is never absent[5] indicates that post-colonial readings of the colonial sources should have been grounded on critical assumptions about the relationship between colonial and post-colonial literatures, recognizing the tentative nature of these assumptions and the political implications of authors' choice of language and implied audience.

Partly seeded from experiences with those who had a rather different opinion of the Naga past,[6] *The 'Savage Other' in Naga Historiography: Condition and Paradigm*[7] seeks to address an aspect pertaining the 'savage other' that anthropologists, administrators, and missionaries from the West paradoxically constructed as the image of the early Nagas[8]—there is a condition and a paradigm that dictated, and still dictates the notion of the savage other in Naga historiography. The condition and paradigm is just another way of explaining the understandings and scholarships that have developed over decades, or perhaps centuries, on savage societies.

There are stray mentions that neighbours of the Nagas considered them as the savage other. M.M. Clark wrote that she and her husband, E.W. Clark was informed by the Assamese, "... They (the Nagas) are savages, sahib, village warring with village, constantly cutting off heads to get skulls".[9] However, it was the arrival of the 'colonial agencies' (British military officers and administrators, American and Welsh missionaries, as well as anthropologists from other parts of Europe) that formally initiated it. 'Savage/savagery', a label which has persisted to impose itself as a historical identity on the early Nagas, requires an explanation (instances in texts as well as by the media[10]). This may help in associating the constructed image of the early Nagas with the received understanding of the same in the post-colonial context.

I

Discussing historiography on Nagas besides Naga history is, perhaps, a perennial exercise, especially when Naga history seemed as if it emerged out of nowhere after a big hiatus.[11] This misty 'History' suddenly seemed clearer with the coming of the colonial agencies who churned out a substantial number of monographs, documents and reports. They became sources for later writers on the Nagas. However, Naga history as early as the 1940s was, more or less, a descriptive affair; information on the culture, traditions and social life was deemed enough to qualify as history, a striking nature in Naga historiography. To a critical present day scholar, they are seen as mere documentations than history. Post-1940 writings fared no better; history became political in tune with the need of the time,[12] but not the methodologies. They still lacked analytical categories—all that is different was contested in the terrain of facts. While doing so, most writers on the Nagas overlooked an aspect that demands an immediate redressal—perceiving the early Nagas as the 'Savage Other' in the post-colonial context.

The role of colonial creation and discourse on exotic, degenerate, and savage societies like the Maoris of New Zealand as studied by Pat Moloney,[13] aborigines of Australia by Simon Ryan,[14] the American Indians by Phil Bellfry[15] and Howard Mumford Jones,[16] and the Iberian discourse by Toby Freund[17] need not merely be overlooked as studies on cross-cultural encounters; they are examples of othering within contexts that have been contested and substantiated. However, for people(s) of the Indian subcontinent who have been marginalized by the so-called 'tribalist' discourse in understanding the past of communities without written sources, such kind of lapse in contesting their historiography has meant an erasure of their authentic identities by superimposing constructed or perceived identities over the passage of time.[18] Given the fact that historical writings have their moorings in sources irrespective of their reliability or un-reliability, the ascendancy of writing and views on the Nagas is no exception to this.

II

(Nagaland) ... is a land full of headhunters and warmongers.[19]

Societies, throughout the ages, have experienced tremendous upheavals; upheavals in the forms of eventful unrests; bloodshed in the garb of war, terrorism, and genocides. Somewhere back in time, in a secluded corner of the north-eastern part of India, the early Nagas actively indulged in a practice called 'headhunting' till the same was discouraged after the coming of the British administration. In one of the few areas in the world where acute observers have documented, the Europeans found this practice (headhunting) to be the most 'bizarre practice'.[20] In doing so, they either forgot or unconsciously ignored a fact that in Europe and elsewhere in the globe—around the same era—numerous lives were lost in gory battles as compared to the few heads taken by the Nagas. This practice along with the observations by Europeans that the Nagas were 'naked,'[21] 'filthy', 'treacherous', 'barbarians', and 'heathen'[22] (to consider a few) however brought in a generalization that the early Nagas were 'savages'.

Julian Jacobs opined that these numbers of features particularly made the Nagas interesting to European observers and presented administrators and anthropologists with one of their major challenges. By the turn of the 20th century, the Europeans were well aware of the logic of the system and could recognize that if headhunting was rapidly abolished (as it had been in other parts of the Empire) it would be the equivalent to destroying money, markets and the profit motive in a capitalist society. There would be little point to life any more. Yet the "western conscience could not condone the cruelty, nor was the pax Britannica very plausible in a world of almost ceaseless feuding."[23] This is where the observers tried to study, modify and re-shape the institution of the Nagas.

However, the mutual relations between these strikingly different points of view which run through the literature can be considered as posing the broadest questions concerning ethnological relativism and the preservation or destruction of existing modes of thought which emanates from oral as well as written traditions.[24] This stream of perceived progress then becomes a parcel within the modes of thought in perceiving or studying any society. And for those many who have not yet come across, but have heard of Nagaland, the Nagas and Naga history, they often have a misconception—that the Nagas still practice 'headhunting'. And hence the very mention of 'Naga' often leads one to unconsciously relate the word to 'warriors', 'feared headhunters', and 'savages'.

Reports in the media have often represented north-east India, particularly Nagaland as a land full of unrest, to the extent of commenting on 'bizarre' food habits of the Nagas. However, it does not mean that media is always biased—Baruah's lament, "... The North-East; unknown, remote, exotic and barbaric ... and at best, a region to be regarded as a museum piece, a subject of anthropological study,"[25] clearly indicates that outside opinions have sidelined the Nagas from mainstream Indian society;[26] Jug Suriya also admittedly "... entered Nagaland burdened with preconceptions and prejudices".[27] But the writer realizes that the Nagas themselves have lamented that most of the non-Nagas consider them as "those naked, dog-eating, headhunting savages," and hence have difficulty in finding acceptance with the 'others'.

There is a silent and an ongoing opinion confined within individuals on the question whether the 'early Nagas' were savages:

> (Our Naga ancestors were not savages) .... It was a term to demonize a society hitherto converted to Christianity.[28]

> ... when they (British) came here, they tried to term the Nagas as 'savages' without understanding the inner dynamics of the Nagas' culture.[29]

But there were others who had a different explanation to this fact:

> Definitely, we were 'savages'! That was before the coming of Christianity.[30]

> Even Our Naga Scholars use the term (savage).[31]

> ... we lived a primitive and brutish life in our villages, uncivilized and unlettered ... the only form of contact between the Nagas was through the savage practice of head hunting ... .[32]

The opinion that the early Nagas were indeed savages has therefore led some to justify the Naga society before and after contact with 'civilization'. While Epao wrote, "Nagaland was once as dark as Sheol, the reason being the influence of demons was very great. The whole atmosphere was of fear which affected the daily life of big and small alike in addition to lawlessness in society ...".[33] Bendangyabang stressed that "(Christianity) in the long run opened the minds of 'savage' and 'wild' people and began to change their social and cultural life".[34] These suggests that within Nagas as well as some non-Nagas who have over the decades written and commented on the early Naga, there is an effort to address a 'before' and 'after' dichotomy, an argument highlighted by Adas.[35] Though it cannot be ascertained whether the dichotomy asserted in post-colonial context on the early Nagas is a conscious one, it indicates that there is a discourse highlighting departures between the 'early' and the 'modern' Naga society. After all, it becomes a priority to justify the progress that the 'Naga society' has achieved in terms of 'modernity'.

Ethnographic Discourse on the Early Naga

> ..., we have become accustomed to packaging our past and identifying it with labels. Such labels, even where they may include a variety of activity and experience, tend to force interpretation into a single category so that the infinite shades of difference within them disappear. When this happens, the historical perspective comes to be governed by the tyranny of labels: a condition which requires the historical unpacking of the categories and redefining of the contents.[36]

Traditions exist and persist only if created. In the historical context, the Nagas were brought to the notice of the Europeans[37] around the second quarter of the nineteenth century, and the coming of the Europeans is considered to be the beginning of writings on the Nagas whose history relied on oral traditions. The writings were, however, limited to the British officials who had first felt the need to identify the Nagas before any intercourse took place.[38] Ever since then, Europeans have struggled to make sense of the apparent 'ethnographic chaos' they perceived around them.[39] In spite of this, a significant body of descriptive writing by surveyors, soldiers and administrators, anthropologists and missionaries was inherited.

Although the writings were, on many occasion, patronizing, they persistently emphasized the obviously exotic features of Naga society. To the modern eye, it was still ethnocentric, and the validity of the information given by the Europeans, especially their transcripted versions of the oral renditions of the Nagas remains doubtful.[40] The European textualization of the early Nagas as savages plausibly indicates an analogical exercise in categorizing some non-European societies considered 'still' inferior than some other inferior societies. With the persistent association of this term with the early Nagas, it became a colonial reference to the Nagas.

The sources of Naga history is peculiar—majority of textual sources rest on anthropological monographs left by anthropologists, British administrators and military officers. Renditions of oral tradition of the Nagas, though incorporated, were confined within narration and translation of love songs, and at stray instances, the tales and songs of valour sans the history of the clan, nor the community or the village. This selective textualization of the oral tradition into texts had its long-term effect. In course of time, some oral sources that never went into the textualizing process either becomes too exaggerated, insignificant, or forgotten.[41] With the written tradition overshadowing its oral counterpart, and with the slow transition from a non-literate to a literate society which witnessed an unconscious disinheritance of the oral tradition by the Nagas themselves, historical memory suffered a severe lapse. In due process of transcription, only those oral traditions that have been textualized became a static source of reference.

The role of anthropology in viewing the practices of different cultures with an eye to their place on the scale of advancement employed methods like display of tools placed in sequential order, from simple general purpose devices to more specialized artifacts, so that the audience could follow the movement from the primitive to the complex. Anthropological treatment of the 'savage' was employed as the normative scale,[42] but with empirical and scholarly approach.

Cohn notes that "in the colonial history ..., there were explicit efforts to construct an 'official ethnography' at the moment that anthropology was beginning to be defined as a distinctive form of knowledge. Anthropologists developed practices through which they sought to cross the colonial influence by describing what they took to be authentic indigenous cultures. Their epistemological universe, however, was part of the European world of social theories and classificatory schema that were formed, in part, by the state projects to reshape the lives of their subjects at home and abroad".[43] Beattie also noted that the British social anthropologists restricted 'ethnography' to those studies of mostly pre-literate people and their cultures that attempt to explain their present in terms of their remote past.[44]

Though the colonial officers' task was to maintain a record for their administrative convenience, their records of the Nagas relied on a framework set by anthropologist, who, after studying the 'exotic' and 'savage' societies in the African continent, the native Americans, the natives of the Caribbean, and the aborigines of Australia, re-employed the same methods in studying and co-relating their model with other societies. In following this framework, the *colonial* observers not only situated themselves at the top of the scale of advancement and the 'others' to a position lower down but ethnographic artifacts were also considered as the 'material embodiment' of the social-cultural complexities of the other cultures.[45]

The European discourse on the early Naga as the 'savage other' emerged in a similar context and it influenced the post-colonial outlook and historiography on the Nagas. The impact of some of European sources were great; they shaped the received understanding of the Naga in the years to come (in the post-colonial era), especially when their information travelled throughout the West. While Haimendorf's treatment of the Naga as the savage operated within a anthropological framework,[46] eurocentric worldview operated in Clark's narration of a thematic triumph of Christianity as enlightenment 'from darkness to light': "... in this rude population—largely demon-worshippers—is found a virgin soil, the richest in all this valley for gospel seed-sowing".[47] Similarly, Dalhousie's minute of 1851 also expressed 'dissent' against control over the 'savage inhabitants' which was 'costly and unproductive'.[48] There is another of Dalhousie's view on the Nagas: "... hence after, we should confine ourselves to our own ground; protect it as it can and must be protected; not meddle in feuds or fights of these savages ...".[49] There is a implication here; ethnographic symbolisms on social processes have gone beyond the discipline of anthropology, especially with the usage of ethnographic labels.

Some post-colonial writings on the Nagas exhibit similar approaches like their colonial predecessors. One may often find that some contemporary writings and views equate headhunting with savagery[50] though there is vagueness in the way the European writers equated headhunting with savagery.[51] Post-colonial replications of views and observations made by European writers indicate that the 'presentist' bias is too obvious and that there is a lineal connection between present day concerns and writing of history. The repetitions also imply that their writings operated under the paradigm of the colonial construct indicating that most of the post-colonial arguments are circular; they neither went beyond mololinear and chronological explanations, nor contested concepts, portrayals and labels.

It may be assumed that most colonial writers were products of the positivist school; they were influenced by Rankean notions of history and progress. Western history, since the mid-seventeenth century, had then sought refuge in empirical approaches. And most of the historians from the West thought that approaches to history had matured under the positivist and Rankean umbrellas.[52] This development was not exclusively confined to the West; it affected other Western scholars researching elsewhere in different parts of the world during that time. It is obvious that the Europeans who came to the north-eastern part of India also had the notion of the other, established by Western scholarship. Nagas were a part of this temporal context. If Pat Moloney's argument that the early Victorians were not only simply producing crude rationalizations for the exploitation of the other nations, but also the discourse of savagery and civilization was one of which Europeans were forming and fabricating their identities,[53] then, most of the post-colonial writers on the Naga history were not able to make a departure from the European discourse that was concerned with the construction of the self and the other.[54]

European methodology, though positivist and Rankean while writing the Nagas, was then deemed 'sophisticated' and relevant to the need of their time—it served their purpose.[55] In the post-colonial perspective, with the emergence of alternative methodologies of looking into history, the empiricist methodology of the colonial writers could not serve much relevance to the purpose of the later writers. Yet the post-colonial writers' adherence to the empiricist methodology resulted in documented narratives and descriptions with little or no attempts to explain and interpret societal changes. The renditions sans theoretical and interpretative methodologies have indeed reduced Naga history to a repetitive exercise. The problem lay not in the European sources; it lay in the received understanding of the same by post-colonial writers.

The 'Savage Other'

> that is the most interesting ethnological race of people divided by 500 or 1000 years from the rest of India.[56]

The European understanding of the 'savage' is a culmination of developments over centuries; the concept predates the European colonization of North America by several millennia.[57] Greeks, like all ancient civilizations, were believed to have portrayed themselves as living at the centre of the world and all (barbaric) others as residing in a geographical and cultural periphery.[58] Bellfry says that along with the ancient concepts and connotations of the word 'savage', one should also consider the situation in Europe as early as the late fifteenth century which led to the development in the discourse on the savage societies.[59] Columbus is believed to have invented the notion of the 'savage native' when encountering the indigenous people of the Caribbean; also to be the first to apply the current Eurocentric interpretation by cataloguing the things they lacked. To him, it appeared the natives had no clothes, no laws, no religion, no weapons, no customs, and no private property. Consequently, he believed they were barbarians and savages.[60]

Another discourse on the 'savage' developed in Spain and Portugal in the late fifteenth century. By a declaration of the Papal Bull in 1493, the church granted the kings of Spain and Portugal the rights to settle and possess vast tracts of what are now Africa and the Americas. This initiated encounters with hundreds of new societies, leading to multiple definitions of the other, especially the "stench, miserable-ness, dishonesty, and ugliness of the Khoisan" that need to be civilized. While his perceived 'savagery' also justified their authority over the new acquisitions,[61] it also brought about the need to fit the strange inhabitants into their scheme of 'universal history'.[62]

With the defeat of the Spanish Armada by the English in 1588, North America witnessed a new wave of European colonizers, who, by the seventeenth century accepted the belief in the savage nature of the continent's peoples.[63] An American Indian uprising in Virginia in 1622 was put forth as proof of native savagery. Over time, the equation of American Indians with savagery[64] became formalized into a generalized philosophy scholars now refer to as *savagism*.

According to the tenets of this outlook, Indians are emotional rather than rational; morally and culturally deficient; uncivilized; genetically inferior; untrustworthy (although individuals have the potential to be 'noble'); generally lazy and indolent; and often immorally sensual in their nature.[65] Significantly, the discourse of ignobility and unredeemable savagery dominated discussions of the Cape, like the American Indians, until the very end of the eighteenth century.[66] And, as early as the 19th century, savages were recognized as varying greatly in their moral and physical conditions.[67]

Intellectual discourse treated the savage at another level—for Montesquieu, the savages were generally 'hunters';[68] for Morgan, tribes that never attained the art of pottery were to be classed as 'savages';[69] for Montaigne, it was a total lack of 'civilization';[70] for Adam Smith, savagery was a condition of 'vagrant liberty';[71] for Winick, it was a state of society characterized by a hypothetical cultural stage in which there are 'no crops or language'; and for Gordon Childe, the savage was a label to describe the earliest human organization in which gathering and hunting was predominant. Vico's opinion on 'what history on societies should be' further informs us:

> ... in order to find the key to reinterpreting traditions, we must remember that minds at a given stage of development will tend to create the same kind of products. Savages at all times and in all places, are savages in mind; by studying modern savages, we can learn what ancient savages were like, and then find out how to interpret the savage myths and legends that conceal facts of remotest ancient history.[72]

This provides us the key understanding on how every civilized nation was presumed to have its remote origin in the savage condition, and how savagery itself was represented as the childhood of more civilized nations. It was considered as a mirror to the features of their own progenitors. While on the one hand the savage state was the antithesis of their commercial and civilized society, it was also a picture of their infancy. It would excite nostalgia and romanticism, but also embarrassment and rejection.[73] It also presumably defined a type of society ancestral to more advanced forms, or the analogy of an evolutionary history of some natural species.[74]

Norbert Elias also gives an interesting insight on how certain practices, manners, codes of conducts, and gestures spanning from the twelfth century onwards gave rise to what the West considered, a civilized society with its antithesis. He says that Erasmus' treatise on manners—that stressed on modes of behaviours considered civilized like bodily carriage, gestures, dress, facial expressions, table manners, bodily culture, and manners at holy places, banquets, meetings, amusements, and bedchambers—engaged 'elite' sections of Western societies to redefine the 'self', juxtaposed against the comparative 'other'.[75] Similarly, Freund opines that the publication of Carolus Linnaeus's *Systema Naturae* in 1735 inaugurated a movement to classify the 'natural world' into an ordered system of European knowledge. This enterprise included 'scientific' treatment of racial differences and it 'mixed character with anatomy', creating a 'natural' racial hierarchy; "an explanatory scheme capable of objectifying nature and representing it to the knowing, synthesizing human subject". Freund contends that this new discursive endeavour brought with it a moralizing imperative to aestheticize and cultivate the 'dark continent' and its peoples, to alleviate their natural savagery and primitive ways through the injection of Western culture.[76]

Europeans defined themselves and correlated the world according to what they perceived themselves to be. Kuper contended that "by the second half of the nineteenth century, Europeans believed themselves to be witnessing a revolutionary transition in the type of their society". Marx defined a capitalist society emerging from a feudal society; Weber was to write about the rationalization, the bureaucratization, the disenchantment of the old world; Durkheim about the change from mechanical to organic forms of solidarity. Each conceived of the new world in contrast to 'traditional society'; and behind this 'traditional society' they discerned a primitive or primeval society.[77] The discourse on 'savage societies' can be, then, seen as a binary construction of 'self' and 'other' within the 'New World' discourses that consistently sought to disassociate and systematically distance the encountered natives from having to share a discursive space with the European observer.

The dialectic of westward exploration engaged in an active discussion and re-consideration of humanity, was therefore aimed at properly locating 'the inferior societies' similar to the 'American Indians' within the Eurocentric cosmos. Freund's opinion that the discourse on noble savagery "would become an enduring motif in Western thought in the nineteenth century,"[78] seemingly emerges as one of the strongest contender in the representation of other societies.

Perception and Portrayal of the Early Nagas: The Condition and Paradigm

The 'other' in the Naga context is simple as well as complicated at the same time—simple, because the history of the early Naga has been a normative comparison of the past and the present by some Naga and non-Naga writers alike; complicated, because this subject emerges not only from constructs by colonial writers, but also replications of the colonial constructs by Nagas and non-Nagas in the post-colonial period. However, the usage of the 'savage' slot as a 'floating concept/label' has never been the bone of contention among the post-colonial scholarship, nor has it been considered a potential to imprint itself in Naga history.

Explaining the dynamics that went into the perception and portrayal of the Naga as the savage other has never been easy since then. As for a understanding of Naga historiography (especially in the context of post-colonial critique towards colonial historiography), post-colonial scholarship, in a determination to deconstruct colonial historiography may be said to have established some long arguments that—colonial historiography is all about marginalizing other societies, hence having an edge over them; it is all about civilizational superiority (racial and cultural); ideologically, the superiority privileges them to dictate the history of a weaker/subjugated society as such the subject societies were made to view their society through the Western construct; and the privilege makes them the proponent of the 'White Man's Burden', a justification for colonialism as well as on potential regions to be colonized and civilized. Post-colonial scholarship thus alleges that these reasons highlighted the long term psychological intimation by the colonial rulers on the 'other' societies that were made to acknowledge that they were 'inferior'.

However, these conventional understanding of colonial historiography can be considered to have operated within a context—a condition and a paradigm. The 'condition' is all about the long genealogy of development in the West since antiquity that crystallized into a particular worldview about the savage other. It concerned defining the 'self' through the 'other', as well as the belief that 'savagery' of the 'other inferior' societies were rendition of their (the 'civilized' societies') ancestors. And beyond the 'conditioned' perception and portrayal of other societies as savage societies, there lies a 'paradigm'. The paradigm, in this case, is the paradigm of 'difference'—colonial observers and writers ensured that there was ample distance between them and the 'observed'. Most of the Europeans who wrote on the Nagas lived and interacted with them, have appreciated their ways of life. But, while the Europeans acknowledged and highlighted the hospitality, the generosity and the bravery of the Nagas, they also ensured that the Nagas were simultaneously portrayed as savages. The question here is why the Europeans were contradicting their views on the Nagas. How plausible is it that the 'savagery' and the 'goodness' of the Nagas can be complementary to each other?

Despite their close association with the Nagas, there still existed residual forms of savagery in the Nagas—the rudeness in agricultural practices, social life and the unrelenting inter-village warfare—or their view that the aptitude of the Nagas has to be improved by intercourse with civilization. There was a fear of being influenced by the perceived 'savagery' of the observed; this made them delineate themselves from the observed. Encapsulated in this is a determination to be always different from the Nagas. This paradigm of difference was a justification, not to the Nagas but to their European counterparts, as such M.M. Clark had been graciously introduced by S.A. Perrine in the *Examiner* as "... the first woman messenger of the Cross to a savage tribe of head-takers in the Assam range of the Himalayas."[79]

There was a need to address their readers back in Europe that in spite of living and working among the Nagas, they were still Europeans, different from the Nagas. It assured the audiences in the writers' homelands a justification and the belief of the persistent savagery of the observed societies.

Peter Robb says that in the course of the nineteenth century, as evangelical, romantic and utilitarian influences grew, and as the British rule became more established, the difference was emphasized.[80] The fact that J.P. Mills contended that the "Naga customs and practices is incomparably better than that of a Western city dweller"[81] though he still considered the Nagas as savages validates this assertion. In doing so, the difference was highlighted, and similarities were drawn, a similarity noted by Clark, "... There is much that suggests a comparison with our own North American Indians, as they were in their days of their prowess. Human skulls were as honourable trophies as ever were scalps to the American savage".[82] This corresponded to their mental understanding of societies they considered as inferior to their rightful level of societal progress. Had the Nagas been not considered inferior, the treatment would have been quite contradictory, as observed in the case of Haimendorf who exclaimed, "... I would soon be among real 'savages' ...".[83] although at the same time he spoke about the holy men in Benares, "... there were indeed many such completely naked men sitting cross legged in the streets of Benares, hardly noticed among the other ascetics and beggars ...".[84] It may therefore be thought-provoking to ponder on why the 'naked men' in Benares not considered as savages.

The condition and paradigm therefore justified Western perception and portrayal of the early Nagas. With centuries of development in their understanding of savage societies, the colonial writers addressed to a preconceived audience with undertones that appealed to the then accepted worldview of the West towards 'inferior' or 'peripheral' societies.[85] The discourse on the Nagas which often employed derogatory metaphors and allusions was the product and extension of a discourse developed in the West that stands justified within this parameter.

In a society that did not have indigenous literary elite, the replacement of an indigenous worldview by the Western worldview initiated a possible mirroring of the past from the enlightened European perspective as well as another stream of 'othering' within the Naga communities; the emergent and new literary Naga elites (christianized and introduced to the Western ideal of progress) began to look into their past in derogatory terms. M.M. Clark reinforces this with what she believed to have seen in the features of the hill tribes 'soften', and as they mirrored the new hope, she 'no longer saw the savages' to whom she 'first came'.[86] Succeeding generations extended the colonial perception and portrayal of the early Nagas: "the victory of Christ in the mind and lifestyle of Nagas led to the ultimate victory in setting all the animists free from bondage of superstition and fear. This is a drastic change from polluted human environment into a creative and helpful society".[87] Again, "(the) gospel has changed the entire culture of the people from dao and spade to technology and from headhunting to soul winning; from rude language to refined one, from hatred to love and from savage to civilized life ...".[88] The process of negation within the respective Naga communities, we may safely assume as Haimendorf observed, began when "the Naga saw his own customs condemned by the missionaries; he learns to despise his own tribe and cultural inheritance. Christianity and Naga culture seem to him (the Naga) opposite poles".[89] He presents clearer evidence to this context from his interaction with a Naga convert on their discussion of the 'Morung';[90] the convert is said to have viewed, "how could a Christian boy sleep in these houses of the heathen? ... To use them would be against our rules".[91]

With the mental universe of the post-colonial mind overshadowed by the colonial construct, replication and the persistence of the early Naga as the savage other remain colonial legacies that post-colonial scholarship overlooked. The condition and paradigm, as discussed earlier, indicates manifold implications of the failure by post-colonial scholarship. Firstly, it may be borne in mind that social science methodologies call in for a different set of addressing the audience. Since the colonial sources on the Nagas might have come about mostly due to sheer interest the Nagas generated on the Europeans and also due to administrative expediencies, their methodologies relied more on Rankean and Positivist approaches, descriptive ones. Moving up to the post-colonial context, these sources have not served to much relevance.

Secondly, ethnography which literally means 'writing about people'[92] was then the established form of study in the West. However it is not uncommon in ethnography for researchers to be outsiders to the community or culture being described[93] as Goldbart opined. Colonial ethnography was backed by ideologies which addressed and complemented the colonial worldviews over the then inferior societies. Considering these with Hustler's view that many of the early ethnographic studies and exhortations are regarded as methodologically naive and perhaps even romantic in their attempts to capture the 'natural' worlds of their 'subjects'[94] sums up the failure of the post-colonial writers to grasp the accountability of ethnographic information inherited from the colonial sources on Naga historiography.

Thirdly, there is an anomaly in synonymously associating the early Naga as the savage in the light of Taylor's argument that things in themselves signify nothing; "... It is only when they become integrated in our own mental universe that they acquire historical meaning".[95] The mental universe of the post-colonial mind then was overshadowed by the colonial construct. The generalization that the early Nagas were savages—in the colonial and then in the post-colonial context—was a process of this discourse.

Mark Salber had argued: "if temporal distance is a defining condition of all form of historical representation, an analysis of the ways in which histories of different types have confronted the problem of distance in all its modifications would seem to be an important focus for historiographical study".[96] Since post-colonial historiography could not fully grasp and contest or do away the discourse on the 'others' while confronting the colonial writings, the colonial intervention in the post-colonial writings made the post-colonial writers on the Nagas strangers of the pre-colonial and colonial past of the Nagas.

Finally, the premise that the requirement of the 'historical unpacking of the categories and redefining of the contents'[97] as Thapar had argued in context of labels have not been taken into account in the case of historiography on Nagas. That the early Nagas have been labeled as savages was mediated through the prism of the colonial observer or author conditioned by the Western worldview, this perception was transformed into literature. The early Naga as the savage became a historical symbolism.

With popular opinions obscuring the notion of the savage other, the context seems clear; post-colonial critiques allege colonial historiography to have initiated a new set of othering[98] in a society whose history was written by the 'civilizing west'. But if the dynamics of such discourse was understood within their parameters—time, space, and context—there are possibilities that reconsidering post-colonial critiques on colonial constructs would instead partially vindicate the established colonial perception and portrayal of the early Nagas. Indeed, the persistent discourse of the early Nagas as the savages other in the colonial sources 'conditioned' most of the post-colonial writers. For, a sensible consideration arguably indicates that the colonial construct of other inferior societies was also justifiable, though the metaphors and allusions to portray these societies were often derogatory at the same time.

Notes

1. Karl Mannheim, *Ideology and Utopia*, Routledge and Kegan Ltd., New York, 1936, (Reprint), 1976, p. 247.
2. A. Waller Hastings, "Historical Background: European Colonization and the Colonial and Postcolonial Worlds", http://www.northern.edu/hastingw/colonialhistory.htm. (Accessed 28th August, 2005).
3. Ibid.
4. Morang Bell, "Images, Myths and Alternative Geographies of the Third World", in Derek Gregory and others (ed.), *Human Geography: Society, Space and Social Science*, Palgrave & Macmillan: New York, 1994, p. 188.
5. Claude Levi Strauss, *The Savage Mind*, The University of Chicago Press: Chicago, 1966, p. 3.
6. It so happened, like in many other occasions, a scholar, in the midst of an interaction remarked, "I am glad that at least out here in Hyderabad, Nagas can't chop off my head!", The remark, though light-hearted, confirmed a doubt that the speaker had 'preconceived' information about the Nagas that was communicated either through text, media, or hearsay. Nagas are no exception to this; there are some Nagas who still consider the past of their ancestors as being embroiled in savagery.
7. This paper is an excerpt from my M. Phil. Dissertation, "Perceiving the savage in Historiography on Nagas", submitted to the Department of History, University of Hyderabad, December 2005. I am deeply indebted to my supervisor, Dr M.N. Rajesh, for his constant encouragement and valuable inputs, and to Prof Rila

Mukherjee, for patiently going through this paper and suggesting necessary inclusions and deletions.

8. In this case, we will be referring the 'early Nagas' to those Nagas belonging to the pre-British and the colonial eras in the present state of Nagaland. The nomenclature and the etymology of the term 'Naga' is still problematic for those who are critically researching the 'identity' of the Nagas. Hoverer, the term 'Naga' is used loosely in this paper for the sake of convenience. The 'Nagas' are a conglomeration of sixteen recognized 'tribes' in Nagaland, a north-eastern state of the Union of India.
9. M.M. Clark, *A Corner in India*, American Baptist Publication Society: Philadelphia, 1907, Christian Literature Center: Gauhati [*Sic*], (Reprint), 1978, p. 1 and pp. 9–10.
10. Four respondents—in interview sessions—opined the role of media in exaggerating and over-hyping the portrayal of the Nagas. This, we can presume, might explain a part of retaining, perpetuating and exemplifying the exoticism of a particular society by the media which is seen as the replication of the exotic discourse on many other societies by the Europeans.
11. This is not the only problem plaguing Naga historiography. Apart from the problem of periodization, the 'assumed' loss of script and the absence of a concise Naga history per se has baffled writers on the history of 'Nagas'. They are yet to arrive to a consensus on the question of 'origins' and 'migrations' of the Nagas. This mystery has continued ever since the Europeans initiated, but failed to grapple it, leaving a big hiatus in Naga history. The helplessness to this context has often led post-colonial writers on Nagas to accommodate various versions of myths and legends of the oral tradition while discussing the origins and migrations of the Nagas—the Nagas themselves have different versions of their origin and migrations. For most of the Aos, they believe in the version that they originated from 'Longterok' (six stones), while the other groups of Nagas uphold the version that they originated and dispersed from a place called 'Khezakenoma'.
12. This is because history began to be referred again and again by the Nagas in the height of separatist tendency (that heightened in the 1960's) to claim that the Nagas and the Naga inhabited areas were never a part of Indian Union.
13. Pat Moloney, "Savagery and Civilization: Early Victorian Notions", *New Zealand Journal of History*, Vol. 35, No. 2, October 2001.
14. Simon Ryan, *The Cartographic Eye*, Cambridge University Press: Australia, 1996.
15. Phil Bellfry, "Encyclopedia of North American Indians", http://college.hmco.com/. (Accessed 10th September 2005).
16. Howard Mumford Jones, *'O' Strange New World: American Culture, The Formative Years*, New York: Viking Press, 1964.
17. Toby Freund, "The Occidental Tourist: Discover, Discourse, and Degeneracy in S. Africa", *Michigan Journal of History*, Fall 2001, http://www.umich.edu/~historyj/papers/fall2001/freund3.html. (Dissertation, accessed 6/10/05).
18. In a similar tone, Sartre had opined that discourses such as the 'colonial' discourse, in the name of civilization, not only aimed to keep enslaved people at a respectful distance, but it also sought to deny legitimate voices them by "liquidating their traditions, language and culture." See, Jean Paul Sartre, *Colonialism and Neocolonialism*, Routledge: London and New York, 2001, p. 142.

19. Frans Welman in Dijanna Curica (ed.), "Enter the Forbidden Land", http://www.nagalim.nl/html/. ©2002–2003, (Accessed 17th August 2004).
20. But all aspects of Naga life had its ritual significance: all activities, from simple household and economic tasks from dancing to feasting. The 'spirits', which they believed to have had controlled the realities of the life of the Nagas, needed constant appeasement. Julian Jacobs opines that the human head, "the seat of wisdom and the human soul was the repository and conductor of power". This was true, whether the head was that of a child, a man, a woman, alive or dead. They believed that, he who owned other's head gained prosperity in this world, the esteem of his folk, and a guaranteed happiness in the after-world. Success and merit in every field depended on taking the heads. Moreover headhunting was practised for the fertility of their lands, prosperity of their villages, or for enhancing their social standings (of the Naga warriors). Life was given its central purpose by the quest for heads. Boys would not become men without the ritual tattooing only to be undertaken after a successful headhunt; girls would not be attracted to men without the splendid headhunting dances and decorations.
21. Not all the Nagas were considered 'naked' except by some; Haimendorf in his *Naked Nagas* identified the Konyaks as such (he had observed that apart from a loin, the Konyaks rarely covered their bodies). Whatever the reason of this depiction, his view somehow became the marker of the later European view of the Konyaks and their contemporaries, the Rengmas as the 'naked' Nagas.
22. These are general views of the Europeans who observed the Nagas in their writings—the colonial officials in their reports and diaries, the anthropologists in their monographs, and the missionaries in their correspondences and books on the Nagas.
23. Julian Jacobs, "The Nagas: Hill Peoples of Northeast India", http://www.alanmacfar lane.com/ bamboo_ naga_front/T15.htm. (Accessed 20/10/2005).
24. Ibid.
25. Bonita Baruah, "The North-East: The India we don't Know", Special Report, *Sunday Times Of India*, Hyderabad, October 10, 2004.
26. Though Nagaland is, at present, a state in the Indian Union, it is often mistaken to be a foreign 'country' much to the amusement of the Nagas.
27. Jug Suriya, "No dogs, please, we're Indians", Special Report, *Sunday Times of India*, Hyderabad, October 10, 2004.
28. Excerpt of interview with Imna Imchen, Managing Director, Cosyne, Midlane, Dimapur on 18th March 2005.
29. Excerpt of interview with Dr Victor Babu, Senior Lecturer, Department of History and Archeology, Nagaland University, Kohima on 4th March 2005.
30. Excerpt of interview with Theja Meru, Director, Dream Café, Kohima on 18th February 2005.
31. Excerpt of interview with Dr N. Venuh, Reader, Department of History and Archeology, Nagaland University, Kohima on 18th February 2005.
32. S.C. Jamir, *Bedrock of Naga Society*, Nagaland Pradesh Congress Committee, (2nd edition), July 2000, pp. 7–8.
33. Veprari Epao, *From Naga Animism to Christianity*, Hindustan Print-o-Print: Dimapur, (2nd edition), 1998, p. 20.

34. A. Bendangyabang Ao, *History of Christianity in Nagaland: Social Change, 1872–1972*, Shalom Ministry Publications: Bangalore, 1998, p. 272, (This was made in the context of Naga society).
35. Michael Adas, "Imperialist Rhetoric and Modern Historiography: The Case of Lower Burma before and after Conquest", *Journal of South East Asian Studies*, Vol. 3, 1972. In this paper, he suggests a 'before and after dichotomy' that was employed to highlight the development that the coming of British rule has ushered on the Burmese subjects. This, he says, can also be relevant in the study of erstwhile colonized society.
36. Romila Thapar, "The Tyranny of Labels", in Aloka Parasher-Sen (ed.), *Subordinate and Marginal Groups in Early India*, Oxford University Press: Delhi, 2004, p. 349.
37. Mostly British administrators, officers on special duty, and anthropologists in the Naga inhabited areas. However, for convenience sake, American missionaries are also listed in this category.
38. See Verrier Elwin, *Nagaland*, Research Department, Advisers' Secretariat: Shillong, 1961, p. 19. He quotes Alexander Mackenzie: "the Assam valley is surrounded north, east and south by numerous savage and warlike tribes...", Evidently, mental geography first began to map the Naga inhabited areas even before physical explorations and surveys took place.
39. Amongla Imsong, Myths and Ancient History: Case Study of Ao-Naga Myths, (Unpublished M. Phil Dissertation) Department of History: University of Hyderabad, 2004, p. 2.
40. This skepticism complements Samuel's argument: "spoken word can easily be mutilated when it is taken down in writing and transferred to the printed medium". See Raphael Samuel, "Perils of the transcript", in Robert Perks and Alistair Thomson (ed.), *The Oral History Reader*, Routledge: London and New York, 1998, p. 389.
41. Moyer's opinion may be well considered in this context: "Trained to depend on written records, traditional historians have been known to shudder in horror at the potential problems and inherent weaknesses of oral history. What of the failings of human memory? What of the human tendency to impose a narrative structure on events that may not be closely connected? What of the self-serving motives of the story teller? What of the power relationships between interviewer and interviewee that affect what and how events are reported? What of the differences between the spoken and written word? What of the inaccuracies that creep into meaning when trying to put a conversation onto paper?" Judith Moyer, "Step-by-Step Guide to Oral History", ©1993, (Revised), 1999 http://.dohistory.org/on_your_own/toolkit/ oral_History.html., Also see Linda Shopes, "What is oral history?" http://historymatters.gmu.edu., (Both accessed on 17th October, 2005).
42. Kuper says that the 'anthropological treatment of other cultures' was already taking place in the West. See Adam Kuper, *The Invention of Primitive Society: Transformation of an Illusion*, Routledge: London and New York, 1988, p. 8.
43. Bernard S. Cohn, *Colonialism and its Forms of Knowledge: The British in India*, Oxford University Press: New Delhi, 1997, pp. 11–12.
44. John Beattie, *Other Cultures*, The Free Press: New York, 1968, p. 19.
45. Ibid.

46. Though he equates savagery with headhunting, he nevertheless identified the close connection of headhunting with its significance—attachment with fertility of the land, prosperity of the community, and a warrior's initiation into a better social status in the community. See, Christoph Von Furer Haimendorf, *The Naked Nagas*, Spectrum Publications: Guwahati, (Reprint), 2004, p. 15, 63, 204.
47. M.M. Clark, op. cit., fn. 9, p. 45.
48. Dalhousie cited by Mackenzie, See Alexander Mackenzie, *The North East Frontier of India*, (1884); photo reproduction, Mittal Publications: New Delhi, 1999, p. 45.
49. Dalhousie as quoted by B.C. Allen in *Gazetteer of Naga Hills and Manipur*, Mittal Publications: New Delhi, 2002, first published in Shillong, 1905, p. 16.
50. To consider one such writer, Jamir, who equates these labels as one, See S.C. Jamir, op. cit., fn. 32, p. 8.
51. This comes from a general reading of some early European writings on the Nagas. M.M. Clark, for instance, did not equate headhunting of the Nagas with savagery though she did mention some other practices along with headhunting which went into a general understanding of the Naga as the savage.
52. There is a similar argument by Sharma who says that the European writers were products of the "seventeenth and eighteenth century intellectual development in Europe" which was "dominated by the search for scientific truth and thus for objectivity of knowledge". See, Manorama Sharma, *History and History Writing in North East India*, Regency Publications: New Delhi, 1998, p. 5.
53. Pat Moloney, op. cit., fn. 13, pp. 153–172.
54. Kindly note that not all post-colonial writers fall within this category.
55. Cohn says that writing on the colonial subjects became a part and parcel of the empire because acquiring and having knowledge about the subjects (their language, culture and traditions) served their administrative purpose. Having intricate knowledge about the ways of life of the subjects was mostly generated by the numerous and keen ethnographic studies and observations undertaken by the administrative officers, anthropologists and the missionaries. Therefore, there was inherently no necessity for theoretical analysis or discussion apart from describing the society and social life of the subjects, an exercise which served the purpose of collecting information on the subject societies. See Bernard S. Cohn, op. cit., fn. 43, ibid.
56. Kuklich's remark on the Nagas, Earl Winterton cited by Verrier Elwin, op. cit., fn. 38, p. 58.
57. Phil Bellfy, op. cit., fn. 15, ibid. Roget (ed.), "The New Thesaurus", (3rd edition), *American Heritage Dictionary*, 1996–2004, http://.www.yourdictionary.com. (Accessed 10th September 2005). Ernst Breisach, *Historiography: Ancient, Medieval and Modern*, Chicago and London: The University of Chicago Press, 1983, p. 2.
58. John Bellamy Foster, "Empire of Barbarism", Dec., 2004, http://www.findarticles.com/p/articles/mi_m1132/is_7_56/ai_n9483626. (Accessed 11th August 2005), Also see, Phil Bellfry, op. cit., fn. 15, ibid., Andrew Roberts, "Extracts from Montesquieu", http://www.mdx.ac.uk/www/study/xmon.htm. (Accessed 8th November, 2004). Here Roberts says that Montesquieu ascribes the similarity between 'savage' and 'barbarous' nations. Montesquieu nevertheless points out a difference: "... There is this difference between savage and barbarous nations: the former are dispersed clans, which for

some particular reason cannot be joined in a body; and the latter are commonly small nations, capable of being united. The savages are generally hunters; the barbarians are herdsmen and shepherds."

59. Phil Bellfy, op. cit., fn. 15, ibid.

60. Ibid., Also in Ken Ficara and Robert J. Howe, "On the 500th Anniversary of Columbus", "Discovery of America", October, 1992, http://www.panix.com/~ficara/writing/columbus.html. (Accessed 18th October, 2005). Also see, Russell Grigg citing Darwin in "Darwin's Savages", *Creation Archive*, Vol. 21, Issue 3, (Accessed 17th March, 2005) http://www.answersingenesis.org/creation/v21/i3/darwin.asp. Charles Darwin, who arrived in *Tierra del Fuego* at the southernmost tip of South America (as part of his world tour aboard H.M.S. *Beagle* in 1832), is said to have observed the difference between 'civilized' and the 'savage' societies: "I could not have believed how wide was the difference between savage and civilized man: it is greater than between a wild and domesticated animal, inasmuch as in man there is a greater power of improvement".

61. Toby Freund, op. cit., fn. 17, ibid. http://www.umich.edu/~historyj/papers/fall2001/freund3.html. (Accessed 6/10/05).

62. Ernst Breisach, *Historiography: Ancient, Medieval, and Modern*, Chicago and London: The University of Chicago Press, 1983, p. 178.

63. Plymouths' governor, William Bradford, expressed this deeply embedded notion when he declared in 1617: "The unpeopled countries of America [are] devoid of all civil inhabitants, where there are only savage and brutish men, which range up and down, little otherwise than the wild beasts of the same". See Toby Freund, op. cit., fn. 17, ibid.

64. It is obvious from E.W. Clark's remark: "Now a few words about these savages of the hills (the Aos and Angamis). They are run of blood and war. Their fighting is all hand to hand, with big knives and spears ... But as our [American] Indians prized a scalp, so these men glory in the head of a warrior; and as, among some of the tribes, a man is hardly considered a man till he has taken human life ..." See excerpt of letter from E.W. Clark to Bronson in H.K. Barpujari, The American Missionaries and North-East India: 1836–1900 AD, Spectrum Publications: Guwahati, 1986, p. 267; Also in Mr Clark's letter, December 5, 1851, Sibsagor cited by A. Bendangyabang Ao, *History of Christianity in Nagaland: A Source Material*, Shalom Ministry Publications: Bangalore, 1998, p. 50.

65. However, these views goes against the then popular understanding of the 'noble savage' which was characterized by traits such as living in harmony with nature, absence of crime, innocence, inability to lie, physical health, moral courage, and lack of sexual inhibitions. See, *"Noble Savage"*, http://encyclopedia.laborlawtalk.com/Noble_ savage., (Accessed 19th March, 2005).

66. Liebersohn cited by Freund; See Toby Freund, op. cit., fn. 17, ibid.

67. Pat Moloney, op. cit., fn. 13, p. 154.

68. Andrew Roberts, op. cit., fn. 55, ibid., Also see Charles de Montesquieu (1752), "The Spirit of Laws", http://www.marxists.org/reference/subject/philosophy/works/fr/montesqu.htm (Accessed 8th November, 2004).

69. L.H. Morgan, *Ancient Society*, University of Arizona Press: Tuscon, Arizona, 1985. Henry Holt & Co., p. 9.

70. Nina Strohminger, *"Montaigne's Noble Savagery"*, Brown University, 2002, http://www.victorianweb.org/courses/nonfiction/montaigne/strohminger.html. (Accessed 15th March 2005).
71. Adam Smith cited by Pat Moloney, op. cit., fn. 13, p. 154.
72. Vico cited in E. Sreedharan, *A Textbook of Historiography: 500 B.C. to A.D. 2000*, Orient Longmans: New Delhi, (Reprint), 2005, pp.105–106; Also see, Marnie Hughes-Warrington, *Fifty Great Thinkers in History*, Routledge: London and New York; First Indian Reprint, 2004, pp. 340–341.
73. Pat Moloney, op. cit., fn. 13, p. 158
74. Opinion by Professor Vinay Kumar Srivastava, U.P.E. Visiting Professor, Department of Anthropology, University of Delhi, 14th October, 2005.
75. Nobert Elias, *The Civilizing Process*, Blackwell Publishers, 1994; (Revised edition), 2000, Oxford: UK, pp. 47–61.
76. The label of dark continent was also applied to Ethiopia even though the Ethiopians had a script, embraced Christianity during the biblical period (one of those present during the birth of Jesus is said to be an Ethiopian), and had a continuous monarchy dating from the time of Menelik-I who was a historical personality and said to be the progeny of Queen Sheba. See A.H.M Jones and Elizabeth Monroe (ed.), *History of Abyssinia*, Kessinger Publishing: Montana, 2003, pp. 12–14 and p. 187.
77. Adam Kuper, op. cit., fn. 42, p. 4.
78. Toby Freund, op. cit., fn. 17, ibid.
79. Ibid., p. 54.
80. Peter Robb (ed.), *The Concept of Race in South Asia*, Oxford University Press: Delhi, 1997, p. 29.
81. J.P. Mills, "The Effect of the Naga Tribe of Assam of their Contact with Western Civilization", Fifth Pacific Science Congress, Victoria, Vancouver, 1933, cited by Tuisem A. Shishak, "Nagas and Education", *Nagas' 90: Souvenir*, Literature Committee, Nagas 90, February 8–11, 1990.
82. M.M. Clark, op. cit., fn. 9, p. 103.
83. Christoph Von Furer Haimendorf, op. cit., fn. 46, p. 2.
84. Ibid., p. 8.
85. Younghusband's assertion that the western ideologies of modernization and development continue to impose an identity on non-western societies, may well be taken into consideration. F.E. Younghusband, cited by Bell; See Morang Bell, op. cit., fn. 4, ibid.
86. M.M. Clark, op. cit., fn. 9, p. 88.
87. Veprari Epao, op. cit., fn. 33, p. 31.
88. Ibid., p. 100.
89. Christoph Von Furer-Haimendorf, op. cit., fn. 46, pp. 54–55.
90. Male dormitory ('Naga way of life' was imparted in the morung).
91. Christoph Von Furer-Haimendorf, op. cit., fn. 46, p. 51.
92. David Hustler, "Ethnography", in Bridget Somekh and Cathy Lewin (ed.), *Research Methods in the Social Sciences*, Vistaar Publications: New Delhi, 2005, p. 16.

93. Juliet Goldbart, "Ethnographic Interviews: An Outsider Looking In", in Bridget Somekh and Cathy Lewin (eds.), *Research Methods in the Social Sciences*, Vistaar Publications: New Delhi, 2005, p. 16.
94. David Hustler, op. cit., fn. 75, p. 17.
95. Barbara Taylor, "How Far, How Near: Distance and Proximity in Historical Imagination", *History Workshop Journal*, Issue 57, Spring 2004, p. 118.
96. Mark Salber, "Distance and Historical Representation", *History Workshop Journal*, Issue 57, Spring 2004, p. 125.
97. Romila Thapar, op. cit., fn. 36, p. 349.
98. It does not mean that the Nagas did not have their own criteria of the 'other'; 'Nagas' belonging different villages or clans had their own definition of the 'other'.

18 Rethinking the Concept of Tribe Construction and Re-construction of *Adivasi* Identity

NETRAPAL SINGH

In the recent decades the idea of tribe is immensely focal theme of the social anthropology or cultural anthropological in the tradition of world anthropological discourse. Primarily to define sociological and anthropological concept, i.e., tribe, race, and caste are an anthropologist's job which comes from the existed norms of societies. But the discipline of anthropological history has been entered into the anthropological discourse as a form of critical observer in the discipline of social historiography. The approaches of a social anthropologists and anthropological historians are different, but the destination of intellectual practices are not unlikely different. Anthropologist discusses the present and historian the past of particular society, but, both work widely as a complementary units.

F.G. Bailey and Andre Beteille have seriously worked on the concept of tribe in India. The views of both the intellectuals are nothing but it is an analogy from colonial thoughts into post-colonialism. Bailey's paper published in *Contribution to Indian Sociology* in 1961 in which he made efforts to define tribe in opposition to caste citing the markedly distinct assumptions of isolation, language, religion (animism), economic backwardness, and finally the claim for original inhabitation (Adivasiness) of tribes in India (Bailey, 1961: 7–19).[1]

The most serious efforts were made by Beteille to identify and define the term 'tribe' in the context of India. His first article was published in 1960, and second in 1973.[2] In these articles he adopted two assumptions, isolation and language to define 'tribe' out of five assumptions given by Bailey. He gives emphasis on the transition of 'tribe' to caste. In this direction he is uneasy to distinguish 'tribe' from caste. He argues that tribes are not always easy to distinguish from castes, particularly where the two modes of organization meet. The earlier accounts of the people of India show a preoccupation with the identification and description of various tribes and castes in the population, without any clear criteria between the two kinds of units. What are acknowledged as castes are freely described as tribes, and vice versa? The transformation of tribes into castes has been documented; undoubtedly, the opposite process also took place, though it can not be easily documented.[3]

His third article published in the *European Journal of Sociology* in 1986 with more ambitious arguments. In this paper, he is critical to Sahlin's definition of tribe, tribe as a segmental organization'[4] and Godelier's 'tribe as a type of society', and 'a stage of evolution'[5] and Fried's idea of 'tribes as a secondary phenomena'[6] in the Indian context. Beteille goes on to discuss various points, i.e., language, endogamy, kinship, tribes' relationship with state and civilization, tribal absorption into caste and Hinduism or Hinduization and Hindu method of tribal absorption of tribe, regarding less for definition but more for identification of tribes in India. He finally defines that being a tribe has been move a matter of remaining outside of state and civilization, whether by choice or necessity, than of attaining a definite stage in the evolutionary advance from the simple to the complex. Therefore, we cannot dismiss as anomalous the Indian practice of regarding the tribes a large assortment of communities, differing widely in size, mode of livelihood and social organization. They all are tribes because they all stood more or less outside of Hindu civilization (Beteille, 1986: 316).[7]

Beteille's definition and treatment of tribes suffers from serious pitfalls. He takes the dual responsibility of defining and identifying the tribes in India. He adopts historical approach rather than evolutionary approach. Firstly, historical approach faces difficulty against an evolutionary approach, when he adopts the thesis if transition of tribe to caste and Hinduism, because he perceives the practices of both caste and Hinduism as the advance stages of human evolution. This is a methodological failure with Beteille's concept of tribe. And secondly, he compares 'tribes' only with 'Hindu Civilization' not with Indian civilization in India. Thirdly, he considers 'tribes' out of civilization though they have ever been the part of Indian civilization but might not be the part of Hindu civilization as well.

Some significant and natural questions may arise here. Are the concepts like tribe, caste and Hinduism appropriate to deal with the tribal (Adivasi) societies in India? Was there only a Hindu civilization? Was there only a Hindu state in India by nature? Was there only single method, 'the Hindu method' of tribal absorption or other possible ways were they in India? Was indigenous culture transformed or hegemonies by claims? Who constitute 'tribal' (Adivasi) culture in India?

Colonial observations state that the myth of tribe and history of terminology practises of the term 'tribe' is not more than one and half century old. By the 1840s the indigenous or tribal (Adivasi) people began to be described usually as 'aboriginal, forest or hill tribes'. But by the 1860s the distinction between caste and tribes had almost entirely crystallized (Bates, 1995; Skaria: 1997).[8]

Contemporary historical and anthropological studies appropriate 'tribe' as colonial construct (Beteille, 1986; Guha, 1998: 428; De Valle, 1992; Skaria, 1997: 730; 1999).[9] What was the purpose of the construction of tribe? It was primarily related with the theory of race in European societies. As the development of geology and the science undermined the authority of Church, and political and social change appeared to be destabilizing Western societies, the concept of race was invoked to support threatened hierarchies, both in colonies, and metro poles (Hariss, 1968: chap. 4).[10]

In India the theory of race is linked with caste and caste is linked with tribe by seven racial types of castes in colonial ethnography (Risley, 1901).[11] These were the indigenous elites who appropriated racial anthropology to justify South Asian hierarchy on the one hand and to assert partly with the European upper classes on the other (Guha, 1998: 428).[12] "Both condensation and understanding have been taken over from late colonial ethnography, and used to justify a project—that of paternalistic uplift of tribes (however defined) that had also began under colonialism. Equally, their history is seen as constituted by two events—on which took place thousand of years ago, when they were driven into forest, and second in contemporary times, when they were being excluded from them, between these two they dwelt untouched by history" (Guha, 1998: 431).[13]

Ajay Skaria appropriates the colonial politics of time (anachronism) and gender to justify its rule and domination. The intersection of several characteristics and hierarchies defined the anachronistic space occupied by savage or primitives. Basic amongst these from the mid-eighteenth century was the hierarchy of modes of substance. Hunting was considered the lowest stage in social evolution; it was succeeded by pastoralism and agriculture, and industry was the cultivation of development. One characteristic that was shared by many groups that eventually became 'tribe' was their dependence on hunting (Skaria, 1997: 730).[14] Besides, these modes of substance, a new phenomenon, the gender became assumption to define tribes in relation with Hinduism. The tribes have been considered as outside Hinduism. The masculinity and nature of violence linked with tribes (Bhils) in western India, and metaphors of feminity were normally used by the British to describe both Hinduism as a religion and Hindus as a people (Skaria, 1997: 732–39).[15]

Susana de Valle in her brilliant study on Jharkhand reveals the mythical construction and problem of the colonial thesis of 'tribe'. As a myth it was related with caste. In India, 'tribe' is clearly a colonial category in origin and content. It has been formulated in the context of Hindu model of caste-ideology, a context observable in the conceptualization of Adivasi 'backwardness' in the alternative espoused for social mobility (De Valle, 1992: 32).[16] 'Racial', 'ethnic' and 'tribal' stereotypes were forged, conflicting a variety of mode of production, forms of social organization and cultures ignoring the complexities, dynamism, history and civilizational patterns of societies thus catalogued (De Valle, 1992: 27).[17]

The concept of 'tribe' is highly problematic in its practice in Susana's view, because it ignores societal macro level, historical process and structural transformation. The term 'tribe' creates a confusion between idealized and reality because it was constructed out of ideas about what societies were thought to be have been in the pre-colonial past. Thus, categorization of Adivasi in pre-capitalist societies of pre-colonial India as 'tribe' is, at best, out of place and at worst, a historical and sociological groundless (De Valle, 1992: 30, 76).[18] Such mythical concepts become suitable instruments for the state-ist concept of nation-state where only one possible cultural model of one history, one language and one social project predominates (De Valle, 1992: 20).[19]

Susana cites the alternative of ethnicity at the place of 'tribe' because of its historical and ideological significance. Two salient faces of the phenomenon are differentiated by her: (1) Ethnicity can serves an element of support for the hegemony of the dominant classes and of the state, (2) Ethnicity can also be a counter-hegemonic forces in the instances where ethnic ascription and economic and political subordination correlate (De Valle, 1992: 16).[20] In both the cases she places the role model of the adivasi societies of Jharkhand.

Caste: Colonial Invention and the Mother of Sociological Discourses

During the post-colonial period social anthropological and historical writings have emerged by the colonial administrators invented or constructed 'caste' discourse in India through Orientalistic process. For an example, Ronald Indan and Nicholas Dirks are exponents of colonial theory of invention of caste.[21] Ronald emphasizes on the 'essentialist' view by arguing that British obsession with caste is seen to have created an 'essentialist' India, a 'pre-enlightened, world where superstition and darkness reign, with poverty, exploitation, and political chaos as the result? This essentialism robbed Indian of their 'agency', treating them as trapped in an unchangeable world of extremes (Inden, 1990: 83–4).[22]

This process of caste construction as the principal modality of Indian civilization appropriates as much as from the role of British Orientalists, administrators, officials, and missionaries as it does from Indian reformers, social thinkers and political actors. In Dirks' view, colonialism was itself a cultural project of control. Cultural forms in societies newly classified as 'tradition' were reconstructed and transformed by colonial knowledge, which created a new categories and oppositions between colonizers and colonized, European and Asian, modern and traditional, West and East (Dirks, 2002: 9).[23]

In a remarkable work like the colonial theory of caste invention have been questioned. For centuries, South Asians have found ways to make caste or caste like identities serve them in changing and often threatening circumstances. As a means of coping with a diverse and unpredictable social and physical environment, the titles, symbols and lifestyles of caste have proved to be remarkably durable and adaptable. So if caste is neither an Orientalistic fiction nor a shameful crime to be disguised or ignored in discussing India's history, it must be a fit subject for historical exploration (Bayly, 1999: 7).[24]

In medieval period Bhakti movement was centred around caste hierarchies and its exploitive natures. Saurabh Dube in his study on Satnamis of Chhattisgarh drew attention that caste identity prevailed in pre-colonial India. Here the growing rigidity of concerns of purity and pollution that worked against the Chamars and thus informed the construction of Satnampanth was not conjured by the colonial regime, but had its beginnings in pre-colonial Chhattisgarh ruled by Marathas (Dube, 1998: 214).[25]

With the colonial knowledge, it was also the post-colonial Western and Indological scholarship which projected the caste as ultimate essence of Indian society. Dumont, the ghost of Indian sociology emerged tallest among them. He has identified that the caste system as the fundamental institution of Indian society, and represented caste as 'objective totality' implying religious and political views. The whole course of Indian history confirms the hierarchical relationship between the principle of religion, represented by the Brahman, and principle of temporal power, represented by the "Kshatriya King—'political disunity for the sake of religious unity" (Dumont, 1970).[26]

In such a view, the identification of caste as the fundamental institution of Indian society, allowed India to be conceptualized as one, despite the observed regional and historical variation. Representing two poles of Indian social system, Veena Das argues that equality and reciprocity have the same importance as hierarchy in the system. The whole point of drawing attention to move practices of the lower castes which stood opposition to Brahmanic practises was to interrogate the notion of a system or of a totality which privileged the world view of the Brahman, giving his Brahmanic world view the status of the truth objective rather than treating it, as a site of contest. Positioning the Brahman as the only voice, Dumont was in fact participating in the creation of a master narrative of Indian society that saw Brahman world views as somehow representing the whole Indian system (Das, 1999: 29, 35).[27]

Burghart represents the more exotic views on Dumont's thesis of objective totality. The singularity of homo heirarchicus lies not in Dumont's representing the Brahman's view on Hindu society but in his limitating the Brahman's representation of Hindu society (Burghart, 1990: 288).[28] Dominant's discourse of caste in India represents theoretical aspect rather than empirical realities of Indian societies. In vernacular mind caste is not only caste (Jati), this is a Samaj (society), a complete social unit. The term Samaj (society) denotes the meaning of an independent or discrete unit with its distinct socio-political institutions. Caste preferably is an elite construction. But the caste gives a sense of an order of social hierarchy.

In a sense, Susan Bayly appropriates, Dumont's formulation is nothing less than a synopsis of Hindu civilization itself, in which he saw as being animated by unique and coherent structure of 'core values' (Bayly, 1999: 14).[29] Historian S. Dube contextualizes Dumont's conception in historical process with the Satnamis of Chattisgarh and derives the fallacy of it. An exclusive emphasis on the ritual hierarchy of purity and pollution is ultimately a matter of religious value, or a sole preoccupation with the ritual centrality of kingship, or, indeed, the judicious construction of a bipolar model where, depending on the context, the Brahman or the dominant caste can reign power. All affords towards the construction of a synthetic theory of caste in South Asia tend to obscure the intermeshing of different axis of dominance, elaborated over time in the constitution of power in caste society (Dube, 2001: 214).[30]

Hinduism: Birth under British Colonialism

The term Hinduism as it is being practised in dominant intellectual and popular discourse, what meaning it denote and what historical legacy it possesses? Is the term Hinduism a construction? Until Indian civilization was defined relatively to the world outside, there was no need for a concept of 'Hindu' at all. That word and to some extent the very concept of the Hindu seems to have been supplied by Persian, Europeans and Central Asians rather than Indian themselves (Mendelson and Vicziani, 1998: 27).[31] Legacy of the term Hindu very much questioned in historical sense and applicability. The process of Indian civilization can not be appropriately represented by such terms.

The term Hindu, although is of a much older vintage than Hinduism, had originally a geographical connotation [an Iranian misinterpretation of the river *Sindu* (Indus) and the people of the lands around and beyond it] but which was gradually applied to the non-Muslim in habitant of subcontinent, and then used by the British (as entered the English language in Seventeenth Century) to designate who were not Muslim or Christians was appropriated by Brahmanic elite to identify their religion (Omvedt, 2003: 222; Dube, 2001: 4).[32]

It was only in the 19th century that the category of Hinduism and Hindu, in conjunction with each other, came to clearly specify an Indian's religious affiliation and this involved a twin birth but a single conception, a conception that wás largely Christian, but far from immaculate because of its colonial implication (Dube, 2001: 4).[33]

From the textual discovery of 'Hinduism' in the 18th century, though the various institutional methods deployed by colonial rule throughout the 19th century in which Hinduism both as doxa and praxis was defined by upper caste elite in relationship to colonial and national contexts and imperatives, to the birth of a post-colonial Hindu nationalism, the relationship of religion has undergone massive redefinition (Nicholas, 2001: 297–98).[34]

The struggle for the construction of Hinduism in colonial Indian has two mutually complementary ways. The first was directed against the backward elements of tradition, culture and ideology and was expressed in terms of the reformation and regeneration of socio-religious institutions. The second was an attempt to contend with colonial culture and ideology (Panikker, 1995: 58).[35] The first way was highly influenced by colonial culture, ideology and institution and Indian elite readily adopted colonial conceptions. Orientalism filled the fantasy and the freedom sought by European Romanticism, particularly in its opposition to the more disciplined neo-classicism. The cultures of Asia were seen as bringing a new romantic paradigm (Thapar, 2003: 4).[36]

Historians appropriately have contributed to this aspect of colonial impact. Farquhar mentions, "The estimating forces are almost exclusively Western, i.e., the British government, English education and literature, Christianity, Oriental research, European science and philosophy and the material elements of Western civilization" (Farquhar, 1967: 433; Majumdar, 1965: 89).[37] In a significant study Charles Heimsath came to final conclusion that Indian elites not only adopted the Western ideas but too methods of organization to colonial inspiration (Heimsath, 1964: 46).[33] In David Kopf's attribution, 'the Bengal renaissance was a result of the contact between British official and missionaries on the one hand and the Hindu intelligentsia on the other (Kopf, 1969: 1).[39] Thus, it was colonial way to construct Hinduism in 19th century colonial India.

Some reactions came from nationalist historians against colonial rule which fall under second path. Recognizing the role of colonial rule, Susobhan Sarkar made his focus that "foreign conquest and domination was bound to be a hindrance rather than a help to subject people's regeneration" (Sarkar, 1970: 150).[40] Similar kind of emotional observation came from A.K. Bhattacharya. "Imperialism raised barriers in the Indian mind against critical ideas from the

West because these ideas came from those sources that were holding India down (Bhattacharya, 1962: 29).[41]

In the construction of Hinduism, Orientalism and utilitarianisms worked as the catalysts for India upper caste elites. The discovery of Indian past by Orientalists and its glorification by linguistic affinity between Sanskrit and some European language like Greek and Latin by William Jones, chronological relationship between the ancient texts the Puranas and Bible, Racial affinity of Europeans with Indian upper-caste (Aryan Race theory by Max Muller)[42] and depiction of Indian values as spiritual and European values as materialistic; and utilitarian critical evaluation of India, i.e., James Mill's periodization of Indian civilization into Hindu (ancient), Muslim (medieval) and British (not Christian but modern),[43] and theory of Oriental despotism and Gandhian movement became the major aspects of the construction of Hinduism by upper caste elites.

Co-existence: Tribe and Territory

The identification of 'tribes' is being discussed in their relationship with state and territory in Indian historical tradition. Beteille compares Islamic historical tradition with Indian. It is appropriated, following historian Kosambi's observations regarding sense of history, that, the Indian intellectual tradition lacked the historical sense before Muslim introduction. Though Kosambi confined only with Brahmanical literature, i.e., *Ramayana, Mahabharata* and *Puranas* (Kosambi, 1975: 2; Beteille, 1986: 308).[44] He mixes Indian intellectual tradition with Brahmanical intellectual tradition. Contrary to Beteille and Kosambi's view, Romila Thapar defends Brahmanical intellectual tradition for a sense of history (Itihasa Purana tradition). She argues, Itihasa literally means 'thus it was' and Purana refers to that which belongs to the past (Thapar, 2003: 134).[45]

Rejecting both the views Gail Omvedt has accused the orthodox Brahmanic perspective of Itihas-Purana tradition which had been continued from early century CE to the time of Mughals in India. In this tradition, Buddhist literature, which gives historical descriptions of the period, was wiped out of India. Manuscripts of Buddhist literature preserved in Cylon, Tibet, and China. Though history was not an early 'science' in Buddhism as it was in China, still Buddhism did foster a historical approach: the early Pali texts show an orientation to a fairly sober description of historical events and the monasteries were institutions of potentially great autonomy. The Buddhist chronicles (Dipavamsha and Mahavamsha) of Sri Lanka give an account of India's greatest emperor, Ashoka; the Brahmanical sources barely mentions his name (Omvedt, 2003: 165–66).[46]

This does not come to grips with the fact that what is preserved in India has been the Brahamanical, 'concept of its past' and not that of a nebulous society. The concept of the past as revealed in Buddhist sources is quite different from the one revealed in Brahmanical sources, not to mention those of other Indian traditions or preliterate indigenous groups within India. Moreover, the very different conception of the past is embodied in Buddhist literature has been erased in India itself (Omvedt, 2003: 166).[47]

Recent excellent historical studies have revealed the sense of history in oral traditions among indigenous societies (tribes), most probably Buddhist in

Western and north-eastern India.[48] Though, such histories are recent ones but represent a distinct prospective.

In traditional historical and anthropological writings, the whole Indian civilization in early past has been appropriated in two socio-cultural modes: *Jana* and *Jati* (Ray, 1973; Bose, 1971).[49] In this historiography *Janas* were identified with tribes and *Jatis* (castes) with Hindu civilization. Naharraryan Ray identified two sets of Janas in Indian historical tradition, one as tribes and another who were at relatively higher level of socio-economic and political organization of aesthetic and religious culture (Ray, 1973).[50]

Sociologists appropriate the meaning of *Janas* as 'communities of people' rather than the 'tribes'. Xaxa determines that the terms of reference in tribal studies are not to be such categories as caste, peasanthood and social heterogeneity but groups or communities such as the Bengalis, the Assamese and the Gujaratese. The counterparts of tribes are not castes or peasants but communities or societies incorporating castes and peasants. The later are not whole societies but only elements of wholes. Tribes, on the other hand, are societies each with their own language, territory, culture, customs, and so on. They must be compared with other societies and not, with castes (Xaxa, 1999: 1524).[51]

Subsequently, in Hindu nationalist view, historical significance of 'tribal' dynasties in historical past had been reduced to a negligible level. The centralized states overcome the existence of tribal politics and if they emerged as the independent state, the only possible model of state was Hindu model. Beteille has declared that as the state became more powerful and society better organizes, the scope available to tribal lineage to establish new dynasties become more restricted. But the state was not the most durable product of Hindu civilization. The weakness and decay of states always left room for the emergence of tribal chiefs whose aim was to create not tribal chiefdoms so much as kingdoms after the Hindu model (Beteille, 1986: 309).[52] In this proposition, made by Beteille, Buddhist and Islamic notions of state have been ignored.

In Indian civilization, Mauryan and Mughal empires have been appropriated as centralized states at polity level, and undoubtedly ever biggest in pre-colonial India. Evidences from Greek writings and the Asokan edicts clearly suggest that the Mauryan period in the sub-continent saw a contact between peoples and cultures on a scale and intensity that has not been known before (Aloka, 1998: 173).[53] In terms of religious policies both states were not Hindu states. Mauryan state was Buddhist and Mughal Islamic. Authority historians on Mauryas, Thapar and Fussman proposed their hypotheses on the nature of Mauryan administration and territories in Indian subcontinent.

Thapar appropriates whole Mauryan Empire into three administrative levels: the metropolitan state, the core areas and, peripheries (forest and hill areas). She demonstrates that the area of Magadha under the metropolitan state is high powered, centralized bureaucratic control and the nucleus of the empire. The metropolitan state is juxtaposed with other categories of territories. Metropolitan state conquered the core areas aiming at the territorial expansion and resource mobilization for the necessities of metropolitan state. In condition of insufficiency of resources from core areas, then the peripheral areas come under territorial expansion and exploitation. The peripheral areas were inhabited by forest tribes (Thapar, 1997: 317–19; 1987: 3–4).[54]

Fussman made alike divisions of Mauryan Empire, and concludes that the Mauryan Empire was made up of (a) territories administered directly by crown; (b) kingdom conquered or won over, and; (c) tribes and republics with some degree of internal autonomy. These tribes existed before the Mauryan Empire and they survived its dissolution. It left a greater or lesser degree of autonomy according to the place and circumstances so that 'history and geography precluded the constitution of a unitarian state, which is not a reality even in the twentieth century (Fussman, 1987–88: 71–72).[55]

In a significant historical study, Aloka has revealed multi-dimensional relationship of Mauryan state with forest tribes. He too, questions the propositions made by Thapar and Fussman and, strongly suggested that however powerful an ancient empire, it always had difficulties in containing diverse ethnically powerful populations. Geography and perceived existence of hostile tribes defined the frontiers of empire and both had to be mastered for the expansion and integration of the state. Thus, the growth of empire and process of territorial acquisition and assimilation went along with defeat and subjugation of tribal and frontier people, a marginalization of their ways of life (Aloka, 1998: 174).[56]

Most striking fact, Aloka reveals, is related to the territorial areas occupied by civilized and 'tribal' polities during the Mauryan period and later. He reveals that the Jaina tradition, which was systematized later (after Mauryan period) around the fifth century AD, during the reign of king Sampai (Samprati), contains references to many countries other than the sixteen Mahajanapadas. The Pannavana (Prajanapana) consequently thus listed twenty-five-and-half countries, with their important cities, as more inhabited by the Arya and fifty-three countries of the Milakkha or barbarian (Aranyacara, Atavi and Atavika tribes). Most of the Milakkha or tribal tracts were mountainous and forested in the subcontinent (Aloka, 1998: 178).[57] It shows that a large area of subcontinent was under autonomous forest polities. References in *Arthashastra* reveal that the Atavika tribes had their own territories and had all the facilities that a strong kind could have. Ashokan edicts and *Arthashastra* discussed the political autonomy of Adivasi polities, their confrontation with centralized state, and in return centralized state's approach towards these Adivasi polities (*Arthashastra* 8.4.43, Aloka 1998: 179).[58] It is clear from the reference of edicts that Asoka's *Dhamma* policy made a deep impact on forest tribes (Ativikas). Asoka's edicts mention the names of 'tribal' societies like the Yonas, Kambojas, Nabhakas, Bhojas, Pitinikas and Andhras (Aloka, 1998: 185).[59]

In the traditional historiography Mughal Empire has been described as highly centralized with fully developed agrarian system. 'Tribal' polities and agrarian systems had been disappeared from Mughal state and agrarian system in such historiography. The recent historical writings have filled this gap. A study reveals that the gross cultivated area during the reign of Akbar was unlikely to have been more than 55 per cent of the gross cultivation in 1909–10 (Moosvi, 1987: 65).[60] In geographical terms, it would represent even smaller proportion when placed against the territorial extent of Mughal empire. Large proportion of the empire though uncultivated, were however unlikely to have been totally devoid of human population. Many such areas were, in all probably inhabited by such societies (tribal) for whom settled agriculture has not yet became a primary means of livelihood (Chetan, 1988: 321).[61]

Such societies and polities were existed in different parts of 'Mughal India' in the subcontinent. In the Punjab the Jats, Khukhars, Gujjars, Chakkars, Junjuhars, and Bhattis in Sind, the Nahmadis, Nazharis, Kalmatis, Pahwars and so on in Western; and Dakkan India the Kolis, Bhils and Gonds were that kind of distinct communities as well autonomous agrarian polities. Some of their chiefs minted coins in their names such as Summa chief Jam Hal of Kakrala and established tribal monarchy (Sodhas of Umarkot). Most of the chiefs of such polities had their independent army and some times attacked the imperial Mughal state (Chetan, 1988; Zaidy, 1989).[62]

In central highlands, some 'tribal' politics, especially Jawar (*Koli*) and Ramnagar (*Bhil*) in medieval India were the finest examples of autonomous state formation and for competitive survivals and participation in main stream political economy of empires. These polities unfold over 500 years as forest chiefs fought and negotiated with the Sultanate of Gujarat, the Portuguese Estado, the Mughal Empire, the Maratha states and finally the British Empire (Guha, 1999: 8).[63]

Regarding relationship between centralize state, i.e., Marath and Bhil polities in seventeenth and eighteenth centuries it has come out that Bhil polities always were not at lower end with Maratha state in western India. Maratha state shared the sovereignty with Bhil polities in Dangs. Since around the late 18th century, there had been a sharing of fees collected from timber nakas or toll stations located in the villages with at least two major Dangi chiefs, those of Ghadvi and Dherbavti (Skaria, 1998: 205).[64] Rajkumar Hans in his study on Broach in Gujarat reveals that the Girasias claimed a fourth or a third share of revenue; and held half the land under cultivation (Rajkumar, 1987: 62).[65]

State Formation and Tribe

Another proposition made by Beteille, was a Hindu model for emergence for 'tribal' dynasties. He has argued that what is characteristic of the relationship between tribe and civilization in India is that there was virtually no way in which a tribal dynast could legitimize its rule without becoming Hinduized(!). This is an exaggeration of a small part of truth. Earlier, Surjit Sinha was pioneer among Indian anthropologist who founded and popularized the Rajputization theory of state formation for tribal dynasties in central India. "State formation in the tribal belt of central India is very largely a story of the Rajputization of the tribes" (Sinha, 1995: 305).[66] But, he did not make it final truth like Beteille. Though Sinha is critical towards ethnographers for ignoring historical process, but, his model of Rajputization itself is based on myths and genealogies and used mostly ethnographical and anthropological material in spite of historical material in pre-colonial India.

Ajay Skaria has revealed completely a distinct process of state formation of 'Bhil Raj' at top, and Bhilization in general in pre-colonial and colonial Western India. His arguments are based on proper historical material. He has demonstrated that Rajput chiefs were quite willing to marry into powerful Bhil lineages. Claiming and participating in the wildness of being Bhil, was not something that only *Janglijatis* like Koknis did even Rajputs were fascinated by, and claimed their involvement in enactments of wildness (Skaria, 1998: 213).[67] Except this, ritually superior Dangi communities the Bhils like Gomits, Chodharis, Valvis or Koknis made their claim to be part of Bhil Raj, and claimed to be Bhil (Kokni Bhil). Skaria calls this process Bhilization (Skaria, 1998: 204; 1999: 113),[68] which is contrary to Rajputization. On the other hand, kinship ties were less significant among Rajput lineages in the initial stages of power building for often the founder of a lineage would have migrated to a new territory with a small number of kinsmen. Only in the later stages of developmental cycle of a Rajput lineage when it had succeeded in dominating the sizable area of land, did a large body of kinsmen organized into stratified and distinct tiers appear (Fox, 1971: 70, 75).[69] In medieval Andhra politically prominent Kakatiya dynasty and many of the leading warrior families made no pretensions to Kshatriya status rather they proudly claimed their descent from Sudra status because they are the bravest or the purest (Talbot, 2001: 51).[70]

Sumit Guha in his valuable study on central highland forest polities, covering a span of period since Delhi Sultanate to the post-colonial state, has placed three interacting but distinct models of tribal state formation as well as their competency for substances. The first, follows Sinha's argument, was achievement of transition to Rajput kingdom by a regional chiefdom, but failed and lost to history. In the second, the regional chieftancy made transition to Rajput kingdom but lost its links to the local forest elite and was marginalized by competition from third. The third, was a tribal clan chieftancy that sustained itself by retaining its kinship ties with the local dominant forest tribe and avoiding pretensions to Rajput status (Guha, 1999: 8).[71]

Contrary to the transitional approach, integrative approach of state formation has also been recorded too in medieval and pre-colonial states. An early explanation of integrative approach can be appropriated from C.U. Wells' study on medieval Chattisgarh kingdoms, where, these kingdoms were successful in maintaining legitimacy because they retained local tribal organization and local chieftaincies. The system of *garhs* (political and administrative divisions centred around a fort) derived from the earlier tribal clan territories which Rajput ruler standardized (Wills, 1919: 199).[72] Thus, a system of feudalism superimposed on a earlier tribal organization (Wells, 1919: 235, 255).[73] This is a type of incorporation of tribal political and administrative institutions. Kulke in his work on Orissa, appropriated the incorporation of socio-cultural tribal institutions in to system of centralized states where he talked of vertical and horizontal legitimizations. Vertical legitimization was achieved through an appropriation of indigenous deities into royal cults, while horizontal legitimization whose stakes were prestige and acceptance within other kingdoms, involved bringing a Brahmans and building temples. The two processes were not separable as successive stage but co-existed (Kulke, 1986).[74] Brahman were intended to provide administrative and ideological specialists to counter centrifugal feudal forces (Kulke, 1986: 135).[75] Thus, the incorporation of Brahmans into royal cults was not only for religious reasons or for the competition with other kingdoms.

In the process of state formation in Bastar, Kakatiya had achieved the hegemony through two mechanisms—the ritualization of *corvee*, service by forest tribes to the king and kingdom, as both right and obligation and the materiality of ritual within *Dussehara* (a tribal festival, but in north India it has been appropriated as Hindu festival with distinct connotation)—the integration through labour of different groups within the kingdom, and the integration of their Gods, like Danteswari, a tribal Goddess (Sunder, 1997: 54–55).[76] The result was that the rulers adopted 'tribal' gods and change them, and the tribal in turn adopt these changed gods and change them, and so it goes on in endless mimesis we might equally see the Hindus as over determined aboriginals (Sunder, 1997: 62).[77]

In medieval and pre-colonial period, Kulke, has described the ways of tribalization of princely courts in Orissa. Appropriating this process, he talks about three distinct types of tribal deities: first, the martyr-istadevata (represents the initial violent coercion, killing of 'tribal' human being by princely king), to establish royal power; second, the most powerful 'tribal' rastradevata or royal istadevata (symbolizes the aspect of the infinite power over state as a whole) and third, 'subsidiary' istadevata represent the local aspect of power over a particular part of social groups of the state (Kulke, 1993).[78] Further, he argues that by accepting the royal istadevata (tubulatory 'tribal' goddess) the raja became the legitimate ruler of the state as a whole (Kulke, 1993: 136).[79] It is significant character of the relationship between 'tribe' and civilization in India that by no ways 'Hindu' dynasties could legitimized its rule without becoming tribalize.

Language and Tribe

Language has been assumed as one of the significant criteria to define or identify tribes in India. On the basis of language scholars made efforts to establish the relationship between tribes and civilization. In India language has been imagined at two levels: static or literary language mean national or regional language (civilized language), and non-static languages or local languages (tribal language) or non-literary language. In an assumption national or regional languages fixed with 'civilized' and religious identities, like Sanskrit and Hindi with Hinduism or Hindus, Urdu and Persian with Islam or Muslims, and tribal/non-literary languages with 'tribal' and animism. It is also assumed that 'tribal' languages have lost or in transition to lost to static/literary or languages. The bilingualism is also imposed on tribes to justify their transition. Are these imaginations appropriate to define the 'tribe'?

Literary languages are mechanized and standardized forms of local or tribal dialects. Civilized states always have been involved itself in the standardization of dialects for constructing literary forms. The standardization of dialects to literary usually seems to be standardization of civility of speaking communities. Literary national (i.e., Hindi) or regional (e.g., Tamil, Oriya, Bengali etc.) languages are the common forms of local dialects, even yet, distinct dialects have been spoken by various communities. How can, communities who speak local dialects which construct Hindi, Tamil or any literary language, be given the status of 'tribal' and 'uncivilized'? In Madhya Pradesh, Nimari language constituted of Bhili, Bareli, Bhilali (tribal) and local dialects of Hindi, and alike Malwi. Those who speak Bhili, Bhilali and Bareli they have been considered as 'tribes' but those who speak Nimari and Malwi considered as Hindus?

It seems that with linguistic boundaries, the smallness of speaking population is bound to identify the tribe. This test is also inappropriate. Nearly 880, or linguistic boundaries, languages are spoken in India. But all populations who speak these languages have not been considered as 'tribes'. It seems constructive rather than natural because in less than a hundred years an area which was covered by a mass of small dialects gets restructured linguistically into two or three regions using the highly self-conscious languages of their respecting high cultures (Kaviraj, 1997: 24).[80]

Hardly any community would be found without religion in India or elsewhere. Hindi, English and Urdu are not only spoken by Hindus, Christians and Muslims. Each of them is spoken by different religious communities Hindu, Christian, Buddhist, Islamic etc. In north-east 'tribes' speak English as well as their mother-tongue. In central and western India 'tribal' communities speak their mother-tongue as well as national/regional languages like Hindi, Gujarati, Marathi. Bilingualism should not only confine with 'tribal' communities. In the linguistic model of floral figuration De Swaan talks of metropolitan elites (literate) with central language and local populations (illiterate) with peripheral language. Mediation between these two was carried out by local or regional elites, literate as a rule, and bilingual fluent in both the regional and central language (De Swaan, 1990).[81]

Secondary Phenomenon and Tribe

Anthropologists appropriated tribes as secondary phenomenon in India. In the model of secondary phenomenon 'tribes' do not represent a definite type of society in itself and get the organizational framework and identity from outside source (Fried, 1968; Beteille, 1986).[82] It is almost certain that such secondary phenomena have increased in scale and intensity from the middle of the nineteenth century to the present, and the idea of ex-criminal tribes, if not criminal tribes, sounds of definitely modern. Indeed there is a reason to believe that both detribalization and retribalization occurred in the distant as well as the recent past (Beteille, 1986: 310).[83]

In the model of secondary phenomena, both the views: Fried's view of 'tribes' as not a definite type of society and, identity formation from outside source; Beteille's transition view where transformation only take place among 'tribes' by following detribalization and retribalization, touches only single aspect. It could hardly be viewed that 'tribes' have no identity and always get identity from outside. Transformation acquires in every society. Chetan Singh concludes that structural change in tribal societies, however, could not have been a matter of concern for tribal alone. So close a relationship did tribal pastoralism bear with the sedentary and commercialized agrarian society of Mughal Punjab, and so inextricably linked were its economic interests with those of later, that fundamental shifts in the structure of any of these societies could hardly have left the other unaffected. To view these societies as constituting two separate worlds in themselves would, probably, be quite far from the truth (Chetan, 1988: 340).[84]

Identity formation is interactive and communicative between societies. In India from early past, Zimmerman reveals the process, the differentiation that began to occur was socio-cultural as well as technological, and the communities of the river plains, the forest, the savanna, the desert, and the high mountains coevolved in continuous interaction evolving both conflict and cooperation over the next two millennia. Each community's habitat was a resource for it: a resource defined not merely in economic, but in political and cultural terms. The boundaries and aspirations of communities were defined by the presence of other communities, other way of living-identities generated by contrasts; and one of most crucial of these contrasts was between the civilized and their domesticated landscape, and the savage in their wild woods (Zimmerman, 1987: Chapter 1–3).[85]

In historical process 'tribal' communities cannot be regarded in dominant discourses as animists. All societies have been integrated by some kind of religious faith. In the long past, two different cultures—the Indic and the Vedic, and a mix of ethnic and linguistic groups, came together in the period of social tumult and momentous transformation in north India. With the growth of an economic surplus, cities and kingdoms had come with increasingly social strain, class divisions and pressure on the older, move equalitarian 'tribal' and lineage-based societies of the region. Two major political forms appeared by the time of Gotama; the stratified but still 'tribal' *Gana-Sanghas*, and emerging monarchial kingdoms. Gana-sanghas, one of which Gotama was born, were oligarchies. While these have been called 'tribal republics' and they were in fact democratically and collectively governed, they were nevertheless incipient class societies themselves (Gail, 2003: 27–28).[86]

Religion, Conversion and Tribes

It is highly misconceptualized in the Hindu nationalist narrative that Indian civilization has been a Hindu civilization from ancient to the modern times. In special context of the relationship of 'tribe', they always have been discussed with 'Hindu' civilization and caste as the potent reality. The idea of division of Indian society into tribe and caste or animist and Hindu is completely vague because first, it removes other real qualifications and merits of Indian civilizations, and secondly it is a colonial construct to fit colonial policies to rule India, and for colonial convenience. In post-colonial state colonial constructions suited ruling elites.

Contemporary studies show that *Ancient India was not 'Hindu India' but Buddhist India* (Omvedt, 2003: 118; Thapar, 1969: 7; Davids, 1997).[87] The decisive period for the formation of continuous 'thread' of history was the first millennium BCE, and that to a very large degree of the thousand years after this representing a civilization dominated by Buddhism. Hinduism is not an oldest and dominant religious faith in ancient India. Hinduism had its beginning at the end of the first millennium of CE with the adoption of the *Bhagwat* cult (*Vaishnavism*) and the absorption of the Shiva cult (known for a long time as the *Pashupatis*) while the *Dhammashastra* (for example *Manusmriti* and *Arthashastra*) were manifestos for the type of society Brahmanism sought to bring into being. But Brahmanism was not the determining force in Indian society. For a millennium after the time of Buddha, his *Dhamma* remained the major determinant of Indian civilization though in conflict throughout with the Varnashrama Dharma of a developing Brahmanism which it opposed (Omvedt, 2003: 125).[88]

Tribal communities in anthropological discourse had been depicted as animist or without any established religion in India? Is it appropriate? Colonial ethnographers and anthropologists started cataloguing Indian indigenous or Adivasi communities 'tribe' with animism and rest of the population into caste with Hinduism in the late nineteenth and early twentieth centuries.[89] Such divisions were mostly practiced in census operations. Of course, the hyper real categorization of Indian communities into tribe and castes was colonial but was based on Brahmanical view. There are several accounts of such evidences in colonial knowledge and practice where former had been considered as socially inferior or outcasts (Malcolm, 1823, 1970: 2; Steele, 1868: 93; Gorden, 1994: 151).[90]

In the first millennium BCE, two contending and conflicting socio-religious traditions *Samana* (Shramana) and Brahmanism were emerged. Thapar demonstrates ideological confrontation. *Sramanism* (Samananism), a term covering a variety of Buddhist, Jaina, *Ajivika* and other sects, denied the fundamentals of Brahmanism such as Vedic *Sruti* and *Smriti*. Organizationally, Brahmanism had its base in the householder Brahmanic elite, while the samana had their base in the wandering hermits and medicants drawn from various castes. Brahamanic philosophers were passed down through a guru-disciple tradition that was at times loose but was generally identified with caste hierarchy; a disciple from lower castes would normally not be admitted. It was secretive. In Gail's view, Buddhism was best identified with Samana tradition (Omvedt, 2003: 51).[91]

In the context of mode of materialist production, the samana tradition attested rather to an excess energy in society; it was the existence of a material surplus in the rising agricultural society that made it possible for many to exist without production or to live off extracted products of the forests and their questioning was evidence of a dynamic society bursting normal bounds of its cultural and social framework (Omvedt, 2003: 31).[92] Thus the samana tradition can be most importantly identified with the Adivasi forest communities with lower castes (earlier best known untouchables but now Dalits). Untouchability was also a form of religion prosecution, for this exclusion was common to Brahmanism as well as to some *Sramami* sects, the *Candala* being a category apart (Thapar, 2000: 74).[93] Earlier, Ambedkar already had spoken that untouchables were untouchable because they were adherents of Buddhism in historical past (Ambedkar, 1948).[94]

Buddhism and Jainism had dominant ideological and cultural influence on wider plain and forest communities in the first millennium BC and the first millennium AD in Indian subcontinent. Most importantly, today what we called tribal communities were greatly influenced by these philosophies. Thus, Buddhism and Jainism, reflects a situation of detribalization in which they attempt to reach out across castes to be wider range through their universal ethic (Thapar, 2000: 104).[95]

In Mauryan period large populations of frontier and forest areas had heavily transformed into Buddhism. For this transformation, Asoka adopted the peaceful conquest by morality rather than military politics. For the promotion of *Dhamma* into forest areas, and among forest communities Asoka appointed the *Mahamatras* of *Dhamma-Mahamatras* are occupied with all sects in establishing *Dhamma*, in promoting Dhamma, and for the welfare and happiness of those who are devoted to *Dhamma* (even) among the *Yonas, Kombojas*, and *Gandharas*, and whatever other western borders (Kosambi, 1975: 202).[96] The influence of Buddhism upon the empire was not greater than the influence of the empire upon Buddhism (Kosambi, 1975: 204).[97]

Gadgil and Guha appropriate historically the eco-friendly religious and cultural aspects of Buddhism and Jainism with special regards of forest 'tribes' and 'untouchables'. They state that Buddhism and Jainism had begun to play a role in once again designing social convention which promoted the prudent use of resources. In past, such conservation practices would have been founded on earlier ones, inherited from food gathering societies. Apart from their appeal to traders, these religions perhaps appealed most to the lower social strata composed largely out of food-gathers (Gadgil and Guha, 1992: 88).[98]

Brahmanism reflects a completely apposite view to Buddhism and Jainism in regard forest protection and appropriation of the inhabitants. In epics, the forest was the context of at least three activities: the hunt, the hermitage, and the place of exile ... . The *vana* was the unknown territory, peopled by *raksasas*. Here the hero slaughtered indiscriminately. Families of tigers and deer were killed, and severely wounded elephants trampled the forest. So fierce was the slaughter of animals that predators and pray refuse took together. One is remained of another vivid description of destruction of forest—the *Khandava vana* was burnt by *agni*. Further, she argues that Hindu Gupta rulers had changed Asoka's policy of moral conquest (*Dhamma* policy) towards forest tribes. In the Allahabad stone pillar inscription of Samudragupta, in the fourth century AD Samudragupta is said to have reduced the atavika-rajas or forest chiefs to servitude (Thapar, 2001: 4, 12).[99] In Hindu nationalist writings, Gupta period is projected as the period of Hindu Renaissance. But far from the Guptas reviving nationalism, it was nationalism that revived the Guptas (Kosambi, 1975: 313).[100]

Contrary to Hindu nationalists' taken for granted view, in medieval period tribes converted into Islam. Richard Eaton in classical work in Bengal Frontiers, demonstrates four conventional theories of conversion to Islam in India: first, the religion of the sword thesis (forcible conversion); second, the royal patronage thesis (self-interested conversion for the benefit of being Muslim under a Muslim king); third, the 'religion of social liberation' thesis (Islam being an equalitarian religion attracted low caste converts fleeing the oppression of Brahmanic varnashrama society) and; fourth, immigrant thesis. However, he rejects first three theses. The rejection of first three theses came on the ground that the mass of poorer Muslims are found not at the centre of Muslim rule, but in the northeast and northwest, at peripheries. In rejection of third, and establishing 'migration' thesis, he argues that most of the mass converts had never really been Hindus. They were basically hunting, fishing, gathering peoples who went directly from a tribal culture to that of Islam. Most of these tribes such as the Rajbanshis, Pod, Candal, Kuch and other indigenous people who had little formal contact with literate representatives of Brahmanism (Eaton, 1997: 76).[101]

Eaton does not restore the value of social liberation thesis. Omvedt establishes it in case of untouchable *Candalas* or *Namsudhas* in Bengal. Historically she finds relationship of untouchable *Candalas* (officially Scheduled Caste) with indigenous Proto-Munda speakers as well as Mundari-speaking, the *Santhal* (officially Scheduled Tribe). The application of the word the *Candal* was not only restricted to east of Bengal but also practised in Gangetic plains as well as central India. She logically appropriates indigenous Namasudras in East Bengal as Buddhist. These people learned the values of equality from Buddhist traditions rather from Rousseau or Jefferson (Eaton mentions the names of Rousseau and Jefferson for learning fundamental quality from them by indigenous people, 1997: 117). The 'tribes', instead, converting into discriminatory religion Brahmanism, they converted into Islam, a religion with egalitarian and equalitarian traditions (Omvedt, 2003: 180–81).[102]

Talbot's path breaking study on medieval Kakatiya Andhra resembles the socio-religious and expending agrarian process with Eaton's study on medieval frontier Bengal. He argues that like Bengal, medieval Andhra was characterized by agrarian expansion, the migration of agrarian people to new lands, and the growing assimilation of non-agrarian peoples. Public identities (king and other identities) stressed occupation and individual achievements far more than caste or territorial affiliations in Kakatiya Andhra. The transformation of occupational identities such as *Ko(m)pu* and *reddi* into hereditary 'caste' labels did not occur in Andhra until, at least, the late seventeenth century (Talbot, 2001: 86).[103] Hindu identity did not appear in the case of Kakatiya Andhra. In Kakatiya Andhra, social identities were not expressed in terms of Varna or Jati. Tablot argues that social identities represent earned statuses rather than ascribed ranks (Tablot, 2001: 85).[104]

In an alternative model to Indian social system, pre-colonial society was actually centred on the king rather than being a Brahmanical/hierarchical system based on levels of ritual purity. In case of Kakatiya Andhra, Talbot follows this model. Depolitization occurred after the British eliminated the pivotal role of the king—who had integrated an extensive re-distributive system that united the various sectors of society. His disappearance caused the economic, political and social hierarchies to differentiate, which in turn gave rise to village that were far more self-contained, each with their own Jajmani division of labour—a remnant of the original redistributive network, but not an inherent feature of traditional India itself (Fuller, 1977: 105–8; Dirks, 1989: 65–72).[105] Likely, the displacement of the king caused the social sphere to become autonomous and led to Brahman ascendance in the social order (Dirks, 1987: 59).[106] Consequently, the perspective provided by Sanskrit texts, Brahman experience and elite culture in medieval states has attained a privilege in the framework of civilization that it does not deserve in history (Ludden, 1994: 6–7, 11).[107]

Vandeville emphasized that till medieval period in north and eastern India, a large number of low artisan (*julaha* and *koris*) and allied indigenous communities had already adhered to the Buddhist creed. Specially, in Eastern India Buddhism was the adherence of large population under the statehood of Buddhist Pala kings till the 12th century. Buddhist artisan communities such as *julahas* or *koris* in Islam were superficial rather than real because they retained their Buddhist customs and practices. More importantly, Muslim missionaries 'Sufis' were under deep influence of somewhat degraded form of Buddhism (Vaudeville, 1993: 72).[108] Furthermore, from early medieval ages, Buddhism was in practice in its some crude form in North India and Nepal by the preaching of the Fanatic Buddhist Sahajiya Siddhas and the Nath Yogis or Gorakhnathis. The great God Shiva (*macchendra,* or *minanath* in the Bengali tradition) identified with Buddhist icon *Avalokitesvara,* the ancient protector of Nepal (Vaudeville, 1993: 73–74).[109] In Western and Central India *Siva* is the best identified god of 'tribes' (Russell and Hiralal, 1916; Skaria, 1998; Ilaiah, 1996).[110]

Gail Omvedt argues that the Bhakti movements show a clear conflict with Brahmanism and the caste and gender hierarchies it involved, but they also show an almost overwhelming degree of Brahman dominance. Thus the conflict between Buddhism and Brahmanism took place in a different way and had a very different significance consequently, the Bhakti movements in many ways reflected the social conditions of the long millennium between the 8th and 18th centuries (Omvedt, 2003: 215).[111] The ideology and teachings of Bhakti saints is largely appropriated and practised among the untouchables and 'tribes' in India,[112] as they had their historical attachment with Buddhism.

Colonial and post-colonial historiography labeled the 'tribes' as animist or without the faith in any existing religion. Historically to an extent animism could be identified with Buddhism. Rhys Davids concludes that animistic beliefs as to tree worship mentioned in pre-Buddhist literature formed part, at the time of the rise of Buddhism, of the religion of the people. They were rejected by the early Buddhists. But they continued to form part of the religion of more of the people who were influenced by the new teachings. And one or two of them found their way back into one or other of the later schools of Buddhism (Rhys Davids, 1903: 226).[113] Later, the *Bodhi Vriksa* (wisdom tree), which is called the *Assattha* or *Pipal* tree, became sacred in the memory of the master Buddha (Rhys Davids, 1903: 230).[114] In Madhya Pradesh, Rajasthan and Gujarat, tree and grain worship is highly sacred and practiced among Bhils and other tribal on the occasion of every festival, and significant ritual. The Pipal tree is also highly sacred among the Chamars of Uttar Pradesh. At the time of rise of Buddhism, Nagas are related with the spirit of Banyana tree and the tree is the dwelling place of Nagas (Rhys Davids, 1903: 232).[115] In his recent philological study, Marmat shows that the all indigenous communities (Sudras/Dalits/Adivasi/OBCs/SC/ST) are of Naga origin in India (Marmat, 1996).[116]

'Transformation' of Tribe and Caste

In India the concept of 'tribe' has been treated in Brahmanical view in British colonial and Hindu nationalist social anthropology. Buddhist view of society is entirely missing. Buddhist scholar, Rhys Davids appropriates that the Brahman view, in possession of the field when Europeans entered India, has been regarded so long with reverence among us that it seems almost impenitence now. The writings of orthodox Brahmans, like Manu and other, are taken too seriously and without a sneer. So, they formed the key—stone of arch of social life in India. They are the only proper authorities. Why trouble about these miserable heretics (Rhys Davids, 1988: III–IV)?[117]

Consequently, Brahmanical view represents 'tribes' (including Dalit-Bahujan) as: beings whose cultural consciousness and ideology have no identity. Their history, language, philosophy, skills, knowledge of science and technology were all rendered invisible. The reason for this is the institution of caste. As a consequence, caste arrested them and their consciousness within it. They saw it that the very idea of caste negated the idea of history. Their history therefore became non-history (Ilaiah, 1996: 66).[118]

Though, tribal society has its own distinct features, cultural and ideological consciousness apart from Hindu society. Tribal society resembles with Indic or Buddhist notions of society. Scholars accept that tribal society is egalitarian, homogeneous, undifferentiated and un-stratified. Contrary to this, traditional caste Hindu society is heterogeneous, differentiated and stratified. At the same time it is both hierarchical and segmental. This hierarchy and segmentation is authorized and justified by 'sacred' traditional Brahmanical texts.

In Hindu society if *Varnashrama-dharma* and *Caste-dharama* do not function normally, Hindu lawmakers assigned the king to implement them forcefully. Historian R.C. Majumdar says that Manu lays down that the king should carefully compel Vaishya and Shudras to perform the work prescribed for them. Again every caste should practice the duties that have been mentioned as belonging to it and that have been practiced by ancestors and should otherwise be punished by the king (Majumdar, 1969: 385).[119]

Contrary, tribal society was not abode by such obligations and birth-determined caste or occupational identity. The division of labour in tribal society is unconditional, practical and changeable. Simply tribal society is *moral-conduct-based* society. Buddhist philosophy comprises these characteristics. This *moral-conduct* (*kamma*) is explained in Buddhist canon *Sutta-Nipata* that one who lives by keeping cow is a farmer or *kassiko*; one who lives by handicrafts is a *sippiko;* one who lives by selling merchandise is a *vanijjo*; one who lives by services done for hire is a *pessiko* or a wage-worker; one who lives by warfare is a *yodajivo* or soldier; one who lives by sacrificial rite is a *yajako* or priest; one who rule is a monarch or *Raja* (Omvedt, 2003: 76).[120]

Hindu nationalists have taken tribes for granted as Hindus. Anthropologist N.K. Bose propagated the idea of 'Hindu Method of Tribal Absorption'.[121] Beteille extends this argument that there are, firstly castes of tribal origin in areas in which the caste based division of labour is well established and these include both agricultural and artisan groups. But they ... also the ... phenomenon, namely the growth of occupational specialization and the emergence of caste—like groups in the interior of a tribal area (Beteille, 1986: 312).[122]

Ambedkar rejects the argument that caste is not just merely a division of labour. It is also a division of labourers (Ambedkar, 1979: 47).[123] Definitely, there is a division of labour among tribes but without the resemblance with caste—Hindu society. In Central India, Bhila, Bhilala, Barela, Gond, Kol, Agaria, Kamar, Munda, Santal; in northeast, Naga, Mizo, Apatani, Khasi, and Garo practice various occupational specializations regarding agriculture and artisanal activities. But they are still known by their local/regional and cultural identity not by occupational. A study on Bihar shows that Lohra, Agaria, Asura, Kamar and Marya practice the occupation of blacksmith and carpenter from medieval period. Yet they identified themselves as Kamar, Agaria, Asura and Marya instead of blacksmith (*Lohar*) and carpenter (*Badhai*) (Shukla, 2003).[124]

Historian D.D. Kosambi generalized the concept of 'castes from tribes' by putting his argument that the entire course of Indian history shows tribal elements are being fused in to a general society. This phenomenon which lies at the foundation of the most striking Indian feature, namely caste, is also the great basic fact of Ancient Indian history (Kosambi, 1975: 27).[125]

Sociologists and historians strike off this idea that caste is a universal phenomenon in ancient Indian history. Buddhism reflected and propagated a casteless, open society. In general there is too much concern even for birth, in spite of references to the nobility of a *khatiya* origin. The power shown by *varnashrama dharma* at certain periods and in certain regions should not be 'read' into all of India or projected unrealistically backward in time (Omvedt, 2003: 118, 126–7, 133–340).[126] Nicholas Dirks put his argument differently that caste is a modern phenomenon, that it is, specially, the product of encounter between India and Western colonial rule. It was under the British 'caste' became a single term capable of expressing, organizing, and above all: systematizing India's diverse form of social identity, community and organization (Dirks, 2002: 5).[127] If there are 'castes from tribes' then why are castes among Brahmans and Kshatriyas?

R.S. Sharma holds the view that caste proliferation took place in early medieval period. Several castes originated in Hinduism from varnas itself. He seeks four reasons for origin of castes. First, the origin of castes among Brahmans came through by their identification with family, male ancestors names, *gotras*, Vedic learnings, and finally with the village (the local territory) from where they came. Second, in *kshatriya varna* castes originated by emerging a new concept of *Rajputhood* and racial affinities like Calukya, Candellas, Palas, Parmars, Tomars, Gharwals. Third, thousands of mixed castes have been produced as a result of the connection of Vaishya women with men of lower castes. Fourth was the religious affiliation. The parallel between multiplication of sects and that of caste in medieval India is very close, and former helped the later (Sharma, 1999: 26–27).[128]

About a different perspective, contrary to the universalization of socio-economic origin of caste in Indian history, sociologist G. Aloysius awares us, to understood caste as non-deterministically and in its historical and geographical perspective:

First of all *varna-caste* is primarily recognized as a kind of social formation in single type of eco-zone—the riverine valley of subcontinent. Second, even here, the social formation in the primary Ganga valley was not only bifurcated but of mutually antagonistic nature (the state forms and the *gana-sanghas*). Third, the opponent submergence and collapse of the relatively secular-flexible stratification of *gana-sanghas* under the pressure of monarchy and its religious varna hierarchy was not a matter of natural or internal evolution, but a result of historical confrontation and the vanquishing of one social formation by the other after much contestation and resistance ... . Fourth, in its movements of conquest and encompassment had become merely a cognitive and ideal with the actualization limited to and development actual power (Aloysius, 1999: 157–58).[129]

Irfan Habib, Marxist historian, extends Kosambi's sophisticated theory of the origin of 'castes from tribes' following Kosambi's traces. He stress that tribes are often rigorously endogamous ... who avoid marrying outside the tribe. And weavers, butchers, and other had strong tendencies to be endogamous (Habib, 1995: 165, 174).[130] He further argues that the end product of the fission of tribes was not only the caste but endogamy as well, as a tribal characteristic too. The fusion of tribal societies into general society also took place in Buddhism, Christianity, and Islam in Asian, African, European and Australian countries other than India. Why tribal societies could not transformed into rigid caste system and endogamic character in these societies? In responding such questions, Kosambi's theory of 'castes from tribes', and Habib's theory of 'endogamy from tribes' in Indian context have been failed to answer.

In sociological interpretation, Ambedkar explained the origin of caste and endogamy through psychological and mechanical perspectives. Contra to 'tribes', caste and endogamy are Brahmanical characteristics. Psychologically, endogamy or the close door-system was a fashion in Hindu society, and as it had originated from Brahman caste, it was wholeheartedly imitated by non-Brahman sub-divisions, who in turn became endogamous castes. It is the infection of 'imitation' that has turned them into castes. He further argues, first Brahmans closed the door then other found it close against them (Ambedkar, 1979: 18).[131] Mechanically caste in singular number is an unreality. There is no such thing as caste. There are always castes. While making themselves into a caste; the Brahmans, by virtue, created non-Brahman castes (Ambedkar, 1979: 20).[132] In Western Madhya Pradesh the *Bhagoria Marriage* have been practising among inter-tribal societies Bhil, Bhilala, Barela, Tadvi, Mankar and Gond for a long centuries.

A debate was started in 1940s over the religious identity of 'tribes' in India. That was basically, religious and cultural identity which decided the positioning of 'tribes' in administrative policies, i.e., isolation or protection, assimilation, and integration of nation state. The isolationists or protectionists (the British administrators, anthropologists) confirmed the distinct religious identity and ideology of 'tribes' but the assimilationists (Hindu nationalist anthropologists) labeled them as part of Hinduism. The protectionist position is represented by Verrier Elwin.

Verrier Elwin restlessly worked among the tribes on their culture and religion, which he found them distinct from Hinduism. He personally experienced the attitude and approach of Hindu nationalist—Congress politicians and Gandhian movement. He observed that it seems to be the aim of the Congress politicians to bring the aboriginals within the Hindu fold and then to treat them as Hindu. This company of vegetarians and teetotallers would like to their own bourgeois and Puritan doctrines on froe wild people of forest. On the other hand, myself consider the aboriginals to be pre-Hindu and that adoption of Hinduism will be a major disaster for them (Guha, 1999: 105).[133] Historian Guha reveals that Verrier was so fed up with their caste and humbug and prohibition that at times he felt like fleeing India for 'one of the Buddhist countries like Burma or Cylon' (Guha, 1999: 108).[134]

G.S. Ghurye in his book *The Aborigines—"So Called"—and Their Future* (1943) later changed to *The Scheduled Tribes* attacked on Elwin's prepositions of 'National Park'[135] in his *The Baiga* (1941). According to Ghurye, Elwin was 'no-changer' and 'revivalist' (Ghurye, 1963: 173).[136] Tribes, Ghurye pointed out, had long been involved in Hindu religious movements and structures of authority. The only proper description of these people was that they are 'the imperfectly integrated of Hindu society'. Anthropological accuracy demanded that they be called 'backward Hindus' rather than 'aboriginals' (Ghurye, 1963).[137]

Elwin, later, made it clear that he was in favour of integration but distinct from Congress-Hindu nationalist approach. He revealed that the aboriginal problem cannot be apart from the general village problem. The great majority of Indian village are still illiterate; they are still attended to anticipated and economically injurious social, religious and agricultural habits; they have little medical assistance, meagre educational facilities, bad communication; they are exploited and oppressed just as aboriginals are. It is evident that there is little possibility of protecting them although locally it may often be possible to ameliorate their lot by special treatment. The twenty million aboriginals need what all village India needs—freedom, prosperity, peace, good education, medicine, a new system of agriculture and fare deal under industrialization. He argued that it is rather pathetic; there is little of the isolationist or no-changer here (Elwin, 1960: 32).[138]

Hindu nationalist and Gandhian, anthropologist N.K. Bose claims that Hindu society when absorbing a new tribe or while creating a new jati by differentiation of occupation, always guaranteed or tried to monopoly in a particular occupation to each caste within given religion. It was according to the principles of caste system which had been set by the Hindu law givers of ancient India (Bose, 1994: 174).[139] Tribal economic systems, he argued, were technologically backward and that they were sucked into the larger economic arrangements caused to viable under demographic and other pressures (Bose, 1994: 174).[140] Andre Beteille, pupil of N.K. Bose, defends his argument: the tribes that have been affected the most by the Hindu method of tribal absorption are the ones in the interior hills and forest areas where influence from other civilizations whether Islamic or Chinese have been feeble or absent. The Hindu method of tribal absorption did not seek to efface the tribal identity fully or in short time and the end product was a caste usually of lowest rank but not a deviant group (Beteille, 1986: 314–15).[141]

Anthropologist Haimendorf analyzed the Hindu method of tribal absorption. No doubt, there were instances of individual and small tribal groups being absorbed within the caste system of Hindu India, but such cases of assimilation attracted little attention and did not give rise to any special problems. On the part of Hindu society, there was no conscious drive to assimilate or reform the aboriginals, and later seems to have shown little eagerness to exchange their own style of life with that of their Hindu neighbour (Haimendorf, 1960: 1).[142] The value system of many aboriginal tribes differs fundamentally from orthodox Hindu society, and even those middle Indian tribes have adopted certain Hindu beliefs and practice forms of worship akin to Hindu ritual, do not subscribe to Hindu social values (Haimendorf, 1960: 3).[143]

In Indian civilization for a thousand years long 'tribal' economies had been sustained with full-hold. Dr Ramdayal Munda, noted Adivasi scholar and leader, appropriate superior characteristics of Adivasi economies. The Adivasi economy is based on the principles of communal collectivism. Commonly, the Adivasi society had always been the owner of *Jal, Jungle,* and *Jameen* (water, forest and land) and other properties. Individual rights had been absent from Adivasi economy. Most importantly Adivasi economy is for sustenance but modern economy is only for individual profits (Munda, 2002: 33).[144] Kancha Ilaiah, political scientist and Dalit intellectual, makes distinction that Adivasi culture is productive and Hindu culture is unproductive (Ilaiah, 1996: 119).[145] He describes it: we (Dalit-bahujans including 'tribes') differ from them (Hindus) because we are skilled producers, productive instrument makers, creative builders of material basis of society. Hinduism and Brahmanism represent the world-view of atrocious 'others' who have been parasites and whose role has been positive and constructive (Ilaiah, 1996: 167).[146]

In cultural contexts, tribes' acute sense is superior to that of many plains' populations, and their uninhibited and spontaneous approach to inter-personal relations contrast significantly, with more formalized and restrained behaviour pattern of traditional society. The retentions of many basic tribal values and ideas do not impede a change over to modern technologies and methods of production (Haimendorf, 1960: 5).[147]

Sociologist M.N. Srinivas, student of G.S. Ghurye, gave the concept of 'Sanskritization' which nearly seems as an aspect of N.K. Bose's concept of Hindu Method of Tribal Absorption. He says, "Sanskritization is the process by which a 'low' Hindu caste or tribal or other groups, change its customs, rituals, ideology. And, ways of life in the direction of high, and frequently, twice-born castes. Generally, such changes are followed by a claim to a higher position in the caste hierarchy than that traditionally conceded to the claimant caste by the local community. The claim is usually made a period of time, in fact, a generation or two, before the 'arrival' is concerned" (Srinivas, 1995: 6).[148]

Subaltern historians and sociologists have rejected the theory of 'Sanskritization' (Hardiman, 1987; Ilaiah, 1996; Shyamlal, 1997; Skaria, 1999; Dube, 2001).[149] David Hardiman in his classical work on the Devi Movement of 1922 in South Gujarat among Adivasis demonstrates that by leaving the meat-eating and liquor-drinking, the Adivasis do not claim to caste status, but, they claim to equality of status with caste-Hindus. In such practices Adivasis attacked the power of neighbouring dominant communities. The ambiguity of 'Sanskritization' seems when a tiny section of Adivasis who claim Kshatriya status but continue 'impure' customs such as meat-eating and liquor-drinking. The theory of 'Sanskritization', in emphasizing only the aspect of 'purification', facts to take account of the sharp challenge to the existing social structure which forms a necessary part of such movements and historical interpretation (Hardiman, 1987: 159–60).[150] 'Sanskritization' also abstracts caste from deeper economic process and does not seek the level of violence inflicted Adivasis and their ideas (Pati, 2001: 4205).[151] Hardiman reveals that Adivasis adopt the socio-religious values to earn the political status or political power but not to earn the social status in the caste-hierarchy.

Contemporary studies compel to notice that a single theory of socialization in India is impossible to found in implication. Kancha Ilaiah does profound the process of *Dalitization*[152] of indigenous societies in India; Skaria reveals the process of *Bhilization*[153] in Gujarat; and sociologist, Shyamlal demonstrates *De-Sanskritization/ Bhangiaization*[154] of 'upper-castes' into 'lower castes' in Rajasthan contrary to 'Sanskritization'. In Nimar of Madhya Pradesh Bhils, Bhilalas, and Barelas have been organizing various *Sanskritik Sammelans* (cultural fairs) and leading socio-political and cultural movement to identify and establish the original Adivasi culture with distinct symbolization. It can be called *Adivasization* of indigenous societies (Singh, 2002).[155]

Tribal identity cannot be taken for granted as Hindu. In a recent paper Bismoy Pati traces the historical and logical understanding of Adivasi conversion in Orissa. He argues that logic of re-conversion of Adivasis to Hinduism is mistaken and unjustified because adivasis never born as Hindus. The *Feudalization/Hinduization/ Oriyaization* has been the ways of conversion to Hinduism but not as the processes of re-conversion in India. The way of Hinduization emerged as a contested site between the colonial feudal order and Gandhian nationalism (Pati, 2001: 4209).[156] It is also propagated, that 'tribes' converted only into Hinduism. It is evident that in medieval India tribes converted to Islam under Islamic rule (Eaton, 1995)[157] and Christianization took place during colonial period. In northeast India, Eaton reveals the conversion of the Nagas into Christianity during this period (Eaton, 1984).[158]

Buddhist notions and values are deeply rooted among the indigenous societies in India. And a most remarkable part of 'tribal' populations in India is still Buddhist. In northeast Arunachal Pradesh; in north, Himalaya region; in north, some centres like Gaya, Vaishlai in Bihar and Varanasi, Allahabad, Mathura in Uttar Pradesh; in northwest, Laddakh; in Central India, Ujjain, Sanchi, Bhilsa, and Vindhyachal region; in south and east some parts in Maharashtra, Andhra Pradesh, Karnataka, and West Bengal and Orissa still maintained Buddhist culture and its institutions. Many Buddhist institutions had been derived on the lines of 'tribal' institutions such as *Sangha* (a form of traditional Adivasi sabha). A famous *gatha* gave the essence of Buddhism "showing the cause and its negation" (Kosambi, 1975: 171).[159] Outside India, Buddhism influenced the Cylon, Burmese, Chinese, Japanese, Korean, Mongolian and Russian civilizations in the world.

An ascetic is an oldest Indic religious institution in India. In Hindu nationalist view it is depicted as Hindu and as a means of spread of Hinduism in the interior tribal areas. Ghurye described that sometimes the forest retreat of a saint or an ascetic became a famous centre of pilgrimage ensuring a regular flow of traffic through the tribal area surrounding it. This traffic might influence the religious life of the tribal people even when they remained largely outside the organization of economic activities based on caste. There is a evidence of deep-rooted and widespread Hindu beliefs and practices throughout the tribal areas in the interior of India (Ghurye, 1963).[160]

Contrary to Ghurye's Hindu nationalist view, Khare demonstrates that the ascetic order is originally a Buddhist which juxtaposes to Brahmanical order (Khare, 1984: 33).[161] He argues that Indic ascetism raises the sights of the untouchable (indigenous) thinker towards an alternative, and not merely a surrogate, cultural ideology. The non-Brahman ascetic is also the anti-Brahman ascetic and that he alone is the 'original' ascetic, the supreme mystic, the true visionary, and the savior since he alone could be the messiah of social equality, hence also of love and social justice. He represents a forceful moral critique of caste-ordered hierarchy and its excesses and subverts unjustified inequality by launching alternative symbolization (Khare, 1984: 23).[162] The ascetic in principle upholds the unconditional equalitarian world view, and Brahman upholds the conditional, the hierarchical (Khare, 1984: 23, 28).[163] Against the forest and interior areas, he reveals, a north Indian indigenous Chamar community is Buddhist, even though it had been living in a metropolitan city Lucknow within 'Hindu Civilization'. The Buddhist or indigenous culture could not be effaced after the thousands of year efforts of Hindu method of absorption! All these historical discourses will help to the ethnographer to make a theoretical notion on caste and tribe before entering his/her research.

Notes

1. F.G. Bailey, "Tribe and Caste in India", *Contribution to Indian Sociology*, 5, 1961.
2. Andre Beteille, "The Definition of Tribe", *Seminar*, 14 (October 1960); on the concept of tribe, 1973, in Beteille, *Six Essays in Comparative Sociology*, New Delhi: OUP, 1986.
3. Beteille, op. cit., No. 2, pp. 79–80.
4. M.D. Sahlin, "The Segmentary Lineage: An Organization of Predatory Expression", *American Anthropology*, LXIII, 1961, pp. 322–45.
5. M. Godelier, *Perspective in Marxist Anthropology*, London: Cambridge University Press, 1977, translated from French: Horizons, *trajets Marxist en anthropologie*, Paris: Maspero, 1973.
6. M.H. Fried, *The Notion of Tribe*, Menlo Park: Cummings Publishing Co., 1975.
7. Andre Beteille, "The Concept of Tribe with Special Reference to India", *European Journal of Sociology*, 27, 1986, p. 306.
8. Crispin Bates, "Race, Caste, and Tribe in Central India: The Early Origin of India Anthropometry" in Peter Robb (ed.), *The Concept of Race in South Asia*, New Delhi:

Oxford University Press, 1995; Ajay Skaria, "Shades of Wildness: Tribe, Caste and Gender in Western India", *Journal of Asian Studies*, 56 (3), 1997.

9. Beteille, op. cit., No. 7; Susana De Valle, *Discourses of Ethnicity: Culture and Protest in Jharkhand*, New Delhi, 1992; Sumit Guha, "Lower Strata, Older Races, and Aboriginal People: Racial Anthropology and Mythical Past and Present", *Journal of Asian Studies*, 57 (2), 1998, pp. 432–441; Ajay Skaria, op. cit., No. 8; by same author, *Hybrid Histories*, New Delhi: OUP, 1999.
10. Marvin Harris, *The Rise of Anthropological Theory*, New York: Thomas Crowell, 1968, Chap. 4.
11. H.H. Risley, *Census Report of India*, 1901.
12. Sumit Guha, op. cit., No. 9, p. 428.
13. Ibid., p. 431.
14. Skaria, op. cit., No. 8, p. 730.
15 Ibid., pp. 732–39.
16. De Valle, op. cit., No. 9, p. 32.
17. Ibid., p. 27.
18. Ibid., pp. 30–76.
19. Ibid., p. 20.
20. Ibid., p. 16.
21. Ronald Inden, *Imagining India*, New Delhi: OUP, 1990; Nicholas B Dirks, *Castes of Mind: Colonialism and the Making of India*, New Delhi: Permanent Black, 2002.
22. Inden, op. cit., No. 21, pp. 83–84.
23. Dirks, op. cit., No. 21, p. 9.
24. Susan Bayly, *New Cambridge History of India*, Vol. 3: *Caste, Society and Politics in India from the Eighteenth Century to the Modern Age*, Cambridge: Cambridge University Press, 1999, p. 7.
25. Suarabh Dube, *Untouchable Pasts: Identity and Power among a Central Indian Community, 1780–1950*, New Delhi: Vistar Publications, 2001, p. 214.
26. Louis Dumont, *Homo Hierarchicus*, New Delhi: OUP, 1970.
27. Veena Das, *Critical Events*, New Delhi: OUP, 1999, p. 29.
28. Richard Burghart, "Ethnographers and their Local Counterparts in India in Localizing Strategies" in R Fardon (ed.), *Regional Traditions of Ethnographic Writing*, Edinburgh: Scottish Academy Press, 1990, p. 268.
29. Bayly, op. cit., No. 24, p. 14.
30. Dube, op. cit., No. 25, p. 214.
31. Oliver Mendelsohn and Marika Vicziani, *The Untouchables: Subordination, Poverty and the State in Modern India*, Cambridge: CUP, 1998, p. 27.
32. Gail Omvedt, *Buddhism in India: Challenging Brahmanism and Caste*, New Delhi: Sage Publication, 2003. p. 222; Dube, op. cit., No. 25, p. 4.
33. Dube, op. cit., No. 25.
34. Dirks, op. cit., No. 21, pp. 297–98.
35. K.N. Panikkar, *Culture, Ideology, Hegemony: Intellectual and Social Consciousness in Colonial India*, New Delhi: Tulika, 1995, p. 58.

36. Romila Thapar, *The Penguin History of Early India: From the Origin to AD 1300*, New Delhi: Penguin, 2003, p. 4.
37. J.N. Farqhar, *Modern Religious Movements in India*, Delhi, 1967, p. 433; R.C. Majumdar (ed.), *British Paramountcy and Indian Renaissance*, Vol. X, Bombay: Popular Press, 1965, p. 89.
38. Charles Heimsath, *Indian Nationalism and Hindu Social Reform*, Princeton: Princeton University Press, 1964, p. 46.
39. David Koff, *British Orientalism Bengal Renaissance*, Berkeley: Berkeley University Press, 1969.
40. Susobhan Sarkar, *Bengal Renaissance and other Essays*, New Delhi: Manohar Publications, 1970, p. 150.
41. A.K. Bhattacharya, Akshay Dutt, *Pioneer among Indian Rationalism, Rationalist Annual*, 1962, p. 29.
42. Max Muller, *India What Can Teach Us*, New Delhi: Rupa & Co., (1869–2002).
43. James Mill, *The British History of India*, New York, 1968.
44. D.D. Kosambi, *An Introduction to the Study of Indian History*, Bombay: Popular Press, 1975, p. 2; Beteille, op. cit., No. 7, p. 308.
45. Thapar, op. cit., No. 39, p. 354.
46. Omvedt, op. cit., No. 32, pp. 165–66.
47. Ibid., p. 166.
48. Skaria, op. cit., No. 9. Ajay Skaria has revealed the history of Bhils of Dangs in Gujarat on the basis oral genres; Stuart Blackbum, "Colonial Contact in the 'Hidden Land': Oral History Among the Apatanis of Arunachal Pradesh", *Indian Economic and Social History Review*, 40 (3), 2003. Stuart Blackbum appropriated the oral history among Apatani tribes of Arunachal Pradesh.
49. Niharranjan Ray, *Nationalism in India*, Aligarh: Aligarh Muslim University, 1973; N.K. Bose, *Tribal Life in India*, New Delhi: National Book Trust, 1971.
50. N. Ray, op. cit., No. 76, p. 123.
51. Virginius Xaxa, "Transformation of Tribe in India: Terms of Discourses", *Economic and Political Weekly*, 34 (24), 1999, p. 1524.
52. Beteille, op. cit., No. 7, p. 309.
53. Aloka Parasher-Sen, "Of Tribes, Hunters and Barbarian: Forest Dwellers in Mauryan Period", *Studies in History*, 40 (2), 1998, p. 173.
54. Romila Thapar, *Asoka and the Decline of Mauryas*, New Delhi: OUP, 1997, pp. 317–19; by same author, *The Maurya Revisited*, S.G. Deuskar Lectures in Indian History, 1984, Calcutta, 1987, pp. 3–4.
55. Gerard Fussman, "Central and Provincial Administration in Ancient India", *Indian Historical Review*, 14 (1–2), 1987–88, p. 48.
56. Parasher-Sen, op. cit., No. 63, p. 174.
57. Ibid., p. 178.
58. Ibid., p. 179.
59. Ibid., p. 185.
60. Sheerin Moosvi, *The Economy of the Mughal Empire, 1595: A Statistical Study*, New Delhi: OUP, 1987, p. 65.

61. Chetan Singh, "Conformity and Conflict: Tribes and Agrarian System of Mughal India", *Indian Economic and Social History Review,* 23 (3), 1988, p. 321.
62. Sunita Zaidi, "The Mughal State and Tribes in Seventeenth Century Sind", *Indian Economic and Social History Review,* 26 (3), 1989; Chetan Singh, op. cit., No. 86.
63. Sumit Guha, *Environment and Ethnicity,* New Delhi: OUP, 1999, p. 8.
64. Skaria, op. cit., No. 8, p. 205.
65. Rajkumar, Hans, Agrarian Economy of Broach District During First Half of the Nineteenth Century, Ph.D. Dissertation, Department of History, M.S. University, Baroda, 1987, p. 62ff.
66. Surjit Sinha, "State Formation and Rajpoot Myth in Tribal Central India" in H. Kulke (ed.), *State in India 1000–1700,* New Delhi: OUP, 1995, p. 305.
67. Skaria, op. cit., No. 8, p. 213.
68. Ibid., p. 113; Skaria, op. cit., No. 8, p. 204.
69. Richard Fox, *Kin, Clan, Raja and Rule,* Berkeley: University of California Press, 1971, pp. 70, 75.
70. Cynthia Talbot, *Precolonial Indian in Practice: Society, Religion and Identity in Medieval Andhra,* New Delhi: OUP, 2001, p. 51.
71. Sinha, op. cit., No. 63, p. 8.
72. C.U. Wills, "The Territorial System of the Rajput Kingdom of Medieval Chattisgarh", *Journal of Asiatic Society,* 15, 1919, p. 199.
73. Ibid., pp. 325–255.
74. Harman Kulke, "Royal Temple Policy and Medieval Indian Kingdoms" in Eschman, Kulke and Tripathi (eds.), *The Cult of Jagannath and the Religious Tradition of Orissa,* New Delhi: Manohar Publishing House, 1986.
75. Ibid., p. 135.
76. Nandini Sundar, *Subaltern and Sovereignty: An Anthropological History of Bastar 1854–1996,* New Delhi: OUP, pp. 54–55.
77. Ibid., p. 62.
78. Harman Kulke, *Kings and Cults: State Formation and Legitimization in India and South Asia,* New Delhi: Manihar Publishers, 1993, p. 118–33.
79. Ibid., p. 135.
80. Sudipta Kaviraj, "Imaginary Institution of India" in Ranjit Guha and Partha Chatterjee (eds.), *Subaltern Studies Vol. VII: Writing on South Asian History and Society,* New Delhi: OUP, 1997, p. 24.
81. A. De Swan, Political and Linguistic Integration, IDPAD Seminar, 1990.
82. M. Freid, On the Concept of 'Tribe' and Tribal Society" in L. Helm (ed.), *Essays on the Problem of Tribe,* Washington: American Anthropological Society, 1968.
83. Beteille, op. cit., No. 6, p. 310.
84. Singh, op. cit., No. 61, p. 340.
85. Francis Zimmerman, *The Jungle and the Auroma of Meats,* Berkeley: University of California Press, 1987, pp. 1–3.
86. Omvedt, op. cit., No. 32, pp. 27–28.
87. Romila Thapar, Harbansh Mukhia, Bipan Chandra, *Communalism and Writing of Indian History,* New Delhi: Peoples' Publishing House, 1969, p. 46; T W Rhys

Davids, *Buddhist India*, New Delhi: Motilal Banarsidas, 1903, (rpt.), 1997; Omvedt, op. cit., No. 32, Chap. 4.

88. Omvedt, op. cit., No. 32, p. 125.
89. D.J. Ibbeston, *Report on the Census of Punjab*, Vol. I, 1881; G. Campwell, *The Ethnography of India*, 1865; W. Crooke, *Tribes and Castes of North-West Provinces and Oudh*, Calcutta, 1896; H.H. Risely, *Introduction and Ethnographic Appendices, Census of India*, Vol. I, Calcutta, 1903; H.H. Risely, *Tribes and Castes of Bengal*, Vol. I, Calcutta, 1891; R.E. Ethnovan, *The Tribes and Castes of Bombay*, 3 Vols., Bombay: Government Central Press, 1920.
90. John Melcolm, *A Memoir of Central India including Malwa*, 2 Vols., Delhi: Sagar, 1970, 1823, p. 191; Aurthur T. Steele, *The Law and Customa of Hindu Castes of Dakkan*, London, Smith Elder, 1868, p. 93; S.N. Gorden, *Marathas, Marauders, and State Formation in Eighteenth Century India*, New Delhi: OUP, 1994, p. 151.
91. Omvedt, op. cit., No. 32, pp. 27–28.
92. Ibid., p. 78.
93. R. Thapar, *The Past and Prejudice*, New Delhi: National Book Trust, 2000, p. 13.
94. B.R. Ambedkar, *The Untouchables*, New Delhi: Amit Book Co., 1948,
95. Thapar, op. cit., No. 93, p. 104.
96. Kosambi, op. cit., No. 44, p. 202.
97. Ibid., p. 204.
98. Madhav Gadgil and Ramachandra Guha, *This Fissured Land*, New Delhi: OUP, 1992, p. 88.
99. R. Thapar, *Perceiving the Forest: Early India*, Studies in History, 17 (1), 2001, p. 4.
100. Kosambi, op. cit., No. 44, p. 313.
101. Richard M. Eaton, *Rise of Islam in Bengal Frontier, 1204–1760*, New Delhi: OUP, 1997, p. 76.
102. Omvedt, op. cit., No. 28, pp. 180–81.
103. Talbot, op. cit., No. 95, p. 86.
104. Ibid., p. 85.
105. Christopher J. Fuller, "British India or Traditional India? An Anthropological Problem", *Ethnos*, 3–4 (4), 1977, pp. 105–8; Nicholas Dirks, "The Original Caste: Power, History and Hierarchy in South Asia", *Contribution to Indian Sociology*, 23 (1), 1989, pp. 65–72.
106. Nicholas Dirks, *The Hollow Crown: The Ethnography of Indian Kingdom*, Cambridge: Cambridge University Press, 1987, p. 59.
107. David Ludden, "History Outside Civilization and Mobility of South Asia" *South Asia*, 17(1), 1994, pp. 6–7 and p. 11.
108. Charlotte Vaudeville, *A Weaver Named Kabir*, New Delhi: OUP, 1993, p.72.
109. Ibid., pp. 73–74.
110. R.V. Russsell and Hiralal, *Castes and Tribes of Central Provinces*, 2 Vols., London, 1916; Skaria, op. cit., No. 8, 1998; Kancha Ilaiah, *Why I Am Not A Hindu*, Calcutta: Samya, 1996.
111. Omvedt, op. cit., No. 32, p. 215.

112. Asha Shukla Chaube, "Technology and Culture Among the Iron Workers of Bihar During the Seventeenth and Eighteenth Centuries", *Indian Economic and Social History Review*, 6 (1), 2003.
113. Rhys Davids, op. cit., No. 115, p. 226.
114. Ibid., p. 230.
115. Ibid., p. 232.
116. Awantika Prasad Marmat, *Vedkaleen Nag Jateon, Rajao tatha Sanskriti ki Khoj*, Ujjain: Nagsmiriti Prakashan, undated.
117. Rhys Davids, op. cit., No. 115, pp. III–IV.
118. Kancha Ilaiah, Productive Labour, Consciousness and History: The Dalit-Bahujan Perspective, in Shahid Amin and Dipesh Chakrawarti (eds.), *Subaltern Studied IX: Writing on South Asian History and Society*, New Delhi: OUP, p. 66.
119. R.C. Majumdar, *Corporate Life in Ancient India*, Calcutta: Firma KLM, 1969, p. 385.
120. Omvedt, op. cit., No. 32, p. 76
121. N.K. Bose, "The Hindu Method of Tribal Absorption", *Science and Culture*, 8, 1941, pp. 188–94.
122. Beteille, op. cit., No. 7, p. 312.
123. B.R. Ambedkar, *Dr. Babasaheb Ambedkar Writings and Speeches* Vol. I collected by Vasant Moon, Bombay, Government of Maharashtra, 1979, p. 47.
124. Shukla, op. cit., No. 112.
125. Kosambi, op. cit., No. 69.
126. Omvedt, op. cit., No. 3, p. 118 and pp. 126–7, 133–4.
127. Dirks, op. cit., No. 121, p. 5.
128. R.S. Sharma, Social Change in Early Medieval India circa AD 500–1200: the first Devraj Channa Memorial Lecture 1969, New Delhi: Peoples' Publishing House, 1969, pp. 20–26.
129. G.S. Aloysius, "Caste in and Above History", *Sociological Bulletin*, 48 (1–2), 1999.
130. Irfan Habib, *Essays in Indian History: Towards Marxist Perception*, New Delhi: Tulika, 1995, p. 165.
131. Ambedkar, op. cit., p. 18.
132. Ibid., p. 19.
133. Verrier Elwin quoted in Ramchandra Guha, *Savaging the Civilized*, New Delhi: OUP, 1999, p. 105.
134. Ibid., p. 108.
135. Verrier Elwin, *The Baiga*, New Delhi: Gyan Publishing House, 1941, 1986, p. 515.
136. G.S. Ghurye, *The Scheduled Tribes*, Bombay: Popular Press, 1963, p. 173.
137. Ibid., p. 160.
138. Verrier Elwin, "Issues in Tribal Policies Making", *Seminar*, 14 October 1960. All arguments have been made from Romesh Thapar (ed.), *Tribe, Caste and Religion in India*, New Delhi: Macmillan, 1977, p. 32.
139. N.K. Bose, *The Structure of Hindu Society*, translated from Bengali with an introduction by Andre Beteille, New Delhi: Orient Longmans, 1975, 1994, p. 174.
140. Ibid., p. 174.
141. Beteille, op. cit., No. 7, pp. 314–15.

142. C. Von-Furer Haimendorf, "Tribal Problems in India", *Seminar,* 14 October 1960. All arguments have been made from R Thapar (ed.), op. cit., No. 138, p. 1.
143. Ibid., p. 3.
144. Ramdayal Munda, *Adivasi Asitatva aur Jharkhandi Asmita ke Sawal,* Delhi: Prakashan Sansthan, 2002, p. 33.
145. Ilaiah, op. cit., No. 110, p. 119.
146. Ilaiah, op. cit., No. 118, p. 167.
147. Haimendorf, op. cit., No. 142, p. 5.
148. M.N. Srinivas, *Social Change in Modern India,* New Delhi: Orient Longmans, 1995, p. 6.
149. David Hardiman, *The Coming of the Devi: Adivasi Assertion in Western India,* New Delhi: OUP, 1987; S. Dube, op. cit., No. 25; Kancha Ilaiah, op. cit., No. 110; Shyamlal, *From Higher Caste to Lower Caste: The Process of Asprashayeekaran and the Myth of Sanskritization,* Jaipur: Rawat Publications, 1997; Skaria, op. cit., No. 9.
150. Hardiman, op. cit., No. 181, pp. 159–60.
151. Bismoy Pati, "Identity, Hegemony, Resistance: Conversion in Orissa, 1800–2000", *Economic and Political Weekly,* November 3, 2001, p. 4201.
152. Ilaiah, op. cit., No. 110.
153. Skaria, op. cit., No. 9.
154. Shyamlal, op. cit., No. 181.
155. Netrapal Singh, Adivasi Resistance in Nimar: An Assertion from Below, M, Phil. Dissertation, (MHOW, Dr Babasaheb Ambedkar, National Institution of Social Sciences, DAVV, 2002).
156. Pati, op. cit., No. 151, p. 4209.
157. Eaton, op. cit., No. 101.
158. Richard Eaton, "Conversion to Christianity among Nagas, 1876–1971", *Indian Economic and Social History Review,* 21 (1), 1984, pp. 1–44.
159. Kosambi, op. cit., No. 44, p. 171.
160. Ghurye, op. cit., No. 136.
161. R.S. Khare, *The Untouchable as Himself: Ideology, Identity and Pragmatism among the Lucknow Chamars,* Cambridge: Cambridge University Press, 1984, p. 33.
162. Ibid., pp. 23–28.
163. Ibid., pp. 25–28.

IV

Social Development and Ethnographic Discourses

19 The Rational and the Relative

History and Tradition in the Construction of Social Knowledge

UPENDRA

Initial Arguments

When one is asked about the constitution of social knowledge, one would say that it constitutes several rules (legal as well as customary), rational principles, social structures, functional mechanisms, historical events, institutional frameworks, and last but not the least the foundational ideas. This is a general understanding of what constitutes social knowledge. Apart from this, there are two other ways of approaching this issue. On the one hand, many philosophers would argue that social knowledge contains autonomous body set of ideas and principles. On the other hand, there are other set of philosophers who have emphasized on the rationality of valuing the growth of ideas through traditions. For instance, the debate between philosophers and social scientists on the issue of foundations of social sciences reveal that the former claim that prediction and explanation is possible with *law-like* explanations that have autonomous *universal* value, while the social scientists would emphasize on the *relative* aspect that is subject to historical-social contingent factors. Only then we can capture the real aspect of plurality and diversity that is fundamental to each and every tradition.

The belief is that there is something called social reality that drives us to understand it in different yet legitimate perspectives. The current paper will not go into the discussion whether the notion of *social reality* is meaningful to be assumed. Rather, the paper is grounded in the assumption that there is social reality irrespective of whether it has autonomous value or constructivist value. The notion that social reality is objective is countered by the notion of contingent social reality or temporal social reality.

The question that would immediately follow is whether this social reality is tradition-independent or tradition-dependent. Before answering this question, one should have a clear explanation of what social reality is. The fact is that one cannot really have a singular explanation of social reality. The reason may be that the issues that constitute social explanation repel the form of law-like explanation.[1] Is social reality different from social knowledge? We can say that social reality is the understanding of various infinite social processes that explain the individual behaviour and the manner in which it differs from one social formation to the other. It also contains all those fundamental *basic* principles that can be called as *common social knowledge*.

There are arguments that social reality is constructed through historical social facts only and there is no such thing called tradition-independent body of social knowledge. If we admit this as an inescapable given reality, then we have to address the issue of rational construction of knowledge. Theorists of social knowledge, irrespective of anthropologists, sociologists, historians and political scientists, have to tackle the problem of *rationality of traditions* or rationality defined by tradition. Here, the emphasis would be on the explanatory aspect that is attached to social knowledge and concept formation. The linkage between concept formation and social knowledge that the latter has certain rational foundations. It further implies that social knowledge also constitutes some generic knowledge. Let us take the example of moral conflicts related to issue of rightful actions over several issues such as abortion, religious freedom, euthanasia, homosexuality, pornography etc.

The central unit of any social explanation is human being and human behaviour. The conflict between rational foundations and the relativist foundations is over the rational behaviour of the human agents. If we take into account any of the above-mentioned issues, the question is whether individual is determined by rationality-reason for her/his behaviour or whether her/his behaviour is subject to social norms of a particular time and space. We can invoke an question here: What difference would it make for the understanding of social knowledge with the following comparison; human agents generally behave in such and such a manner from persons that belong to *Indian* or *American* society. This conflict can be traced to the conflict between rational foundations of *liberalism* and the contextualist foundations of *communitarianism*.

If there is a social reality who would better explain this social reality. There is an interesting argument here. If philosophers tend to explain social reality, the dominant aspect would be rational construction of *justifiable* knowledge that is both mind-independent and tradition-independent in nature.[2] The point of reference would be always universal knowledge. If we leave it to anthropologists, historicists, sociologists, economists, political scientists etc., then we cannot avoid the mentioning of culture, community, tradition and relativity at large. Theodore Schatzki brings out an interesting point here. Though philosophers make the pronouncements of objective reality (physical reality), we expect the scientists to say more about the nature of physical reality. On the other hand, social reality is about the nature of social existence. Should we say that the obligation to explain the social phenomenon should be left to anthropologists, sociologists, economists etc.?[3]

Understanding social reality through traditions is supposed to be required due to one main reason. The reason is that several ongoing life patterns of different people, cultures, and societies at various stages have to be taken into account to explain various developments in our life patterns. In one way, this kind of understanding helps us to narrate the gradual change in human perception, growth of knowledge, and the change in the manner we treat different social problems. These social problems are part of moral problems that challenge the very subject matter of moral reasoning. To bring forth the issues mentioned above, a historical account of, say, social and political philosophy gives the idea how we treat these issues in a different manner from time to time.

The issue is not as simple as stated above and will not easily justify the historical relativist approach to social knowledge. These social problems are also philosophical problems simultaneously. The philosophers account would persistently emphasize on the foundational aspects that drive these contingent factors. Though social circumstances highlight contingent conditions, defenders of universal rationality claim that the definition of what is moral does not change according to the social situation. What is important to philosophy is the importance of valid and justifiable knowledge. The issue is why relativism cannot provide us a justifiable social epistemology or body of social knowledge. Besides, we should also explain what it means to say that *what is moral* or *what is rational* are not independent of specific social formations.

The relativist approach is appropriate to anthropologists, sociologists, political scientists etc., as this approach enables them to capture the actual essence of diverse nature of live patterns. It is also appropriate because the values and beliefs are themselves very radically different. Besides, the diverse nature of human life also explains two important things. They are *incommensurability* and *irreducibility* of cultures and histories. The proponents of this argument would say that one cannot measure or judge all cultures with a rational eye. For instance, they would claim that what is rational in one society *A* regarding *capitol punishment* will differ from society *B*. This is because these two societies have their own respective social values or normative principles. These specific normativism themselves decide the nature of moral right and wrong. As the fundamental normative structures are different in these two societies, they are incommensurable to each other. Hence, different societies may have different value-assertions over the same moral problem.

It may right that the normative foundational structures of different societies are deep rooted in their respective intellectual and non-intellectual traditions. Yet, this does not legitimize such a relativity as is seen in many of the theories of social sciences. The proponents of the relativist approach should also reflect upon the extent to which empirical facts are important in theorizing about social knowledge. There are certain issues that bother every society. These are, as already mentioned above, issues that pertain justice, equality, freedom, and reality. There are several sociological and philosophical issues involved here. The issues are how should we define equality and egalitarianism, model distributive justice, define rational and moral behaviour, the accounts of collective life, formation of life-projects and self-realization. These issues call for the interaction of ideal (rational) and the non-ideal (empirical) circumstances to come out what is better alternative than the other; not only in normal conditions but also in times of conflict.

On the issues mentioned above, communitarians and cultural theorists would say that the knowledge of the particular traditions and their gradual growth is important in digging out best alternatives. For instance, with respect to the Rawlsian theory of justice, many critics have argued that social justice cannot be conceived with the kind of rational-neutral foundationalism adopted by Rawls. In order to know the social reality of inequality, we should know the past historical factors also. This is nothing but the *social embodiment* of tradition. The argument from rationality will not be convinced fully from the above discussion. The issue here would be whether rationality should determine the human behaviour or the human behaviour should define rationality? The concern for rationality and social knowledge is not about the social dimensions of social knowledge but the very nature of social knowledge.

Let us come back to the point of *foundations* of social knowledge. We can also ask that apart from the *social embodiment* of tradition, we have to define the basic structure of social knowledge. For instance, moral epistemology is about the foundations of morality. It is guided by certain foundational formal rules such as one ought to be moral, one ought to be honest, one should not cheat others etc. Human beings are rational and moral when they follow these under all conditions. It is very illogical to say that one can be honest in situation *x*, but not in situation *y*. Thus, morality is not defined out of our convenience and whims to follow it. Similarly, social knowledge is supposed to have rational foundations whose basic structure is compatible to all social contexts.

Rationality supplemented by reason is supposed to have the characteristic of timelessness. This makes knowledge more and more justifiable. The problem with relativism is that it has no fixed points. The question how can we claim something as rational if it is determined by mere temporal factors like culture and tradition? Does relativism contain claims that are contrary to reason and rationality? What is need is a proper location of historical understanding vis-à-vis the force of reason and rationality.

The dispute between the rational approach and the relativist approach is unending. While the former emphasizes the importance of tradition-independent knowledge that has both the characteristics of timelessness and force of objective reason, the latter shows the inevitability of treating cultures and traditions as integral to the construction of knowledge. For the former, rationality itself is to counted as a tradition as the latter locates rationality *within* traditions. How could we resolve the tension? For this, we have to answer three important questions: What is this *socially embodied* knowledge? Can we understand the body of knowledge without making reference to traditions, histories and cultures? What kind of influence can we say understanding knowledge has on history and tradition?

In answering the above three questions, the current paper takes cognizance of the complications involved in taking either of the stands. The author is also aware of the fact that the body of social knowledge as a whole is not determined by neither relativist approach alone nor is grounded in the rationalist approach alone. One cannot even imagine where one single tradition explains all the social processes or the nature of social existence. The argument will centre around the supposition that the construction of social knowledge requires both these approaches. Such a kind of claim would mean that some aspect (may be the *narrative*) of social knowledge involves the description of difference and diversity. Yet, it cannot avoid the foundational principles that are basic to all perspectives in framing the ideas.

In this process, incommensurability may lose its significance amidst plurality. The following section will contain the discussion on MacIntyre's notion of *tradition* as not only an intellectual one but also that of representing one single culture or set of practices. This would help us to understand how to conceptualize notions such as justice, equality, morality, rationality, reason and social explanation at large. The argument would not confine, as MacIntyre did, to search for a better tradition that would explain all the aspects. The better answer for this could be restricted sense of tradition-dependence. Nevertheless, there is no claim that we can resolve the *deadlock* of how to weigh one account or perspective with another in a rational manner. The author admits that this cannot be resolved at all. The scope of social knowledge should be such that we have to include in social explanation the must possible extent of rival accounts and competing theories. The obligation of the social scientists or philosophers is not confined to mere search for ways to tackle problems, contradictions and paradoxes.

Tradition-Dependent or Tradition-Independent?

MacIntyre's works especially *Whose Justice? Which Rationality?*[4] and *After Virtue*[5] have a specific understanding of tradition, which would mean the source of idea or a perspective. In the former, he talks about the significance of four traditions, i.e., Aristotle's theory. Aquinas's synthesis of Aristotelean and Augustinian Christianity, the seventeenth and eighteenth century Scottish tradition, and liberalism.[6] Each of this tradition has a respective account of moral and social life. MacIntyre talks about a range of questions such as inequalities, compensation for past injustices, capital punishment and other matters related to justice. These are part of the nature of social existence and are seen in several important rival and competing traditions. MacIntyre's treatment of tradition is intellectual traditions and the change in the concept formation. These intellectual traditions are embedded in various forms of social life.

In the paper, MacIntyre's interpretation of rational justification and the rationality within traditions will be discussed. The issue is whether we can have rational answers to the issues mentioned and of those mentioned in the beginning of the paper. MacIntyre interprets the significance of rationality the force of reason as advocated in the entire liberal philosophical tradition. What is the difference in his account and the account of liberalism? The liberal philosophical account (which MacIntyre's calls as *post-Enlightenment reason*) resides in rational justification, i.e., justification through irrespective out of social context.[7] It follows what can be called as tradition-transcendent notion of rationality

On the contrary, MacIntyre seems to explain that what is rational is defined within a tradition. He further argues that what counts as a good reason dependent on the tradition of debate one is standing in.[8] He also talks about the notion of rationality taking different shapes in different traditions. For instance, in explaining the nature of moral disagreement MacIntyre introduces the notion of emotivism that can conform rationality (he treats rationality and emotivism as two intellectual traditions). According to this doctrine, all moral judgments are result of expressions of preference, feeling or attitude.[9] Further MacIntyre discusses the manner in which these different traditions deal with the reasoned objections caused by them. This point of MacIntyre provokes serious discussion. It is true that different traditions have their accounts of rationality with their respective tools of organizing their objections. It would mean that within a time frame there is an independent conception of rationality, or it may be called as tradition-dependent rationality. In that case, MacIntyre's thesis could be linked to the idea that truth and rationality are outcomes of a particular form and period of social construction.

Tradition and constructivism seem to have an intimate relationship in such account of tradition-dependent rationality. MacIntyre's tradition-dependent reason and rationality not only indicates perspective based conception, but also historical and time-bound conception. Social constructivism in some sense is not free from arbitrary constructivism. Paul Boghossian discusses similar point discussing that social knowledge cannot be reduced to relative knowledge as he feels that social constructivism of reality is more or less arbitrary.[10] From the point of view of *realism*, truth is independent of whether one believes it or not. This is generally attributed to the understanding of physical reality or natural facts.

There is a difference in the comprehension of natural facts and social facts that in turn brings the difference between physical reality and social reality. But can we perceive social reality as independently constituted or is it only a product of different forms of social construction? Unlike the nature of epistemology of natural sciences, social reality cannot escape from social constructivism, which may result from the contestation of rival accounts or perspectives or intellectual traditions. This may not take much effort for the philosophers also to get convinced about the nature of perceiving social reality. Yet, they may not get convinced with the claim that rationality is confined to a particular understanding of a particular intellectual tradition.

In the examples of abortion, homosexuality, pornography etc., we witness the arguments of moral permissibility and social permissibility. The tradition-dependence argument would suggest that the permissibility and non-permissibility of these issues are dependent on what a particular theory claims and defends as rational. In this sense, abortion may be permissible in society *A* because it is *fundamentally* free society with socially liberal values and a society that has adopted these values gradually. On the other hand, abortion may be impermissible in society *B* because its social structures are located in rigid and dictatorial values. Tradition-dependent account of relativism may make both these accounts morally right as they belong to two different set of norms. This could be treated as *multiple rationalities*. However, the philosophical account would object as they consider a set of human values to be independently applicable to all human beings irrespective of whether we believe it to be empirically right or wrong. This pertains even to the issues that MacIntyre deals with in his both the works.

Multiple rationalities *prima facie* as a concept seems interesting, but does it has any convincing account of tradition-dependent rationality? There is lot of apprehension due to the reason that there is no perfect way to resolve the conflict between different accounts that prevail at the same time. This kind of a fix can be seen in the issues mentioned above. In matters of moral reasoning philosophers would claim that *multiple rationalities* makes less sense. By stating this they would say that morality, justice or virtue is not dependent on human nature. On the other hand, relativists emphasizes that one should take account of differences in human thinking, human nature, beliefs and values that guide society, and the fundamental diversity. It would enable us to unearth the reason why there are different rationalities or in other words, rationality of traditions in MacIntyre's sense.

There is confusion between the approach of relativism and that of the rational approach. The subject matter of social knowledge can be divided into various levels. The rational approach deals with certain aspects, like the foundational principles that guide this social knowledge. The relativist approach is more appropriate for that aspect of the knowledge which has more descriptive element like narratives, histories, cultures, and practices of various groups, societies and communities. It conveys that *embeddedness* is more important, which in reality we cannot overlook. Tradition-dependent account of the growth of ideas also indicates incommensurability. It is very difficult to say that traditions or the intellectual traditions should have some kind of commensurability. There is also a situation that there are different rival accounts within a single perspective or intellectual tradition. The differentiation between the rational and the relative approach would enable us to realize that the plurality does not make incommensurability a necessary principle.

Discussing the contention between right and good, MacIntyre makes a mention of rational superiority of traditions. According to him, rational superiority to other traditions comes not in the feat of arguing the others down, but in having the conceptual resources to explain convincingly one's own tradition success and the other tradition's failure in meeting this kind of challenge.[11] This argument of MacIntyre would bring problem to himself as his idea of intellectual tradition is tied to the notion of tradition in the historical sense. MacIntyre is right in stating that one need not involve in arguing the others down. But showing the other tradition's failure in meeting certain kind of challenge is as good as arguing them down. Arguing his own examples of justice and morality, there are certainly many rival accounts of how to deal with the issues such as distributive justice, egalitarianism, social empowerment etc. Besides, when it is difficult to accommodate rival accounts at a same time, it is ambiguous how we are able to find flaws in each intellectual tradition. It is also not clear how tradition-dependence rationality resolves the epistemological crises. The later needs rational foundational principles for its explanation. In this sense, the questions invoked in *Whose Justice? Which Rationality?* become counter-questions to the position of MacIntyre himself. How would he respond to the situation where the *liberal democratic* tradition itself meets all the requirements? The only difference is that MacIntyre makes an a priori assumption that liberal democratic tradition is flawed for its tradition-transcendent rationality and neutral foundations.[12]

MacIntyre claims that his notion of *tradition-dependence* is not relativism proper at all. From the complications that are addressed above, we can ask whether this notion of tradition-dependence can escape from relativism.

MacIntyre has a response for this. He states, the historical particularities of traditions, the fact that each is only to be appreciated by a relationship to a particular contingent history, does not of itself mean that those histories cannot extend to and even flourish in environments not only different from but even hostile to those in which a tradition was originally at home.[13] This point of MacIntyre seems very strong but with an exception. The exception is that an intellectual tradition can extend from time to time only in two ways, they should be either successful (as attributed to the liberal-democratic tradition) or when they have adopted to the changing conditions. Does the latter mean that an intellectual tradition can sustain by modifying its *basic core*? This question has no easy answer as such. MacIntyre is right in saying that the occurrence of epistemological crises requires imaginative new theories and concepts, no just reflection on old ideas. This method does not have fixed rational conceptions and conceptual universals. This methodology always takes care of contingent social conditions.

MacIntyre has an advantage here. He talks of development of a tradition through stages. This point of his, i.e., the requirement of new imaginative theories has an implicit mechanism of commensurability of different intellectual traditions. Commensurability, here, would mean that the interaction of various intellectual traditions to resolve the epistemological crises.[14] The situation is not as simple as MacIntyre explains it to be. Though he talks about rationality relative to tradition than rationality *per se*, the alternative that we can go for *rational* choice among the rival traditions creates doubt whether he prefers cross-tradition rational approach. To allow rational choice among the rival traditions is to admit intertraditional or tradition-dependent account of rationality.[15] Another apprehension is whether tradition-dependence of MacIntyre's rationality avoids perspectivalism? The manner in which MacIntyre's arguments proceed to resolve the epistemological crises, tradition-dependence would certainly be more like envisaging *perspectivalism*, where explanation is bound to depend on a specific intellectual tradition. Nevertheless, MacIntyre's thesis can avoid *relativism* if and only if answers to questions such as morality, justice, and self-realization are not confined to mere specific empirical historical traditions. In other words, the intellectual tradition should be in some sense be independent from historicism. This, however, does not mean a total detachment from the historical facts.

This is related to the position taken above on how rational and the relative approaches have their respective roles in the construction of social knowledge. The advantage and disadvantage of tradition-dependent rationality and tradition-independent rationality cannot be overlooked if we really recognize their respective roles in conceiving knowledge. One should not overlook the advantage of a historical approach that is a treasure house of how intellectual traditions grow in various stages in response to various challenges. In this aspect, MacIntyre scores positive despite there are certain confusions. It conveys the message that there is a necessity of different rival accounts of several aspects of social enterprise.

Jennifer A. Herdt makes an interesting point with respect to this conflict between tradition-independence and tradition-dependence. According to Herdt,

"... the best way to resolve these contradictions is to move beyond the dichotomy between tradition-dependent and tradition-independent norms. Norms of practical rationality can be things that emerge historically as a particular time and place without being tradition-dependent in the sense of being dependent for their validity on a particular tradition".[16] This point of Herdt seems appropriate despite the author's critical appraisal of MacIntyre's position. The nature of social existence that we have been with respect to manifold issues can be understood from the perspective of practical rationality that may be embedded in any form of social explanation and intellectual tradition. This approach provides a balancing perspective that takes account of tradition-dependent and tradition-transcendent approaches assuming them to have their own respective significances.

Rational and Relativist Dimensions

The rational approach in reality is not oblivion to the historical growth of intellectual tradition and historical growth of knowledge. However, the constructivist aspect of social knowledge seems very deceptive due to the reason that truth and reality that epidemiologists point out may be subjected to arbitrary subjectivism or extreme relativism. It could be as MacIntyre points out those different relative rational dimensions that never intersect. In the construction of body of social knowledge we can afford to accommodate the *descriptive* nature of social reality. However, it is too good to accommodate *normative* relativism that claims deep incommensurability and a total incompatibility of cultures and traditions. The underlying idea is though the understanding of social reality gets constituted amid plurality and diversity, the nature of social existence as part of social explanation should not be reduced to *hardcore* incommensurabilities.

The discussion in the above section was concluded with an agreement that in what way tradition-transcendence and tradition-dependent approaches are relevant to the construction of social knowledge. Yet, there will be even more opposition to the claim that social sciences cannot be freed from relativism and certain ambiguity due to the very nature of its subject matter. One has to treat this point carefully. The proponents of this claim would say that it is difficult to say that social reality in totality is so and so. It has so many things in its fold that really complicates the explanatory aspect of it.[17] It will not be defended here that one has to adopt the rational approach for the sake of explanatory convenience. No approach that explains social existence can afford to overlook overarching social formations and social formations embracing plurality of lives. However, the plurality of life patterns does not restrict or negate the possibility of reasoning about what is good and right for the individuals in society.

The MacIntyre's approach of tradition-dependent non-relativism is only partially successful as we have explained the ambiguities in his position. Nevertheless, one can make an attempt to construct a rational foundational principle that explains social reality that could be extended to further contexts with or without modification owing to the changes in the social situations. There is Cretan aspect of social knowledge that possesses autonomous value. This aspect constitutes foundational principles that may not be subject to ramification, at least not so frequent when compared to the social situations. Only when we allow certain foundational knowledge to be autonomous, then we can be able to set up criteria to explain social phenomena. And also we would be able to avoid arbitrariness in distinguishing from right beliefs and wrong beliefs. It means that law-like principles do not change with changes in social circumstances. In the sense of Herdt, the approach of practical rationality is far more appropriate in the context of necessity of both tradition-transcendence and tradition-dependence.

We will come to the issue of whether philosophers should intervene in explaining the nature of social existence or is it left to anthropologists, sociologists, political scientists etc.? This question of Schatzki is very interesting. We can finally say that it is mere stupidity to say that explaining the nature of social existence is the job of only social scientists, As mentioned in the first section, most of the ambiguities in social explanation calls for more than fact-based observation and thinking. Besides, most of the problems that anthropologists, sociologists, and political scientists encounter have a philosophical dimension equally and sometimes more important enough. After all the discussion, it will not be committed that the rational approach would, in totality, defeat the relativist approach. Nevertheless, relativism is relevant as far as descriptive and narrative aspect of various social knowledge systems is concerned. The understanding of social knowledge should be such that it has to do with the process of managing rival accounts and competing theories. The obligation is not just to tackle several problematic situations, paradoxes and contradictions.

Notes

1. Finn Colin, *Theory and Understanding: A Critique of Interpretative Social Science*, London: Basil Blackwell, 1985. John Skorupski, "Explanation and Understanding in Social Sciences", in *Explanation and its Limits* (Royal Institute of Philosophy Supplement, 27), (ed.), Dudley Knowles, Cambridge: Cambridge University Press, 1990, pp. 119–134 at 123.
2. For example one can refer to John Searle, *The Construction of Social Reality*, New York: The Free Press, 1995. Also see Paul Boghassian, *Fear of Knowledge: Against Relativism and Constructivism*, Oxford: Oxford University Press, 2006.
3. See his paper, "The Nature of Social Reality", *Philosophy and Phenomenological Research*, 49.2, December, 1988, pp. 239–260 at 241.
4. Notre Dame: Notre Dame University Press, 1988.
5. Notre Dame: Notre Dame University Press, 1984.
6. Julia Annas, "MacIntyre on Tradition", (Review of *Whose Justice? Which Rationality?*), *Philosophy and Public Affairs*, 18.4, Autumn, 1989, pp. 388–404.
7. The whole Kantian and the Neo-Kantian moral philosophy believes in *rationality* understood as time-independent as well as tradition-independent in nature. The liberal philosophical tradition attached to this believes in similar notions of rational moral justification for all those moral conflicts that pertain to several issues.
8. Julia Annas, "MacIntyre on Traditions", p. 392.

9. Alasdair MacIntyre, *After Virtue*, p. 12.
10. See his *Fear of Knowledge: Against Relativism and Constructivism*, Oxford: Oxford University Press, 2006.
11. Julia Annas, "MacIntyre on Traditions", p. 302.
12. MacIntyres' claim is that attempts to find neutral grounds to elucidate practical rationality as such have failed and can be expected to continue to fail. See Jennifer A. Herdt, Alasdair MacIntyres' *Rationality of Traditions*, p. 527.
13. Julia Annas, "MacIntyre on Traditions", p. 391.
14. Herdt mentions that some epistemological crises are not resolved at all, some are resolved from within, and some are resolved by a turn to a rival tradition. See Alasdair MacIntyres', *Rationality of Traditions*, p. 528.
15. Herdt opines in a similar way. The author argues that MacIntyres' theory of rational choice among the rival traditions cannot be possible without abstracting from the particular epistemological crises, ibid., p. 536.
16. See Jennifer A. Herdt, Alasdair MacIntyres' "Rationality of the Traditions and Tradition-Transcendent Structure of Justification", *The Journal of Religion*, 78.4, October, 1998, pp. 524–546 at 525.
17. See Theodore Schatzki, "The Nature of Social Reality".

20 Political Economy of Drought and Sustainability

A Village Study in Chittoor District of Andhra Pradesh

P. RAGHUPATHI, K. GANGARATNAM AND V. SUBRAMANYAM

The sustainable development is a complex of activities which could be expected to improve the human condition in such a way that the management of natural resources to ensure the long term productive capacity of the resource base and to improve the long-term wealth and well-being that derives from the alternative resource use systems. Broadly the concept of sustainable development is concerned mainly with the increasing material standard of living conditions of the poor at the grass-roots level. Further quantitatively this could be measured in terms of access to more food, education, health, sanitation, water and increasing real income. The primary objective of sustainable development is to reduce the absolute poverty and to maintain social stability. The concept, when applied to agriculture, refers to the development in agriculture sector, without extreme pressure on existing resources like land, forests and water bodies. But whether such controlled development in agriculture is economically viable and socially acceptable?

Agriculture is one of the important components of sustainable development. Sustainable agriculture is rooted in a set of values that reflects awareness about ecological and social realities and a commitment to respond appropriately to that awareness. It emphasizes design and management procedures that work with natural processes to conserve all resources and minimize waste and environmental damage while maintaining and improving farm profitability. The need for agricultural practices to be economically viable to meet human needs for food and to be concerned with quality of life is the general concern. Sustainable agriculture is not linked to particular technological practice. Nor is it an exclusive domain of organic farming. Rather, sustainable agriculture is thought of in terms of its adaptability and flexibility.

Moreover, the promotion of sustainable agriculture and rural development requires some major changes to create the conditions for sustainable agriculture and rural development. The major objective of sustainable agriculture and rural development is to increase food production in a sustainable way and enhance food security without causing much harm to the environment. This will involve education initiatives, utilization of economic incentives and the development of appropriate and new technologies without neglecting the traditional farming techniques, thus ensuring stable supplies of nutritionally adequate food, access to those supplies by vulnerable groups and production for markets; and finally employment and income generation to alleviate poverty.

Agriculture is the mainstay of the Indian economy and about two thirds of the total working population is employed in this sector. Many changes have been taking place to maintain sustainable agriculture in different ways. However, there is no everlasting solution to lead sustainable agriculture across the country, consequently, agriculture is lagging behind resulting in around 40 per cent of rural population still living below poverty line. It may be attributed that due to ecological imbalances in particular, low rate of rainfall, gambling of monsoons play a significant role in leading the agricultural sector towards sustainability. Because of these circumstances, sustainability varies from state-to-state and from region-to-region. Andhra Pradesh is one such state with three regions; each region has its own strategy to maintain sustainability in agriculture. Many strategies are followed for sustainability of which crop diversification occupies an important role due to various reasons.

There are many factors such as physical factors; irrigation facilities and economic factors that influence the cropping pattern of which physical factors play a significant role. Physical factors like climate, rainfall, weather, etc., influence cropping, apart from these economic factors like prices, income, size of land holdings, availability of inputs, insurance against risk, tenure and government policies have also direct influence on the cropping. Therefore, cropping pattern has inseparable relation with agricultural sector. It is attributed that in accordance with ecological imbalances crop diversification is taking place in which income generation is the main objective. By shifting of copping pattern, other sectors like animal husbandry sector is also coming up as a plausible solution for rural development. Therefore, in the case of livestock, most production comes from confined, concentrated systems, i.e., agriculture and its allied activities. Hence, the concept of sustainable agriculture is not only confined within the farm boundary but has strong connections and interlinks with the expanding rural economy.

In this context, this paper attempts to analyze the crop diversification that led to sustainability of rural mass in various ways. And how it paves the way for livestock development, which in its turn leads to further development of dairy cattle. Moreover, how the dairy cattle is becoming as a significant and subsistence occupation to all the sections of population at village level as a whole and how agriculture, crop diversification and animal husbandry are cyclically depend up on each other.

Profile of the Panchalamarri Village

Panchalamarri village is located in the Chittoor district (Rayalaseema region) of Andhra Pradesh, which is subjected to periodical chronic adverse seasonal conditions. The village is a multi-caste village consisting of Reddy, Balija, Chakali, Kurba, Besta, Mangali, Muslim, Yerukala, Mala, Madiga and Vadde castes. Most of the land resources are owned by the Reddys. Among the other castes mentioned above Mala and Madiga are the lowest in the caste hierarchy.

Panchalamarri is situated about 1.5 km away from Madanapalli—Thamballapalli road, at a distance of 34 km (about one hour bus journey from

Madanapalli Town) from Mandanpalli towards north and 4 km from Thamballapalli towards northwest. Panchalamarri possesses about 1.81 per cent of the total land area of the Thamballapalli mandal, and its population is 2.66 per cent of the total population of the mandal. The working force of the village forms about 58 per cent of the total population of 832 and the dependency rate is 42 per cent, it is plausible high.

Pattern of Agricultural Growth

Panchalamarri is a medium size village with 213 households of which 181 (84%) householders are cultivators and 17 (about 8%) were labourers. The average size of holdings is 1.87 hectares. The entire sown area in the village is either unirrigated or irrigated. About 44 per cent of the total land is irrigated by tube wells. The major crops grown in this village are paddy, groundnut, mulberry, and fodder for cattle. Groundnut is the dominant crop accounting for 78 per cent of the cropped area. Very high crop intensity in the village is due to a large area being under groundnut cultivation. Paddy is the second important crop accounting for about 11 per cent of the cropped area. Another 3 per cent of the cropped area is covered by fodder. The relative area under fodder crop cultivation is due to the importance of dairy farming in the village. It needs to mention that about 70 per cent of the farmer reported sale of milk as subsidiary source of income.

Last two decades witnessed rapid change in the agricultural economy of the village. The most significant change is the massive reduction in the average farm size. In 1970 there were 100 hectares operated by only nine cultivating households. Of the total holdings, only one household owned 59 (about 59%) hectares in size and another one household had 13.5 (13%) hectares in size and there were no household below one acre. On the contrary, there was no household, which possessed 59 hectares alone by 2000. Therefore, a large reduction in the average size of holdings has been taken place due to subdivision of households resulting from increase in population and the break-up of joint family. This can be witnessed from Table 1, out of 55 sample households in 2000, 34 (66.67%) households belonged to less than one hectare size group, one household constituted large farm (over 19 hectares) and there were three households below one hectare. Apart from these, there were four landless households the details of which were unable to be compared against 1970 statistics, as there was no single household covered particularly from this category. As a result of subdivision of holdings, large farmers controlled only 12 per cent of the cultivated area in 2000 as against 62 per cent in 1970. Apart from these changes, impact of Land Ceiling Act during 1987–88 also played a significant role in bringing out a breakthrough in the distribution of land holdings.

The availability of limited irrigation facility has helped in crop intensity and in improving crop pattern and crop yields. The introduction of high yielding verities of paddy has led to a large increase in area of groundnut cultivation indirectly. Consequently, yield per acre of paddy is now 32 bags in 2000 as against to 20 bags in 1980. Farmers particularly who have adequate water facility have now preferred to allocate some land to cultivate both fodder and groundnut crops even in an acre of land. Therefore, it is evident that farmers expect more income from dairy cattle rather than cultivating paddy crop. The increase of both farm income, generated by green revolution and dairy income, has resulted more in substantial investment in human and animal labour saving technology (tube well and tractors). There are four tractors, two tillers and 69 tube wells in this village. These machines have significantly reduced the demand for animal and human labour for tillage, irrigation and transportation.

Change in Cropping Pattern

Cropping pattern can be defined as the proportion of area under different crops at a point of time, changes in this distribution over a period of time, and factors determining this change in distribution.[1] Factors like nature of soil, type of climate, extent of rainfall, etc., determine the crop pattern of this village. Apart from these factors, prices of agricultural commodities, incomes of farmers, size of holdings, availability of inputs and nature of land tenure are the important factors in determining cropping pattern. Since both land and cropping pattern have inseparable relation, landholdings are discussed in the Table 1.

Table 1 *Sizewise Distribution of Landholdings of Sample Households in Panchalamarri Village During 1970–2000*

Landholdings Size Group	*1970*			*2000*		
	Number of Sample Households	*Total land under occupation (in hectares)*	*Average size of Holdings*	*Number of Sample Households*	*Total land under occupation (in hectares)*	*Average size of Holdings*
Landlessness	—	—	—	4	0	0
Below 1 acre	—	—	—	3	2.15	0.72
1–5 acres	3	4.25	1.42	34	84.26	2.48
5–10 acres	4	23.85	5.96	13	66.12	5.09
10–20 acres	1	13.5	13.5	1	19.12	19.12
51 acres and above	1	59	59	—	—	—
Total	9	100.6	11.18	55	171.65	3.37

Source: A.S.O. and Mandal Records, Thamballapalli Mandal, Chittoor District (A.P.).

Land is limited in area. Its ownership determines social status and economic opportunities. By and large, agriculture land has occupied a significant place at village level. Furthermore, most of the villagers are treating land as a prime source for their prestige. Therefore, every one in the present study village is longing for more land to have more economic opportunities. It cannot be denied that landlords are becoming moneylenders in general and Panchalamarri village is no exception. As per Table 1 the average size of holding between 10–20 acres increased from 13.5 acres in 1970 to 19.12 acres in 2000. Similarly, the average size holding above 51 acres has completely vanished since 2000. Importantly, the average size of holdings was 11.8 hectares in 1971 from nine sample households as against 3.37 hectares in 2000 from 51 sample households. It is found that due to Land Ceiling Act only few households got benefited, but it is not implemented effectively. It is said that majority of the land which was given away through Land Ceiling Act is of no use. Most of the land is not being cultivated, as it is located close to the forest and swarm with bushes and stones.

As far as cropping pattern is concerned there are two main crop seasons in this region, i.e., Khariff and Rabi which have been determined primarily by rainfall. The Khariff season starts in the middle of May and banks heavily on the southwest monsoon. The Rabi starts in the middle of October, as the southwest monsoon retreats and the northeast monsoon takes over. Pre-monsoon rains (March-May) are important for the sowing of Khariff corps like autumn rice. The main monsoon (June to September) covers the growth and harvesting of Khariff crops. Post-monsoon rains (October to December) are essential for Rabi crops. If the monsoon is delayed or weakened, it may lead to drought conditions.

Both rainfall and climate have influenced the changes that occurred in cropping pattern. The percentile change in area under each crop is varying over a period of three decades. It was observed that there was a considerable change taking place particularly between food crops and cash crops. The trend of diversification was favourable towards cash crops during the period 1970–71 to 2000–01. The overall compound growth rate of commercial crops was 2.24 per cent as against—4.39 per cent of food crops (Table 3), therefore, area under food crops had drastically declined. However, the area under groundnut cultivation among cash crops had grown remarkably from 143 hectares in 1970–71 to 267 hectares in 2000–01 (Table 2), whereas the area under paddy cultivation among food crops had declined substantially from 75 hectares to 36 hectares during the same period. Similarly, the compound growth rate of groundnut was 2.17 per cent as against 2.34 per cent of paddy. During the Khariff season the cropping pattern is favoured both food crops as well as cash crops in general, but groundnut was the most preferred crop. On the contrary, during Rabi season crop diversification has favoured paddy mostly. However, as a cash crop groundnut is being preferred and cultivated, as it requires less amount of water when compared to the paddy. Therefore diversification in the cropping pattern took place wherein high value crops like groundnut, and mulberry gradually replaced relatively less remunerative crops like jowar, maize, bajra, ragi, and castor. Therefore, the year 1990–91 has to be noted because the area under groundnut cultivation has rapidly increased by twofolds from 151 hectares in 1980–81 to about 300 hectares in the year 1990–91 itself.

Despite the study village being adversely affected by periodical drought, it has still little source of irrigation, but not up to the mark. Area under tanks continuously increased since 1981 onwards. On the contrary, area under tanks has vanished since 2000 due to the shortage of rainfall (Table 4). However, irrigated area under tube wells has been continuously increasing since 1991. About 53 tube wells out of 70 are being used as an irrigation source for cultivation to both cash as well as food crops. The tremendous decline of well irrigation during the period of 1991–2000 was mainly because of switching over to tube wells irrigation. And about 60 per cent tube wells of the total are not working properly particularly in Rabi season and dry up. The first tube well was drilled in 1983 by Vemanarayana Reddy, then he got enough water at the depth

Table 2 *Cropping Pattern in the Panchalamarri Village through Decades*

(area in hectares)

Name of the Crop	*1970–71*	*1980–81*	*1990–91*	*2000–01*
I. FOOD CROPS				
Paddy	75.81 (22.99)	63.19 (15.85)	79.81 (16.94)	36.74 (10.72)
Jowar	8.44 (2.56)	4.01 (3.05)	13.11 (2.79)	—
Maize	0.61 (0.81)	0.23 (1.17)	3.47 (0.74)	—
Ragi	13.40 (4.06)	10.21 (3.09)	10.76 (2.28)	—
Bajra (Sajja)	68.71 (20.84)	14.73 (2.28)	11.11 (2.35)	7.88 (2.30)
Others	5.82 (1.76)	3.82 (1.51)	6.80 (1.44)	5.10(1.49)
Sub Total	172.79 (52.39)	134.07 (26.95)	125.06 (26.55)	49.72 14.51)
II. CASH CROPS				
Groundnuts	143.32 (43.46)	151.02 (62.74)	298.91 (63.45)	267.41 (78.04)
Sugarcane	0.89 (0.27)	0.81 (4.70)	18.01 (3.82)	—
Castor	3.19 (0.97)	2.01 (0.50)	1.97 (0.42)	—
Chillies	3.79 (1.14)	2.08 (0.43)	2.34 (0.50)	1.11 (0.32)
Mulbary		1.79 (2.04)	9.76 (2.07)	18.63 (5.44)
Sub Total	151.19 (45.84)	157.71 (70.41)	330.99 (70.26)	287.15 (83.80)
III. OTHERS				
Onions	0.82 (0.25)	0.89 (0.48)	2.10 (0.45)	1.21 (0.53)
Vegetables	2.25 (0.68)	1.98 (1.63)	8.12 (1.72)	3.46 (1.01)
Miscellaneous crops betel, gardens etc.	2.74 (0.84)	2.24 (0.53)	4.79 (1.02)	1.12 (0.33)
Sub Total	5.81 (1.77)	5.11 (2.64)	15.01 (3.19)	5.79 (1.69)
Grand Total	329.79 (100)	296.89 (100)	471.06 (100)	342.66 (100)

Sources: (1) Census of India 1971, Special Survey Reports on Restudy Villages, Panchalamarri
(2) V.A.O., Panchalamarri Village
(3) A.S.O. Records, Mandal Revenue Office, Thamballapalli

Note: Figures in parentheses are percentages.

Table 3 *Compound Growth Rates of Paddy and Groundnut in Panchalamarri Village, 1971–2000*

Crop	*1971*	*2000*	*Compound Growth Rates*
Paddy	71.81	36.74	–2.34
Groundnut	143.32	267.41	2.17
Food crops	172.79	49.72	–4.39
Commercial crops	151.19	287.15	2.24
Others	5.81	5.79	–99

Source: Field Survey.

of 120 feet. On the contrary the depth of tube wells crossed over 450 feets in 2000, however farmers are unable to get adequate water at present. Though the depth exceeds beyond 450 feets there is no hope that the tube well would work and provide adequate water all through the year, hence the farmers are so reluctant to drill tube wells. At this juncture, majority of the farmers give considerable importance to cash crops particularly those require less quantity of water for which groundnut is profitable in both ways. As a result, both, the new technology and the green revolution have influenced and played significant role in the agricultural pattern.

Table 4 *Sourcewise Area Irrigated In Panchalamarri Village 1971–2000*

Source of Irrigation	*1981 (in hectares)*	*per cent to the total*	*1991 (in hectares)*	*per cent to the total*	*2000 (in hectares)*	*per cent to the total*
Tanks	68	75.56	120	54.55	—	—
Wells	22	24.44	25	11.36	15	14.29
Tube wells	—	—	75	34.09	90	85.71
Total	90	100	220	100	105	100

Sources: (1) Census of India 1971, Special Survey Reports on Restudy Villages Panchalamarri.
(2) Mandal Revenue Records, Thamballapalli Mandal, Chittoor District

It is estimated that the cost of installing a tube well point is between Rs 10,000 and 20,000 and another Rs 30,000–40,000 for electric motor, amounting to a total of nearly Rs 50,000–70,000. Based on the basis of land mortgage system, farmers are provided loans from the bank for nearly 50 per cent of their potential value of land, which means offering tube wells loans to unirrigated areas, while valuing it at the price of irrigated land.

There was only 43.50 per cent irrigated of the net area sown in 1981, and it has marginally increased to 44.18 per cent in 2000. Interestingly, over a period of one decade irrigated area has rapidly increased from 90 hectares in 1981 to 220 hectares in 1991 (Table 5). It has taken place exclusively by increasing number of tube wells during the same period. But, irrigated area has been continuously declining as both tube wells and open wells began to dry up. And only a very few hectares is cultivated under the open well and almost all open wells have dried up since water table got declined.

Table 5 *Area Irrigated in Panchalamarri Village During 1981–2000*

Year	*Irrigated Area (in hectares)*	*Net Area Sown (in hectares)*	*per cent Area Irrigated to Net Sown Area*
1981	90	206.89	43.50
1991	220	251.06	87.62
2000	105	237.66	44.18

Source: Collected from Field Survey.

Cost of Cultivation between Paddy and Groundnut Crops

Cost of cultivation is estimated through labour requirement according to operationwise cost. Apart from operationwise cost, we have taken into account both fertilizers and pesticides cost as well. Same method is applied for both paddy and groundnut crops. As far as operations are concerned, paddy is having twelve operations whereas groundnut has only five operations. Therefore, there is a considerable difference even in operations between these two crops. Another development is that the labour requirement has continuously increased through the decade. It is said that the main reason is, to increase number of operations (for instance, weeding and to reduce working hours) in agricultural activities. For instance, a labour had to work for about 10 hours and even more sometimes in 1980 whereas in 2000 it has reduced to only 8 hours. Similarly, operations like weeding absorb more labour since it has to be operated time and again in order to enhance the crops production.

Requirement of labour for paddy cultivation increased from 81 in 1980 to 95 by 2000 (Table 6). Female participation in all operations in every decade has increased as against the male, which is due to seasonal migration of male workers. Female workers have now replaced in male agricultural activities, which were led by male workers earlier. Similarly in the case of groundnut crop, labour requirement has increased from 40 in 1980 to 52 in 2000 (Table 7). Since 1980, the same trend, as in paddy crop, is seen in participation of male and female workers in agricultural activities. Unlike paddy, even children services are greatly utilized pertaining to the groundnut cultivation. Though paddy has more operations, a remarkable change has taken place in increasing number of labourers according to operationwise. Fourteen labourers have increased in paddy operations as against to 12 in groundnut crop. Among various operations transplantation, weeding and harvesting plays a significant role in padduy cultivation resulting in the absorption of more labourers.

Increasing number of labourers for both crops has also ultimately led to increase the cost of cultivation. Cost of cultivation has been rapidly increased since 1980 onwards. It has increased to Rs 4,620 per acre in 2000 as against just Rs 918 in 1980 (Table 8) as far as paddy is concerned. Similarly, for groundnut cultivation, it has increased from Rs 601 per acre in 1980 to Rs 2,880 in 2000 (Table 9). It is observed that the cost of cultivation has tremendously increased more than five times for paddy crop as well as more than four times in groundnut crop over a period of two decades. Accordingly, the cost of cultivation for paddy is as high as Rs 1,740 when compared to groundnut crop. The first and foremost thing that is to be done, in order to get high yield is weeding. Therefore, weeding plays a significant role in bringing high yields, and it takes place whenever weeds grow more in the crop irrespective of limited time. However, during 1980s farmers were not concentrating much on weeding operations, hence they had only received small quantity of yield. Similarly, during 1980s all farmers used to use their own manure by which they did not feel as if they invested more on fertilizers. On the contrary from 1990 onwards, usage of fertilizers/pesticides has grown considerably high which enhanced investment on agriculture, apart from this, series of weeding is inevitable. In addition, compared to groundnut, paddy crop needs more pesticides and fertilizers. Number of workers increased from 10 to 13 for weeding operation alone for both paddy and groundnut crops. Thus, weeding can be performed generally twice and thrice and more in some cases in accordance with seed growth in the field.

Table 6 *Labour Requirement Per Acre for Different Operations of Paddy During 1980–81, 1990–91 and 2000–01*

Operations	*1980–81*			*1990–91*			*2000–01*		
	Male	*Female*	*Total Number of Labourers*	*Male*	*Female*	*Total Number of Labourers*	*Male*	*Female*	*Total Number of Labourers*
Tilling prior to transplantation	3	—	3	4	—	4	5	—	5
Cutting the contours	2	—	2	2	—	2	3	—	3
Tilling at the time of transplantation	3	—	3	3	—	3	—	—	—
Puddler	—	—	—	—	—	—	1	—	1
Levelling	1	—	1	1	—	1	—	—	—
Transplantation	5	15	20	6	15	21	8	15	23
Weeding (twice)	—	10	10	—	11	11	—	13	13
Harvesting	5	15	20	6	15	21	8	15	23
Threshing	11	—	11	12	—	12	13	—	13
Trampling grass	—	5	5	—	5	5	1	4	5
Winnowing	—	2	2	—	3	3	—	4	4
Storage of grass	3	1	4	3	2	5	3	2	5
Total	33	48	81	37	51	88	42	53	95

Source: Data Collected from Village Farmers (Meti-Rythulu).

Table 7 *Labour Requirement Per Acre for different Operations of Groundnut During 1980–81, 1990–91 and 2000–01*

Operations	*1980–81*			*1990–91*			*2000–01*		
	Male	*Female*	*Total Number of Labourers*	*Male*	*Female*	*Total Number of Labourers*	*Male*	*Female*	*Total Number of Labourers*
Tilling prior to seeding	10	—	10	11	—	11	12	—	12
Tilling at the time of seeding	2	2	4	2	3	5	2	4	6
Guntaka	1	—	1	1	—	1	1	—	1
Weeding	—	10	10	—	11	11	—	13	13
Harvesting	10	5	15	11	6	17	12	8	20
Total	23	17	40	25	20	45	27	25	52

Source: Data Collected from Village Farmers (Meti-Rythulu).

Secondly, reducing working hours also gave rise to increased cost of cultivation. It happens due to reduce number of working hours. During 1980–81 agricultural labourers used to work about 11 hours in a day, i.e., from morning 7.30 am to evening 6.30 to 7 pm with two times meals a day. The whole scenario was completely changed in 2000 and unlike in 1980 workers generally engaged in the field at about 9.30 am to 10 am and returned to home by 6 pm at any cost. Above all, the conventional practice of attached labour has completely vanished which has helped the labour class to get rid of all their constraints. This has resulted in the demanding high wages from labour class, which eventually led to increased cost of cultivation as well as labour requirement.

Farmer gets high yield in accordance with his effort importantly by bearing all the above-mentioned expenses. As a result, there is a change that has taken place not only in terms of quantity but in terms of price as well. During 1980s only 20 paddy bags were produced in an acre of land and it increased to 30 bags in 2000 (Table 10). Similarly, 15 groundnut bags were produced in 2000 as against to only 10 bags in 1980. So, in during the course of time, many changes have taken place with regard to these two crops. It was only Rs 175 per bag for paddy in 1980 and it has increased to Rs 410 in 2000. Similarly, in the case of groundnut, it has increased to Rs 6,100 in 2000 as against to only Rs 120 in 1980. Change in the rate of increase in the price is Rs 235 for paddy and Rs 490 for groundnut over a period of two decades. So, the rate of increase in price is high in the groundnut rather than paddy.

It is observed that due to low production of groundnut in the different parts of the state, price might be hiked and also consumption of groundnut oil (as an edible oil) for household needs either directly or indirectly is growing more in recent years resulting increased high prices. More so, direct result of delay in monsoons for the past ten years, which results crop failures sometimes

Table 8 *Cost of Cultivation of Paddy by Operationswise During 1980–81, 1990–91 and 2000–01*

Operations	*1980–81*					*1990–91*					*2000–01*				
	Male	*Total Wage Rate*	*Female*	*Total Wage Rate*	*Gross Expen-diture*	*Male*	*Total Wage Rate*	*Female*	*Total Wage Rate*	*Gross Expen-diture*	*Male*	*Total Wage Rate*	*Female*	*Total Wage Rate*	*Gross Expen-diture*
Tilling prior to transplantation	3	27	—	—	27	4	80	—	—	80	5	150	—	—	150
Cutting the contours	2	18	—	—	18	2	40	—	—	40	3	90	—	—	90
Tilling at the time of transplantation	3	27	—	—	27	3	60	—	—	60	—	—	—	—	—
Puddler	—	—	—	—	—	—	—	—	—	—	1	30	—	—	30
Levelling	1	9	—	—	9	1	20	—	—	20	—	—	—	—	—
Transplantation	5	45	15	105	150	6	120	15	225	345	8	240	15	375	615
Weeding (twice)	—	-	10	70	70	—	—	11	165	165	—	—	13	325	325
Harvesting	10	90	10	70	160	6	120	15	225	345	8	240	15	375	615
Threshing	11	99	—	—	99	12	240	—	—	240	13	390	—	—	390
Trampling the grass by cattle	—	—	5	35	35	—	—	5	75	75	1	30	4	100	130
Winnowing	—	—	2	14	14	—	—	3	45	45	—	—	4	100	100
Storage of grass	3	27	1	7	34	3	60	2	30	90	3	90	2	50	140
Cattle manure	20 bullock carts each at the rate of Rs 10				200	10 bullock carts each at the rate of Rs 30				300	10 bullock carts each at the rate of Rs 50				500
Fertilizers	75				75	800				800	1460				1460
Pesticides	0				0	50				50	75				75
Total					918					2,655					4,620

Source: Collected from Field Survey.

Table 9 *Cost of Cultivation of Groundnut by Operationswise During 1980–81, 1990–91 and 2000–01*

Operations	*1980–81*					*1990–91*					*2000–01*				
	Male	*Total Wage Rate*	*Female*	*Total Wage Rate*	*Gross Expen-diture*	*Male*	*Total Wage Rate*	*Female*	*Total Wage Rate*	*Gross Expen-diture*	*Male*	*Total Wage Rate*	*Female*	*Total Wage Rate*	*Gross Expen-diture*
Tilling prior to seeding	10	90	0	0	90	11	220	0	0	220	12	360	0	0	360
Tilling at the time of seeding	2	18	2	14	32	2	40	3	45	85	2	60	4	100	160
Guntaka	1	9	0	0	9	1	20	0	0	20	1	30	0	0	30
Weeding	0	0	10	70	70	0	0	15	225	225	0	0	20	500	500
Harvesting	10	90	5	35	125	10	200	10	150	350	20	600	10	250	850
Cattle manure	20 bullock carts each at the rate of Rs 10				200	10 bullock carts each at the rate of Rs 30				300	10 bullock carts each at the rate of Rs 50				500
Fertilizers	75				75	250				250	500				480
Total					601					1,450					2,880

Source: Collected from Field Survey

and reduced cultivated area of groundnut crop in some parts of drought-prone areas are the main reasons to increase high prices for groundnut crop. Above all, there is no high yielding varieties as many as in paddy, therefore, only two or three varieties are available in groundnut, whereas more than seven varieties are available in paddy.

Table 10 *Productivity Per Acre of Paddy and Groundnut Crops*

(in bags)

Year	*Paddy*	*Groundnut*
1980–81	20	10
1990–91	25	12
2000–01	30	15

Source: Information Collected from Field Survey.

Over a period of two decades, paddy cultivation brought income from Rs 3,500 to Rs 12,300, whereas the income increased by groundnut cultivation from Rs 1,200 to Rs 9,150 only (Table 11). The main reason to increase both productivity as well as income per acre for paddy crop is firstly, the availability of various high yielding varieties, secondly, the high usage of fertilizers and pesticides and thirdly, the introduction of short term crops, i.e., four months crops.

Table 11 *Income Per Acre of Paddy and Groundnut Crops*

Year	*Paddy*			*Groundnut*		
	No. of Bags	*Price per Bag*	*Total Income*	*No. of Bags*	*Price per Bag*	*Total Income*
1980–81	20	175	3,500	10	120	1,200
1990–91	25	250	6,250	12	300	3,600
2000–01	30	410	12,300	15	610	9,150

Source: Collected from Field Survey.

Significance of Livestock in Rural Transformation

In the present study, village majority of the population are employed to a large extent based on milch cows rearing. Farmers belonging to all classes treated it as their main as well as subsidiary occupation and some of them revealed it as their main occupation as well. Therefore, over a period of three decades, there was a tremendous increase in dairy cattle population. Farmers feel that possessing of a single milch cow is equivalent to having an acre of land; therefore, a milk cow value is equal to an acre of dry land value. Generally, an acre of land brings an amount of Rs 15,000 on an average per annum if it is cultivated. Far from it, a milk cow could bring more income without any constraints and hard labour. So every farmer moves towards earning income in a simple way, i.e., by having a milch cow.

Farmers have another advantage, if the existing milch cow gives less quantity of milk that can be sold soon. Punganur is the main and well-known town where every Tuesday and Wednesday cattle fair takes place in which sellers and buyers participate not only from different parts of the state but also from neighbouring states as well. This town is located just about 60 km away from the village. Generally merchants even from neighbouring states such as Tamil Nadu, Karnataka and Kerala attend this fair and purchase good and high yielding milch cows. This fair and place is famous for dairy as well as drought cattle for exchanging.

Dairy Cattle Population in the Village

Growth

Table 13 shows the compound growth rates of cattle population in the village from 1971 to 2000. The following formula was used to estimate the compound growth rate (CGR):

$$\text{CGR} = [\text{antilog}(\log P_n - \log P_0/\text{No. of years}) - 1] \times 100$$

$$P_n = P_0 (1 + r)^n$$

where:

P_n = Population of the livestock in '*n*' period (current year),

P_0 = Population of the livestock in the base year,

r = growth rate, and

n = time in years.

Kapu (Reddy) caste possessed 81.05 per cent in 1971 and 61.65 per cent in 2000 (Table 12) of total livestock from all categories. It is clear from the data that the greater part of livestock was possessed apparently by Kapu caste as their population occupies about 76 per cent of the total village population. Moreover, of the 214 bullocks 179 (83.6%) were possessed by 68 Kapu households in 1971, while in 2000, 110 out of 174 were possessed from 114 households. The compound growth rate of bullocks was –0.72 per cent during 1971 to 2000. Over a period of three decades this has declined tremendously. So the impact of mechanization of agriculture has been supplanted in place of traditional method of cultivation, as a result importance and usage of bullock for agricultural activities has declined tremendously. Far from it, number of cows, has been predominantly doubled among various caste groups. Similarly, the compound growth rate of cows and milch cows was found to be positive, i.e., 1.54 per cent and 3.78 per cent respectively (Table 13). In absolute terms, total number of cows increased from 157 to 260 and milch cows alone increased from 45 to 132. It is found that number of milch cows have increased for about threefolds rather than cows. It is reported that income in every month can be derived from dairy cattle rather than others. Therefore, it should be noted that not only increased number of cows alone but milch cattle as well. There is large-scale reduction in the number of sheep and goats and the compound growth rate is negative as high as –4.54 per cent, it is caused due to economic problem, i.e., the gestation period which ranges from 1 to 2 years.

Rearing dairy cattle become a self-employment for most of the households. However, prior to 1980s it was neither their main occupation nor subsidiary

Table 12 *Castewise Ownership of Livestock in Panchalamarri 1971 and 2000*

Caste	1971 Livestock by Type								2001 Livestock by Type								
	No. of House-holds possess-ing cattle	Bullocks	Cows	Buffaloes	Sheep & Goat	Total milch cattle	Total	per cent to the total	No. of House-holds possess-ing cattle	Bullocks	Cows	Buffaloes	Young stock under 3 years	Sheep & Goat	Total milch cattle	Total	per cent to the total
Muslim	—	—	—	—	—	—	—	—	1	2	1	—	1	2	1	7	0.86
Chakali	—	—	—	—	—	—	—	—	2	3	2	—	—	4	1	10	1.23
Balija	1	6	10	5	20	4	45	5.02	7	14	7	—	3	14	2	40	4.93
Yerukala	1	2	—	—	—	—	2	0.22	1	2	-	—	—	—	—	2	0.25
Vadde	2	—	4	—	—	2	6	0.67	4	6	4	—	2	7	1	20	2.47
Kuruba	3	—	2	—	22	—	24	2.66	6	4	18	—	8	3	12	45	5.55
Brahman	—	—	—	—	—	—	—	—	—	—	—	—	—	—	—	—	—
Kapu (Reddy}	68	179	125	96	291	36	727	81.05	114	110	172	—	51	47	94	474	61.65
Christian	2	3	1	—	—	—	4	0.45	—	—	—	—	—	—	—	—	—
Mangali	4	2	5	2	—	2	11	1.23	5	3	12	—	5	12	4	36	4.44
Mala	13	14	8	2	20	—	44	4.90	19	20	25	—	11	6	9	71	10.23
Madiga	5	—	10	—	2	—	12	1.34	7	02	7	—	3	—	1	13	2.84
Besta	5	8	2	—	11	1	22	2.44	9	8	12	—	6	6	7	39	5.55
Total	104	214 (23.85)	167 (18.62)	105 (11.71)	366 (40.80)	45 (5.02)	897 (100)	100	175	174 (22.90)	260 (34.35)	—	90 (11.89)	101 (13.34)	132 (17.44)	757 (100)	100

Sources: V.A.O., Panchalamarri Village
Census of India 1971, Special Survey Reports on Restudy Village Panchalamarri

Table 13 *Compound Growth Rates of Livestock in Panchalamarri Village, 1971–2000*

Livestock	*1971*	*2000*	*Compound Growth Rates*
Bullocks	214	174	–0.72
Cows	167	260	1.54
Buffaloes	105	0	—
Sheep and goats	366	101	–4.54
Milch cows	45	132	3.78
Young under 3 years	0	90	—
Total	897	767	0.59

Source: Collected from Field Survey.

occupation, but it became occupation for most of the households after 1990s. With this, a large portion of their total household income is derived from dairy cattle. At last, this process has adversely affected buffaloes, and as a result buffaloes population has reduced to nil in 2000 as against 105 in 1971. With the introduction of Jersey cows, more or less every household has at least one single Jersey cow, with which they are earning lucrative income of nearly Rs 35–80 per day (at the rate of Rs 7 per litre). As a result the increased rate among various caste groups pertaining to milch cattle is 36 to 94 in Kapu, 0 to 12 in Kuraba, 0 to 9 in Mala, 1 to 7 in Besta and 2 to 4 in Mangali castes in the order of magnitude during 1971–2000. Responses from farmers show that there is no risk in maintaining a single cow instead of a pair of bullocks and it is somewhat easy too.

Labour Absorption in Cattle Keeping

For the maintenance of livestock number of tasks have to be carried out. These tasks are generally grazing of animals, collecting grass, bathing of animals, cleaning cattle shed, milking and feeding the various feedstuffs. It is noted that in the maintenance of cattle there was no hired labour in all classes, i.e., small, medium and large at this village level. One of the important aspects is, the whole family involves in all operations irrespective of age. However, female participation is confined to grazing, collection of grass, milking, cleaning sheds. It is reported that about 70 per cent of operations are performed by female with regard to milch cows whereas male does only little work. However, this entire nature of practice for two decades was different, when both male and female were involved actively more or less equally in taking care of the dairy cattle. It is observed that majority of the male population is engaged in agricultural activities, and most of the dry land turned out to be wetland. It is evident that bore wells were increased from nil to 90 within a short span of ten years. Male labourers concentrate more on agricultural activities, whereas female labourers take care of dairy cattle rearing.

Mode of Acquisition of Cows

There is a variation among different classes in acquiring cows. Since Reddy caste is dominant in the village, they purchase milking cows out of their profits incurred by cultivation. And this is the only caste availed loans advanced by the bank and other caste groups are not even aware of this facility. Unlike Reddy caste, the rest of the caste groups purchased milking cows exclusively out of their savings coupled with the earnings of other activities like daily labour. It is also observed that a very few depend upon moneylenders for financial assistance in acquiring dairy cattle. Even government agencies provided financial assistance to landless families to acquire the dairy cattle through the schemes as a part of the poverty alleviation schemes. However, such schemes did not work out effectively for whom they are meant to be. Wide variation was also found in the type of animals reared by various classes. Reddy caste families in this village are found to be rearing Holstein Friesian (HF) and Jersey crosses, whereas Jersey and Sindhi cross-breeds are generally reared by all classes. Few families also maintain indigenous dairy cattle. Farmers can build their milch animals herd either by raising female calf or by getting animals on exchange arrangements. On the other hand, farmers have much awareness about artificial insemination through which a high yielding milch calf could be produced even by local breeds. So such development in artificial insemination techniques have contributed to significant changes in the cattle breeding practices followed by the farmers and in the breed composition of their cattle.

Income Through Dairying

The minimum quantity of milk yield from dairy cattle is 2 litres and maximum is 16 litres per day. The price of one litre milk in this village is Rs 7 only. According to this, the annual income from dairying ranged from as low as Rs 8,640 to as high as Rs 20,160. The overall mean annual income through dairying in all classes in this village is Rs 14,400. The income earned by dairying has a lion share to the total income of the family. Most of the families are earning between 50 and 75 per cent of their income from dairying. There are also few families who earn beyond 75 per cent of their income from dairying. It is also to be noted that no single family is found which derives less than 25 per cent of its income from dairying. This emphasizes the significance of dairy cattle for the landless families too.

Utilization of Dairy Income

Sale of milk turns out to be an important occupation, which provides regular income to the farmer. Therefore, this is an important reason for most of the dairy farmers to continue rearing dairy cattle. This income is being utilized particularly for purchase of food items and other household requirements in marginal and middle class families. However, it is also utilized to repay the loans in high class families and some amount of it is saved for precautionary measures. More so, it becomes a vital source of income for occasions like marriage of daughters, repayment of loans and education for children etc., and this is very much true in the case of landless families.

Crop Diversification and its Impact on Dairy Cattle Development

An effort is made to ascertain how exclusively crop diversification gave rise to dairy cattle development. As majority of the farmers have cultivated groundnut crop which saves enough money. Unlike paddy crop, many operations of groundnut crop are performed either by own labour or by exchange labour. As a result, saving is more rather than expenditure in case of groundnut crop cultivation. Ultimately, saved amount is being invested again on purchasing milch cows, which in its turn lead to dairy farm. Apart from this, there are other reasons to be noted. If groundnut straw is used as a feed for dairy cattle, according to farmers, there is an increase from 100 ml to 250 ml in a day a compared to paddy grass. In addition to this, groundnut requires less amount of water than paddy. Various other crops like jowar, maize can be cultivated as mixed crops in the same area of groundnut crop, whereas in paddy crop it is highly impossible to cultivate mixed crops. Though various short term and high yielding verities have emerged in paddy crop, they are not producing plausible quantity of grass. As a result, the quantity of grass produced by high yielding and short term paddy crop is very low when compared to the indigenous verities. However, local or indigenous verities are not in practice presently, therefore, this is one of the reasons to switch over to groundnut crop cultivation. Having observed the above analyses, it can be said that paddy cultivation does not effectively support the rearing of dairy cattle. It should also be borne in mind that because of this, food crops like ragi, bajra, jowar and maize have completely vanished. Therefore, crop diversification took place wherein groundnut occupies a significant place, which now clears all constraints. Consequently, the whole village economy has switched over from food crop to commercial crop cultivation.

Focusing on how groundnut is becoming an important source in developing dairy cattle than paddy. It has to be noted that, firstly, as far as labour requirement per acre is concerned, paddy requires 95 labourers whereas groundnut requires only 52. Secondly, productivity per acre also vary between these two, and a yield of 30 paddy bags can be produced and only 15 bags of groundnut can be produced in the same size of land. However, there is a difference between these two crops even in earning income as well, according to recent rates, in absolute terms, a paddy bag comprising 75 kg is priced at Rs 410 only whereas 35 kg of groundnut bag cost is Rs 610. However, it is completely different, in estimating income according to acrewise. So, paddy crop brings income per annum about Rs 1410 more than groundnut from one acre of land. Though paddy gives more income it is not satisfied in other matters. It should be noted that paddy cultivation is not accessible to all class farmers and it is limited only to some classes and majority of them are large farmers. More so, large farmers who are using bore wells are cultivating paddy. Far from this, all classes irrespective of class and caste cultivate groundnut. Even, small and marginal farmers who have an acre of dry land maintain single milch cow, and even landless labourers are no exception to this. Large farmers and those who have both wet and dry land maintain two milch cows on an average. It is observed that every farmer who has bore well, allocate about 10 cents of total land in which hybrid grass is being grown. They assume that hybrid grass helps in producing more milk.

During 1980, different crops like jowar, ragi, bajra, and maize were being grown as food crops even in dry land apart from groundnut. However, all food crops were vanished barring paddy by 2000. Some extent of land is allocated to develop dairy farm even in wetland. In addition to this, cultivation of some commercial crops like mulberry and tomatoes are also introduced in which mulberry is also one sort of fodder crop. Consequently, area under paddy cultivation has also reduced from 63 hectares to 36 hectares by 2000.

Forest Land Converted as Cultivable Land

Cattle feed is available from cultivable land in general and uncultivable land in particular. The main source of fodder includes: uncultivable wastelands, fallow lands, common pastures, grazing grounds and forest areas. It is observed that there was 101 hectares under forest in 1971(Table 14); however, all the area was brought into cultivation and there was no land under forest category by 2000. All the forest land transformed into various lands of which largely around 63 hectares turned out to be a land under miscellaneous category. Moreover, permanent pastures, grazing land, barren and uncultivable land together occupies about 35 hectares in 2000 as against nil in 1970. Now, it is clear that there is an extensive land for grazing cattle apart from other reasons. According to the information gathered from villagers, a large chunk of land was distributed under Land Ceiling Act and simultaneously forest land was also distributed to the landless. In 1989–90, major part of the forest land was transformed into cultivable land in which most of the landless households got benefited. However, within a short span of time most of the landless households have done away with cultivation. In addition to this, due to inadequate water facility, menace of wild animals, lack of financial assistance in order to bring that land under cultivation, majority of the land became barren and uncultivable. And in the remaining land, groundnut is the one and only crop, which is cultivated out of food crops. Therefore, it may be conducive effect, which enables them to nurture dairy cattle. Landless labourers, marginal and small farmers are utilizing more of this land and it has become a main source to feed their dairy cattle.

Conclusions

The following conclusions emerge from the foregoing discussions

> In this study village, dairy cattle are maintained only for milk, which becomes an important panacea for all their financial constraints. Farmers have chosen groundnut crop rather than paddy as it contributes in yielding milk in high quantity. Though paddy is dominant in terms of productivity and income per acre and it requires more water, which is really inadequate at this village level. As a result, majority of the farmers are unable to cultivate paddy and it is limited only to large farmers alone (i.e., 53 households out of 213). Unlike paddy crop, all farmers, irrespective of large, medium and small, are cultivating groundnut.
>
> On the one hand, groundnut does not need more labour on the other it requires less usage of fertilizer and pesticides, when compared to paddy. So it contributed to the villagers preferring more groundnut cultivation. Therefore, a poor family comprising of five members could cultivate and perform all operations in an acre of groundnut crop without hiring any labour, but it is highly impossible in the case of paddy cultivation. Since groundnut supports much to the dairy cattle advancement, it is being cultivated extensively and as a result, most of the forest land has turned

Table 14 *Land Use Pattern in Panchalamarri Village: 1971–2000*

Category	*1971*		*1981*		*1991*		*2000**	
	Area (in hectares)	*per cent to total geographical area*	*Area (in hectares)*	*per cent to total geographical area*	*Area (in hectares)*	*per cent to total geographical area*	*Area (in hectares)*	*per cent to total geographical area*
Total geographical area	513.14	100	513.14	100	513.14	100	513.14	100
Forest	101.17	19.72	—	—	—	—	—	-
Barren and uncultivable land	—	—	—	—	—	—	18.74	3.65
Land put to non-agricultural uses	80.94	15.77	56.66	11.04	30	5.85	12.50	2.44
Permanent pastures and other grazing lands	—	—	—	—	—	—	16.67	3.25
Land under miscellaneous tree crops and groves not included in the net area sown	—	—	—	—	—	—	62.73	12.22
Cultural waste	22.66	4.42	142.85	27.842	103.00	20.07	4.17	0.81
Other fallow lands	—	—	—	—	—	—	—	—
Current fallows	—	—	—	—	—	—	—	—
Net area sown (for the year)	308.38	60.1	313.63	61.12	380.14	74.08	398.33	77.63

Source: District Census Handbooks, Chittoor, 1971, 1981 and 1991
* Collected from A.S.O. Mandal Revenue Office, Thamballapall

out to be groundnut fields. Conspicuously, groundnut was supplanted by food crops like bajra, maize, jowar and ragi, consequently all these crops have vanished except paddy. Moreover, the first and foremost thing to be required for rearing dairy cattle is, availability of grazing grounds, but it is no longer a problem at this village level.

Acknowledgement

We are thankful to Professor D. Narasimha Reddy, Department of Economics, University of Hyderabad for his supervision and cooperation.

Note

1. Analysis is confined to during 1971–2000; however, due to unavailablitiy of data since 1971, results were drawn from 1981 to 2000 particularly for labour requirement, cost of cultivation, income per acre, productivity per acre etc.

References

Ahuja, Vinod (ed.), (2004), "Livestock and Livelihoods: Challenges and Opportunities for Asia in the Emerging Market Environment", National Dairy Development Board.

Barnabas, A.P., (1999), "Globalisation and Transformation of Indian Rural Social Structure", *Indian Journal of Public Administration,* Vol. 45, No. 4.

Bhowmick, B.C. and Sharma, A.K., (2002), "Livestock in Assam: Its Importance, Income and Employment Generation Potential", in Birthal, P.S., Kumar, Anjani and Tewari, Laxmi (eds.), *Livestock in Different Farming Systems,* Agricultural Economic Research Association (India) and Advance Publishing Concept, New Delhi.

Birthal, P.S. and Singh, M.K., (1995), "Structure of Rural Income Inequalities: A Study in Western Uttar Pradesh", *Indian Journal of Agricultural Economics,* Vol. 30, No. 2.

Birthal, P.S., (2002), "Technological Change in Indias' Livestock Subsector: Evidence and Issues", in Birthal, P.S. and Rao, P. Parthasarathy (eds.), (2002), *Technology Options for Sustainable Livestock Production in India,* National Agricultural Economics and Policy Research, New Delhi, International Crops Research Institute for the Semi-Arid Tropics (ICRISAT), Patancheru, Andhra Pradesh and International Livestock Research Institute, Addis Ababa.

Dandekar, M.N., (1988), "Transformation in Agriculture and Rural Development", *Journal of Rural Development,* Vol. 7, No. 5.

Das, Someswar et al., (2004), "Role of Women in Livestock Farming", *Kurukshetra,* 52 (9), July.

Gandhi, R.S. and Singh, A., (2004), "Crossbreeding of Cattle for Enhancing Milk Production under Sustainable Livestock System in India", *Indian Dairyman,* 56 (7), July.

Hann C. de, et.al. (2001), Livestock Development, Environment, Poverty and Global Food Security, World Bank, Washington, DC.

Kumar, Ghosal Ratan, (1992), "Transformation in the Pattern of Asset Holding of Rural Households in West Bengal during 1961–62 to 1981–82", *ArthaVijnana*, Vol. 34, No. 4.

—, (2004), "Dynamics of Transformation of Rural Workforce Structure in India since 1961", *Indian Economic Journal*, Vol. 52, No. 1–2.

—, (2005), "State and Transformation of Rural Workforce Structure in West Bengal, 1961–2001", *Indian Journal of Labour Economics*, Vol. 48, No. 4.

—, (2006), "Dynamics of Transformation of the Rural Workforce Structure in West Bengal, 1961–2001", *Man and Development*, Vol. 28, No. 2.

Indian Society of Agricultural Economics, (1989), *Livestock Economy of India*, Bombay: Oxford and IBH Publishing Co. Pvt. Ltd.

Kanaka, Sundara Rao D.S.K., (2004), "Livestock Services and the Poor: An Alternative Service Strategy through Visakha Livestock Development Association in North Coastal Andhra Pradesh", in Morrenhof, Jan (ed.), *Livestock Services and the Poor*, Papers, Proceedings and Presentations of the International Workshop held at Bhubaneswar, India, October 28–29, 2002 edited by Jan Morrenhof, Vinod Ahuja and Ashok Tripathy, Switzerland: Swiss Agency for Development and Cooperation.

Kumar, A., Ali, Jabir and Singh, H., (2001), "Trade in Livestock Products in India: Trends, Performance and Competitiveness", *Indian Journal of Agricultural Economics*, Vol. 56, No. 4.

Kurien, C.T., (1980), "Dynamics of Rural Transformation: A Case Study of Tamil Nadu", *Economic and Political Weekly*, Vol. 15, No. 5–7.

Mishra Chaturanan, (1993), "Role of Rural Labour in Socio-Economic and Political Transformation of India", *Indian Journal of Labour Economics*, Vol. 36, No. 1.

Misra, S.N. and Sharma, Rishi, K., (1990), *Livestock Development in India: An Appraisal*, Institute of Economic Growth, New Delhi: Vikas Publishing House Pvt. Ltd.

Patel, R.K., (1993), "Present Status and Promise of Dairying in India", *Indian Journal of Agricultural Economics*, Vol. 48.

Pradhan, Promodini, Ahuja, Vinod and Venkatramaiah, P., (2004), "Livestock Services and the Poor in Orissa", in Morrenhof, Jan (ed.), *Livestock Services and the Poor*, Papers, Proceedings and Presentations of the International Workshop held at Bhubaneswar, India, October 28–29, (2002), edited by Jan Morrenhof, Vinod Ahuja and Ashok Tripathy, Switzerland: Swiss Agency for Development and Cooperation.

Rao, C. Niranjan and Nair, K. Narayanan, (2003), "Change and Transformation in Rural South India: Findings from Village Studies", *Economic and Political Weekly*, Vol. 38, No. 32.

Saleth, R. Maria, (1997), "Occupational Diversification among Rural Groups: A Case Study of Rural Transformation in Tamil Nadu", *Economic and Political Weekly*, Vol. 32, No. 30.

Satyanarayanan, T.V., (2001), "Technology Transfer for Transformation of Rural Areas", *Yojana*, Vol. 45, No. 1.

Shukla, R.K. and Brahmankar, S.D., (1996), *Impact Evaluation of Operation Flood on Rural Dairy Sector*, New Delhi: National Council of Applied Economic Research.

Singh, Ajit Kumar, (1984), "Dynamics of Rural Transformation in UP: Some Preliminary Findings", *Man and Development*, Vol. 6, No. 1.

Somayajulu, V.V.N. and Mahanth, K., (1984), "Rural Transformation in Two Districts of Andhra Pradesh", *Social Change*, Vol. 14, No. 4.

Singh, Surjit, (1996), "Rural Social Transformation in India: Some Thoughts", *Anvesak*, Vol. 26, No. 1.

Vyas, V.S., (1989), "Occupational Diversification in Rural Areas: An Aspect of Rural Transformation", *IASSI Quarterly*, Vol. 8, No. 1.

Waldie, Kevin and Ramkumar, (2002), *Landless Women and Dairying: The Opportunities for Development within a Poverty Perspective*, Rajiv Gandhi College of Veterinary and Animal Sciences, Pondicherry, India.

21 Land and Dalits

A Village Study

E. KRISHNA RAO

Agriculture plays a vital role in the process of economic development of a country particularly, in the initial stages of development. Agriculture, in addition to supplying required food and fodder, also promotes industrial development by supplying necessary raw materials. Agriculture growth promotes the purchasing power of the agricultural workers and thereby increases the demand for industrial goods leading to industrial development and increase in non-farm employment. This important agriculture sector development is essentially depends on the land tenure system, availability of irrigation and other inputs like fertility of land and technology. Land being a factor of production in all the stages of the economy and it also plays a diabolical role in the life of rural people. Being the main source of subsistence, land is metamorphosed into a socio-economic reality. After the Second World War, number of the free nations emerged, predominantly having agrarian economy. As a result, most of the countries went gone for the land reforms to reduce the existed inequalities in the land distribution pattern. Socialist countries like China decided for the elimination of landlordism by bringing all land under the control of the state, wherein Japan under the occupation army headed by General Mac Arthur and Taiwan eliminated the feudalism, demolished non-farming landlordism, protected the tenants and ensured egalitarian redistribution of land under the leadership of President Chiang Kai Shek (Sukumar Das, 2000). Meanwhile democratic countries like India also implemented several land reforms to reduce inequalities in land distribution pattern and bring out the economic equality in the Indian society.

The Indian agrarian structure has been characterized by great inequalities in the ownership of land. A small number of big landlords owned large extent of land while millions of marginal and small peasants owned small amount of land. And also the Indian agriculture has close relation with the caste hierarchy, large landowners belonged to the so-called upper castes, the cultivators belonged to the middle castes and the agricultural workers mostly belonged to the weaker sections such as Scheduled Castes and Scheduled Tribes. Under these peculiar conditions, after the independence, Indian government gave top priority to the abolition of intermediatery land tenure system. At the time of independence in India, agricultural land was administered under three systems such as

Zamindari, Mahalwari and *Rayotwari*. The Zamindari system covered nearly 57 per cent of land, the Mahalwari system prevalent 5 per cent of land and Rayotwari system covered nearly 38 per cent of land. In the intermediary system by fixing abnormal rents Zamindars used to extract surplus from the peasants. The Zamindars were required to pay only fixed amount in terms of land tax to government, the rest they use it for their extravaganza. The Zamindars never showed interest in the development of the land and also never participated in the process of production. On the other hand the tenants also did not pay interest to develop the land due to several reasons such as: (i) They have no control over the piece of land, which was cultivated by them for any stipulated time as it can be taken away by Zamindars at any time and it may leased out to other person without showing any reason. (ii) Even if a tenant produce more, it was quite likely that it might be appropriate by Zamindars by collecting high rents in the absence of any rent regulation. The Indian government felt that to protect the interest of the tillers to land and to bring the equity in the agriculture, the abolition of intermediatery land tenure system was necessary. Even the five year plans also gave the top priority to land reforms which included abolition of intermediaries, tenancy reforms, imposition of ceilings on landholdings and distribution of surplus land, allotment of government land, consolidation of holdings and protection of lands of Scheduled Castes and Tribes (Nancharaiah, 2000).

At the initial stage of implementation of intermediary land tenure abolition act, Zamindars resisted by moving to courts. Indeed the Indian government could overcome their resistance through necessary constitutional amendment in early 1951. Moreover the Zamindars were economically strong but politically weak and they were away from the people and land as they were mostly living in urban areas and enjoying their wealth. These factors helped the government to overcome the resistance of Zamindars and successfully abolished the intermediary land tenure system. The Andhra Pradesh state has peculiar features than India. The Andhra Pradesh state has been constituted with three distinct regions. The Telangana region has a high proportion of tenancy due to the prevalence of pervasive absentee landlordism. The costal Andhra was marked by high density of population, and ownership of land has generally been restricted to less than half of the households, and a large proletariat has existed. The Rayalaseema region has a high incidence of tenancy and a large number of poor owning small plots of land. With this background in Andhra Pradesh, several land legislations have been made to augment the production and to reduce the inequalities in the distribution of land. The following are the most important of them:

1. Andhra Pradesh (Andhra Area) Estates Land (Reduction of Rent) Act, 1947: The major objective of this Act was to provide for reduction of rents payable to *ryots* in estates approximately to the level of assessment levied of lands in Ryotwari area in the neighbourhood.
2. The Madras Estate (Abolition and Conversion into *Ryotwari*) Act, 1948: It provided for the repeal of the permanent settlement, the acquisition of the rights of land: holders in permanently settled and certain other estates in the province of Andhra and the introduction of the *Ryotwari* settlement in

such estates. 'Estate' means a Zamindari or under-tenure or an *Inam* Estate. This Act extends to the whole of the state of Andhra.

3. The Andhra Pradesh (Telangana Area) Tenancy and Agricultural Lands Act, 1950. The major objectives of this Act are: (1) to regulate the relations of landlords and tenants of agricultural lands (2) to regulate alienations of land (3) to prevent excessive sub-division of agricultural holdings (4) to provide for the legislation of co-operative farm, and (5) to empower government to assume in certain circumstances management of agricultural lands.
4. Andhra *Inams* (Abolition and Conversion into Ryotwari) Act, 1956 to abolish and convert certain *Inam* lands into Ryotwari lands. It extends to the whole of the state of Andhra but applies only to *Inam* lands.
5. Andhra Tenancy Act of 1956 provides for the payment of fair rent by cultivating tenants and for fixing the minimum period of agricultural leases in the state
6. The Andhra Pradesh ceiling on Agricultural Holdings Act, 1961 provides for the imposition of ceiling on agricultural holdings ranging from 27 acres to 324 acres depending upon the class of land.
7. The Andhra Pradesh Land Reform (ceiling on Agricultural Holdings) Act, 1972, which provides for a ceiling areas of one standard holding ranging from 4.05 hectares (10 acres) to 10.93 hectares (about 27 acres) in the case of wetland and from 14–16 hectares (35 acres) to 21–85 hectares (54 acres) in case of dry land.

With the aim of providing minimum source of income and promote social and economic status of the poor landless people, the government distributed the surplus land made available from land ceiling. As on September 30, 1996, about 52.13 lakh acres had been distributed at all India level. Of these, about 18.08 lakh acres of land was distributed to SCs, 7.31 lakh acres to STs and 26.74 lakh acres to non-SC/ST persons. A total of 51.21 lakh beneficiaries have been so far covered of which 18.49 lakh were SCs, 7.19 lakh STs and 25.53 lakh non-SC/STs. The land distribution per beneficiary in the SC category household comes to 0.977 acres, which was less than corresponding 1.047 acres for non-SC/ST households (Thorat, 2001). The extent of land redistribution was 43 per cent of agricultural land in China, 37 per cent in Taiwan, 32 per cent in South Korea and 33 per cent in Japan, whereas in India it was only 1.23 per cent of the operational area. At Andhra Pradesh state level as on September 30,1996 an area of about 5.90 lakh acres was distributed among 5.21 lakh beneficiaries. Out of which, 41.51 per cent were SCs, 17.7 per cent were STs, 32.9 per cent were BCs and OCs were 8.01 per cent at Andhra Pradesh state level. At the time of early reforms 4,42,750 declarations were filed, out of which surplus land was detected in only 64,911 cases, covering an area of 16.63 lakh acres. Based on appeals, revisions, major sons' share, etc., the net surplus land was reduced to about 8.21 lakh acres. Out of this surplus land, possession of only 5.91 lakh acres was taken over by the government, leaving a balance of 2.29 lakh acres yet to be taken over at Andhra Pradesh state alone (Venkata Subbaiah, 2004). It is estimated that all efforts taken together including *Bhoodan* and distribution of government wasteland accounted for less than 10 per cent of the cultivated land (Shankaran, 1994). The small magnitude of the declared surplus was due mainly to the poor legislation with large number of loopholes. Thus, the opportunity for a more equitable distribution of land was missed. Land reforms in India abolished all forms of intermediataries in terms of landholdings viz., *Zamindari, Inamdari* and *landlord* system. Those tilling the lands at the time of the abolition of intermediatars were conferred ownership rights and tenants were given protection. The protection and enlargement of control and command over land are crucial issue for the poor. It may not be possible that all rural poor can be accommodated but there is scope for utilizing the wasteland for providing access to the poor and also eliminating the biases against the poor in land relations. The desire to possess land is strong among the poor as ownership of land denotes one's social status. As per 1995–96 agricultural census report, 72 per cent of SCs recorded as agricultural labourers. Due to loopholes of land reforms, still most of the land is concentrated among some castes and classes.

With this background in this paper, an attempt has been made to analyze the land distribution pattern of Andhra Pradesh state level in general, particular to Dalit community as well as at village level. It also examines the impact of landlessness on socio and economic conditions of Dalits at micro level, and factors affecting the landlessness of Dalits. This study observe land holding particulars for ten years period, i.e., 1989–90 to 1998–99 at village level and 1970–71 to 1995–96 at Andhra Pradesh state level. For this study we have selected a hamlet namely Jammula Palem from Prakasam district to observe the land distribution pattern and occupational distribution and estimate the Dalits' socio-economic position. The present study is based mainly on primary and secondary data. The primary data on operational holding, occupational distribution, labour employment and wages etc., collected at the village level. These primary data are collected from the village through interviewing the heads of the selected households. Out of the total village households of 760, the number of sample households are 95, i.e., 13 per cent from each category of households in the village. The 95 households are selected on the basis of 'random sampling method'. Out of which landless households are 33 (28 from SC and 5 from BC), marginal farmers households are 30 (3 from BC and 27 from OC), small farmers households are 20 (17 from OC and 3 from BC), medium farmers households are 9 (8 from OC and 1 from BC) and large farmers households are 3 (all from OC).

Here we have divided sampling households into five groups such as:

(1) Landless labourers[1] (those who are not having land)
(2) Marginal farmers (who are having 0.1 acres—2.5 acres of land)
(3) Small farmers (who are having 2.51 acres—5 acres of land)
(4) Medium farmers (who are having 5.1 acres—10 acres of land) and
(5) Large farmers (who are having 10 acres or above land). We also used the Gini-coefficient technique to calculate the land distribution variation between Dalit community and other communities.

Land Distribution Pattern at Andhra Pradesh State Level by Sizewise and Social Groupwise

Let us examine the land distribution pattern of Andhra Pradesh state level since 1970–71 to 1991–92 with respect of operational holdings and ownership holdings. These data on distribution of operational holdings is revealing itself. But it could be more useful to consider the distribution of ownership holdings thrown up by National Sample Survey Organisation (NSSO). The land reform laws enacted in the state, though could not lead to realization of much surplus land, they have had the effects of blocking further accumulation of land by the big landlords. It could be observed from the Table 1 that the marginal holdings constitute 47.29 per cent of the total holdings but control only 9.28 per cent of total operated area in 1970–71. Small holdings constitute 19.4 per cent of total holdings and control 11.74 per cent of total operated area. Marginal and small holdings together constitute 66 per cent of total holdings but control nearly 21 per cent of total operated area in 1970–71. On the other hand, medium and large holdings together constitute about 14 per cent of total holdings but control 57 per cent of total operated area during the same period. This shows that at Andhra Pradesh state level also land distribution skewed in 1970–71. By 1991–92, marginal holdings significantly increased. Their percentage in total holdings increased to nearly 60 per cent but area operated under their control increased to 18 per cent of total operated area. On the other hand, medium and large holdings declined to 6 per cent but they control 33 per cent of total operated area. It indicates that during 1970–71 to 1991–92 inequalities in the land distribution increased despite land reforms. In case of ownership holdings same thing retain during 1970–71 to 1991–92. Marginal and small ownership holdings increased from 79 per cent to 88.8 per cent but controlling area increased from 23 per cent to 43.7 per cent during the same period. On other hand, medium and large ownership holdings declined from 10 per cent to 3.7 per cent and their controlling area decreased from 55.7 per cent to 32 per cent of total own area during the same period (Table 3).

Table 1 *Operational Holdings and Operated Area by Different Size Groups in Andhra Pradesh State Level, 1976–77 to 1995–96 (Nos. in lakh, Area in lakh hect.)*

Size group	*1976–77*		*1980–81*		*1986–87*		*1990–91*		*1995–96*	
	Nos	*Area*	*Nos*	*Area*	*Nos*	*Area*	*Nos*	*Area*	*Nos*	*Area*
Marginal	28.69 (46.6)	13.36 (9.3)	38.04 (51.6)	18.86 (13.1)	44.6 (54.1)	20.54 (14.5)	52.11 (56.1)	23.69 (16.4)	63.0 (59.4)	29.04 (20.2)
Small	12.52 (20.3)	18.36 (12.8)	15.91 (21.6)	24.12 (16.8)	17.14 (20.8)	24.54 (17.3)	19.72 (21.2)	28.26 (19.5)	22.62 (21.3)	32.29 (22.5)
Semi-medium	10.72 (17.4)	29.93 (20.8)	11.74 (16.0)	32.61 (22.7)	12.54 (15.2)	33.91 (23.9)	13.45 (14.5)	36.4 (25.2)	13.95 (13.1)	37.36 (26.0)
Medium	7.53 (12.2)	46.47 (32.3)	6.46 (8.8)	39.79 (27.8)	6.57 (7.98)	38.65 (27.2)	6.44 (6.93)	37.77 (26.1)	5.63 (5.3)	32.31 (22.5)
Large	2.09 (3.4)	35.68 (24.8)	1.55 (2.10)	27.95 (19.5)	1.46 (1.77)	23.94 (16.9)	1.18 (1.27)	18.48 (12.8)	0.83 (0.8)	12.73 (8.85)
All	61.55 (100)	143.8 (100)	73.7 (100)	143.33 (100)	82.3 (100)	141.5 (100)	92.9 (100)	144.6 (100)	106.3 (100)	143.7 (100)

Source: Report on Agricultural Census of Andhra Pradesh, 1995–96.

Note: Figures in parentheses indicates the percentage.

Table 2 *Percentage Distributions of Operational Holdings and Operated Area according to Size-Class of Andhra Pradesh State: NSSO (rural)*

Size-class (ha)	1970–71		1981–82		1991–92	
	Nos	Area	Nos	Area	Nos	Area
Marginal (below 1.0)	47.29	9.28	48.64	10.25	59.27	17.54
Small (1.0 to 2.0)	19.14	11.74	22.13	15.37	21.38	23.34
Semi-medium (2.0 to 4.0)	18.23	21.91	15.51	21.08	13.16	26.23
Medium (4.0 to 10.0)	11.87	31.32	10.80	60.20	5.38	23.49
Large (10.0 and above)	3.47	25.75	2.92	23.10	0.81	9.40
All classes	100.0	100.0	100.0	100.0	100.0	100.0

Source: Various NSSO reports on landholdings of Andhra Pradesh

Table 3 *Percentage Distributions of Ownership Holdings and Area Owned According to Size-class for Andhra Pradesh State: NSSO (Rural)*

Size-class (ha)	1970–71		1981–82		1991–92	
	Nos	Area	Nos	Area	Nos	Area
Marginal (below 1.0)	65.30	9.92	67.49	11.26	76.41	21.30
Small (1.0 to 2.0)	13.65	13.16	14.03	15.29	12.35	22.44
Semi-medium (2.0 to 4.0)	11.22	21.19	10.01	20.70	7.46	24.15
Medium (4.0 to 10.0)	7.57	30.15	6.69	29.83	3.38	24.06
Large (10.0 and above)	2.26	25.58	1.78	22.92	0.39	8.06
All classes	100.0	100.0	100.0	100.0	100.0	100.0

Source: Various NSSO reports on landholdings of Andhra Pradesh

Gini-coefficients for operational and ownership holdings (rural) at Andhra Pradesh level by NSSO for different years are presented in the Table 4. Gini coefficient slightly decreased from 0.603 to 0.599 in 1970–71 to 1981–82 and further decreased to 0.576 in 1991–92 in case of operational holdings. In case of ownership holdings Gini-concentration increased to 0.73 in 1970–71 to 0.74 in 1981–82 and further retains it in 1991–92 respectively.

Table 4 *Gini-coefficient of Operational and Ownership Holdings*

Year	Operational holdings*	Year	Operational holdings**	Ownership holdings**
1976–77	0.572	1970–71	0.603	0.73
1980–81	0.552	1981–82	0.599	0.74
1986–87	0.545	1991–92	0.576	0.72
1990–91	0.528			
1995–96	0.498			

Source: Table 1 and NSSO report 1992.
Note: *As per agricultural census data,
** As per NSSO data

Dalits and Agriculture

Dalits comprise scheduled castes and scheduled tribes population. About three-fourths of the SCs live in rural areas where the main source of income is either cultivation of agricultural land (as self-employed farmer), wage labour or some type of non-farm wage of self-employment. As per 1991 census, scheduled castes constitute 15.93 per cent of the total population and scheduled tribes constitute 6.31 per cent of total population at Andhra Pradesh state level. About 17.31 per cent of SC population and 7.60 per cent of ST population live in urban areas as against 26.9 per cent of general population that is more than 83 per cent of SC population and about 93 per cent of ST population lives in rural areas as against 63 per cent of general population. Almost 25.89 per cent of SC population and 13.66 per cent of ST population are literates as against 44 per cent of general population that is more than 74 per cent of SC population and about 86.4 per cent of ST population are illiterates as against 56 per cent of general population. The work participation rate of SCs, defined as the percentage of SC population participating in the work of total scheduled caste population is 51.08 per cent and that of STs is 54.03 per cent as against 45 per cent among general population in 1991. This may happen due to the high participation rate among SC (46.7%) and ST (50.65%) women. It is also to be noted that as per 1991 census, 85 per cent of SC main workers and 83 per cent of ST main workers depend on primary sector only 68 per cent of general workers depend upon primary sector. More than 72 per cent of SC main workers and about 44 per cent of ST main workers were reported as agricultural labour as against only 41 per cent among general workers (Statistical Abstract of Andhra Pradesh, 2000). With the high dependency of SC/ST on agriculture, let us examine the landholding situation and occupational distribution of Dalits at Andhra Pradesh state level.

Table 5 *Percentage Distribution of Operational Holdings and Operated Area of Different Social Groups in Andhra Pradesh*

Category	*1976–77*		*1980–81*		*1986–87*		*1990–91*		*1995–96*	
	Nos	*Area*	*Nos*	*Area*	*Nos*	*Area*	*Nos*	*Area*	*Nos*	*Area*
SC	13.4	6.9	12.6	6.9	12.2	6.8	12.73	7.48	12.12	7.42
ST	6.3	6.2	6.4	6.3	6.4	6.7	6.88	7.23	7.11	7.56
Others	80.3	86.9	81.0	86.8	81.4	86.5	80.39	85.29	80.77	85.02
Total	100.0	100.0	100.0	100.0	100.0	100.0	100.0	100.0	100.0	100.0

Source: Various issues of Report on SC/ST Land Holdings.

Table 5 explains the operational holdings and area operated by different groups since 1976–77 to 1995–96 at Andhra Pradesh state level. It could be seen from the table in 1976–77 SC households constituted about 13.4 per cent of total holdings but control only 6.9 per cent of the area, while others constitute about 80.3 per cent of total holdings but control 87 per cent of total operated area in 1976–77. By 1995–96 the percentage of SC holdings declined to about 12 per cent and their controlling area share slightly increased to 7.4 per cent. While the percentage of others holdings retain same, i.e., 80.7 per cent and their operated area share slightly declined to 85 per cent of total operated area. In 1976–77, ST operational holdings constituted 6.3 per cent of total holdings and control 6.2 per cent of total operated area. By 1995–96 their holdings increased to more than 7 per cent while their share in area also increased to 7.5 per cent. The position of ST households in terms of operational holdings is better than SC households at Andhra Pradesh state level as well as all-India level.

It could be seen from the Table 6 that, most of the SC farmers are marginal and small. In 1976–77 marginal and small holdings of SCs constituted 83 per cent (control nearly 46% of total operated area of SCs) of total holdings and their percentage tremendously increased to about 91 per cent (control nearly 67% of total operated area of SCs) in 1995–96. On the other hand, medium and large holdings declined from 4.7 per cent (control nearly 29% of total operated area of SCs) to 1.4 per cent (control nearly 10% of total operated area of SCs) during the same period. Their average size of holdings also significantly decreased from 1.19 hectares to 0.83 hectares during the same period (Table 7). In 1976–77, marginal and small holdings of STs constituted 59 per cent of total ST holdings and their percentage also significantly increased to about 77 per cent in 1995–96. On the other hand, medium and large holdings declined from 16.6 per cent to 10 per cent during the same period. Their average size of holdings also significantly declined from 2.32 hectares to 1.44 hectares during the same period (Table 9). One can conclude from these tables most of the SCs and STs are marginal and small farmers, since 1976–77 to 1995–96 their controlling area also decreasing. Due to lack of irrigation facilities, high cost of cultivation, high cost of mechanization, these vulnerable sections were loosing control on their lands. Most of the SCs and STs are selling their land to other caste people and becoming as agricultural labourers for their livelihood.

Table 6 *Percentage Distribution of Operational Holdings and Area Operated by Scheduled Castes in Andhra Pradesh*

Size group	*1976–77*		*1980–81*		*1986–87*		*1990–91*		*1995–96*	
	Nos	*Area*	*Nos*	*Area*	*Nos*	*Area*	*Nos*	*Area*	*Nos*	*Area*
Marginal	64.8	22.3	67.7	27.6	70.1	30.4	70.67	31.98	73.46	37.15
Small	19.0	23.1	18.9	26.2	18.0	26.4	18.43	28.28	17.75	29.74
Semi-medium	11.5	26.0	10.2	25.2	9.1	24.5	8.70	24.40	7.39	22.51
Medium	4.1	21.5	2.9	15.2	2.5	14.6	2.03	12.38	1.32	8.82
Large	0.6	7.1	0.3	5.5	0.3	4.1	0.17	2.96	0.08	1.78
All groups	100.0	100.0	100.0	100.0	100.0	100.0	100.0	100.0	100.0	100.0

Source: Various issues of Report on SC/ST Land Holdings.

Table 7 *Average Size of the Hoperated by Scheduled Castes (in hectares)*

Size groups	*1976–77*	*1980–81*	*1986–87*	*1990–91*	*1995–96*
Marginal	0.41	0.43	0.41	0.41	0.42
Small	1.45	1.46	1.40	1.40	1.39
Semi-medium	2.69	2.62	2.56	2.56	2.53
Medium	6.21	5.66	5.59	5.58	5.53
Large	14.65	16.48	14.41	16.00	19.00
All groups	1.19	1.06	0.95	0.91	0.83

Source: Various issues of Report on SC/ST Land Holdings.

Table 8 *Percentage Distribution of Operational Holdings and Area Operated by Scheduled Tribes in Andhra Pradesh*

Size group	*1976–77*		*1980–81*		*1986–87*		*1990–91*		*1995–96*	
	Nos	*Area*	*Nos*	*Area*	*Nos*	*Area*	*Nos*	*Area*	*Nos*	*Area*
Marginal	38.2	8.5	43.8	11.7	45.9	12.4	47.83	14.36	51.59	17.94
Small	21.0	13.3	23.1	17.2	23.2	18.6	24.80	21.65	25.33	24.84
Semi-medium	24.2	27.2	21.6	30.0	20.3	29.5	18.90	30.70	16.98	31.0
Medium	14.3	35.5	10.2	31.0	9.4	29.7	7.67	26.49	5.70	21.90
Large	2.3	15.5	1.30	10.1	1.2	9.8	0.80	6.80	0.40	4.32
All groups	100.0	100.0	100.0	100.0	100.0	100.0	100.0	100.0	100.0	100.0

Source: Various issues of Report on SC/ST Land Holdings.

Table 9 *Average Size of the Holdings Operated by Scheduled Tribes (in hectares)*

Size groups	*1976–77*	*1980–81*	*1986–87*	*1990–91*	*1995–96*
Marginal	0.52	0.51	0.49	0.49	0.50
Small	1.47	1.42	1.44	1.43	1.41
Semi-medium	2.62	2.65	2.62	2.66	2.63
Medium	5.82	5.77	5.70	5.65	5.53
Large	15.62	14.49	14.47	13.72	15.67
All groups	2.33	1.91	1.80	1.64	1.44

Source: Various issues of Report on SC/ST Land Holdings.

Occupational Distribution among Different Social Groups

The changes in the occupational distribution during 1971–1991 at Andhra Pradesh state level for different social groups could be seen from the Table 10. It is evident from the table that during 1971 to 1981 there was an increase in the percentage of SC workers as cultivators from 14.66 per cent to 17.41 per cent while percentage of SC agricultural labourers declined from 73.04 per cent to 68.24 per cent. In case of general workers, the percentage of cultivators declined from 34.43 per cent to 32.73 per cent. Percentage of agricultural labourers also declined from 38.24 per cent to 36.78 during the same period. Regarding the non-farming workers, it increased from 12.3 per cent to 14.35 per cent in case of SC workers, while it increased from 27.3 per cent to 30.49 per cent in case of general workers. Thus, there is some marginal improvement in the SC workers as cultivators and also non-farming workers. This indicates some upward mobility of SC workers also. This may be attributed to redistribution of wasteland and surplus land under 20–Point Programme in 1970s (Nancharaiah, 2000). But during 1981–1991 the percentage of SC cultivators declined from 17.4 per cent to 12.77 per cent, while there was an increase in the percentage of SC agricultural labourers from 68.24 per cent to 72.05 per cent. In case of workers of general population also, percentage of cultivators declined from 32.73 per cent to 27.44 per cent while the percentage of agricultural labour increased from 36.78 per cent to 40.78 per cent. Percentage of non-farming workers increased from 30.49 per cent to 31.69 per cent indicating occupational shift. In case of STs, there was significant increase of cultivators from 37.05 per cent to 43.21 per cent while the percentage of agricultural labour declined from 50.40 per cent to 43.72 per cent during 1971–1981, by 1981–91 the percentage of cultivators slightly declined from 43.21 per cent to 41.19 per cent while the percentage of agricultural labour increased from 43.72 per cent to 46.52 per cent. Anyhow during 1971 to 1981, their share in non-farming workers increased from 12.55 per cent to 13.07 per cent and again it declined to 12.29 per cent in 1991. This shows that at Andhra Pradesh state level agricultural workers were slowly shifting to non-farming activities. The above analysis reveals that in Andhra Pradesh state level most of the Dalits are landless and they totally depend upon their agricultural labour work for their livelihood. The implemented land reforms also could not provide more land to the needy persons. In this connection let us examine the Dalits socio-economic position at micro level, i.e., village level.

Table 10 *Occupational Distributions at Andhra Pradesh State Level*

Category	*Percentage in total main workers of SCs*			*Percentage in total main workers of STs*			*Percentage in total main workers general population*		
	1971	*1981*	*1991*	*1971*	*1981*	*1991*	*1971*	*1981*	*1991*
Cultivators	14.66	17.41	12.77	37.05	43.21	41.19	32.45	32.73	27.44
Agri. labourers	73.04	68.24	72.05	50.40	43.72	46.52	38.24	36.78	40.87
Non-farming workers	12.3	14.35	15.81	12.55	13.07	12.29	29.31	30.49	31.69

Source: Statistical Abstract of Andhra Pradesh, 1971, 1981, 1991

Socio and Economic Conditions of the Selected Hamlet

For this study we have selected a hamlet namely Jammula Palem from Prakasam district. Jammula Palem is a multi-caste village, inhabited by Brahman, Kamma, Muslim, Komati Yadava, Kamsali and Mala castes. Kammas are politically and economically dominated caste in the hamlet. This hamlet is totally agriculture hamlet. The total hamlet is constituted with 760 households, out of which 260 households are landless (200 from SCs and 60 from other castes) and remaining 500 households have land. A very important feature is that the total scheduled caste (200 households constitute about 26 per cent of total households) households are depending upon their labour work for their subsistence because no one has land and after the agricultural season they go for work in tobacco companies. Out of 500 landholders 238 are marginal farmers, 182 are small farmers, 60 are medium farmers and 20 are large farmers. The total arable area of the hamlet is about 1,329 acres. The major crops of this hamlet are tobacco, eucalyptus, paddy, sesamum and subable. The total hamlet is constituted with 3,585 persons. Out of 3,585, 1,789 (49.9%) is male and the rest of 1,796 (50.09%) is female. By social group among the total population 1160 are SCs of which 49.15 per cent are males and 50.86 per cent are females (Table 11). Male literacy level (55.25%) is more than the female literacy (44.74%) level in 1998–99 irrespect of social group in the hamlet. Out of 1,160, SC persons 549 literates (59% male and 41% female) and 611 (40% male and 60% female) peoples illiterates. Among BCs, out of 719 persons 392 are literates (60% male and 40% female) and 327 are (40% male and 60% female) illiterates, whereas out of 1,706 OC persons 885 are (51% male and 49% female) literates and 821 are (49.4% male and 50.5% female) illiterates during 1998–99. In this hamlet BC (54.52%) and OC (51.8%) social group literacy level is higher than the SCs (47.32%) literacy level. Social and economic backwardness may be one of the reasons for high illiteracy among the SC households.

Table 11 *Population Particulars of Selected Hamlet*

Social group	*SC*	*BC*	*Others*	*Total*
No.of HH	200 (26.31)	130 (17.1)	430 (56.57)	760 (100)
Male	570	363	856	1,789 (49.4)
Female	590	356	850	1,796 (50.09)
Total population	1,160 (32.5) (100)	719 (20.0) (100)	1,706 (47.53) (100)	3,585 (100.0)
Literates	549 (47.08)	392 (54.52)	885 (51.87)	1,826 (100.0)
Male	324	235	450	1,009 (55.25)
Female	225	157	435	817 (44.34)
Illiterates	611 (52.40)	327 (45.4)	821 (48.12)	1,759 (100.0)
Male	246	128	406	780 (44.34)
Female	365	199	415	979 (55.65)

Source: Household Survey by Author, 2000,V.A.O, Jammula Palem.

Note: Figures in parentheses indicates the percentages.

Table 12 *Social Groupwise Percentages of Literates and Illiterates in Selected Hamlet*

Social group	*Percentage in total population of SCs*		*Percentage in total population of BCs*		*Percentage in total population of OCs*		*Total*	
	Male	*Female*	*Male*	*Female*	*Male*	*Female*	*Male*	*Female*
Literates	59.0	40.9	59.9	40.0	50.8	49.1	55.25	44.74
Illiterates	40.2	59.1	39.1	60.8	49.4	50.5	44.34	55.65
Total	100.0	100.0	100.0	100.0	100.0	100.0	100.0	100.0

Source: Household Survey by Author, 2000, VAO, Jammula Palem.

Land Distribution Pattern of the Selected Hamlet

Table 13 presents the land distribution pattern of selected hamlet since 1989–90 to 1998–99. Marginal and smallholdings together constitute nearly 53 per cent of total holdings but control about 45 per cent of total operated area in 1989–90. On the other hand, medium and large holdings constitute nearly 15 per cent of total holdings but control about 55 per cent of total operated area during the same period. This implies that land distribution was skewed in 1989–90 in the hamlet. By 1998–99 marginal and smallholdings slightly increased to 55.2 per cent under their control area also slightly increased to 54.69 per cent. On the other hand, medium and large holdings declined to 10.5 per cent of total holdings but control nearly 45.29 per cent of total area. 10.5 per cent of medium and large holdings controlling 45.29 per cent of total land indicate that in the hamlet land has been under the control of few landlords. We can get the clear picture from the Table 14. It explains the social groupwise land distribution pattern of the hamlet in 1998–99. This hamlet constituted with 26.3 per cent of SC households, 17.10 per cent of BC households and 56.57 per cent of OC households. These 26.31 per cent of SC households are not controlling single cent of land, these all are landless labourers. About 17 per cent of BC households are controlling 14.29 per cent of total land and remaining 85.70 per cent of land is controlled by 56.57 per cent OC households in 1998–99. Since long time, these 26.31 per cent of SC households are not having land and they totally depend upon their labour work. One of the SC respondent reported that he had 5 acres of land 15 years back, but he sold it to Kamma farmers due to lack of investment. 20 Komati caste families reported that during 1989–90, they were controlling land but after that they sold it because they shifted from agriculture to commerce and trade activities. These community people are running some shops and they are giving money to the farmers during the cultivation season at higher interest rates. In this hamlet, the land has been transferred from non-cultivated communities to cultivated communities, moreover the land has been transferring between the non-SCs only. In this hamlet the Andhra Pradesh state government has been distributed the house plots to SC, BC and OCs. But till now the government has not taken any initiative action to implement the land ceiling act and distribute the cultivable land to the SCs, who are the landless.

Table 13 *Land Holdings of Selected Hamlet*

Size of holdings	1989–90		1994–95		1998–99	
	Number	Area	Number	Area	Number	Area
Landless	245 (32.2)	—	260 (34.2)	—	260 (34.21)	—
Marginal	228 (30.0)	170 (12.8)	235 (30.9)	248 (18.7)	238 (31.31)	265 (19.9)
Small	172 (22.6)	430 (32.3)	180 (23.7)	456 (34.3)	182 (23.9)	462 (34.8)
Medium	89 (11.7)	455 (34.2)	65 (8.5)	395 (29.7)	60 (7.9)	372 (28.0)
Large	26 (3.4)	274 (20.6)	20 (2.6)	230 (17.3)	20 (2.6)	230 (17.3)
Total	760 (100)	1,329 (100)	760 (100)	1,329 (100)	760 (100)	1,329 (100)

Source: Household Survey by Author, 2000, VAO, Jammula Palem.
Note: Figures in parentheses indicates the percentages.

Gini-coefficients for operational holdings of selected hamlet are presented in Table 15. It could be seen from the table that Gini-coefficient slightly decreased from 0.62 in 1989–90 to 0.60 in 1994–95 and further retains it in 1998–99 respectively (including landless). If we exclude landless, Gini-coefficient slightly decreased from 0.44 in 1989–90 to 0.40 in 1994–95 and further it decreased to 0.39 in 1998–99 respectively.

One can estimate the socio and economic position of households through literacy and earning position. Tables 16 and 17 present the literacy and earning position of 95 sample households. The total population of sample 95 households stands as 534 persons. The total land of sample households was 269 acres, of which 1 acre is not cultivable and remaining land was cultivated in 1998–99. The average size of land holdings is 4.33 acres. It is 2.83 acres if landless households are included. For marginal farmers it is 1.56 acres, whereas for the large farmers it is 16.50 acres. Large holdings, which constitute about 3 per cent of total holdings, control about 20 per cent of the total land, while marginal holdings, which constitute about 32 per cent of total number of holdings control only about 19 per cent of the total land. This indicates that the distribution of land is skewed in the village under study. Out of the total 534 sample population, the numbers of literates are 292 (54.68%) and remaining 242 (45.31%) persons are illiterates. Among the samples high illiteracy rate has been concentrated (58.04%) among the landless labourers. The literacy level among the small farmers shows the highest (60.83%) by 59.25 per cent medium, 58.04 per cent marginal and 54.68 per cent among large farmers. Economic backwardness may be one of the reasons for high illiteracy rate among the landless labourers. The number of earners and dependents among different size groups of sample farmers has been presented in the Table 16. Out of the total 534 sample population earners are 392 (73.40%) persons and dependents are 142 (26.59%). The percentage of dependents in case of landless labourers is highest (35.35%). This shows the poor economic condition of this group. The dependents percentage among other category of farmers like marginal, small, medium and large is 20.97 per cent, 23.33 per cent, 20.37 per cent and 15.78 per cent respectively.

Table 14 *Social Groupwise Land Holdings in Selected Village, 1998–99*

Size of holding	*Social group*							
	SC		*BC*		*OC*		*Total*	
	Nos.	*Area*	*Nos.*	*Area*	*Nos.*	*Area*	*Nos.*	*Area*
Landless	200 (76.9) (100)	—	40 (15.4) (30.8)	—	20 (7.7) (4.6)	—	260 (100) (34.21)	—
Marginal	—	—	42 (17.6) (32.3)	39 (14.7) (20.5)	196 (82.4) (45.6)	226 (85.3) (19.8)	238 (100) (31.31)	265 (100) (19.9)
Small	—	—	38 (20.9) (29.2)	95 (20.5) (50.0)	144 (79.1) (33.5)	367 (79.5) (32.2)	182 (100) (23.90)	462 (100) (34.8)
Medium	—	—	10 (16.7) (7.7)	56 (15.0) (29.5)	50 (83.3) (11.6)	316 (85.0) (27.7)	60 (100) (7.89)	372 (100) (28.0)
Large	—	—	—	—	20 (100) (4.6)	230 (100) (20.2)	20 (100) (2.6)	230 (100) (17.3)
Total	200 (26.3) (100)	—	130 (17.1) (100)	190 (14.3) (100)	430 (100) (100)	1,139 (100) (100)	760 (100) (100)	1,329 (100) (100)

Source: Household Survey by Author, 2000, V.A.O., Jammula Pale.
Note: Figures in parentheses indicates the percentages.

Table 15 *Gini-coefficient Ratios*

Year	*Including landless*	*Excluding landless*
1989–90	0.621	0.448
1994–95	0.605	0.404
1998–99	0.600	0.394

Source: Computed from Table 14.

Table 16 *Literacy Level among Sample Households*

Size of holdings	*Literates*	*Illiterates*	*Total*
Landless	91 (45.09)	107 (58.04)	198 (100)
Marginal	83 (58.04)	60 (41.95)	143 (100)
Small	73 (60.83)	47 (39.16)	120 (100)
Medium	32 (59.25)	22 (40.74)	54 (100)
Large	13 (54.68)	6 (45.31)	19 (100)
Total	292 (54.68)	242 (45.31)	534 (100)

Source: Household Survey by Author, 2000.

Table 17 *Sizewise Dependents and Earners among Sample Households*

Size of holdings	*Dependents*	*Earners*	*Total*
Landless	70 (35.35)	128 (64.64)	198 (100)
Marginal	30 (20.97)	113 (79.02)	143 (100)
Small	28 (23.33)	92 (76.70)	120 (100)
Medium	11 (20.37)	43 (79.62)	54 (100)
Large	3 (15.78)	16 (84.21)	19 (100)
Total	142 (26.59)	392 (73.40)	534 (100)

Source: Household Survey by Author, 2000.

Wage Determination

The farmers with the consultation of *Mutamastris*[2] generally determine the wage rates after the plantation is over in the hamlet for all crops such as tobacco, paddy and plants. It is found that, each labour group is having one Mutamastri, who controls the entire group. He sends the labour to the work as per requirement. The decision of employment is totally depend upon the Mutamastris. And there is no direct relation between the workers and farmers regarding work and payment. The Mutamastri is working as mediator. Here we observed from field survey that the farmers in front of Mutamastris after the end of plantation season would determine the wages. The wages increase is totally depending upon the farmer's grace and not demand. Here Mutamastri will not play any active role in the determination of wages. Sometimes he requests the farmers to increase the wages, they may agree or may not agree for his proposal. In the determination of wages large farmers (*landlords*) play vital role. If they agree to increase the wages, then only remaining farmers will agree to increase the wages. We observe from the field survey that this type of wage determination system has been developed in this hamlet due to landlessness of labourers (all SCs are landless) and they do not have any other source for work. Due to landlessness only, the labourers are unable to demand the increase of wages as proportionate to their normal consumption. In the hamlet all SC households totally depend upon the labour work for their subsistence. These SC Mutamastris also reported that they use to go neighbour villages for the tobacco plantation, because these villages start little bit earlier than this hamlet, at that time they demand the higher wage from the neighbour village farmers because the relation between Mutamastri as well as labours is tentative. For this work they get wage on the same day itself and more wage than their native village wages. They also provide transport. We observed from the field survey that in their own village these labourers have some informal relation with Kamma landlords, i.e., barrowing money for unexpected expenses such as marriages, health problems and children education, that's these labourers are unable to demand the farmers to increase the wages. This is also observed that the Mutamastri is getting two wages (one as a labour and another one is as Mutamastri), that's why he is also not pressurizing the farmers to increase the wages.

Wage Rates for Different Crops

To calculate the wage rates per day, we have interviewed 3 local Mutamastris, 8 labourers and 20 farmers (i.e., 8 marginal, 5 small, 5 medium and 2 large) additional to the samples. In many areas, the market wages are lower than minimum wages and minimum wages fixed in many states, in turn, are lower than minimum subsistence wage. Although different state governments have revised the minimum wages, the wages fixed still remain very low for the unorganized workers. In most cases, the statutory minimum wages fixed and their revisions do not seem to have taken into consideration the minimum requirements of a worker's family to rise above the poverty line. In many states, the actual wages are 50 per cent of the minimum subsistence wage. According to some calculations, a fair wage works out to Rs 125 per day providing, minimum wages, which forms part of employment security (Dev, 2001).

With this view let us examine the wage situation in the selected hamlet in 1998–99. The overall wage variation is quite high in case of tobacco cultivation. Average wage per day for plant cultivation for male workers was Rs 60 whereas Rs 45 for female worker in 1998–99, in paddy field male labour is getting per day on an average Rs 65 and female labour is getting Rs 46, whereas it is Rs 69 and Rs 50 in tobacco field during the same period. In the case of paddy and tobacco also wages are unequal between male and female worker but the variation is less than the variation in plant cultivation. The highest amount of wage per day is being paid to the male worker for cutting leaves (Rs 80) and curing (Rs 75) of tobacco cultivation. And the lowest amount wage of Rs 25 per day is given to the female workers for grading tobacco (Table 18).

Wage Discrimination

In tobacco, paddy and plants fields male labourer were getting on average Rs 65.74, Rs 62.60 and Rs 55.82 in 1994–95 and it slightly increased to Rs 69.62, Rs 65 and Rs 60.6 per day in 1998–99, whereas female worker were getting Rs 46.10, Rs 42.50 and Rs 41.50 in 1994–95 and it also increased to Rs 50, Rs 46.87 and Rs 45.38 per day in 1998–99 respectively for same work and for same working hours. In this context, we can easily understand in tobacco fields male labourer are getting more wages than other fields, similarly female workers are getting more wages in paddy fields than other crops. In tobacco fields male worker gets wage Rs 50 and female worker gets Rs 45 at the plantation operation, similarly child male labour gets Rs 30 and child female labour gets only Rs 25 per day for the same operation in 1998–99. In paddy cultivation for transplantation male worker gets Rs 60 and female worker gets Rs 50 per day. Here, there is no child labour in paddy. For the pumping of pesticides in tobacco fields and paddy fields male labourer paid a wage of Rs 70 per day in 1998–99. In case of cutting operation, male and female workers are being paid same wages Rs 75 for tobacco cultivation. But in paddy cultivation there is a slight difference between male and female labour wages for reaping operation. For reaping, male worker is paid Rs 55 and female worker is paid Rs 50 per day. For crops (tobacco, paddy and plants) male labour wages are more than female labour wages on an average. Similarly tobacco male (Rs 69.60) and female (Rs 50) labourers are paid higher wage more than in other crops. If we observe the average wages of tobacco, paddy and plants, tobacco labourer are paid higher wage (male Rs 69.60 and female Rs 50) per day than other crops such as paddy (male Rs 65 and female Rs 46.80) and plants (male Rs 60.60 and female Rs 45.30) in 1998–99. It is observed from the study that since 1989–90 to 1998–99 the labour wages has been increasing slightly in all fields such as tobacco, paddy and plants. At the same time the food grains prices (which is staple food for labourers) has been increasing rapidly during the same period.

Table 18 *Daily Wage for Different Operations of Cultivation of Tobacco and Plants in 1989–90, 1994, 1998–99*

(in Rs)

Year	*Paddy*		*Tobacco*		*Plants*	
	Male	*Female*	*Male*	*Female*	*Male*	*Female*
1989–90	—	—	56.5	39.69	49.23	36.36
1990–91	—	—	57.53	40.36	51.23	37.72
1991–92	—	—	59.92	41.81	51.47	37.72
1992–93	—	—	62.32	43.93	53.17	39.54
1993–94	—	—	63.78	43.96	55.23	40.45
1994–95	62.60	42.5	65.74	46.18	55.82	41.54
1995–96	62.75	43.45	65.74	46.18	56.55	41.61
1996–97	63.28	44.95	67.33	47.68	57.94	42.76
1997–98	63.39	46.54	68.92	49.18	59.5	44.38
1998–99	65.0	46.87	69.62	50.0	60.68	45.38

Source: Household Survey by Author, 2000

Employment Opportunities for Different Social Groups

We also calculated the labour employment days per acre by social group for different operations of different crops. It could be seen from the Table 19 that in all crops more female labour is used than male labourers. The female labourers are specialized in some aspects relating to the process of tobacco and paddy cultivation. For example, the grading of tobacco and plantation of paddy for which the female labourers are most efficient than their counterpart male labourers. The labour requirement vary from crop to crop. Paddy crop require (per acre) 43 labour for entire processing whereas tobacco crop need 59 labourers and plants cultivation need only 31 labourers. In the hamlet, social status is also plying a pivotal role in the getting of employment opportunities. For one acre of paddy crop cultivation farmer require 43 labourers, out of total labours they are utilizing 18 from SCs and 25 from other social group (BCs and OCs). In case of tobacco cultivation their requirement is 59, out of which 22 from SCs and 37 from other social labourers. For plant cultivation they need 31 labourers, out of which 11 from SCs and 20 from other social group. In total, these three crops required 133 labourers per one-acre cultivation, out of which 51 SCs and 82 others are getting employment. This shows that SC and other social group labourers are not getting equal employment days in the hamlet. Other social group laboures are getting nearly 31 employment days more than SCs. The SC Mutamastri reported that, at the time peak season only they are getting regular employment. After that the formers are giving first priority to the BCs, if they require more then only the SC labourers will get employment.

One can easily say that the social status is one of the main factors to get labour employment in the hamlet.

Table 19 *Social Groupwise Employment Days in Different Fields*

Social group	*Paddy*			*Tobacco*			*Plants*		
	M	*F*	*T*	*M*	*F*	*T*	*M*	*F*	*T*
SCs	8	10	18	9	13	22	6	5	11
Others	11	14	25	18	19	37	12	8	20
Total	19	24	43	27	32	59	18	13	31

Source: Household Survey by Author, 2000, VAO, Jammula Palem.

Summary and Conclusions

This study observed that in the selected hamlet land has been concentrated among the non-SC/STs and land has been passed from non-cultivated communities to cultivated communities during the study period. In 1998–99, 17 per cent of BC households control 14.29 per cent of total area and 56.57 per cent of OC households control 85.7 per cent (particularly Kamma caste) of total area in the hamlet and 26.31 per cent of SC households are not controlling single cent of land, they all are landless agricultural labourers. Moreover that, these SC households totally depend upon their labour work for their subsistence. On the other hand, 10 per cent of medium and large farmers control nearly 45 per cent of total land, while 31.34 per cent of marginal farmers control only 19.9 per cent of total land, indicates that the land distribution has skewed by sizewise as well as caste wise in the hamlet during study period. At Andhra Pradesh state level SC holdings in total holdings declined from 13.4 per cent to 12.12 per cent and their controlling area in total area slightly increased from 6.9 per cent to 7.42 per cent during 1976–77 to 1995–96. But ST holdings in total holding and area slightly increased and the other castes holdings also increased from 80.3 per cent to 80.77 per cent and their controlling area slightly decreased from 86.9 per cent to 85.02 per cent during the same period respectively. This implies that in the post-independence period inequalities in the distribution of land has increased despite land reforms at Andhra Pradesh state level as well as village level. Although intermediate land tenure system could be effectively removed through Zamindari abolition, equity in the agrarian structure could not be brought (Nancharaiah, 2000). At Andhra Pradesh state level still 75 per cent of SCs are agricultural labourers and among the SC landholdings nearly 91 per cent are marginal and small holders. In the case of landholdings STs position is better than SCs at state level. However, the quality of their land is inferior to that of others.

The pre-dominantly agriculture character of Andhra Pradesh has led to the domination of the landholding castes in a kind of patron-client network which is a major hindrance in the egalitarian development of the country, and this can only be rectified through thoroughgoing and rational implementation of land reform polices. In this connection, it is suggested that the Andhra Pradesh state government should implement the radical land reforms and distribute fertile land to the landless SC/ST people. In the context of Andhra Pradesh, if sufficient land is to be generated for the landless poor then the existing land ceiling which is 58 acres of dry land and 18 acres of wet land per family, must be reduced. A state level agriculture labourers' movement will be needed to fix new limits of 15 acres of dry land and 6 acres of wetland per family, in order to bring about more significant distribution of land to the landless poor in the state.

The quality of land is also important, most of the studies observed that nearly 60 per cent of land which has been distributed by the government through land reforms since independence, is uncultivable, hill land and unfertile land. In this context the government should take the quality of land as an important issue and give the first priority to the villages where the total SC/ST communities do not have land to the distribution of land.

Peculiar wage determine system has been existed in the hamlet. The farmers in front of Mutamastris after the end of plantation season would determine the wages. The wages increase is totally depending upon the large farmers' grace and not demand. Here Mutamastri will not play any active role in the determination of wages. In the determination of wages large farmers (*landlords*) play vital role. If they agree to increase the wages, then only remaining farmers will agree to increase the wages. These landless SC labourers also use to go neighbour villages for the tobacco plantation, because these villages start little bit earlier than this hamlet, at that time they demand the higher wage from the neighbour village farmers because the relation between Mutamastri as well as labourers is tentative. For this work, they get wage on the same day itself and more wage than their native village wages. One can easily say that this type of wage determination system has been existed in this hamlet due to landlessness of labourers (all SCs are landless) and they do not have any other source for work. Due to landlessness only, the labourers are unable to demand the increase of wages as proportionate to their normal consumption. And they were also fear about unexpected expenses such as marriages, health problems and children education, at that time the landlords only the final source to overcome these expenses. If they demand more wage at the time of determination, they may give money or may not give money at their bad needed time. Add to landlessness of Dalits this may be one of the reasons unable to demand reasonable wages.

One of the important features we have observed in the hamlet, there is quite high variation between the SC labour employment days and other social group employment days in different fields, nearly other social group labourers are getting more than 31 employment days per acre for these three crops such as paddy, tobacco and plants. This may happened to social backwardness and landlessness of SC households, the upper caste land owners are giving the first employment priority within their caste labourers only, after they need excess labourers then only they are going to engage the SC agricultural labourers. In this connection, it is suggested that the Andhra Pradesh state government should provide alternative employment through the self-employment programmes to these landless SCs. It is also observed that the illiteracy rate among the SCs is very high than the other social groups in the hamlet and 25 per cent of child labour engaged in the cultivation of tobacco crop and processing. It is suggested that the state government should provide the necessary incentives for encouraging the education of the rural SC child.

Acknowledgements

I am thankful to my Supervisor Professor G. Nancharaiah for his continuous suggestions and advises to develop this research paper.

Notes

1. In this paper, those who do not have land for cultivation and are totally depend upon their labour work for their subsistence, we considered as landless laboures. But in land and caste in South India, the author Dharma Kumar considered that some of these labourers may own some land themselves, but these minute holdings cannot afford even bare subsistence for a family and the major part of the labourers' income is derived from working on land owned by others. In this sense these labourers are landless.
2. This is a Telugu word, we can call him as a labour group leader or team leader. Generally the *Muta* constitute with nearly 30 labours (male and female) who controls the entire group is called as a Mutamastri. Generally the Mutamastri emerge on the basis of caste, among the caste also they emerge on the basis of surnames. In this hamlet each social group is having 2–5 Mutamastris. In this hamlet SC social group is having more Mutamastris than other social groups He works as a mediator between the farmer and labourers. He uses to collect the wages from the farmers. In every year with the presence of all social group Mutamastris only the farmers decide the wage rates for male and females.

References

Bedi, Narinder, (1996), "Land to the Tiller: Peasant Struggles in Ananthapur District", in Yugandar, B.N. (ed.), *Land Reforms in India*, Vol. 3, New Delhi: Sage Publications, 271–284.

Dev, Mahendra, (2001), "Performance, Issues and Policies", in *Social and Economic Security in India*, (eds.), Mahendra Dev and others, Institute for Human Development, 27–59.

Francis, C., (1996), "Land Reforms: An Overview", in Yugandar, B.N., (ed.), *Land Reforms in India*, Vol. 3, New Delhi: Sage Publications, 57–68.

Krishna, Radha, (2004), Agricultural Growth, Employment and Poverty: A Policy Perspective, Presidential Address, 43rd Annual Conference of Indian Society of Labour Economics, organized by Institute for Social and Economic Change, Bangalore, 18–20.

Kumar, Dharma, (1992), *Land and Caste in South India*, New Delhi: Manohar Publications.

Murthy, C.S., (1998), *Land Lease Market in Agriculture*, New Delhi: Commonwealth Publishers.

———, (2004), "Land Reforms in Soft State Policy Options for Sustainable Agricultural Development", in G. Gopal Reddy (ed.), Pre-Conference Volume,

Institutional Policy Options for Sustainable Agricultural Development, National Seminar organized by Department of Economics, Osmania University, 75–87.

Nancharaiah, (1988), *Land and Caste*, Bombay: Himalaya Publishing House.

———, (2000), "Agrarian Reforms and Agrarian Change: Fifty Years of Independence", in K.R. Gupta (ed.), *Issues in Indian Economy*, Vol. III, New Delhi: Atlantic Publishers and Distributions, 63–92.

———, (2000), "New Economic Policy and its Effects on Dalits in India" in K.P. Kumaran (ed.), *Impact of Economic Reforms on SCs and STs*, Hyderabad: NIRD, 55–72.

Population Census Report of Tangutur, (1991), Assistant Statistical Officer, Tangutur.

Rao, Krishna. E., (2001), Globalization of Agriculture and its Impact: with a Special Reference to Tobacco: A Village Study, Unpublished thesis, submitted to University of Hyderabad, Hyderabad.

———, (2004), "Shifts in the Cropping Pattern and its Impact on Tobacco Labour Employment and Wages: A Village Study", in G. Gopal Reddy (ed.), Pre-Conference Volume, Institutional Policy Options for Sustainable Agricultural Development, National Seminar organized by Department of Economics, Osmania University, 61–71.

Report on Agricultural Census of Andhra Pradesh, (1995), Directorate of Economics and Statistics, Government of Andhra Pradesh, Hyderabad.

Report on Landholdings of SC/ST, (1975, 1981, 1986, 1991, 1995), Directorate of Economics and Statistics, Government of Andhra Pradesh, Hyderabad.

Shankaran, S.R., (1994), Rural Poor and Public Action: Some Issues, C.V. Subba Rao Memorial Lecture, A.P. Economic Association XIII Annual Conference, Nagarjuna University, Guntur, December 10–11.

———, (1996), "Introduction", in Yugandar, B.N. (ed.), *Land Reforms in India*, Vol. 3, New Delhi: Sage Publications, 1–27.

Subbaiah Venkata, (2004), "Trends in Agricultural Land Transfers During Post Independence in Andhra Pradesh", in G. Gopal Reddy (ed.), Pre-conference Volume, Institutional Policy Options for Sustainable Agricultural Development, National Seminar organized by Department of Economics, Osmania University, 61–71.

Sukumar Das, (2000), "A Critical Evaluation of Land Reforms in India, (1950–1995)", in Sinha, B.K. and Pushpendar (eds.), *Land Reforms in India: An Unfinished Agenda*, Vol. 5, New Delhi: Sage Publications, 1–44.

Suri, K.C. and Raghavulu, C.V., (1996), "Agrarian Movements and Land Reforms", in Yugandar, B.N. (ed.), *Land Reforms in India*, Vol. 3, New Delhi: Sage Publications, 28–56.

Thorat, Sukhadeo, (2000), "New Economic Policy and its Impact on Employment and Poverty of The Scheduled Castes", in K.P. Kumaran (ed.), *Impact of Economic Reforms on SCs' and STs'*, Hyderabad: NIRD, 21–54.

———, (2001), "Social Security for Scheduled Castes in Organized Sector", in Mahendra Dev and others, (eds.), *Social and Economic Security in India*, Institute for Human Development, New Delhi, 367–385.

22 Improved Biophysical Management and Livelihood Security

Said and Done through Community Watersheds?

R.P. MULA, N.V. THANG, T. WANGKAHART, S.P. WANI AND Y. SUPAMA

Community Watersheds (CW) implemented through an integrated and consortium approach have two-pronged objectives; to conserve and protect natural resources and to enhance livelihood development. This line of thinking in CW projects traced its beginnings in the 1990s when research and development (R&D) practitioners felt the need to give equal attention to productivity enhancements of agricultural breakthroughs like hybrids from germplasm improvement programs and the environments for the benefit of the resource-poor farm households. Hence, CW is dubbed as the means to realize the integration of genetic improvement and natural resource management without losing track of farm households' livelihood.

This is elaborated in the study conducted in 2006 in four nucleus CW sites (Tad Fa and Wang Chai in Khon Kaen, Thailand and Thanh Ha and Huoang Dao in Hanoi, Vietnam). This paper discusses the relationships and the effects of specific interventions in the biophysical resources on the livelihoods and other social aspects of farm households.

Data were obtained through individual farm interviews involving fifteen farmer-respondents in each site and focus group discussions of different groups in the CWs and with implementers.

Watershed activities implemented by the International Crops Research Institute in the Semi-Arid Tropics (ICRISAT) led consortium in two nucleus CWs, viz.; Tad Fa and Thanh Ha started in late 1999 and scaling-out in other two nucleus CWs commenced in 2003. Despite the consortium's recent involvement in the satellites, some significant impacts have already been noted. These are discussed in the succeeding section of the paper.

Farm households have limited livelihood options in the sites prior to the CW project. Livelihoods are eked primarily from farming. Overexploitation of the land due to households' increasing demands has had a deleterious effect on them and the environment. Household members migrated; others continued to farm in degraded lands and in worse cases, they abandoned farming. However, ICRISAT's twenty five years of R&D activities have proven that productivity of rainfed systems can be substantially improved by two to four times through the adoption of improved soil and water technologies. These breakthroughs have been brought to farming communities using CW as an entry point for integrating crop-related technologies with the biophysical achievements. Technological components of the project, which include soil and water conservation and soil nutrient amendments/replenishment, are integrated in crop and livestock (including fish culture) management to sustain productivity and incomes.

ICRISAT's CW model in a Nutshell

The CW model of ICRISAT is guided principally by the Integrated Genetic and Natural Resources Management (IGNRM) approach where the R&D programs consider a balance in agricultural productivity and livelihood opportunities of resource-poor farm households in the semi-arid tropics and rainfed areas. The interlocking constraints faced by Asian farmers (i.e., Thailand and Vietnam) are not just confined on enhancing productivity but also in managing the social, institutional markets and biophysical environments. These include a germplasm assembly for continuous crop improvement program, which attends to various concerns/requirements of an array of users; an integrated watershed management, which is a platform for a holistic management of farm households' resources and problem situations; an innovative means of knowledge sharing, which facilitates exchange for crafting new opportunities; and a unique form of alliance through public-private partnership and consortium approach, which hastens scaling and policy change (Wani et al., 2007: 2–5).

Figure 1 *ICRISAT's Community Watershed Model*

The entire process revolves around the four Es—Empowerment, Equity, Efficiency and Environment, which are addressed by adopting specific strategies prescribed by the four Cs—Consortium, Convergence, Cooperation and Capacity Building (Figure 1).

Starting with the Biophysical Situation

Interventions to increase agricultural productivity in the sites were tailored based on the output of the biophysical characterization and farming system of the watersheds. As gleaned from Table 1, various soil and water management interventions made significant contributions in improving the biophysical system such as increased water level, reduced soil run-off, and changed farming system. In Tad Fa, there was a significant reduction of run-off from 364 millimetre to 169 millimetre and soil loss from 15.3 tonnes per hectare to 12.8 tonnes per hectare in untreated farms compared to treated farms. In Thanh Ha, water levels in wells showed a significant rise, from 1.5 metres to 2.5 metres. With improvements in water availability, soil loss and soil fertility; farmers took on crop diversification and intensification. Farmers' behaviour towards the change in farming system proves that there are opportunities to improve crop productivity and that adaptation farmers made are relevant information for understanding farm households' management (coping strategies) of damaged resources.

ICRISAT's experience shows that opportunities to abate further land degradation and improving water management through CWs is possible. The centre's success story in this regard evolved from a specific focus (i.e., nutrient deficiency) and on-station research activities and later embraced a CW concept. As earlier mentioned, initial activities of the CW projects started by tackling constraints of the biophysical component and slowly building on the other concerns of various interest groups. The significant impacts created by the various interventions are largely due to synergistic participation of consortium members. Harnessing partnerships in community watersheds in spite of the variability of incentives (Spielman and von Grebmer, 2006: 294–296) among members enhanced impact. Taking advantage of the comparative capacity of ICRISAT and partners (national agricultural research system, non-government organizations, community-based organizations, etc.); the former in being non-partisan but pro-poor and the latter as the direct links to farm households; this complementation resulted in significant livelihood impacts. CWs implemented through public-private partnership ensured more vigour and commitment for improving the plight of resource-poor farm households whose livelihood depended on fragile, shallow and eroded soils. Inappropriate land use practices and increasing demand for food exacerbated the situation of rainfed areas. In an earlier study made by Naraongsak (2001), they described the process of soil degradation that happens in rainfed agriculture. The process can take place individually or interactively at different levels of land use hierarchy and its damage so vicious. This has become a cause of concern by institutions where ICRISAT, NARS of Thailand and Vietnam and the Asian Development Bank worked in partnership mode to abate the situation in rainfed areas.

Together with the biophysical characterization of the benchmark sites was the identification of key factors to improve on farmers' productivity. These

Table 1 *Production System of the Different Watersheds in Thailand and Vietnam*

Particular	*Tad Fa, Thailand*		*Wang Chai, Thailand*	
	Before	*After*	*Before*	*After*
Soil type (Somchai Tongpoonpul et al., 2005: 46–67)	Clayey (30 cm, clay ↓)		Sandy (90%)	
Run off and soil erosion (Somchai Tongpoonpul et al., 2005: 46–67)	2001–2003 Crop-based (Untreated): Run-off: 364 mm Soil loss: 15.3 t/ha Tree-based (Treated): Run-off 169 mm Soil loss—12.8 t\ha		2003–2004 Crop-based: Run-off: 210 mm Soil loss: 4.21 t/ha	
Nutrients	Low in fertility	Significant increase in organic matter and N content	Low in fertility	
Water sources	Ponds and wells		Ponds and wells	
Average rainfall (Piara Singh, A.V.R. Kesava Rao and K. Srinivas, 2005)	1220 mm		1231 mm	
Crops (Somchai Tongpoonpul et al., 2005: 46–67)	Maize. Legumes, and fruit trees	Maize, Legumes, Vegetables, Other fruit trees, and vetiver grass	Rice, Sugarcane, Legumes, and Mulberry	Rice, Sugarcane, new varieties of Legumes, Mulberry, vegetables, and *Vetiver* grass
Soil type	Red-yellow Ferralitic	Red-yellow Ferralitic	Red-yellow Ferralitic	Red-yellow Ferralitic
Run-off and soil erosion (N.V. Viet, H.M. Tam, N.T. Chinh, N.V. Thang and A. Ramakrishna 2005: 68–81)		Seasonal run-off due to good infiltration		No data

Cont'd...

Cont'd...

Nutrients (N.V. Viet, H.M. Tam, N.T. Chinh, N.V. Thang and A. Ramakrishna 2005: 68–81)	• Acidic in nature and with very poor organic matter, medium potassium and very low phosphorous content (N.V. Viet, N.V. Thang, A. Ramakrishna and S.P. Wani)	• Micronutrient applications (grow more and comax) in creases groundnut yields by 10 to 24% and soybean yield by 14 to 22%. Rhizobium application reduced N requirement by 15 to 30 kg/ha	• Acidic in nature and with very poor organic matter, medium potassium and very low phosphorous content (N.V. Viet, N.V. Thang, A. Ramakrishna and S.P. Wani)	No data
Water level (N.V. Viet, H.M. Tam, N.T. Chinh, N..V Thang and A. Ramakrishna 2005: 68–81; Personal communication with Piara Singh) -near check dams -away water table		• Significant rise (1.5 to 2.0 m) in water level in wells was recorded in treated watersheds. The water level fluctuations were less and stable water yield during summer. • 200 water harvesting pits • Water tanks		• 2.5–3 m rise in 10 open wells (T.D. Long; N.V. Thang, and S.P. Wani 2005) • 200 water harvesting pits • Water tanks
Average rainfall (N.V. Viet, H.M. Tam, N.T. Chinh, N.V. Thang and A. Ramakrishna 2005: 68–81)		2020 mm		1585 mm (ADB Report 2004)

Cont'd...

Cont'd...

Crops (ADB Reports and TD Long; NV Thang, and S.P. Wani)	Rice, sweet potato, Cassava maize, Groundnut, tea, soybean, fruit Trees	• Improved cultivars of soyabean (DT 12), groundnut (l 16 and l 17), and mungbean (T 135) were expanded to large areas in Thanh Ha watershed during autumn-winter season of 2003 and spring 2004. Soybean and groundnut gave more benefit than maize • Area under maize declined from 380 ha to 148, while area under groundnut, mungbean, and soybean increased from 18 ha to 250 ha changing the crop agro-biodiversity factor from 0.25 in 1989 to 0.6 in 2002. • Crop management practices on groundnut and maize and application of biofertilizers to groundnut, soybean, maize and in Than Ha watershed increased the economic yields of crops by 8–16% with reduced N application. The farmers incorporated the groundnut, soybean and into the maize- and cassava-based systems • Watermelon cultivation using groundwater transported through pipes • Used of polyethylene mulch which resulted in doubling yield like groundnut	Maize, Rice, Cassava, Soybean, Tea	In Vietnam, high yield varieties of soyabean (VX 93) and groundnut (L 14) were sown in additional 50 ha in Huoang Dao watershed. Fruit trees with water conservation technology Used of polyethylene mulch which resulted in doubling yield like groundnut. Introduction of elephant grass as fodder (ADB 2005) Introduction of wild *Arachis* as soil cover in lychee gardens (ADB 2005)

Source: Annual Reports 1978–2004. ICRISAT, Patancheru, Andhra Pradesh, India. 'A Bit of Everything' as a mode of managing resources.

Legend: Before—Prior to implementation of interventions
After—After the Implementation of interventions

include technological constraints, institutional arrangements as well as socio-economic conditions. The appraisal of these factors with the locals provided the platform for a holistic understanding of resources with which the interventions are implemented.

A case in point is the construction of ponds (in some cases rehabilitation of existing ones) and other water harvesting structures like pits, which has not only impacted irrigation. Pond development opened the avenue for facilitating several livelihood opportunities like tending livestock (poultry and swine) to alleviate socio-economic condition. In Thailand, the Department of Land Development (DLD) undertook pond construction/rehabilitation. Khon Kaen University (KKU) provided technical advice for pond protection (planting fruit trees and grass around the pond) and productivity (cultivation of crops and integration of fish). KKU's participation with the CW project provided the means for students' social laboratory where 'learning by doing' pedagogy is practiced. The Office of the Agricultural Research Development (OARD) Region 3 provided the overall coordination of the project. ICRISAT provided additional technical assistance, scaling of insights and most importantly, the exchange of information among consortium members and south-south partners. Farm households and basically the entire farming communities became the active partners and made the final decision. As one farmer from Vietnam claimed, the improvements he observed in his farm on the reduction of soil erosion and retention of moisture because of simple structures like pits, are sufficient incentives to learn and participate in the project.

'A Bit of Everything' as a Mode of Managing Resources

Farm households have different resources (Mula and Niehof, 2000: 97–114; Chambers and Conway, 1992) and these are the means to satisfy a system's demands. Resources, to a large extent, determine the livelihood security of households. Beyond the major factors of production, which are regarded as precursors to farm households' productivity, the ways in which these factors are managed during slack or abundance situations provide invaluable insights in understanding the success of watersheds. Few specific watershed intervention have been included to illustrate the contours and dynamics of CW in relation to its four key elements namely small infrastructure, cropping system, tending livestock and capacity building. In this research, CW served as the platform for integrating biophysical and social interventions for resource-poor farm households.

Small Infrastructures

Field visits reveal that small infrastructures for soil and water management are prevalent in the watersheds. These include ponds, pits, bunds, and check dams. In the different CW sites, farmer-respondents' domestic and irrigation water supply significantly improved as a result of the consortium's effort on small infrastructures.

Prior to the construction of small infrastructures, soil samples were collected and analyzed for physical, chemical and biological properties. Results of the characterization in most parts of the Tad Fa watersheds show high clay content on the topmost layer and sub-layers are generally solid rocks. This has considerable effect on surface and groundwater hydrology and total moisture holding capacity. This indicates the fast draining of excess run-off. Similarly, in Thanh Ha and Huoang Dao watersheds, the most common soil type is the re-yellow ferralitic. Miniralization is rapid and organic substances quickly breakdown resulting in low humus content. Soils are generally clayey with medium to high water holding capacity (Pathak et al., 2002: 32–33, 39)

In Thailand CWs, a number of farmers availed of the support of one consortium member; the DLD in the construction and/or improvement of ponds. Pond sizes range from 4 × 8 to 5 × 10 metres in area with depths of about 1 × 2 metrés. The dependency on rainwater plus some improved system of water impounding has apparently helped in conserving moisture according to farmer-respondents. Water harvesting pits are not so popular in CWs of Thailand as in Vietnam due to the availability of subsidy for ponds and the bigger land areas in Thailand.

In Wang Chai and Huoang Dao watersheds where ponds and pits are recent innovations (only in 2003), farmers have observed improvements like better stand of fruit trees (more robust and better yield) as indicated by a 30 per cent increase in production of their *longan* and *lychee*. In most of the farmers' field at the Huoang Dao watershed, farmers reported that pits of about 1 × 2 metres in area, depth of about half metre, and a distance of about 5 to 7 metres (depending on the contour) have conserved moisture that provided the needed water for their standing crops. According to Long et al. (2005: 135) there are about two hundred water-harvesting pits in Huoang Dao.

There are other untapped resources, which prove to be possible niches to improve productivity. The Uborrat dam in Wang Chai watershed, which is the primary source of irrigation for the lower stream can also be used for fish culture and the water from a waterfall in Tad Fa can be collected for irrigation and domestic use. With some investments in physical structures for collecting and making water resources accessible, these can benefit the locals.

An assured water source combined with improved crop management practices resulted in a remarkable change in the cropping system, an area where most of the farmer-respondents claimed much improvement (Box 1).

Za and Vareedee's cases epitomize that less-endowed resource farmers are more likely to participate in developmental interventions. Their situations show the uncertainty of their livelihoods, which they by all means need to deal with. There is the surfacing of other opportunities to improve livelihood where, for instance, Vareedee built a chain of social networks that led him to become the focal person for information exchange. Coping strategies, specifically adaptation (Davies, 1993: 60–72) and management of resources under a problematic situation (Barnett, 1993: 10–13), are important manifestations for a better understanding of livelihood systems. An insight from these two farmers' cases suggests that watershed interventions need not always be 'new' but can also be traditional and drawn from local resources (Scoones, 1992: 293–314). Many studies have shown that adaptations of farm households in response to a livelihood problem are varied and borne out of their several years of dealing with the situation. Past experience and existing knowledge, in most cases, are drawn upon where responses become sequential. It also suggests that strategies developed do not always represent clear-cut, mutually exclusive alternatives.

Cropping System

The accounts of farmer-respondents and implementing agencies reveal that run-off and soil erosion were reduced and soil health improved with the introduction of new cropping systems that included the following:

Thailand

- Cultivation of tree crops and *Vetiver* grass around ponds and on contour with steep slopes especially in Tad Fa (slope ranges from 5% to 8%)
- Cultivation of other legumes and vegetable crops
- Micronutrient application
- Crop intensification through crop layering and mixed cropping
- Construction of ponds
- Practice of integrated pest management

Vietnam

- Introduction of legumes (improved varieties) and other crops like watermelon to improve cropping system
- Introduction of polyethylene mulching
- Planting of *Glyricidia* and pineapple on contours
- Staggered trenching and groundwater recharging-pits
- Construction of physical barriers (stone bunds, bench terraces, contours) and supplementary physical structures (pits, contour canals, percolation tanks)
- Application of micronutrients

Table 2 shows that from a monocropping system to practice of rotating other crops after the primary crop (rice, maize, and fruit trees), farmer-respondents diversified into new crops and new varieties of legumes and vegetables and other plants like *Vetiver* and *Glyricidia*. Groundnut and soybean areas have expanded. Thanh Ha farmers in 2003 produced groundnut at 0.69 tonne per hectare pod yield in the farmers' practice and 0.94 tonne per hectare in the improved practice. Maize yields increased from 3.4 tonne per hectare grain in the farmers' practice to 3.6 tonne per hectare in the improved practice. In Tad Fa, trials have proven the benefits of groundnut cultivation in increasing the outputs of maize and other cash crops as shown in Table 3.

Glyricidia has been grown on bunds as a vegetative barrier against soil erosion and also as a source of green manure to improve soil fertility. *Glyricidia* in Thanh Ha watershed can withstand extreme climatic conditions like drought and produced a huge quantity of leaf and young branches of about 24 tonne per hectare per month. Further, it is not vulnerable to pests and diseases, and unlike *Leucaena*, which is also a legume-fixing plant, *Glyricidia* does not become a weed and is not invasive. It is a fast-growing perennial tree that can be pruned six to eight times a year and provides 80 to 100 tons of N rich biomass.

Table 2 *Changes in Farming System*

Particulars	*Thailand*		*Vietnam*	
	Wang Chai	*Tad Fa*	*Thanh Ha*	*Huoang Dao*
Cropping System Before (%)				
• Monocropping	100 rice-rice	100 maize-maize	100 rice-rice lower area	100 rice-rice lower area
• Fruit Tree—Maize/Fruit Tree—Vegetables			100	
• Rice—Legume	40	—	—	—
• Rice—Sugarcane	80	—	—	—
• Maize—Vegetables	—	67	—	—
• Fallow	50	100	—	—
• After (%)				
• CP (crop rotation/tree based)	—	11	100	100 (food trees and lumber)
• CN (composting, green manuring, growing crops around pond)	—	11	100	100
• CPT (integrated pest management)	—	11	100	100
• CP + CN	—	56	100	100
• CP + CPT	60	33	—	—
• CN + CPT	100	—	—	—
• CP + CN + CPT	100	100	100	100

Legend: CP—Crop Production
CN—Crop Nutrition (i.e., *Glyricidia*)
CPT—Crop Protection

Source: Primary data.

Farmer-respondents have been made more aware of environment-friendly practices like crop protection guided by integrated pest management and crop nutrition like using *Glyricidia* loppings integrated with crop production.

Based on an input-output estimation (Table 4) of three major crops in Wang Chai watershed, sugarcane has the highest capital requirement. Planting legumes proves to be a viable alternative because of their low input requirement estimated at US $ 3.3/1,600 square metres, good yields and market ability; at the same time legumes render nitrogen to the soil. Rice cultivation, on the other hand, is a major crop in both countries. Even under extreme situation of inadequate water, rice farming is one activity that was not abandoned. Existing norms and values determine, to a large extent, management and interpretation of the environment. This, in turn, will determine how a biophysical resource like land is put to productive use. This is corollary to the findings in rice farming in the Philippines where despite uncertain yield in lahar-laden paddy fields, this

Table 3 *Cropping system in Thanh Ha Community Watershed, Vietnam*

Cropping System	*Net Income (US $)*	*Additional Profit Over Traditional System (US$)*	*% Increase Over Traditional System*
Maize-maize (traditional system)	492	—	—
Maize-soybean	746	254	51
Maize-groundnut	780	288	58
Groundnut-soybean	1,079	587	119
Soybean-soybean	1,068	576	117
Watermelon-mungbean-maize	1,481	989	201
Mungbean-soybean-groundnut	1,106	614	125
Watermelon-mungbean-soybean	1,803	1,311	266

Source: Nguyen Van Viet, Thang N.V., Long T.D., Ramakrishna A. and Wani, S.P., 2005 Nhung Han Che Va Co Hoi Doi Voi San Xuat Tren Dat Doc O Mien Bac Vietnam Agrobiodiversity management in Northern Vietnam. in GS.Vs. Tran Dinh K Long-Ths.Nguyen Van Thang-TS, S.P. Wani (eds). *Cai Tien Quan Ly Nguon Tai Nguyen Thien Nhien Vung Dat Mien Bac Viet Nam* pp. 22–40. Nha Xuat Ban Nong Nghiep.

Table 4 *Input-output Data for Rice, Sugarcane, and Legume in Wang Chai Community Watershed, Thailand*

Particulars	*Crops*		
	Rice	*Sugarcane*	*Legume*
	Planting Date		
	May or June	*March or October*	*November or December*
No. of Ploughing	2	2	1–2
No. of Weeding	1–2	1–2	1–2
Labour Requirement (person days/rai)			
Planting	2–5	1–2	2–3
Fertilizer/Chemical application	1–2	1–3	1–3
Harvesting	3–5	2	2–3
Amount of Fertilizer (kg/rai)	15–40	20–30	25–30
Capital Requirement (baht/rai)	786.2	3,176.6	146.5
Yield	349 kg/rai Home use: 50–75% Sold: 25–50%	8.8 t/rai Sold: 100%	127.5 kg/rai Sold: 100%

Source: Yen et al. (2003) *Baseline Survey of Wang Chai Watershed, Thailand*
1 hectare = 6.25 *rai*.

was not abandoned. In an area where livelihood security means more rice, the prevalence of inadequate water for irrigation will not prevent farmers from its cultivation (Mula and Niehof, 2000).

Intensive cropping best describes Vietnam's farming system. In a small piece of land of about 1,000 square metres, farmers grow around four kinds of crops, mostly vegetables. Vietnam farmers maximize the utility of their small landholdings. According to them, multiple cropping likewise is dictated by a perception that if one crop fails, the other crops could serve as fallbacks (food source and income). This by itself is a form of coping as in the case of Mr Za (Box 1).

Farmers in Vietnam are also engaged in crop nutrition and crop protection management practices that made farming more stable. In Tad Fa, for instance, farmers practice 'layering' where short-maturing crops like vegetables and legumes are interspersed with the fruit trees. This system maximizes the utility of their area. Together with the knowledge of composting, application of green manure, and growing of crops around ponds, livelihoods have improved. This shows the significance of watershed as a means and an end for tapping all possible agroecological niches where substantial food and cash can be obtained.

Tending Livestock

Small and native breed of livestock are also key resources of farm households in the watersheds. Cattle is primarily used for draught power and occasionally sold. Poultry, specifically chicken and ducks, are generally for home consumption and as a source of added cash. The average heads of poultry in Vietnam is almost three times the average production in Thailand. Preference for small livestock is partly a response to problems of grazing (as in the case of Vietnam) and partly due to ease of management, as in tending and selling (Scoones, 1992). Ponds in Vietnam are used not only as source of irrigation but also as sanctuaries for ducks.

The crop area in the CWs of Northeast Thailand is much higher than in the CWs of Vietnam. The highest average crop area per household is in Tad Fa, which is above four hectares. This is slightly higher than what was reported by OARD, which is approximately three hectares. With livestock raising as an important livelihood resource, the need for grazing is imperative. In Vietnam where there is a shortage of grazing areas, cut-and-carry is mostly done. The average crop area for Vietnam is below one hectare, which is similar to the findings of Long et al. (2005: 135, 173–77) estimated at 600 square metres. However, average upland farm area per household is estimated at 1000 square metres. Farmers feed their cattle with crop waste derived from crops grown in peripheral areas as well as those from homegardens. In Thailand, where the settlement pattern is clustered, the boundaries of their homegardens with their field plots are quite distinct. Homegardens serve as sources of food and non-food crops (Mula and Gayao, 1991: 8). Mulberry trees are integral element of their homegardens, which are important for silkworm rearing. Almost every household in Wang Chai watershed, particularly the elderly women, is doing home-based silk weaving. This is a traditional industry and a good source of cash. However, this is a dying industry because of the lack of interest of the younger generations. In turn, this explains the non-maintenance of mulberry trees (a source of food for silkworms) among households. The OARD, a consortium member and implementer, has taken initial steps towards the sustainability of this industry. In Vietnam where settlements are dispersed, homegardens form part of the crop area, which explains the smaller homelots. Interestingly, in spite of the limited area, farmers continue to grow several food crops and grass for cattle. Crops are interspersed with fruit trees.

Box 1 *Farmers' Response to Improved Water Availability*

- Mr Za is forty-five years-old from the midlands of Huoang Dao, with five children to support, and has a land area of about one hectare, which is slightly higher than the average of eight thousand square metres per household. He is primarily dependent on the land. In most cases, he hardly puts the entire area to productive use because of inadequate irrigation. Lately, with his pond widened (5 × 5 metres) and holding some water even during the dry season, several small pits that reduce water flow, and with new crops and improved varieties that can be grown due to conserved moisture, Mr Za claims better prospects of his cropping system. However, his practice of allocating areas for several other crops in one season, a common practice in Huoang Dao and in societies with fragmented land (Castillo, 1999: 198–200), is hinged on the perception that food and income must be ensured. Having more crops means that the failure in one crop could be buffered by the productivity (yield and income) of the other crops. In his farm, there are patches of different crucifers like cabbage, Chinese cabbage, and leeks alongside a bigger area of transplanted rice. He has also tried planting watermelon and adapted polyethylene mulching, which he finds financially rewarding. In his homestead are also some eggplants, herbs (i.e., mint) and fruit trees (i.e., longan). There are also three cattle in the stable, pigs, and chicken at the courtyard.
- In Tad Fa, growing of sunn hemp (*Crotolaria*) as one of the initiatives of the ICRISAT–led CW project is a great stride towards greater livelihood security for Mr Vareedee (one of the respondents). Majority of the households in the area do sunn hemp cultivation. According to Mr Vareedee, sunn hemp grows very well with very little inputs, under poor soil condition, and with very little moisture. Sunn hemp being a legume improves soil structure. The biggest incentive farmers get from its cultivation is a ready market. The DLD buys all farmers' production through its volunteer who is a farmer from the community. To date, the DLD volunteer in Tad Fa has not only become an intermediary to the project implementers but also serves as community's source of agricultural information. Recently, he has also done the legwork for a self-help group (SHG) on sunn hemp seed bank, which has led to a more organized growers association.
- Sunn hemp was introduced in the area sometime in 1999 by DLD. Since then it has become a major crop in the area besides maize. According to a DLD key informant, a net profit of 10,000 baht (US $ 235.3) could be realized from a 20 *rai* (3.2 hectare) area with an estimated production of 1,000 kilograms.
- Indeed, sunn hemp does not only render cash to farm households but also improves soil health. The only disadvantage, according to respondents and DLD staff, is its difficulty in the harvesting and threshing. Farmers have to grapple with extreme itchiness caused by a caterpillar common in the crop.

Capacity Building

A dynamic capacity development programme alongside and to keep pace with the improvements in the different biophysical interventions contributed in the uptake of technologies. Serious consideration of user sensitivity in the capacity development programme where roles, needs and problems of household members are factored in proved to be an invaluable insight. The trainings and cross visits implemented and institutions built improved the confidence of farm households. On the average, farmer-respondents had at least participated in two trainings and regarded these as enriching. In Tad Fa, the integrated pest management (IPM) exposure farmers participated in, were highly appreciated and provided them another option and not just dependency to pesticide application. IPM's popularity was because it involved local materials such as molasses mixed with water. This technology has been very effective for crucifers especially cabbage. As the molasses ferment, this attracts insects especially the diamond backmoth (*Plutella xylostella*). This was introduced in the area by one of the entomologists of OARD.

The capacity building framework, characterized as dynamic and user sensitive, adopted in the CW approach allowed stakeholders to be more grounded with what they saw and made interactions with other stakeholders more meaningful. This has been found to be very significant with women's participation as discussed in Box 2.

Other types of capacity requirement, as expressed by the farmer-respondents include continuous technical support and information, education communication (IEC) materials, as most of these watersheds (Tad Fa and Huoang Dao) are not easily accessible, especially during the rainy season. This adverse situation of the CWs necessitates for popularized and updated IEC materials. All of the farmer-respondents' expressed the need for print material as references and in order for them to be abreast of technologies. In Thailand, the only IEC material received is the newsletter of the DLD, which does not even contain any farm tips. The issue of market price information as expressed by the farmer-respondents of Thailand is a concern that might not be directly addressed by capacity building. However, when farmers are empowered and are able to organize themselves as in SHGs, issues related to marketing and credit facilities are likely to be addressed. Women who had the opportunity to be part of the cross-visits gained some insights about cooperative work (Box 2). These led the women to organize themselves and set up SHGs, which addressed members' basic household needs.

From the above example, it is clear that connectedness and social support can open opportunities for collective action and prospects for livelihood activity. The case in Box 2 also illustrates that social networks assume the function of disseminating information, generating advice, providing access to material resources, and providing an emotional support (Carey, 1988). An array of social benefits came about with increased agricultural productivity. In the four sites, there was gainful activity of other farm households. There was also strong expression of women having more time for their temple visits as well as donation for their community. The training and cross-visits component of CWs

Box 2 *Women's Share in Securing Households' Livelihood*

- Greater exposure and participation of women in watershed activities improved their domains for meeting day-to-day demands of the household. Mrs Supatra of Wang Chai watershed takes the lead in organizing the women in her community to take on projects like fish sauce and soap making, which are two very important commodities for the households. At the time this study was conducted, these activities were at their initial stages. The initial idea, according to her, was to provide requirements for home consumption, especially fish sauce. Later, this could become a potential source of cash as the demand for commodities like fish sauce is high.
- In spite of Mrs Supatra's limited time due to running her convenience store in the village, she still extends help in organizing the women. She says that these initiatives at least can somehow lessen the burden on household expenses. Moreover, she claims that with some modest capital to start with, these activities could enable the women to have their own source of cash and be happier. Mrs Supatra appreciates Ms Yen of OARD who is instrumental in opening this window for strengthening women's capacity. Because of their visits to another province, which forms part of the capacity building in the watershed project, Supatra and the other women have been linked to Mrs Songbay who served as their technical source specifically for soap/shampoo making.

allowed SHG formation among women. This contributed to their self-esteem. On the overall, through the various watershed initiatives, community empowerment was enabled by the creation and/or strengthening of local institutions. This holds true in Wang Chai watershed where several SHGs were formed not only to address their households' requirement but also as sources of added income for the women.

Likewise, the study shows that with improved biophysical management, the elements of the livelihood system fall into places. Initially, food security becomes the foremost concern, which explains its importance in the discussion of livelihood. In the watershed initiatives, a change in farming system like intensive cropping initially means more food and later more income at farm households' disposal. Understanding livelihood and food security issues from the biophysical aspect—the soil and the various elements, was an attempt to equally address environmental protection and conservation. In CWs, there is a close link between resources and the formulation of strategies, which made livelihood and food sustainable with the least damage to the environment.

Insights Learned: Old and New Together

Constant search for what works best for addressing the issue of poverty is a gargantuan quest for anyone. Experiences in the implementation of CW projects have produced a prime insight, nothing novel but best captured by a sincere paradigm shift of doing science with a human face. We need to note:

- Consortium approach definitely works best especially when members are able to do their share and are willing to negotiate. Partnering with an institution that allows taking on other responsibilities without sacrificing one's own primary function is a trait of a genuine consortium spirit. Forging a partnership, for instance, with an academic institution in the case of the two watersheds in Thailand allowed for providing students a social laboratory where they were better grounded with reality. This inculcates among the youth the value of social responsibility and other virtues like protection and conservation of natural resources.
- Interventions to improve biophysical problems like run-off and soil erosion must be done together with the farm households. Awareness building should be dovetailed with deliberate efforts to explain the significance of every intervention, activity, hardware (weather instruments), and/or infrastructure to inculcate ownership among the locals. A strong sense of inclusion in mainstreaming the development of farmers' own communities, taking collective actions to address their problems and constraints, and soliciting a certain degree of guidance from 'outsiders' ensures commitment for greater participation.
- Institutions engaged in the delivery of their social responsibility should have concrete strategies for their phasing-out stage. In this study, there is intense desire for more active extension support like technical assistance, various types of IEC materials and even market-price information. Addressing these concerns are not difficult in community watershed project because of its soft boundaries; where various objectives can be incorporated and sincere partnerships enjoined. This study shows that community watersheds can be a venue for creative synergy and institutional innovations (Hall et al., 2004: 207–10).
- Resource management means exploring underutilized resources not just for agriculture but also for other beneficial undertakings. The Uborrat dam, which is a source of irrigation among those in the downstream part of Wang Chai watershed, can be tapped for fish culture. The waterfall in Tad Fa watershed has potential for harvesting the water for domestic and irrigation purposes and also as an ecotourism destination when provision for access is made.
- On social capital, the strong interest among the locals and even for joint collaborations between and among organizations operating in the area can be explored to advance the initial success of ICRISAT-led community watershed initiatives.
- Vulnerable groups like the ageing population should form part of any development project and need equal attention. Sensitivity to the interest of women, elderly and the children is as important as the increased yield or income we R&D practitioners aspire for.

Acknowledgments

Our sincerest appreciation to the following who have contributed in the conduct of the assessment:

- Thailand: Supatra Donsophon, Somsak Idippong, Banyong Toomsan, Pranee Srihaban, Anuwat Potinam, Somjit Khantasuvan and to the respondents of Tad Fa and Wang Chai watersheds
- Vietnam: Phan Quoc GIa, and to the respondents of Thanh Ha and Huaong watersheds

References

Barnett, T., (1993), *On Ignoring the Wider Picture: AIDS Research and the Sobbing Social Scientist*, Institute of Social Studies, Badhuisweg: The Hague.

Carey, J.W., (1988), "Health, Social Support and Social Networks in Rural Andean Community of Southern Peru", *Journal on Humanities and Social Sciences*, 49 (10), 10.

Castillo, G.T., (1998) "A Social Harvest Reaped from a Promise of Springtime: User-responsive, Participatory Agricultural Research in Asia", in N.G. Roling and M.A.E. Wagemakers (eds.), *Facilitating Sustainable Agriculture: Participatory Learning and Adaptive Management in Times of Environmental Uncertainty*, United Kingdom: Cambridge University Press.

Chambers, R. and Conway, G., (1992), *Sustainable Rural Livelihoods: Practical Concepts for the 21st Century*, Institute of Development Studies, University of Sussex.

Davies, S., (1993), *Are Coping Strategies a Crop Out?*, Institute of Development Studies, University of Sussex.

Hall, A., Sulaiman, R.V., Yoganand, B., Raina, R.S., Clark, N.G. and Naik, G.C., (2004), "Institutional Learning and Change: Towards a Capacity-building Agenda for Research: A Review of Recent Research on Post-harvest Innovation System in South Asia", in A.J. Hall, B. Yoganand, R.V. Sulaiman, Rajeswari S. Raina, C. Shambu Prasad, Guru C. Naik and N.G. Clark (eds.), *Innovations in Innovation: Reflections on Partnership, Institutions and Learning*, Patancheru, India.

Long, T.R., Thang, N.V. and Wani, S.P., (2005), *Cai Tien Quan Ly Nguon Tai Nguyen Thien Nhein Vung Dat Doc Mien Bac Viet Nam*.

Mula, R. and A. Niehof, (2000), "Rural Households in the Philippines: Indigenous and New Systems of Coping with a Lingering Disaster", *Benguet State University Research Journal*, 29, 97–114.

Mula, R.P. and Gayao, B.T., (1991) *Urban and Rural Homegardens in the Highlands of Northern Philippines: The Case of Sweet Potato*, Benguet State University, La Trinidad, Benguet, Philippines.

Naraongsak Senanarong, Precha Cheuwchoom, Chanvid Lusanandana Somchai Tangpoonpal, Charuwat Phoomiti, Suphachai Aticahrt, Somsak Idhipong, Rego, TJ; Praneet Wisertsri, Arun Pongkanjana, Preedee Deeraksa, Pranee Srihaban, Thommasak Sinhhapong, Aran Patanothai, Banyong Toomsan, and Sawaeng Ruaysoongnern, (2001), "Improving Management of Natural Resources for Sustainable Rainfed Agriculture in Thailand", Paper presented at the ADB planning and review meeting, 9–15 December.

Pathak, P., Wani, S.P., Singh, Piara, Sudi, R. and Srinivasa Rao, (2002), "Hydrological Characterization of Benchmark Agricultural Watersheds in India, Thailand and Vietnam", Global Theme Report, No. 2. ICRISAT, Patancheru, Andhra Pradesh, India.

Ross, J., Maxwell, S. and Smith, M., (1994) "Linking Relief and Development", Discussion Paper No. 344, Institute of Development Studies, University of Sussex.

Scoones, I., (1992), "Coping with Drought: Responses to Herders and Livestock in Contrasting Savannah Environments in Southern Zimbabwe", *Drylands and Sustainable Agricultural Programmes*.

Spielman, D.J. and Von Grebmer, K., (2006), "Public-private Partnerships in International Agricultural Research: An Analysis of Constraints", Springer Business Media Inc., The Netherlands, *Journal of Technology Transfer* 31 (2), 294–96.

Wani, S.P., Ramakrishna, Y.S., Sreedevi, T.K., Wangkahart, Thwailkal, Thang N.V., Roy, Somnath, Li, Zhong, Dixin, Yin, Hong Ye, Zhu, Chourasia, A.K. Shiferaw, B. Pathak, P., Singh, Piara, Ranga Rao, G.V., Mula, R.P., Sitaraman, S., (2007), "Greening Drylands and Improving Livelihoods", ICRISAT, Patancheru, Andhra Pardesh, India.

23 Perspectives on Higher Education

Affirmative Action for the Marginalized

MD. IRFAN BASHA

Education is the foremost important thing which brings transformation and far-reaching changes among the marginalized people. Any nation, any community, or any individual cannot prosper and develop without education. Many scholars have referred to the role of education in removal of poverty. There are quite a few studies that stress education as an important tool in the development of human beings. For instance, Carl Weinberg[1] observes, "Education is the major vehicle through which the generation to generation poverty cycle can be broken. The school must provide first the motivation and then the skills, abilities and knowledge that poor youngsters require to break free from the demoralizing and debilitating effects of deprivation". The development of social order increases with the progress of education. Thus, education certainly makes people live their life in a more harmonious way.

Muslim community in India is undergoing educational transition since a decade, but dynamics and the mechanisms through which such transformations are taking place are little understood. Our understanding on educational dynamics of Muslims is rather insufficient, because there is a shortage of empirical research that is carried out exclusively on Muslim population.

The task of education in aiding and facilitating social and economic progress is well established today. The aptitude of inhabitants of a state to improve their skill and perform in an atmosphere where technological and scientific knowledge is rapidly varying is vital for their development. Upgradation in analytical and functional capabilities of youth and children through educational instructions will bring in prospects leading to both personal and collective privileges. Progress in education has tremendous advantage to a marginalized community. It enhances efficiency, increases earnings, boosts democratic participation, upgrades health and improves quality of life. With as many as 280 universities, 13,150 colleges, 8.821 million students, and 0.427 million teachers during 2001–02 as against 32 universities, 695 colleges, and 0.174 million students during 1950–51, India has developed one of the largest higher education systems in the world.

This paper provides a broad perspective on issues relating to the education of Muslims in India and particularly in Andhra Pradesh The Muslims are at a double disadvantage with low levels of education combined with low quality education; their deprivation increases manifold as the level of education rises. In some instances the relative share for Muslims is lower than even the SCs who are victims of a long-standing caste system.

Literacy Rates and the Muslims

The low literacy level of Muslims, SCs/STs and other groups is well documented in research studies. This is shown in the Figure 1.[2] In the mid-1960s literacy levels of both SCs/STs and Muslims were low, and very much poorer than that of 'All Others'. The literacy rate among Muslims in 2001 was 59.1 per cent. This is far below the national average (65.1%). If the SCs/STs, with an even lower literacy level of 52.2 per cent and Muslims, are excluded, the remaining category of 'All Others' show a high literacy level of 70.8 per cent. In urban areas, the gap between the literacy levels of Muslims (70.1%) and the national average is 11 percentage points and in relation to the 'All Others' category it is 15 percentage points. Although the levels of literacy are lower in rural areas (52.7% for Muslims), the gap between the compared categories is also narrower. Although the literacy levels of 64 per cent and 68 per cent amongst male SCs/STs and

Figure 1 *All India-Literacy Rates by Social Groups-2001*

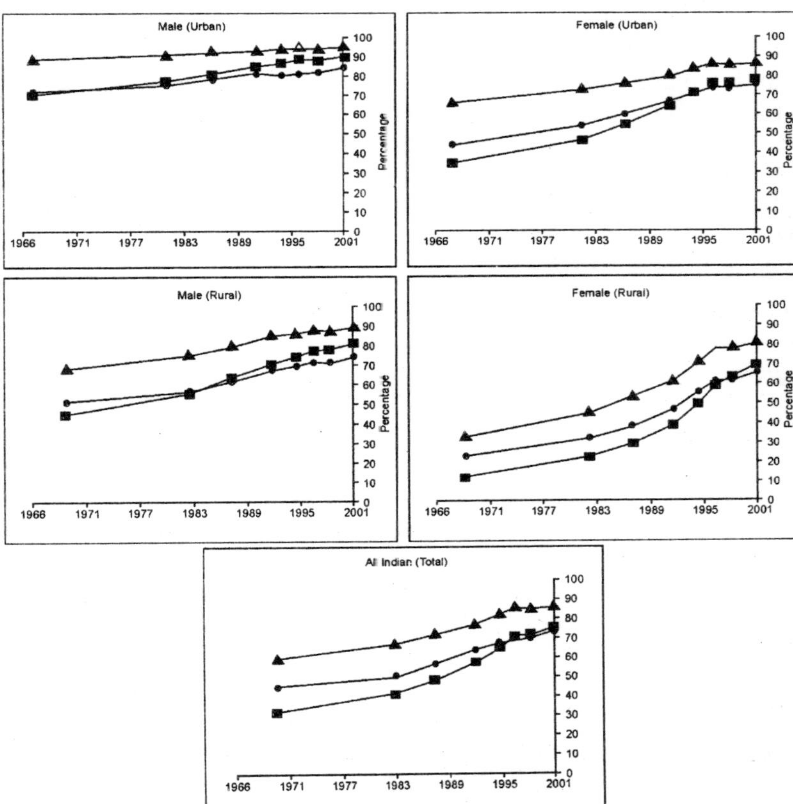

Source: Rajinder Sachar Report, p.55

Muslims respectively are not low, they are far below the level for 'All Others' which is 81 per cent. If we see the literacy levels in time perspective, another interesting feature emerges out, that is the SCs/STs group has achieved more than that of the Muslims in all quarters, be it in urban/rural or in gender composition. It is so because of the affirmative action taken by the government.

While there is a significant rural-urban differential, it was observed that the gap between Muslims and the other socio-religious communities (SRCs) is generally higher in urban areas than in rural areas. Similarly, though Muslim women have lower educational attainments than men, the gap with other SRCs is lower for women. Analysis of time trends indicate that, despite overall improvement in educational status, the rate of progress has been the slowest for Muslims. In other words, while educational attainments of Muslims have improved over the years, it has not been on a pace on par with the other groups.

The changes in educational correlations in these groups imply that SCs and STs have picked up at least some advantages of targeted government and private action supporting their educational progress. This manifests the importance of affirmative action. While the nature of affirmative action that is required needs to be assessed, a sharper focus on school education combined with more opportunities in higher education for Muslims seems desirable. Moreover, skill development initiatives for those who have not completed school education may also be particularly relevant for some section of Muslims given their occupational structure.

Table 1 reports age specific literacy rates computed from the NSSO 61st Round Data (2004–05). The estimates clearly show that in recent years the literacy rates for the SC/ST population have risen more sharply than for Muslims; while persons of the older age groups in the Muslim community had much higher literacy levels, these are higher for SCs/STs in the younger age groups. Therefore, the trends observed in the census data are also evident in the NSSO data (p. 54 in Sachar report).

Table 1 *Literates as Proportion of Population*

Age groups (Years)	*Hindus*			*Muslims*	*Other Minorities*
	General	*OBCs*	*SCs/STs*		
6–13	90.2	80.8	74.7	74.6	88.5
14–15	95.7	87.5	80.0	79.5	91.9
16–17	95.0	85.2	78.6	75.5	91.3
18–22	91.4	76.9	65.0	70.5	85.8
23 and above	74.0	50.6	36.5	46.1	67.0
Total	80.5	63.4	52.7	59.9	75.2

Source: Estimated from NSSO 61st Round, Sch 10, 2004–05.

Table 2 shows a comparative data of the performance of different social groups in primary, middle, secondary, higher secondary, technical diploma and graduation levels respectively. It can be inferred from the above data that the marginalized groups have to go long way to be on par with the dominant groups in their educational status.

Table 2 *Percentage of Groups who Completed at least the Following Levels*

Social Groups	*Primary*	*Middle*	*Secondary*	*Higher Secondary*	*Technical Diploma*	*Graduate (BA)*
All Religions	52	33	21	11	6	5
Muslims	44	24	14	6	3	3
Hindus including SC/ST	53	33	21	11	6	5
Hindu excluding SC/ST	59	39	26	13	7	7
Scheduled Castes	40	22	12	5	2	2
Scheduled Tribes	31	16	9	4	2	1

Source: Census Data, 2001.

It can be seen from the above table that the percentage of Muslims is low at different levels of education. On the whole a variety of socio-economic exclusivities wield a reflective impact on the literacy and schooling, and religion remains relatively of no consequence, substantiating the argument that educational backwardness among Muslims is not owing so much to religious convention as it is because of the explicit layer in which most of them are located that leave education of little or no significance.

Table 3 *Muslim Students in Intermediate Exams in A.P. (2005, 2006 and 2007)*

Year	*No. of candidates appeared*	*No. of candidates passed*	*Pass percentage*	*No. of Muslim candidates appeared*	*No. of Muslim candidates passed*	*Pass percentage*
2005	5,67,270	3,01,493	53.14	41,125	20,503	49.85
2006	5,26,249	3,35,301	57.19	42,616	23,131	54.27
2007	5,75,581	3,58,630	62.30	43,865	25,854	58.93

Source: Public Relations Officer, Board of Intermediate Education, Andhra Pradesh, Hyderabad.

Disparities in Higher Education

In India, a significant proportion of the relevant population still remains deprived of the benefits of higher education and the Muslims comprise an important category of the deprived communities. According to census data, while only about 7 per cent of the population aged 20 years and above are graduates or hold diplomas, this proportion is less than 4 per cent amongst Muslims. Besides, those having technical education at the appropriate ages (18 years and above) are as low as one per cent and amongst Muslims, that is almost non-existent.

Estimates from the NSSO 61st Round Data (provisional) regarding graduate level education, shows that the SCs/STs and Muslims are the most disadvantaged as their respective shares are much lower than their share in the population. In the case of Muslims, their share in graduates is 3.6 per cent while their share in population aged 20 years and above is more than double at over 11 per cent.

Table 4 *Graduates and Diploma Holders by Social Groups*

Social Groups	*Number (in Lakh)*		*Percentage*	
	Graduates	*Diploma and certificate*	*Graduates*	*Diploma and certificate*
Total	376.7	40.5	6.7	0.7
Muslims	23.9	2.7	3.6	0.4
SCs/STs	30.8	4.1	2.4	0.3
All Others	322	33.7	8.8	0.9

Source: NSSO 61st Round data.

The share of technical graduates is significant as it implies the supply of specialized competence accessible in the community/nation. Even as the group of technical graduates is even worse with just about 2 in every 1000 persons being a technical graduate, the performance of Muslims is worse than all the other social groups except SCs/STs, with a sharp disparity existing in urban regions and among the males.

Diploma courses correspond to a lower level of education and skill formation but even at this low level of technical education the overall pattern remains the same with Muslims not doing very well amongst the SRCs, except when compared with the SCs/STs. The gap between Muslims and other SRCs is particularly relevant for such training as Muslims have a substantial presence in the artisanal activities and have the potential, with some technical training, to do well in a variety of emerging and economically viable activities.

State Level Patterns

The all India trend of increasing disparities in Graduation Attainment Rate (GAR) between Muslims and 'All Others' is found to be prevalent in all states. In urban areas, Muslims are falling behind not only vis-à-vis 'All Others', but also SCs/STs in several states. This trend can be observed among both males and females. The rural scenario is equally bad from the perspective of attainment levels of Muslims. In most states, the differential in GAR between Muslims and 'All Others' has increased. In quite a few, SCs/STs have reduced the differential with Muslims, or even overtaken them.

Participation in Institutions of Higher Learning

The proportion of graduate and postgraduate students in different SRCs pursuing higher education in well-known institutions of higher learning is very small.

IIMs and IITs (2004–05 and 2005–06): The data in Sachar Report shows that Muslims constitute only 1.3 per cent of students studying in all courses in all IIMs in India, and in absolute number they were only 63 from out of 4743. In the case of the IITs, out of 27,161 students enrolled in the different programmes, there are only 894 Muslims. the share of Muslims in the postgraduate courses is just about 4 per cent but it is even lower in undergraduate courses at 1.7 per cent.

One possible factor could be low levels of achievement in the CAT examinations while another could be that although the achievement levels are similar across SRCs, not many Muslim candidates took the CAT examination in the first place.

Participation in Premier Colleges in India

The Committee undertook a survey of students currently enrolled in some of the premier colleges offering streams of regular science, arts and commerce courses and the premier medical colleges. The enrolment of Muslims in the regular streams of science, arts and commerce courses is: only one out of 25 students enrolled in undergraduate (UG) courses and only one out of every 50 students in postgraduate (PG) courses is a Muslim. The share of Muslims in all courses is low, particularly at the PG level, and marginal in the science stream. However, it is interesting that the enrolment ratio is higher among girls than boys in UG courses. At the PG level, however, this proportion falls—except in arts courses.

The representation of Muslims in the top medical colleges is only marginally better. It is about 4 per cent of students enrolled in all courses. Most of them are studying at the UG level namely in MBBS, dental, nursing, etc.

Enrolment of Muslim Students in Universities

According to Sachar Report estimates the proportion of Muslim students in the UG courses is about 9 per cent, which is lower than their share in the population, and significantly below that of both the SCs/STs and the OBCs. The participation of Muslims in engineering and medical courses is particularly low.

The status of Muslims in PG courses is equally disappointing. Only about one out of 20 students (5%) is a Muslim. This is significantly below the share of OBCs (24%) and SCs/STs (13%). However, Muslim students typically tend to seek professional courses, followed by commerce; in terms of absolute numbers and relative share they are at the bottom amongst the SRCs.

Given this dismal scenario, it is only too obvious that the state has so far failed to grapple with the reality of the enormous task of educating India's rising generation in socially impartial and universally viable ways. The problem is that many parents are too poor that they would like their children to be wage-earners, but also want to have their children educated.

Table 5 *Status of Muslim Students in Osmania University in Undergraduate level*

S.No.	*Year*	*Total Students in UG courses*	*Muslim Students*	*Percentage*
1.	2004–05	2,10,185*	6,562	3.12
2.	2005–06	2,10,185	6,894	3.27
3.	2006–07	2,10,185	7,125	3.38

*The actual number 210185 is with respect to the year 2006–07. The number of students in earlier years was very close to this number.

Source: Registrar, Osmania University, Hyderabad.

There is a chasm between what the education system is expected to achieve and what it is, in fact, accomplishing, and each of its main objectives remains to be achieved. Education was to be the medium through which equality of opportunity was to be made concrete, yet it remains an endlessly deferred dream for many; investment in education was meant to be a path of greater productivity and growth, yet its potential contribution to economy remains unrealized; education was to be an aspiration for better experience of excellence in all fields, yet it continues to remain a mere aspiration.

India's gross expenditure on education now, by the state and central governments combined, is nearly Rupees one lakh crore or 3.52 per cent of the GDP. Despite the rapid and massive growth of higher education, India has only about 8 to 9 per cent of its relevant age group enrolled for higher education, as against 50–85 per cent in developed countries.

Table 6 *Status of Muslim Students in Osmania University in PG Level*

Year	*Total Students in P.G courses*	*Muslim Students*	*Percentage*
2004–05	45,883*	1,385	3.01
2005–06	45,883	1,422	3.09
2006–07	45,883	1,890	4.11

*The number of P.G. students in the year 2006–07 are 45,883. We have added the No. of students as same in earlier 2 years.

Source: Registrar, Usmania University, Hyderabad.

Table 7 *Acharya NG Ranga Agricultural University*

Course	*Total No. of Students*	*Muslim Students 2004–05*	*Muslim Students 2005–06*	*Muslim Students 2006–07*
Undergraduate Programmes				
B.Sc. Ag	400	9	21	11
B.Sc. (Hort.)	160	2	3	3
B.Tech. (Agr. Engg.)	30	0	0	0
B.Sc. (CA & BM)	40	0	1	3
B.Tech. (Food Sci.)	40	1	0	0
B.H.Sc.	80	10	10	11
Postgraduate Programmes				
M.Sc. (Ag.)	130	0	1	3
M.Sc. (Hort.)	21	0	1	0
Master of Agri Bus. Mgmt	20	0	1	0
M.Sc. (Agri.Bio.Tech)	10	0	0	0
M.Sc. (Envn. Sci. & Tech.)	10	0	0	0
M.Sc. (Home Science)	20	0	0	2
M.Sc. (Food Sci. & Tech.)	15	0	1	0
Ph.D (Ag)	28	0	0	0
Ph.D (Home Science)	16	0	0	0

Source: Administrative Office, Acharya NG Ranga Agricultural University, Hyderabad.

The following is the table containing the data of Muslim students during the last three years. It is estimated that there are 2800 students both in P.G. and research studies now, and the earlier data in the year 2004 was 2,477 students.

Table 8 *Hyderabad Central University*

Course	*Muslim Students in 2004–05*	*Muslim Students in 2005–06*	*Muslim Students in 2006–07*
Postgraduate	62	46	27
M.Phil	17	18	22
Ph.D.	12	19	18
Total	91	83	71

Source: Public Information Officer, University of Hyderabad, dated April 7, 2007.

Suggestions

- The trouble with Indian education revolves around quality, financial support and impartiality, in approach and outturn. As these difficulties have been baffled by the rapid pace of globalization under which the world needs simply educated manpower, the marginalized in India are now victims of double obstruction. Their traditional dispossession keeps them away from quality education; and the stipulation of a knowledge-driven world under globalization set them aside out of the mainstream as social misfits—as the disposable people of society.
- Moreover, the recent trends in enrolments and other educational attainments and Sachar Committee's interactions with the Muslim community are adequate to dispel certain misconceptions and stereotypes with respect to education of Muslims. These need to be highlighted
- Muslim parents are not averse to modern or mainstream education and to sending their children to the affordable government schools. They do not necessarily prefer to send children to Madarsas. Regular school education that is available to any other child in India is preferred by Muslims also. A section of Muslims also prefer education through the English medium, while some others would like the medium of instruction to be Urdu. The access to government schools for Muslim children is limited.
- There is also a common belief that Muslim parents feel that education is not important for girls and that it may instill a wrong set of values. Even if girls are enrolled, they are withdrawn at an early age to marry them off. This leads to a higher drop-out rate among Muslim girls. This indicate that the problem may lie in non-availability of schools within easy reach for girls at lower levels of education, absence of girl's hostels, absence of female teachers and availability of scholarships as they move up the education ladder.
- It needs to be emphasized that the worth of mere literacy is low. Unlike literacy, education is a broad process that enables a person to adopt a rational and questioning attitude and facilitate the recognition of new

opportunities. Education also involves retention and enhancement of these capabilities over a lifetime and the ability to transmit education to the next generation in order to generate the considerable spillover effects documented by social scientists. Therefore, a person must be enrolled into a system of education and remain there for a minimum period in order to derive such benefits.

- Innovative schemes from the government should comprise admission of judiciously selected students from marginalized social groups, granting institutional support, dispensing scholarships, and arranging outreach programmes and regular meetings of group of colleges.
- The government should set up the community polytechnics to impart technical skills by setting them up in predominantly minority concentration areas. And encourage the minorities to own up the responsibility of sending their wards in it.
- The government should give assistance to universities/colleges for starting coaching classes for students belonging to educationally backward minorities.
- To provide vocational courses in higher secondary schools particularly to accommodate marginalized groups and setting up crafts training institutes in predominantly minority artisan concentration blocks, for the children of artisans. Since artisanship is a dominant activity among Muslims, various courses in technical training should be provided to even those who may not have completed schooling.
- A scheme to train in-service teachers from minority institutions in science, mathematics, social sciences, English and career guidance and a scheme for orientation programmes for principals/managers and training programmes for teachers of minority educational institutions have to be taken up on a war footing in a phased manner.
- Challenges of teaching science, mathematics and english will be made on voluntary basis in institutions imparting instructions in Madrasa schools. Socially useful productive Work will also be introduced in these institutions.
- As the enrolment of girls and literacy rate of the Muslim women is the lowest among educationally backward minorities, the government should think of opening of girls' schools, appointment of lady teachers, opening of girls hostels' and providing of incentives in the form of mid-day meals, uniforms etc.
- A training-cum-production centre for crafts exclusively for girls with women instructors in each of the identified minority concentration districts is to be opened.
- In this age of information and communication technologies sweeping the country, the Muslim community is totally out of tune and struggling. The institutions of higher learning in general are not transiting from the arcane structures to the symbols of postmodern society. The universities are finding it hard to cope-up with the requirements of time and technology on the one hand, and the emerging needs of the private sector, corporate

houses and the industry on the other. If that is so, there is very little one can expect from the Muslim minority professional institutions.

- The Muslim community has to relate itself to the emerging opportunities of industry interface, inter-disciplinary approach, pedagogic delivery system, online e-learning and choice-based credit-grading system, quality assurance and provide avenues for computer skills, communication skills, and personality development. They have not made significant efforts to produce inquisitive minds, scientific brains and persons with intellectual attainments and value orientation for higher research pursuits in the field of science, technology and social sciences.
- By and large, the Muslim community has failed to produce smart, dynamic, enterprising, well-grounded and dedicated individuals to carry on the mantles of globalizing world. The advantages of automation, networking, connectivity and pedagogic delivery systems—the hallmarks of knowledge era have not yet received their attention till date.

To conclude, there is no doubt that Muslims of India as a whole pause behind other socio-religious groups in the sphere of literacy and education. Nevertheless, the raison d'être accounting for their educational backwardness are varied and multifaceted, which remain incompletely portrayed in available research. Time and again, we are confronted with vague and tentative interpretation and unconfirmed formulations, which are in general narrow and polemical. Moreover, research regarding Muslim educational backwardness appears to ignore the socio-economic and spatial perspective in which Muslims survive. Situational isolated studies on education fall short of encapsulating their relative standing in relation to other communities.

The policy focus should be in those areas of education where private investment is not adequate to cover the weaker section of the population. While investment and effort from private and voluntary sectors could help in promoting convergence of educational levels of Muslims with that of other communities, the task remains essentially that of the state. Muslims have been not been able to sufficiently reap the benefits of state intervention and growth in education.

We feel that the policies have to sharply focus on inclusive development and 'mainstreaming' of the community while respecting the diversity. There is a pressing necessity to concede diversity in residential, work and educational spaces, apart from enhancing inclusion of the really marginalized groups in 'spaces' created by public programmes and policy interventions.

To lay Muslim education on a speed track, the main requirement is to promote the existing establishments by reassuring fairness and equity in their intake, by intensifying their vital and infrastructure requirements. This includes the recruitment of qualified teachers, and by grounding them in brilliance in quality and disciplinary diversity. The institutions have to address these issues in the presence of active intervention by educationists from outside. The public as well as the private sector with its corporate responsibility should provide adequate financial support and orientation to the educational institutions, backed by institution-friendly monitoring mechanisms.

The need for equity and inclusion in a pluralistic world can never be exaggerated. But the means to ensure fairness and equality of opportunity to create inclusion should be such that diversity is achieved and at the same time the perception of discrimination is eradicated. This can happen only when the significance of Muslims as an intrinsic section of the diverse Indian social mosaic is evenly accepted. When the spirit of commitment is combined with dedicated work, and a new innovative system of education evolves, the outcome in terms of access, equity, and excellence, can be profound.

Notes

1. Carl Weinberg, *Educated Social Problems,* New York: The Free Press, 1971, p. 46.
2. Rajindar Sachar Report on "Social, Economic and Educational Status of the Muslim Community of India", November 2006, pp. 50–58.

24 Poverty and Vulnerability among Tribal People

A Case of Sugalis

ESWARAPPA KASI

I

India has made systematic efforts to alleviate poverty through increased economic growth by using targeted programmes, land and tenancy reforms, participatory and empowerment-based approaches and the provision of basic services (Mehta and Shah, 2003: 491). But development remains unattainable for 350 million of its poorest citizens. Gandhi's vision of development has been undermined through large-scale industrialization, urbanization and modernization (Saxena, 2000a: 6). Since 1951, five-year plans have been adopted to propel India's development in industry and agriculture, and to remedy the political dissension, debt, and infrastructural disarray that plagued the newly independent country (Indian Social Institute, 1988). Development actions have succeeded in exponentially increasing India's industrial, military and agricultural production, its national income and middle class. Yet, in 2001, almost fifty-four years after independence, development has failed to alleviate poverty and related socio-economic oppressions within the most disenfranchised caste, class and tribal communities.

Development institutions continue to assert processes that systematically delegitimize traditional livelihoods by impoverishing the natural resource base upon which the lives of subsistence communities depend (Escobar, 1995). In response to such neglected communities across India are operationalizing frameworks of developmental strategies that link social, cultural and economic well being of the communities. Further, it should be in accordance with the needs and aspirations of the tribal communities which would enhance their livelihood systems and strengthen their coping mechanisms in relation to vulnerability context.

Wikipedia, defines 'vulnerability' as the susceptibility to physical or emotional injury or attack. It also means to have one's guard down, open to censure or criticism; assailable. Vulnerability refers to a person's state of being liable to succumb, as to persuation or temptation. In relation to hazards and disasters, vulnerability is a concept that links the relationship that people have with their environment to social forces and institutions and the cultural values that sustain and contest them. "The concept of vulnerability expresses the multidimensionality of disasters by focusing attention on the totality of relationship in a given social situation which constitutes a condition that, in combination with environmental forces, produces a disaster" (Bankoff et al., 2004: 11).

Vulnerability is the opposite of security. A vulnerable human being is:

1. Capable of being physically (emotionally or spiritually) wounded;
2. Open to attack or damage (physical, emotional or spiritual); and
3. Lacking in defence or support mechanisms (at the levels of state/government, community, household and individual).

Some examples of vulnerable populations are small-scale farmers, fishermen, pastoral nomads, forest populations, slum dwellers, women-headed households, traditionally marginalized groups, landless, and refugees (UNCRD: 1).

Moser defines vulnerability as "insecurity and sensitivity in the well-being of individuals, households, and communities in the face of a changing environment, and implicit in this, their responsiveness and resilience to risks that they face during such negative changes" (Moser, 1998: 1–19).

Current poverty analysis recognizes the need to address vulnerability. Pritchett et al. (2000) find that most poverty measures consider shortfalls in current income or consumption expenditures to determine the poverty line. They argue that these measures do not indicate the vulnerable among the population and therefore it proposes that 'vulnerability to poverty line (VPL)' is the level below which a household is vulnerable to poverty. A household with a risk of experiencing at least one episode of poverty in the near future or has a greater than 50 per cent chance of falling into poverty is considered vulnerable.

Moser (1998), further elaborates that vulnerability is inextricably linked with asset ownership, where the assets are as follows:

1. Labour, which is a valuable asset possessed by most poor people;
2. Human capital, such as education, skills, and health that determine the ability to emerge from poverty and make enhanced use of the labour;
3. Productive assets such as land and housing, and tools for production;
4. Household relations, that determine equitable distribution of resources within a family, for example, ensuring that women have equitable access to food and education; and
5. Social capital, the relationship between households and within communities based on kinship, religion, and mutual interdependence.

Vulnerability and Risk

Key to the discussions of vulnerability and risk in the Chronic Poverty Research Centre (CPRC) literature is the suggestion by Hulme et al. (2001) that:

"What poor people are concerned about is not so much that their levels of income, consumption or capabilities are low, but that they are likely to experience highly stressful declines in these levels, to the point of premature death. This approach suggests that poverty can be seen as the probability (actual or perceived) that a household will suddenly (but perhaps also gradually) reach a position with which it is unable to cope, leading to catastrophe" (p. 9).

This definition of poverty can also be seen as a particularly accurate proxy for a definition of vulnerability, especially due to its emphasis on the risk (whether real or imagined) of being unable to cope. However, in the CPRC literature risk and vulnerability are viewed in different ways. For example, in a discussion of the 'Risk of Market Failure' Bird et al. (2002) highlight that vulnerability to risk may be greater in remote rural areas. This 'vulnerability to risk' is similar to the conception of 'vulnerability to shocks' and views vulnerability as a cause of poverty. For example, in the same paper risk appears to be placed as a precursor to vulnerability. This almost comes across in a linear fashion with risk being the initial step in an assumed chain of events: "there are numerous sources of risk ... which make households more likely to suffer shocks and experience an erosion of assets, deepening their vulnerability to future shocks and damaging their ability to escape poverty" (Bird et al., 2002: 18). This linear depiction of risk and vulnerability (Risk—Exposure to Shocks—Erosion of Assets—Increased Vulnerability to Shocks—Shift into or Persistence of Poverty) contrasts with the earlier conceptions of vulnerability as being a cause, constituent part, and symptom of poverty, and in a sense reduces vulnerability to again being only a cause of poverty. This is not to argue that risk is not central to the processes which create and perpetuate chronic poverty, but that a dominant focus on risks, whether covariant or singular, could sideline equally important structural and idiosyncratic bases to chronic poverty. It is also central to recognize that the outcome of risks depends on how individuals, households, interest groups or communities respond to risk, as an increase in risk can, for some more than others, also increase opportunities.

Discussions of risk and vulnerability can also be found in the overview papers on Sri Lanka (Tudawe, 2002) and India (Mehta and Shah, 2001). Tudawe (2002) argues that a lack of financial capital limits the ability of poor people to 'manage risk and vulnerability' (p. 28). This idea of managing vulnerability is important, and indicates the agency of people in limiting uncertainty through having enough capacity to deal with any exposure to risk and vulnerability. This relates to the difference between the internal and external sides to vulnerability. Mehta and Shah (2001) highlight the relationship between risk and vulnerability through the work of Kozel and Parker (2001). These latter authors categorize the 'poor' into three groups; the destitute poor, the structural poor, and the 'mobile' poor. Interestingly, Kozel and Parker (2001) assert that, while risk and vulnerability were important for all three categories, it is particularly important for the destitute and structural poor. This contrasts with the common 'vulnerability to poverty' use of the 'vulnerability' found in the CPRC literature, which focuses on the 'transient poor', and instead sees the vulnerability of 'chronically poor' as being particularly important.

As risk is central to differing concepts of vulnerability, it seems appropriate to highlight some key distinctions in relation to risk which will be important in latter discussions about how it is best to disaggregate vulnerability for the study of chronic poverty.

Partial and Total Risks

Total risks are those which impact upon a wide spectrum, or the full portfolio, of assets/activities whilst partial risks only influence a particular determinant of well-being (Sinha and Lipton, 1999: 7).

Generic and Specific Risks

Risks can be divided into those which affect large number of people due to geographical location or particular activities (also termed covariate risks) and those risks which are specific to an individual or household (also termed idiosyncratic risks) (Devereux, 2001; Sinha and Lipton, 1999). This is the scale of risk and uncertainty and can be related to macro-(international), meso-(sub-national), and micro-levels (individual) (Devereux, 2001: 509).

Known and Unknown Risks

Risks come in the form of those which are expected or predictable and hence are known to some extent, and those risks which are unexpected, unpredictable, and unknown. Sinha and Lipton (1999) propose the term 'Damaging Fluctuation' (DF) as a description for a known risk whilst an unknown risk is termed as a 'Risky Damaging Fluctuation'. In this respect, a DF can be more or less 'risky' depending on the extent to which is known and can be predicted. The continuum from damaging fluctuations to risky DFs used by Sinha and Lipton (1999) seems useful, and is related to the further distinction between DFs and worsening trends. Devereux (2001) highlights the difference between cyclical risks (such as seasonality), stochastic risks (such as flood-prone locations), and unpredictable downturns (such as financial crises) (Devereux, 2001: 510).

Perception of Risk

Whilst a traditional understanding of the perception of risk would contrast the everyday 'inaccurate' and 'irrational' perceptions of people against the 'real' scientific probability of risk (Oliver-Smith, 1996: 319), Smith (1996) outlines three general modes of understanding risk in relation to hazards:

- Determinate perception: An understanding that seeks to impose order upon the random nature of risks and hazards, often by reference to an order or cycle of events.
- Dissonant perception: Essentially threat denial, this type of understanding questions occurrence of past risks and hazards or rationalizes them as 'freak' events.
- Probabilistic perception: Most closely connected to idea of an information responsive rational evaluator of risk, this type of interpretation acknowledges the random nature of risks and their potential consequences. Often is associated with placing the responsibility of the threat to a higher authority such as God or government (summarized from Smith, 1996: 71).

People, therefore, have a variety of modes of understanding risks and such perceptions will change considering the experience of the individual and the social and cultural setting in which these understandings are formed. In this sense, it should be recognized that "risk perception and assessment are grounded in the cultural norms and values that govern and are embedded in the relationship that human communities have with their physical and social environment" (Oliver-Smith, 1996). Moreover, there is a need to move away from just viewing the perception of risks as being constrained solely by imperfect information but to recognize the relationship between structure and agency which can determine an understanding of, and response to, risk (for example see Wisner, 1993; Kothari, 2002).

Sources of Risk

Henninger (1998) outlines five sources of risk which influence vulnerability:

- Environmental risk (droughts, floods, and pests).
- Market risk (price fluctuations, wage variability, and unemployment).
- Political risk (changes in subsidies or prices, income transfers, and civil strife).
- Social risk (reduction in community support and entitlements).
- Health risk (exposure to diseases that prevent work) (Henninger, 1998: 12).

As Henninger notes, these risks only form part of the equation as the consequence of risk depends on the response by individuals or households to the risk. This relates to the internal and external sides of vulnerability. Sinha and Lipton (1998) offer a review of the empirical evidence of risks by distinguishing between six different types of risky DFs:

- Disease or injury
- Violence, including domestic, criminal, and war-related.
- Natural disaster.
- Harvest failure.
- Terms-of-trade deterioration, especially affecting the price of food
- relative to labour
- Reduced access to productive or income-earning work (Sinha and Lipton, 1999: 8).

Sinha and Lipton (1998) suggest that these categories offer a potential window from which to assess how structural adjustment has influenced the 'poor', and suggest, somewhat contentiously, that adjustment is only likely to affect the last two categories. In this respect they highlight how early adjustment in the form of stabilization plus liberalization will exacerbate both categories of risk, but that through 'economic logic' longer term adjustment will "stimulate faster growth, and lead poor and labour-abundant countries to specialize in labour-intensive activities, in both cases raising the mean income of the poor and thus lowering their vulnerability to any given DF" (p. 9).

There are two key points to be made here. Firstly, the hypothesis that raising the mean income of the poor not only homogenizes a highly diverse social category (for example: will all of the chronically poor be able to partake in such labour-intensive activities) but presumes that an increase in the means of well-being (income) will equate un-problematically to vulnerability reduction. This may not be the case. A major reason for this is highlighted by Sinha and Lipton themselves (p. 9) who acknowledge that increased specialization in income generating activities may actually increase vulnerability as future risks would be total risks as opposed to previously having been partial risks in a diversified portfolio of activities.

Secondly, and more importantly, it can be argued that adjustment has a substantial influence on other areas of risk. This includes a direct influence on the risk associated with a 'Natural Disaster'. Unfortunately Sinha and Lipton (1999) appear to confuse a natural hazard with the potential consequent 'disaster', the connection being an interaction with a 'vulnerable' population. In this respect, adjustment, at any stage, will have an important influence on the scale and severity of a 'disaster' as this is partially defined by the ability of individuals and households response to the hazard. Therefore Sinha and Lipton locate themselves firmly within the behavioural paradigm of understanding disasters. This has particular significance in relation to their conception of 'vulnerability' which is discussed in section 3.6.

The extent to which adjustment is a source of risk for populations is matched by the extent to which governments are also seen as sources of risk. For example, Baulch and Hoddinot (2000) highlight the states role in modifying the "economic, legal and political settings within which the household is embedded" (p. 19) and provide the examples of how macro-economic instability and the rule and law can be important sources of risk. Wisner (1993) illustrates how the state can also be seen as a risk itself through denying the existence of hazard, directing violence towards subgroups within the population, or orientating intervention efforts towards or away from particular locations or populations. It is interesting to note that whilst government itself is highlighted as a source as risk along with government policy, the discussions of structural adjustment as a source of risk highlight only the policies and not the institutions which promulgate these policies.

The present paper tries to proceed answering four questions; what is poverty, who is the poor, why are they poor and how to solve the problem? Based on these questions the present paper has organized into three sections, where first part of the discussion above deals with the brief introduction on the literature on the themes on poverty and vulnerability. The second part tries to explain the statement of the problem and how the problem is viewed by different agencies. The third part of the paper opens up the discussion on village setting, the methodology used in the study and available resources in the settlement. Final part of the paper delineates the conclusions and observations.

II
Statement of the Problem

Poverty is not about income alone. Social, political and even seasonal factors affect well-being from time to time. Women and girls are often particularly vulnerable groups in poor communities. The poor are found in every village, block and district of rural India and in every town and city. They are most numerous in areas where the land is less productive, where water is scarce, where communications are poor or where certain castes or tribes predominate. The poor are increasingly found in towns and cities as people migrate from less productive rural areas to urban areas, where they aspire for better life.

"To be poor is still to be powerless and vulnerable. Life remains a torment for children in the teeming barrio of a developing country's city, for refugees caught up in conflict, for women in a society that still denies them equality and freedom—every day bringing physical and psychological threats. And still too many of the 1.2 billion people living on less than a dollar a day lack even the most basic human security" (Human Development Report, 2000: 7).

The primary objective of the Indian Constitution is social justice. It upholds the dignity of the individual, guaranteeing citizens a fundamental right to equality before the law. It promises that they will not be discriminated against on the grounds of religion, race, caste, sex, or place of birth. It guarantees equality of opportunity in public employment, and assures personal freedoms such as the right to speech, life, liberty and religion.

The Directive Principles take this commitment a step further by instructing the state to secure a wide range of measures, including free legal aid and the citizen's right to work, education and public assistance. They also enjoin the state to ensure a living wage for all workers. Though non-enforceable, the Directive Principles declare:

"The state shall ... strive to minimize the inequalities in income, and endeavour to eliminate inequalities in status, facilities and opportunities" (Unnikrishnan, 2001: 27).

In spite of this, the World Development Report says that over 40 per cent of the population in India lives below the poverty line, and nearly half are still illiterate.

The overall figures for every aspect of development, when broken down, indicate that the poor and those who face discrimination are the worst sufferers and lack access to the basics. As the World Development Report puts it, "Poor women face a double disadvantage in access to resources and voice—they are poor, and they are women" (World Bank, 2000: 11). The Human Development Report 2000 found 'extreme deprivation' especially among rural women from Scheduled Tribes.

In its study of human poverty, the report says that 19 per cent of India's population still lacks access to safe water, a quarter does not have access to health services and as much as 71 per cent lives without access to sanitation. More than half—53 per cent—of all Indian children below the age of five are underweight. There are only 0.4 telephones to every thousand Indians. The top 10 per cent of India's people account for 33.5 per cent of income or consumption. The 10 per cent at the other end of the scale account for a mere 3.5 per cent. Although progress has been made in areas such as literacy and life expectancy, a very large number of people remain excluded from the development that others in the country enjoy.

The World Development Report (2000–2001) noted that "Evidence from India shows that scheduled castes and scheduled tribes are among the structural poor who not only lack economic resources but whose poverty is strongly linked to social identity, as determined by caste. They also have worse social indicators."

The World Development Report (2000: 46) estimated that 44 per cent of the Indian population still lives on less than $ 1 a day. Eighty six per cent live on less than $ 2 a day. Poverty figures are said to be declining but, there are more poor people in India today than the population of the country in 1947. Yet, the government celebrates the swift decline of poverty. Figures cannot communicate what 'living in poverty' means or how it affects human dignity (Sainath, 1996: 18).

People who live in extreme poverty, in which the very basics of life—food, security, sanitation, health care, education, housing and employment—are denied, are automatically denied also the right to live without fear and want. In extreme situations, these conditions might even threaten their right to life itself.

Poverty is seen to impede the progress of nations because large sections of the population remain illiterate and hungry and cannot, therefore, contribute to development and growth. The truth is that the poor have not been given much attention because of the perception that a poor person hardly exists and can only lay claim, modestly, to 'poor' rights. Such perceptions need to be changed. Poverty is much more than mere lack of income. It is deprivation across many dimensions. In floods and famines, it is the poor who are the most affected. In terms of physical security, it is the poor who are most often the victims of arbitrary violence.

Poor people are particularly vulnerable to adverse events that are outside their control. They are often treated badly by the institutions of state and society and excluded from voice and power in those institutions (World Development Report, 2000).

A study carried by the World Development Report 2000–2001 says that "Famines are often the result of crises that affect agricultural production—floods or droughts. How quickly governments respond to such crises depends on many factors. A fundamental one is the level of democracy and the extent to which politicians are held accountable for the efficiency of programmes". A recent study in India shows that the distribution of newspapers can play a big part (Unnikrishnan, 2001: 27). The study says that the higher the circulation, the better the response of the local government. State governments were most sensitive, the study says, to high circulating newspapers in local languages read by the local electorate.

The Voices of the Poor study carried by the World Development Report 2000–2001, says: "In India, the characteristics of credit institutions can deter poor people from seeking loans. Poor people in many regions also report widespread corruption in health care systems. But when facing serious health conditions, they feel they have no choice but to comply with demands for bribes." (World Bank, 2000–01: 12).

Mehta et al. (2003: 502) has rightly viewed that poverty seems to be disproportionately high among historically marginalized groups such as Scheduled Castes and Scheduled Tribes. The multiple deprivations suffered by these groups make it harder for them to escape from poverty. Caste and tribe are structural factors that predispose certain groups to long-term poverty and deprivation. The Scheduled Castes are a collection of castes and some of them are small and marginal farmers, most of them in rural areas work largely as agricultural labourers. The scheduled tribes were identified on the basis of certain well defined criteria including distinctive culture and pre-agricultural modes of production. Sankaran (2000) has rightly stated that the two-thirds of India's bonded labourers are from scheduled castes and scheduled tribes (Quoted in Mehta et al., 2003).

Further, Mehta et al. (2003) mentioned that qualitative research validate the greater vulnerability of scheduled castes and scheduled tribes to poverty. Kozel and Parker (2001) identified a typical poor household as one which is at the low end of the caste hierarchy—most often a member of the scheduled tribe … . Lanjouw and Stern (1991) also postulate a strong correlation between caste and poverty in India. Based on a study, they report that among this group, poverty remains endemic. This is a reflection not only of poor endowments of productive assets, but also of low educational standards, vulnerability and little access to any kind of regular employment (Mehta et al., 2003).

According to Hulme et al. (2001) poverty has many dimensions and the poor suffer deprivation in multiple ways and not just in terms of income. Several forms of human deprivation, including poor survival chances, unjust employment of children, bonded labour, environmental pollution and social exclusion are not related to income in a predictable manner (UNDP, 1997; cited by Mehta and Shah, 2003: 496). The poor also lack access to assets such as credit, literacy, water, and forests.

Vigdis Broch-Due (1995) emphasizes that the concepts of poverty employed in most development analysis are very 'thin', focusing on material and measurable elements, such as income and nutrition. In contrast 'thick' ethnographic work reveals far more complex, multi-layered pictures. The various concepts and definitions of poverty and wealth, or more broadly, ill being and well being, which policy agencies use have emerged in specific cultural and historical contexts. Material deprivation—lack of food and income, poor health—may be important everywhere. But ideas employed by African peoples in particular contexts and selected aspects of material life and also group them with other attributes in distinctive ways, form the natural focus of anthropological work in or around the topic of poverty (cited in Booth et al., 1999).

In discussions about the multi-dimensionality of poverty, it is commonplace that the ways people experience material conditions are mediated through social relations and institutions. Yet anthropological studies emphasize that well being is frequently also conceived or defined in terms of social relations and kin networks, and a person's place in them.

Anthropological work focuses attention on how experiences of poverty and well being vary over the course of people's lifetimes. The developmental cycle of domestic groups (Goody, 1971) was a key concept which drew attention to how opportunities and vulnerabilities might shift through the processes of establishing marriage, having children, children growing up, and ageing. There are links here with economists' ideas about the importance of household size, dependency ratios and so on. However, anthropologists pay attention not only to changes in economic status within developmental cycles, but also to how members at different ages and life stages may be differentially linked into wider kin networks and social relations, and hence be more or less secured and 'supported'.

The present paper deals with the Sugalis (also called Lambadi in the local area), one of the largest and advanced tribes of Andhra Pradesh. They are concentrated in Chittoor, Cuddapah and Anantapur districts of the state. According to Krishna Reddy (1991) Sugalis are not the autochthones of South India. Their original home is believed to be Marwar in Rajasthan. They came into Deccan as transporters of supplies or merchandise for the armies of Delhi emperors in their raids in the south early in the 17th century. Some of the Sugalis returned to the north but some stayed behind and carried on petty trade with their pack-bullocks. They became a useful medium of transaction between the South and the North during periods of peace until 1850s. (cited in Krishna Reddy, 2003: 2). In the 18th century they had also taken up service under the Maratha rulers of Satara, Peshwas of Poona, the Nizam of Hyderabad and the British in their Mysore and Maratha wars.

With the advent of the British rule, the Sugalis gave up much of their traditional occupation of transporting goods due to introduction of mechanized transport, laying of roads and rail lines by the then government. Being poor, illiterate and lacking technical skills, they degenerated and took to crimes like robbery, dacoity, cattle-lifting and kidnapping of children until the middle of the last century. To reform them through persuasion and education was considered impossible by the British administration. Therefore, in order to control their criminal activities, they were brought under the purview of the Criminal Tribes Act XXVII of 1,871 (cited in Rao, 2004: 19). According to Rao (2004) after India became independent, the Criminal Tribes Act was repealed in 1952 and the Sugalis were denotified. Till 1977, they were treated as nomadic tribe in all parts of Andhra Pradesh except Telangana region. However, the list of Scheduled Tribes has been revised by the Scheduled Castes and Scheduled Tribes Orders (Amendment Act) 1976 in order to remove area restriction in respect of the Sugalis.

III
Location and People

Adadakulapalle Thanda is situated in the Adadakulapalle village Panchayat of Penukonda Mandal in Anantapur district, about 10 kilometres from Penukonda, the Mandal headquarters. Adadakulapalle Thanda consists of 165 households belonging to Sugali (Scheduled Tribe). Adadakulapalle Panchayat is reserved for Sugalis. Adadakulapalle Thanda is inhabited by Sugalis only. In Adadakulapalle Thanda the majority of Sugalis forms small farmers. The number of large and marginal farmers is quite few. The crops cultivated are paddy and ragi, which are the staple crops and they constitute the staple diet of all communities. Commercial crop like groundnuts are also grown in the village. Agriculture is their main source of livelihood followed by agriculture labour. Majority of the households follow nuclear type of family system. They have a primary school in the village and four teachers are posted in the school. It has road and transport facility. There is a seven seater auto which runs between Adadakulapalle and

Penukonda. The owner of the auto hails from the Adadakulapalle village. People depend upon the road to transport their produce to the market. Cattle, goat, and sheep are the major livestock in the area. Several varieties of grass along with stocked paddy straw, maize stalk, groundnut and *bhoosa* are used as fodder. Poultry is widely prevalent in the Adadakulapalle Thanda. The Adadakulapalle Thanda has telephone facility in Sarpanch's house. It also has a ration shop under the public distribution system to supply the necessary commodities to the needy people at concessional rates. The president of the Gram Panchayat is from the Scheduled Tribe community.

Protected drinking water is available to all the people of the Adadakulapalle Thanda. Each lane has taps and they have hand pumps within the Thanda, which provide water for the entire year. Health facilities are not easily accessible to the people. They have to go to nearby towns or *Mandal* headquarters. ANM from PHC and PHC personnel come to the village for health check-up often.

Livelihoods of the People

The major livelihoods activities (Table 2) of Sugalis are cultivation, followed by dairying, petty business (running owned and rented autos and kirana shop and hotel). Sugalis do go to agricultural labour, construction or repair works.

The primary livelihood activity of Sugali is cultivation, followed by daily wage labour, and petty businesses such as running one's own or rented auto-rickshaw, kirana (provisions) shop or *angadi* (tea and snacks stall). The majority of them depend on agricultural labour and construction or repair works in and outside the settlement. Cattle, goat, and sheep are the major livestock in the area. Several varieties of grass along with stocked paddy straw; maize stalk, groundnut and bhoosa (powdered rice husk mixed with dried groundnut kernel and molasses) are used as fodder. Individual households raise country chicken in their houses.

The type of land available in the settlement is dry land and only one Sugali farmer has a bore well in his land as against 90 bore wells owned by persons of other communities in the settlement. The rest of the Sugali depend upon the monsoon. Frequent failure of the monsoons has caused out-migration of people to Bangalore and Mumbai to work as construction labour or petty traders. People from the settlement explained that seasonal migration is high among them as the majority of them are marginal farmers and landless agricultural labourers. It is worth mention here that seasonal migration does supplement investable surplus when cash needs are high and sources of institutional borrowings are few (Sah and Sisodia, 2004: 32–33). Almost half of the households in the settlement migrate to towns in the off-season, according to the Gram Panchayat Sarpanch. One informant stated that they are helpless and there is no solution except to migrate to other areas. Younger people migrate to towns in the off seasons and come back to the settlement during the rains, to cultivate the land or work as farm labourers. In the cities and towns, the Sugali face social discrimination as migrants and also face political disenfranchisement as non-locals.

Table 1 *Distribution of Households by Caste/Community*

Type of House	*Type of Castes (No. of Households)*				
	Scheduled Tribe	*Scheduled Caste*	*Backward Castes*	*Other Castes*	*Total*
Stone Houses	98	46	113	75	332
Mud Houses	28	10	21	—	59
Huts	29	04	15	—	48
Total	155	60	149	75	439

Source: Field Data

Table 2 *Available Livelihoods in the Settlement*

Type of Livelihoods	*Total Households in the Settlement*	*Scheduled Tribe (Sugali)*	*% of ST's in the Total*
Wage Labourers/Land less People	237	124	52.32
Agriculture	225	80	35.55
Petty Business	25	10	40.00
Others (Dependents)	25	10	40.00

Source: Field Data

NGO Intervention in the Thanda

An NGO by name Social Education Development Society (SEDS) has been working in the area for the last twenty-five years. It was started in the year 1980; head office is located in Mekalapalle village, which is 15 kilometres from the Mandal headquarters. SEDS facilitates government-sponsored programmes and they have their own programmes in the villages. Initially, they were working in the two Mandals and now their coverage has risen to five Mandals (Penukonda, Somandepalle, Gorantla, Roddam, and Chilamathur) covering 209 villages. According to the manager of SEDS, their main concentration is Scheduled Caste, Scheduled Tribes and other weaker sections in all their villages. Each village have a community level organizer who is based in the village and looking after their works. Likewise, Adadakulapalle is one of their main concentrated villages in the area. Now, the major activities of the NGO are land development programmes, school development programmes, where they construct toilets and plant the trees in the school surroundings, horticulture programmes, women empowerment through the formation of self-help groups (SHGs), water harvesting schemes and to provide minimum wage works to assist the marginal people and landless agricultural labourers. They have initiated the unit, where, all SHGs in the village to start organization called 'Village Organisation'. Village Organisation has started with two people from each SHG in the village. At present, the total strength of Village Organisation is 32 in the village. Village Organisation acts as a nodal agency in the village and undertakes all the developmental works (SEDS, 2004).

Following are the works taken up by the NGO in the village during 2001–2005:

Name of the Activity	*Total Area*
Horticulture	100 Acres
Wasteland Plantation	250 Acres
Water Ponds	68
Fire Tracing	32,988.80sqm
Check Dams Desilting	4
Gurrappa Kunta Construction Work	90,000
Gully Checks	25
Ploughing	29 Acres
Soil Bunding	50 Acres
Seed Dibbling	50 Kg
Avenue Plantation	4 km

Source: SEDS Office, Mekalapalle

SEDS is working for the upliftment of Scheduled Tribe and Scheduled Caste in the village. It is observed from the table that their concentration is more on wasteland plantation, horticulture, water conservation and land development programmes of Sugalis and SCs in the village.

Land Development Programme

Under this programme, wastelands have converted into agricultural fields through soil conservation. Soil conservation works include stone bunding, gully checks, spill ways, woodlots, fire tracing, ploughing, and trenching activities. All these works are being undertaken in the summer season which provides some wage works to the people of the village. Some of the works like stone bunding, ploughing, fire tracing, and trenching, are carried by collecting some contribution from the beneficiaries. For instance, stone bunding activity, NGO provides four people and beneficiary has to one person. Likewise, ploughing, fire tracing and trenching activities where both have to share the work as well as money. Here I am mentioning case, who is beneficiary under the land development programme.

Case Study of a Beneficiary

Ranga Naik, 55-years-old, studied 5th class, has two sons, who are separated after their marriage, has 16 acres of land in the village. The type of land is dry land in nature and do not have water facility before. SEDS have chosen him as beneficiary and started the land development programme in the year 2000 as revealed by the Ranga Naik. Further, soil conservation works have initiated with the help and support from the NGO. NGO also assisted him to go for digging bore well in his land. Later, SEDS people suggested him to for horticulture crop by providing plants of mango, chinta (tamarind), eucalyptus, etc. He also said that there are 340 mango plants in 8 acres of land, 240 tamarind plants in 6 acres of land and eucalyptus in 2 acres of land. Watering to these plants is provided by through water tanker of NGO. Ranga Naik has complained that there is severe problem of forest pigs and cows in the area. To protect the seedlings from the forest pigs and cows, NGO has appointed watcher, beneficiary only, by paying Rs 600 per month as a salary. Due to this problem he has to stay and sleep there in the *polam* (agricultural field) leaving his wife at home, who is alone in the house. He also revealed that his polam is far off from the village, which is nearly 3 km and no electric facility is available for the land. They have complained so many times to the officials but so far they have not done anything as felt by Ranga Naik. Officials have told them that providing electric facility to the fields is difficult since the lands are far off from the village and lanes are not available in the nearby area.

Ranga Naik has told that children's are separated after their marriage leaving parents alone. This is because of the demands and dreams of the young couples as felt by the informant. Further, he mentioned that, they are not practising traditional type of marriages, which used to celebrate for couple of days. Majority of the families of Sugalis are following modern type of marriages, which are just for two days celebrations and that to in the marriage halls. This change is due to the improvement of communication facilities like newspapers, television, radio and also due to the education of the people as felt by the Ranga Naik.

Available Resources in the Village

Following are the common property resources available in the Adadakulapalle Village:

1. Village tank
2. Forest (Unreserved/Revenue)
3. Temple land

Village Tank

Village tank is covered Adadakulapalle village and Adadakulapalle Thanda, where both come under the same Panchayat. Majority of the lands situated under village tank belonging to Adadakulapalle village farmers. People felt that tank was important because for cultivation of crops like Pkm chinta (tamarind), sunflower and often groundnut crops. For cultivation of the crops, they are using tank water. They also said that due to tank, they are not facing the problem of shortage of power; not only that, due to tank, their subsequent wells and bore wells got benefited by increasing groundwater level in the bore wells and raise of water in the open wells.

People who were not having lands under the tank, were also said that it is important for washing clothes (women), watering to cattle, etc. Grass (*Jammu*-local name), which is there in the water is used for making of mats, covering of roof (houses or huts), and construction of sheds to small ruminants. It is also used for fencing of houses.

Another important benefit from the tank is of fishing. Fishing activity is for domestic purposes where all the people of the village do fishing activity individually and also as a group. People, who do fishing activity in a group, share the outcome equally, by giving extra share to the person who brings nets.

People also revealed that, they also use the tank for cultivation of cucumber crop in the tank and cattle grazing whenever tank was dry up. Majority of the beneficiaries were landless labourers, marginal and small farmers. Because of the tank landless people are getting more number of wage days as said by the informants. So villagers felt that tank has given them both direct and indirect benefits.

Unreserved/Revenue Forest

People of the village/Thanda are benefited by the forest by means of fuel wood collection, cattle grazing, collection of Bandaru Aku (which are used for roof/leaves purposes and house fencing) and *bodha* grass (roof and sale purposes). But some people said that, we are not having cattle, so it is not that important for me. Finally people believed that forest is benefited to them but, landless people are not benefited much due to lack of resources.

Temple Land

According to people there are 20 acres of temple land available in the village. Earlier land was given to any farmer for cultivation on the auction basis, which is for one-year duration. According to informants auction is based on the meeting, which is attended by village elders and decides the modalities, terms and conditions and money/amount is on an acreage basis. The amount they get from the farmers was used for development activities of the temple and celebration of temple festivals, rituals in that particular year.

After entering of watershed programme into the village, the situation has changed completely. Villagers conducted Gramsabha and decided to go for raising commercial crop (Pkm chinta) in temple land. Now it is called as 'chinta Topu' (tamarind Topu). Now also, they are using temple land for village development activities but differently. It means that the percentage of income is more than before. They also felt that there are other benefits from tamarind Topu/trees like *chiguru* (used for curry and also they mixed it with *dal*) etc. Generally women collect the chiguru and dry it for few days and they will use this chiguru during non-availability of vegetables or scarcity of vegetable seasons. It is also beneficial by way of giving fuel wood collection to the people.

But Sugalis from the Thanda felt that they are not getting benefits from the resources and access to these resources are restricted accordingly. Except a few benefits from the tank and forest, rest of the benefits are being enjoyed by the Adadakulapalle village people as mentioned by the informants of the Thanda. Thus, vulnerable groups are not benefited from these resources.

IV
Conclusions and Observations

There is a need to understand poverty from the point of view of vulnerability. Vulnerability can be seen both as a cause and effect of poverty experienced by certain deprive section of the society. The causes and consequences of vulnerability can be observed from the ways and means of living of the vulnerable sections in the society. Poverty in the area is closely associated with land and rainfall, but as agriculture is only a part of livelihood, the dynamics of poverty consists of a complex mix of processes, including migration (Eswarappa and Siva Prasad, 2005).

Poverty in the area is closely associated with land and rainfall, but as agriculture is only a part of livelihood, the dynamics of poverty consists of a complex mix of processes, including migration. In order to understand the impact of the developmental interventions of the government and the NGO in ameliorating poverty, this study has taken an anthropological perspective of contextualizing development processes at the ground level. To conclude Eswarappa (2006) argued that poverty and vulnerability coexist and buttress each other and poverty can be understood by analyzing the real life situations and strategies adopted by the people to manage their lives.

References

Bankoff, Greg, Geprge, Freks and Dorothea, Hilhorst, (2004), *Mapping Vulnerability*, Sterling: Earthscan.

Baulch, B., and Hoddinott, J., (2000), "Economic Mobility and Poverty Dynamics in Developing Countries", *Journal of Development Studies*, 36 (6), 1–24.

Bird, K., Hulme, D., Moore, K. and Shepherd, A., (2002), "Chronic Poverty and Remote Rural Areas", Institute for Development Policy and Management, University of Manchester, CPRC Working Paper No. 13, www.chronicpoverty.org.

Booth, David, Melissa Leach and Alison Tierney, (1999), Experiencing Poverty in Africa: Perspectives from Anthropology, for the World Bank Poverty Status Report, Background Paper 1 (1).

Broch-Due, Vigdis, (1995), Poverty and Prosperity: Local and Global Perspectives', Uppsala: Nordiska Afrikainstitutet, Occasional Paper No. 1.

Chatterji, A.P., (1998), Toward an Ecology of Hope, Community and Joint Forest Management in Orissa, Sweden: Scandisconsult Natura AB and Berkeley, Asia Forest Network.

Devereux, S., (2001), "Livelihood Insecurity and Social Protection: A Re-emerging Issue in Rural Development", *Development Policy Review*, 19 (4), 507–519.

Eswarappa, Kasi, (2005), "Socio-economic Development of Sugali: An Anthropological Study from Andhra Pradesh", in the Web Journal 'View Point' No. 7, August-December, Husociology group of University of Hyderabad, Hyderabad, See also www.uohyd.ernet.in/sss/dsociology/view.html.

———, (2006), "Poverty and Vulnerability among Sugali: A Case Study from Adadakulapalle Settlement of Andhra Pradesh", paper presented in the Two Day National Conference on 'Tribal Policy for India', of Mahatma Gandhi National Institute of Research and Social Action (MGNIRSA), during 6–7, January, Hyderabad, India.

Eswarappa, Kasi and Prasad, R. Siva, (2005), "Poverty and Vulnerability among Tribal People: A Case of Sugali", paper presented in the Two-Day National

Seminar on 'Poverty among Tribals', of National Institute of Rural Development (NIRD), Hyderabad, on 12–13 April.

Escobar, A., (1995), *Encountering Development: The Making and Unmaking of the Third World*, Princeton: Princeton University Press.

Goody, Jack, (1971), *The Developmental Cycle in Domestic Groups*, Cambridge: Cambridge University Press.

Henninger, N. (1998), "Mapping and Geographic Analysis of Human Welfare and Poverty—Review and Assessment", World Resources Institute: Washington, DC, http://www.grida.no/prog/global/ poverty/pub/pov_fin.pdf.

Hulme, D., Moore, K., and Shepherd A. (2001), "Chronic Poverty: Meanings and Analytical Frameworks", Institute for Development Policy and Management, University of Manchester, CPRC Working Paper 2, www.chronicpoverty.org.

Human Development Report, (2000), New Delhi: Oxford University Press.

Kothari, U., (2002), "Migration and Chronic Poverty", Institute for Development Policy and Management, University of Manchester, CPRC Working Paper 16, www.chronicpoverty.org.

Kozel, V. and Parker B., (2001), "Poverty in Rural India: The Contribution of Qualitative Research in Poverty", Washington: World Bank.

Krishna Reddy, B., (1991), "Forests and the Sugalis in Andhra Pradesh: Historical and Anthropological Perspective", *Man in India*, Vol. 71, No. 4, 611–619.

———, (2003), Livelihood Strategies of the Sugali Tribal Community in Andhra Pradesh, paper presented at the Interdisciplinary Conference on "Livelihood Strategies Among Forest-related Tribal Groups of South India" held at the Center for Indian Studies, Mysore, during October, 17–19, 2003, under the Auspices of the Department of Social Anthropology, Stockholm University, Sweden and CREDITTe, Bangalore.

Lanjouw, P. and Stern N., (1991), Poverty in Palanpur, *The World Bank Economic Review*, 5 (1), 23–55.

Mehta, A.K. and Shah A., (2001), "Chronic Poverty in India: Overview Study", Institute for Development Policy and Management, University of Manchester, CPRC Working Paper 7, www.chronicpoverty.org.

———, (2003), "Chronic Poverty in India: Incidence, Causes and Policies", *World Development*, 31 (3), 491–511.

Moser, C., (1998), "The Asset Vulnerability Framework: Reassessing Urban Poverty Reduction Strategies", *World Development*, 26 (1), 1–19.

Oliver-Smith, A., (1996), "Anthropological Research on Hazards and Disasters", in *Annual Review of Anthropology*, 303–328.

Pritchett, Lant., Asep Suryahadi, and Sudarno Sumarto, (2000), "Quantifying Vulnerability to Poverty: A Proposed Measure, Applied to Indonesia", Washington: The World Bank, Policy Research Working Paper 2437.

Rao, Venkata P., (2004), *Dimensions of Transformations in Tribal Societies with reference to Andhra Pradesh*, New Delhi: Sarup and Sons.

Sainath, P., (1996), *Everybody Loves a Good Drought*, India: Penguin.

Sah, D.C. and Y.S. Sisodia (2004), *Tribal Issues in India*, Jaipur: Rawat Publications.

Sankaran, S.R., (2000), "Welfare of Scheduled Castes and Scheduled Tribes in Independent India: An Overview of State Policies and Programmes", *Journal of Rural Development*, 19 (4), 507–537.

Saxena, N.C., (2000), "How Have the Poor Done?, Mid-term Review of the Ninth Plan", *Economic and Political Weekly*, October 07, 35 (41).

Sinha, S. and M. Lipton, (1998), *Issue Paper for Discussion*. Brainstorming Workshop on IFAD's Strategic Focus on Poverty. Rome, 20–21 October 1998. IFAD.

———, (1999), "Damaging Fluctuations, Risk and Poverty: A Review", Background Paper for the World Development Report 2000/2001, Poverty Research Unit, University of Sussex.

Smith, K., (1996), *Environmental Hazards: Assessing Risk and Reducing Disaster*, London: Routledge.

Social Education and Development Society: Annual Report of Social Education and Development Society prepared to submit to the donor agencies, 2002–2004, 2004, See also www.seds.org. for further details.

Tudawe, I., (2002), "Chronic Poverty and Development Policy in Sri Lanka: Overview Study", Institute for Development Policy and Management, University of Manchester, CPRC Working Paper No. 9, www.chronicpoverty.org.

United Nations Centre for Regional Development (UNCRD), Vulnerability Analysis and Asset Management, Devyani Mani, http://www.uncrd.or.jp.

UNDP, (1997), *India: The Road to Human Development*. New Delhi: United Nations Development Programme.

Unnikrishnan, Namitha, Press and People: A Manual of Human Rights Reporting in India, 2000–2001, www.britishcouncil.org.

Wikipedia, the Free Encyclopedia: http://en.wikipedia.org/wiki/Vulnerability.

Wisner, B., (1993), "Disaster Vulnerability: Scale, Power and Daily Life", *Geo-Journal*, 30 (2), 127–140.

World Bank, World Development Report 2000/2001, Attacking Poverty, Washington DC: World Bank 2000.

World Bank, *World Development Report 2000/2001, Preventing Famines: The Local Press Matters*. Washington DC: World Bank, 2000.

Contributors

Ankita Arya, Research Scholar, Department of Anthropology, University of Delhi, New Delhi.

Babitha Justin, Lecturer, Department of English, North Eastern Hill University (NEHU), Shillong, Meghalaya.

Basanta Kumar Mallik, Reader, Department of History, Utkal University, Vanivihar, Orissa.

Brian J. Mooney, Faculty & Coordinator, Anthropology, Sociology and International Studies, Paul McGhee Division, School of Continuing and Professional Studies, New York University, New York.

Devesh K. Sahu, Programme Coordinator, Department of Anthropology, PSSO University, Bilaspur.

E. Krishna Rao, Senior Research Fellow, Directorate of Sorghum Research, Hyderabad.

Eswarappa Kasi, ICSSR Doctoral Fellow, Department of Anthropology, University of Hyderabad, Hyderabad.

Haireisim Newme, Research Scholar, Centre for Applied Linguistics and Translation Studies, University of Hyderabad, Hyderabad.

J. Limainla Ao, Research Scholar, Department of History, School of Social Sciences, University of Hyderabad, Hyderabad.

K. Gangaratnam, Research Scholar, Department of Economics, University of Hyderabad, Hyderabad.

K. Venugopal Reddy, Reader, Department of History, School of Social Sciences & International Sciences, Pondicherry University, Kalapet, Puducherry.

Kamal K. Misra, Professor, Department of Anthropology, University of Hyderabad, Hyderabad.

Khurshed Alam, Chief Executive, Bangladesh Institute of Social Research (BISR), Dhaka, Bangladesh.

Md. Irfan Basha, Research Associate, COVA, Charminar, Hyderabad.

Mohan Ramanan, Professor, Department of English, University of Hyderabad, Hyderabad.

N.V. Thang. Project Site Coordinator, Vietnam Agricultural Science Institute (VASI), Hanoi, Vietnam.

Netrapal Singh, Lecturer in History, University of Delhi, New Delhi.

O.G. Sajitha, Assistant Professor, Gujarat Institute of Development Research, Gota, Ahmedabad.

P. Raghupathi, Research Scholar, Department of Economics, University of Hyderabad, Hyderabad.

Panchanan Mohanty, Professor, Centre for Applied Linguistics and Translation Studies, University of Hyderabad, Hyderabad.

R.P. Mula, Post-Doctoral Fellow, International Crops Research Institute for the Semi-Arid Tropics (ICRISAT), Patancheru, Andhra Pradesh.

Ramesh C. Malik, Senior Research Fellow, Centre for Applied Linguistics and Translation Studies, University of Hyderabad, Hyderabad.

Resenmenla Longchar, Research Scholar, Centre for Folk Culture Studies, School of Social Sciences, University of Hyderabad, Hyderabad.

S.P. Wani, Principal Scientist and Project Coordinator, Agroecosystems, ICRISAT, Patancheru.

Sanjukta Dasgupta, Lecturer, Department of History, Calcutta University, Kolkata.

T. Wangkahart, Project Site Coordinator, Office of the Agricultural Research Development (OARD), Region 3, Khon Kaen, Thailand.

Temjenwabang, Research Scholar, Department of History, University of Hyderabad, Hyderabad.

Tutun Mukherjee, Professor and Head, Centre for Comparative Literature, University of Hyderabad, Hyderabad.

Upendra, Research Scholar, Department of Humanities and Social Sciences, Indian Institute of Technology, Mumbai.

V. Subramanyam, Research Scholar, Department of Economics, S.V. University, Tirupati.

Y. Supama, Research Fellow, OARD, Khon Kaen, Thailand.

Yasser Arafath. P.K. Research Scholar, Department of History, University of Hyderabad, Hyderabad.